Insurance Law in Portugal

Insurance Law in Portugal

Maria Inês de Oliveira Martins
Joana Neto Anjos
Joana Vicente
Gabriela Lacerda Assunção
Geraldo Rocha Ribeiro

This book was originally published as a monograph in the International Encyclopaedia of Laws/Insurance Law.

Founding Editor: Roger Blanpain
General Editor: Frank Hendrickx
Volume Editor: Herman Cousy

Wolters Kluwer

Published by:
Kluwer Law International B.V.
PO Box 316
2400 AH Alphen aan den Rijn
The Netherlands
E-mail: lrs-sales@wolterskluwer.com
Website: www.wolterskluwer.com/en/solutions/kluwerlawinternational

Sold and distributed by:
Wolters Kluwer Legal & Regulatory U.S.
7201 McKinney Circle
Frederick, MD 21704
United States of America
E-mail: customer.service@wolterskluwer.com

Printed on acid-free paper

ISBN 978-94-035-0746-0

e-Book: ISBN 978-94-035-0916-7
web-PDF: ISBN 978-94-035-0926-6

Printed in the United Kingdom.

The Authors

Maria Inês de Oliveira Martins is Professor of Civil and Commercial Law in the Faculty of Law at the University of Coimbra, Portugal and a private legal consultant in Portugal and Brazil. She is a member of the University of Coimbra Legal Institute (since 2017); a member of the board of the Portuguese Chapter of the 'Association Internationale de Droit des Assurances' (AIDA); a full member of the Special Commission on Insurance and Reinsurance of the Brazilian Bar Association – São Paulo Chapter; a member of the Supervisory Board of the Institute for Banking, Insurance and Capital Market Law of the Faculty of Law of the University of Coimbra (BBS), the Brazilian Institute for Insurance Law (IBDS), the German-Portuguese Legal Association (DLJV) and the European Law Institute (ELI). She is also responsible for the Section of European Insurance Contract Law of the Institute of Iberian-American Law (IDIBE).

Joana Neto Anjos is a Guest Assistant at the Faculty of Law of the University of Coimbra, teaching Constitutional and Tax Law (since 2016). Anjos is a doctoral student in Public Law (since 2017); member of the Portuguese Chapter of the International Society of Public Law (since 2021); legal advisor to ATAM – local administration workers association (since 2022); Member of the University of Coimbra Legal Institute (since 2018); and has participated in several congresses and conferences, with published work in the field of regulatory administrative law, energy law, constitutional law and tax law.

The Authors

Gabriela Lacerda Assunção is a Judge in Portugal. She graduated from Faculty of Law of the University of Coimbra in 2015 and has a master's degree in Civil Law from the same institution since 2018, with the thesis *Non-pecuniary Loss and the Legal Person as the Injured Party: Reflections on the Protection of Immaterial Interests*. She is a member of the Centre for Biomedical Law, where she specialised in Biomedical Law. She was a researcher between 2014 and 2018; and taught courses regarding confidentiality and public health.

Geraldo Rocha Ribeiro is a Judge and is a Member of the University of Coimbra Legal Institute. Ribeiro is an Associated Researcher at Family Law Centre (Centro de Direito da Família) of Faculty of Law of University of Coimbra and an Associated Researcher of the Biomedical Law Centre of Biomedical (Centro de Direito Biomédico) of Faculty of Law of University of Coimbra).

Joana Vicente is Assistant Professor at the Faculty of Law of the University of Coimbra, teaching Labour Law, Labour Law of Public Administration, Anti-discrimination Law (since 2017); legal advisor to the Judge Chambers of the Portuguese Constitutional Court (2019–2021); national Expert of the European Network of Legal Experts in Gender Equality and Non-Discrimination of the European Commission (since 2020); Member of APODIT – Portuguese Association of Labour Law (since 2013); and a Member of the University of Coimbra Legal Institute (since 2017).

Table of Contents

The Authors 3

Preface 15

List of Abbreviations 17

General Introduction
Geraldo Rocha Ribeiro & Maria Inês de Oliveira Martins 21

§1. General Background Information 21
I. Political System 21
II. Commerce and Industry 24
III. Financial Institutions 25
IV. Currency, Legislation and Monetary Regulations 26
V. Insurance Business, General Organisation and Special Features 26

§2. Historical Background of Insurance and Insurance Legislation 27
I. Before the Commercial Code 27
II. The Commercial Codes of the Nineteenth Century 29
III. Twentieth Century: European Law as a Driving Force for Renewal 30
IV. The Twenty-First Century: The RJCS and the Continuing Role of European Law 35

§3. Sources of Insurance Law 37
I. Legislation 37
A. International Law 37
B. European Law 37
C. National Law 39
II. Governmental Regulations and Regulation by Governmental Agencies 41
III. Private International Law 42
A. Jurisdiction 42
B. Conflict-of-Law Rules 43
1. The Succession of Laws and Their Application in Time 43
2. Definition of the Insurance Contract 44
3. Civil Code (Until 31 December 2008) 45

4. Rome Convention (From 01 September 1994 to 16 December 2009) 46
5. RJCS (From 01 January 2009 until 16 December 2009) 47
6. Rome I Regulation (From 17 December. 2009 until Now) 50
IV. Jurisdiction and Role of Scholarship 60

§4. Dispute Settlement and Arbitration 62

§5. Protection of Vulnerable Parties (In General and in Regard to Insurance) 66
I. Mass Risks Versus Large Risks 66
II. Consumer Protection 68
III. Contracts of Adhesion 70
IV. Protection Against Discrimination 73

§6. Compulsory Insurance 78

Part I. The Insurance Company
Joana Neto Anjos 81

Chapter 1. The Insurance Company: Its Form 81

§1. Mutual Insurance, Premium Insurance and Other 81

§2. Public or Private Nature 83

§3. Factual Data 83

Chapter 2. Access to Business: Authorisation – Requirements and Procedures 85

§1. General 85

§2. Authorisation: Requirements and Procedures 86
I. Insurance Company Limited by Shares 86
II. Mutual Insurance Company 89
III. Insurance and Reinsurance Business by Branch Offices Established in the Territory of EU 89
IV. Insurance and Reinsurance Business by Branch Offices Established Outside of the Territory of EU 90
V. Insurance Companies Operating Through Freedom of Services 93

Chapter 3. Supervision 94

§1. Solvency Control 94

§2. Supervision of Tariffs and Insurance Conditions 96

Chapter 4. Technical Reserves and Investments 98

Chapter 5. Accountancy 100

Chapter 6. Taxation of the Company 102

Part II. The Insurance Contract: General 103

Chapter 1. Generalities
Gabriela Assunção Lacerda, Geraldo Rocha Ribeiro, & Maria Inês de Oliveira Martins 103

§1. Definition of Insurance 103

§2. Rules on Interpretation of Insurance Contracts 106

§3. Categories of Insurance 111

§4. General Principles 114

§5. Inclusion and Content Control of Standard Terms and Condition of Insurance Contracts 116
I. Insurance Contract and Law on SCT 116
II. Protection of Addressees of SCT 117
A. Information Duties and Exclusion of SCT 117
B. Voidness and Prohibition of SCT 119
1. Forbidden SCT: A Principle of the Good Faith 120
2. Contracts Between Businesses or Equivalent Entities and Contracts with Final Consumers 121
C. Procedural Mechanisms 124

Chapter 2. Insurable Risk 125

§1. Risk and Interest 125

§2. Insurable Risks 129

§3. Deliberate Causation of the Insured Event 133

Chapter 3. Formation of the Insurance Contract 135

§1. Pre-contractual Phase 135

§2. Actual Formation of the Contract 137

§3. Validity Requirements 137

§4. Proof of the Contract 138

§5. Insurance Policies 138

Chapter 4. Obligations of the Insured 142

§1. Payment of Premium 142
I. Concept and Setting of the Premium 142
II. Payment of the Premium 142
III. Default on Premium Payments 144

§2. Other Duties of the Policyholder 147
I. Pre-contractual Duty of Disclosure 147
A. Scope of the Pre-contractual Duty of Disclosure 147
B. Consequences of Infringement of the Duty 150
II. Duties During the Contract 152
A. Statutory Duties 152
1. Communication of the Aggravation of Risk 152
2. Mitigation of the Loss 158
3. Communication of the Insured Event 162
B. Contractual Duties 165

Chapter 5. Obligations of the Insurer 168

§1. Main Obligations 168
I. Paying Out the Insurance Money or Performing the Services Promised 168
A. Critical Overview of the Norms on Insurers' Performance and Delay 168
B. Corrective Mechanisms 169
C. Protection of Third Parties' Rights 171
II. Rules Applicable to Indemnity Insurance 171
A. Indemnity Principle: Loss as a Limit 171
B. Multiple Insurance 173
C. Subrogation 174
D. Over-Insurance and Under-Insurance 175
1. Over-Insurance 175
2. Under-Insurance 177
E. Valued Policies 178
III. Rules Applicable to Fixed Sums Insurance 179

§2. Information Duties 180
I. Different Sources of Information Duties 180
II. In Particular, the RJCS as a Source of Information Duties 183
A. General Pre-contractual Duties of Information: Scope 183

B. General Pre-contractual Duties of Information: Consequences of Their Infringement 184
C. General Ongoing Duties of Information 187
D. Special Norms for Personal Insurance 188
E. Administrative Offence under Supervisory Law 188

Chapter 6. Insurance and Third Parties 189

§1. Insurance for the Account of a Third Party 189

§2. Third-Party Beneficiary Clauses 192

§3. Direct Action 192

§4. Group Insurance 192
I. Concept of Group Insurance 192
II. Modalities of Group Insurance 194
A. Contributory and Non-contributory Group Insurance 194
B. Single Insurance Contract or Multiple Insurance Contracts 196
III. Main Points of Regulation 197
A. Modification or Termination of Contracts 197
1. Termination (or Lack of Efficacy) due to Default on the Premium 197
2. Termination by the Insured, Exclusion of the Insured, Termination by the Policyholder and Maintenance of Cover 198
3. Exclusion of the Insured 199
4. Termination of the Contract 199
5. Maintenance of Cover 202
B. Duty to Inform the Insureds 202

Chapter 7. Modification and Termination of the Insurance Contract 206

§1. Modification of the Risk 206
I. Aggravation of Risk 206
II. Reduction of Risk 208
III. Modification of General Background Circumstances 208

§2. General Grounds for Termination of the Insurance Contract 209

Part III. Property and Liability Insurance
Gabriela Lacerda Assunção, Geraldo Rocha Ribeiro, & Maria Inês de Oliveira Martins 213

Chapter 1. Fire Insurance 213

Chapter 2. Loss of Benefits Insurance 217

Chapter 3. Transport Insurance 218

Chapter 4. Liability Insurance 221

§1. Introduction and Legal Framework 221

§2. Types of General Liability Insurance 224
I. Private Liability Insurance 225
II. Professional Liability Insurance 225
III. Commercial Liability Insurance 226
IV. Special Liability Insurance 228

Chapter 5. Motor Vehicle Insurance (*Pro Memoria*) 231

Chapter 6. Legal Aid Insurance 232

Chapter 7. Aviation and Space Insurance 234

§1. Aviation in General 234

§2. Unmanned Aircraft Systems 235

Chapter 8. Theft and Embezzlement Insurance 236

Chapter 9. Agricultural Insurance, Hail Insurance and Livestock Insurance 237

Chapter 10. Catastrophe Insurance 239

§1. General 239

§2. Nuclear Risks 239

§3. Natural Catastrophes 239

Chapter 11. Credit and Caution Insurance 240

§1. Credit Insurance 240

§2. Caution Insurance 241

Chapter 12. Technical Insurance 243

Chapter 13. Miscellaneous Insurance 244

§1. Assistance Insurance 244

Part IV. Compulsory Motor Vehicle Insurance
Gabriela Lacerda Assunção 245

Chapter 1. Applicable Law 245

Chapter 2. Duty to Insure 247

Chapter 3. Insurance Scope 248

§1. Material Scope 248

§2. Territorial Scope 248

§3. Insured Liability: Coverage and Exclusions 248

Chapter 4. Insured Capital 250

§1. Minimum Insured Sum 250

§2. Insufficient Capital 250

Chapter 5. Right of Recourse Against the Insured Person/ Entity 251

Chapter 6. Motor Vehicle Guarantee Fund 252

§1. Material Scope 252

§2. Subrogation 253

Chapter 7. Procedural Rules and Proceedings 255

Chapter 8. Insuring Other Risks 256

Part V. Insurance of the Person
Joana Nunes Vicente & Maria Inês de Oliveira Martins 257

Chapter 1. Workmen's Compensation and Occupational Disease 257

§1. General 257

§2. Workmen's Compensation Insurance for Employees 260

§3. Workmen's Compensation for Independent Workers 264

§4. Workmen's Compensation Fund 265

§5. Compensation due to Occupational Diseases 266

Chapter 2. Bodily Injuries: Personal Accident Insurance 268

§1. Terminology and Scope of the Regime 268
I. Bodily Injuries vis-à-vis Personal Accident Insurance 268
II. Concept of Personal Accident 268

§2. The Personal Accident Insurance Regime 270

Chapter 3. Private Health Insurance 273

§1. Scope of the Regime 273
I. Role of Private Health Insurance in Portugal 273
II. Concept and Possible Forms 273

§2. Regime of Private Health Insurance 274

Chapter 4. Life Insurance 277

§1. Individual Life Insurance 277
I. Concept of Life Insurance Contract and Main Norms Applicable to It 277
II. Special Duties of Information 279
III. Adaptation of the General Norms 281
IV. Third-Party Beneficiary Clauses 286
V. Right to Insurance Benefits, Right to Surrender Value and Other Rights Granted by the Contract 289

§2. Group Life Insurance 291

§3. Life Insurance Savings Products 292

I. Insurance-Based Investment Products 292
II. Capital Redemption Operations 293

Chapter 5. Pension Funds 294

§1. Pension Funds 294

§2. Savings for Education or Retirement Plans 296

Part VI. Private Insurance: Social Security
Maria Inês de Oliveira Martins 299

Part VII. Insurance Intermediaries
Joana Neto Anjos & Maria Inês de Oliveira Martins 301

Chapter 1. Law of Establishment and Supervision 302

§1. General Introduction 302

§2. Registration 302

Chapter 2. Insurance Intermediaries and the Insurance Contract 306

§1. The Impact of the IDF upon the Insurance Contract 306
I. General Duties of the Insurance Intermediaries that Have a Direct Impact upon the Insurance Contract 306
II. The Distinction Between Different Categories of Insurance Intermediaries 308
III. The Dominance of Information Duties 309

§2. Relevant Provisions of the RJCS on Insurance Intermediation 310

Part VIII. Reinsurance, Co-insurance and Pooling
Maria Inês de Oliveira Martins 315

Chapter 1. Reinsurance 315

Chapter 2. Co-insurance and Pooling 318

§1. Co-insurance 318

§2. Pooling 320

Part IX. Taxation of Insurance
Joana Neto Anjos 323

Chapter 1. Taxation 324

§1. Stamp Tax 324

§2. Other Tax: 'Taxas Parafiscais' 324

Chapter 2. Tax Deduction and Tax Benefits 326

Part X. Risk Management and Prevention
Maria Inês de Oliveira Martins 327

Selected Bibliography 329

Index 333

Preface

All statutes and regulations quoted throughout the text can be retrieved at the site of the Official Journal, https://dre.pt, where they can be browsed by their type and number. The site of the Public Prosecution Service for the Lisboa District, https://www.pgdlisboa.pt/leis/lei_main.php, provides for very useful updated versions of the statutes, with indication of all their previous versions.

All regulatory frameworks issued by ASF can be retrieved at the supervisor's website, https://www.asf.com.pt/. In any case, the date of the statute or regulation (the year being indicated after the slash symbol) is that of its official publication. All provisions for which no different source is specified pertain to RJCS.

Unless a different source is provided, all mentioned case law can be retrieved at http://www.dgsi.pt, where it can be browsed by case number.

The text takes into account legal and judicial developments until 15 October 2021.

The text was authored as follows:

General Introduction
§1–3, II – *Maria Inês de Oliveira Martins*
§3, III – *Geraldo Rocha Ribeiro*
§3, IV to §6 – *Maria Inês de Oliveira Martins*
Part I – *Joana Neto Anjos*
Part II
Chapter 1, §1–4 – *Maria Inês de Oliveira Martins*
Chapter 1, §5 – *Gabriela Lacerda Assunção*
Chapter 2 and Chapter 3, §1 – *Maria Inês de Oliveira Martins*
Chapter 3, §2–5 – *Geraldo Rocha Ribeiro*
Chapter 4 and Chapter 5, §1, I – *Maria Inês de Oliveira Martins*
Chapter 5, §1, II and III – *Gabriela Lacerda Assunção*
Chapter 5, §2, Chapter 6, Chapter 7, §1 – *Maria Inês de Oliveira Martins*
Chapter 7, §2 – *Geraldo Rocha Ribeiro*
Part III
Chapter 1 – *Geraldo Rocha Ribeiro*
Chapter 2 and Chapter 3 – *Maria Inês de Oliveira Martins*
Chapters 4, 5, and 6 – *Geraldo Rocha Ribeiro*
Chapter 7 – *Gabriela Lacerda Assunção*
Chapters 8, 9, and 10 – *Maria Inês de Oliveira Martins*
Chapter 11 – *Gabriela Lacerda Assunção*

Chapters 12 and 13 – *Maria Inês de Oliveira Martins*
Part IV – *Gabriela Lacerda Assunção*
Part V
Chapter 1 – *Joana Nunes Vicente*
Chapters 2, 3, 4 and 5 – *Maria Inês de Oliveira Martins*
Part VI – *Maria Inês de Oliveira Martins*
Part VII
Chapter 1 – *Joana Neto Anjos*
Chapter 2 – *Maria Inês de Oliveira Martins*
Part VIII – *Maria Inês de Oliveira Martins*
Part IX – *Joana Neto Anjos*
Part X – *Maria Inês de Oliveira Martins*

This work falls within the lines of research of UCILER, the Institute for Legal Research of the University of Coimbra, of which most of the authors are integrated members. UCILER kindly supported the revision of the text.

List of Abbreviations

ALR	Alternative dispute resolution
ASF	Portuguese Insurance and Occupational Pensions Authority (*Autoridade de Supervisão de Seguros e Fundos de Pensões*)
BFDUC	*Boletim da Faculdade de Direito da Universidade de Coimbra*
Brussels Ia	Regulation (EU) No. 1215/2012 of the European Parliament and of the Council of 12 December 2012 on jurisdiction and the recognition and enforcement of judgments in civil and commercial matters
CIRC	*Código do Imposto sobre o Rendimento das Pessoas Coletivas*
CIRS	*Código do Imposto sobre o Rendimento das Pessoas Singulares*
CMIA	Compulsory Motor Insurance Act, Decree-Law 291/2007, of 21 August 2007
CPR	Constitution of the Portuguese Republic
DCFR	Draft Common Frame of Reference
D&O	Directors and Officers
EBF	Estatuto dos Benefícios Fiscais
EEC	European Economic Community
EEA	European Economic Area
EIOPA	European Insurance and Occupational Pensions Authority
ERPL	European Review of Private Law
EU	European Union
EuCML	*Journal of European Consumer and Market Law*
FAT	*Fundo de Acidentes de Trabalho*

List of Abbreviations

FGA	*Fundo de Garantia Automóvel*
FOS	Freedom of Services
GDPR	General Data Protection Regulation
IAS	International Accounting Standards
IDD	Directive (EU) 2016/97 of the European Parliament and of the Council of 20 January 2016 on insurance distribution
IDF	Insurance and Reinsurance Distribution Framework, approved by Law 7/2019, of 16 January
IFRS	International Financial Reporting Standard
ISP	*Instituto de Seguros de Portugal*
LBIR	Law 147/2015, of 9 September, on the taking-up and pursuit of the business of insurance and reinsurance
LSCT	Decree-Law 446/85, of 25 October, on standard contract terms
Lugano Convention	Convention on jurisdiction and the recognition and enforcement of judgments in civil and commercial matters
MIFID	Markets in Financial Instruments Directive
MIFID II	Markets in Financial Instruments II Directive
Motor Insurance Directive	Directive 2009/103/EC of the European Parliament and of the Council of 16 September 2009 relating to insurance against civil liability in respect of the use of motor vehicles, and the enforcement of the obligation to insure against such liability
PECL	Principles of European Contract Law
PEICL	Principles of European Insurance Contract Law
PFR	Pension Funds Regime (Regime of the setting-up and functioning of pension funds and on the entities that manage them, approved by Law 27/2020, of 23 July)
PPR	*Plano de Poupança Reforma*
PPR-E	*Plano de Poupança Reforma-Educação* PPR-E
PRIIPs	Packaged retail and insurance-based investment products
RabelsZ	*Rabels Zeitschrift für ausländisches und internationales Privatrecht*
RDES	*Revista de Direito e Estudos Sociais*

RES	*Revista Española de Seguros*
RFDUL	*Revista da Faculdade de Direito da Universidade de Lisboa*
RJCS	*Regime Jurídico do Contrato de Seguro*; Insurance Contract Framework, approved by Decree-Law 72/2008, of 16 April
RLJ	*Revista de Legislação e Jurisprudência*
RMP	*Revista do Ministério Público*
ROA	*Revista da Ordem dos Advogados*
Rome I	Regulation (EC) No. 593/2008 on the law applicable to contractual obligations
Rome Convention (1980)	Convention on the law applicable to contractual obligations opened for signature in Rome on 19 June 1980
Rome II	Regulation (EC) No. 864/2007 of the European Parliament and of the Council, of 11 July 2007, on the law applicable to non-contractual obligations
SCT	Standard contract terms
Solvency II	Directive 2009/138/EC of the European Parliament and of the Council of 25 November 2009, on the taking-up and pursuit of the business of insurance and reinsurance
VVG	German Law on the insurance contract
ZEuP	*Zeitschrift für Europäisches Privatrecht*

List of Abbreviations

General Introduction

Geraldo Rocha Ribeiro & Maria Inês de Oliveira Martins[1]

§1. General Background Information

1. Portugal, officially Portuguese Republic, is a country in southern Europe, founded in 1143. The capital is Lisboa (Lisbon). Portugal occupies a total area of 92,212 km^2 and has a population of about 10.26 million people (about 111 people per km^2).[2] The mainland is located on the southwest of the Iberian Peninsula, bordering Spain to the north and east, and the Atlantic Ocean to the west and south. Portugal is a unitary, and not a federal state. It includes two autonomous regions: the archipelagos of Madeira and Azores, in the Atlantic Ocean. Its fundamental law is the Constitution, enacted in 1976 as a result of the Carnation Revolution of 25 April 1974, that ended a period of forty-eight years of dictatorship.[3]

I. Political System

2. As stated in Article 2 of the Constitution of the Portuguese Republic (CPR), the Portuguese Republic is a democratic state based on the rule of law. Sovereignty is distributed by four separate yet interdependent organs: the President of the Republic, the Assembly of the Republic, the Government and the Courts (Article 111 CPR).

---

1. Geraldo Rocha Ribeiro authored §3, III; Maria Inês de Oliveira Martins authored the remaining sections of the General Introduction.
2. *See* https://www.pordata.pt/Portugal and https://www.portaldiplomatico.mne.gov.pt/en/about-portugal (accessed 22 Aug. 2020).
3. A Portuguese version is available on the site of the Official Journal, https://dre.pt/constitution-of-the-portuguese-republic (accessed 22 Aug. 2020).

3. The political system created by the CPR is based on a separation of powers between the president, parliament and government, each possessing identical democratic legitimacy. It is usually characterised as a semi-presidential system, since it combines elements of a presidential system with elements of a parliamentary system.[4]

4. The president is elected by direct and universal suffrage, independent of the political parties, for a term of five years. According to the CPR, the president represents the Portuguese Republic, guarantees national independence, the unity of the state and the proper functioning of the democratic institutions, and is ex officio Commander-in-Chief of the Armed Forces (Article 120.º). The Constitution assigns the president with a broad range of powers, including, at a political level, the power to appoint the Prime Minister, the power to veto legislation, the power to remove the Government and to dissolve the Assembly (Articles 133 and 136).

5. The Assembly of the Republic represents all Portuguese citizens (Article 147). It has a total number of 230 members (Article 13 of the Electoral Law), elected on the basis of a proportional representation system. It is the organ with the broadest legislative powers, some of them exclusive (Articles 161, 164, and 165), and is also endowed with considerable political powers.

6. The government conducts the country's general policy and is the senior body of the public administration (Article 182). The prime minister is appointed by the president in the light of the electoral results for the Assembly of the Republic (Article 187). Although the Constitution grants the president discretionary powers in this regard, the praxis that has meanwhile been consolidated is that of simply appointing the candidate of the winning party.[5] The other members of the cabinet are also appointed by the president, upon a proposal from the prime minister. The Government has political, legislative and administrative powers (Articles 197 ff.) and is responsible before the president the Assembly (Articles 187–196).

7. The courts have the competence of administering justice. Under Articles 209 ff. of CPR, Portugal has two separate sets of courts – the judicial courts and the administrative courts. Provision is also made for other courts – the Constitutional Court (*Tribunal Constitucional*), the Court of Auditors (*Tribunal de Contas*), courts of arbitration (*tribunais arbitrais*) and justices of the peace (*julgados de paz*).[6]

8. The ordinary courts with civil and criminal jurisdiction are the judicial courts, which are organised in three instances. In descending order of hierarchical rank and territorial scope, these are: the Supreme Court (*Supremo Tribunal de Justiça*, with

4. Ana Martins, *Presidential Elements in Government, The Portuguese Semi-presidential system, About Law in the Books and Law in Action*, 2 European Constitutional Law Review, 81 and ff. (2006); differing, Paulo Otero, Direito Constitucional português, II, Organização do poder político, Almedina, (2010), 477 and ff.
5. P. Otero, Direito Constitucional II, 351.
6. *See* https://e-justice.europa.eu/content_judicial_systems_in_member_states-16-pt-en.do?member=1.

jurisdiction over the whole country), the courts of appeal (*tribunais de relação*, one per judicial district and two in the Porto judicial district) and the district courts (*tribunais de comarca*, at first instance).[7]

9. The first instance judicial courts have general jurisdiction in civil and criminal matters and also exercise jurisdiction in all matters not assigned to other courts. They fall into three categories, depending on the subject matter of the action and the amount at stake: courts with general jurisdiction, courts with specialised jurisdiction (criminal cases, family matters, minors, labour law, trade, maritime affairs and the enforcement of sentences) or specific jurisdiction (civil, criminal or mixed divisions; civil or criminal benches; civil or criminal benches dealing with minor matters).

10. The administrative courts settle disputes arising from administrative and tax relations. They include the first instance administrative and tax courts, the central administrative courts (North and South) and the Supreme Administrative Court (*Supremo Tribunal Administrativo*, covering the whole country). Conflicts of jurisdiction between courts are resolved by a *Tribunal de Conflitos*, regulated by law.

11. The Constitutional Court was created in 1982. It is competent in matters of electoral law, as well as in some issues of political relevance, but its central competence is the review of constitutionality and legality (in view of norms endowed with superior legal force and the autonomous regions' statutes) of norms (Article 223). It can exercise its reviewing powers either in regard to a particular interpretation of the norm, arising in connection with a specific court case – 'concrete review of constitutionality and legality', Article 280 –, or in regard to the norm in itself, without connection to any specific case – 'abstract review of constitutionality and legality', Article 281. Moreover, it has competence to review the constitutionality of certain norms before they are enacted – 'prior review of constitutionality', Articles 278.º and 279.º. This applies to norms contained in international treaties or in international agreements, as well as to norms that are to be enacted as a Law or Decree-Law. Finally, the Court can consider and verify whether there is a failure to comply with the Constitution due to the omission of legislative measures needed to make constitutional norms executable – 'unconstitutionality by omission', Article 283.

12. Only certain public entities (and not the ordinary citizen) have legal standing regarding abstract review of constitutionality and legality, prior review of constitutionality and the procedure of unconstitutionality by omission.

13. The Constitutional Court is composed of thirteen justices, ten of whom are appointed by the Assembly of the Republic and three co-opted by those ten. Six of the justices who are appointed by the Assembly of the Republic or are co-opted, must mandatorily be chosen from among the judges of the remaining courts, and

7. *See* https://e-justice.europa.eu/content_judicial_systems_in_member_states-16-pt-en.do?member=1.

the others from among jurists. The term of office of the Justices of the Constitutional Court is nine years and is not renewable (Article 222).

14. In the civil sphere, the ordinary courts with civil and criminal jurisdiction are the judicial courts, which are organised in three instances. In descending order of hierarchical rank and territorial scope, these are: the Supreme Court (*Supremo Tribunal de Justiça*, with jurisdiction over the whole country), the courts of appeal (*tribunais da relação*, one per judicial district and two in the Porto judicial district) and the district courts (*tribunais de comarca*, at first instance).

15. The Court of Auditors is the highest body with the authority to scrutinise the legality of public expenditure, and to review the accounts that the law stipulates must be submitted to it.

16. The Justices of the Peace are governed by Law 78/2001 of 13 July 2001. They are courts with special characteristics and with competence in civil proceedings (namely regarding contracts, ownership and consumption disputes) where the value of the claim does not exceed EUR 15,000.[8]

17. Arbitration is governed by Law 63/11 of 14 December 2011. The law generally follows the standard established by the UNCITRAL Model Law, albeit with a higher degree of detail and some adaptations based on the experience under the previous act on arbitration.

18. Each of the autonomous regions of Azores and Madeira possesses its own political and administrative statute and has its own government. The sovereignty of the Portuguese Republic is represented in each autonomous region by the Representative of the Republic (*Representante da República*) who is appointed by the President, after consulting the Government (Article 230). The self-government organs are the regional executive (*Governo Regional*) and the legislative assembly (*Assembleia Regional*). The assembly is elected by universal suffrage, whereas the president of the regional executive (the *Presidente do Governo Regional*) is appointed by the Representative of the Republic according to the results of the election to the legislative assemblies (Article 231).

II. Commerce and Industry

19. Before the COVID-19 pandemic, and after the public deficit crisis that deeply affected it after the financial crisis of 2008/2009, Portugal was growing at a

8. *See* Mariana França Gouveia, Curso de resolução alternativa de litígios, Almedina, (2014), 317 and ff., and https://dre.pt/dre/detalhe/lei/78-2001-388220.

steady pace, bolstered by exports and also by domestic consumption.[9] The main export destination of its goods and services was by far the Euro area, followed by other European countries.

20. In 2017, tourism accounted for close to half of all service exports. Nevertheless, export of machinery and transport equipment, as well as of manufactured goods, had also acquired importance and accounted for nearly half of the exports of goods.

21. The special ties with Portuguese speaking countries should also be highlighted – especially Brazil and Angola, which in 2019 accounted for over 10% of the stock of Portugal's outward foreign direct investment.

22. Portugal is expected to resume growth after the pandemic.[10] Its considerable reliance on the tourism and hospitality sector does carry some risk, but strong activity in the manufacturing sector and the absorption of European Union (EU) funds are hoped to support investment and exports.

III. Financial Institutions

23. The legal framework of European and national laws applicable to the financial system has grown exponentially in the aftermath of the financial crisis. Some statutory frameworks should nonetheless be singled out, for their central role in shaping the national financial system: first of all, the Act on credit institutions and financial societies (*Regime geral das instituições de crédito e sociedades financeiras*, Decree-Law 298/92, of 31 December); second, the Securities Code (*Código de valores mobiliários*, Decree-Law 486/99, of 13 November) and third, Law 147/2015, of 9 September, on the taking-up and pursuit of the business of insurance and reinsurance (LBIR).

24. At a supervisory level, Portugal follows a tripartite system, with a supervisory body responsible for the banking sector – *Banco de Portugal* (Bank of Portugal), which is the national central Bank –, a supervisory body responsible for the capital markets sector – *Comissão do Mercado de Valores Mobiliários*, CMVM (Securities Market Authority) – and a supervisory body responsible for insurance and pension funds – *Autoridade de Supervisão de Seguros e Fundos de Pensões* (ASF). These three entities are jointly represented at the *Conselho Nacional de Supervisores Financeiros* (National Council of Financial Supervisors), which acts

9. *See* OECD, *OECD Economic Surveys, Portugal*, February 2019 (available at https://www.oecd.org/economy/portugal-economic-snapshot/).
10. *See* OECD, *Economic Forecast Summary*, May 2021 (available at https://www.oecd.org/economy/portugal-economic-snapshot/).

as a macro-prudential supervisory entity. It has mere coordinating and consulting competences, and its powers are limited to the issuing of recommendations.[11]

IV. Currency, Legislation and Monetary Regulations

25. Portugal has been a member of the Eurozone since its establishment. Before having adopted the Euro, the national currency was the 'escudo' and monetary policy was defined by the central bank, 'Banco de Portugal'. As a member of the Eurozone, Portugal is now under the monetary policy of the European System of Central Banks, formed by the European Central Bank and the national central banks of all the EU Members – among them, 'Banco de Portugal' (*see* Articles 119–144, 219 and 282–284 of the Treaty on the Functioning of the European Union).

V. Insurance Business, General Organisation and Special Features

26. According to the ASF, in the first three months of 2021 the global business volume of direct insurance in Portugal was above EUR 2.8 thousand million, having increased 5.4% when compared to the same period of 2020.[12]

27. The different stakeholders taking part in the insurance market are organised in associations. The Portuguese Association of Insurers (*Associação portuguesa de seguradores* – APS) is a non-profit association of insurance and reinsurance carriers present in the Portuguese insurance market.[13] The APS is a member of Insurance Europe and of Global Federation of Insurance Associations. The National Association of Insurance Agents and Brokers (*Associação Nacional de Agentes e Corretores de Seguros*)[14] is a non-profit association of insurance agents and brokers.

28. On the policyholder/insured side, reference should be made to two entities. First, to the Portuguese association for consumer protection (*Associação portuguesa para a defesa do consumidor* – DECO),[15] which has a broad scope of action in the protection of consumer interests and is also active in the protection of consumers of insurance products. Finally, to the Automobile Club of Portugal (*Automóvel Clube de Portugal* – ACP),[16] a private entity whose purpose is the promotion of motor sports and activities and the promotion of the interests of its associates in this regard. Along the more than one hundred years of its existence, ACP

11. *See* Art. 2 of Decree-Law 228/2000, of 23 September, which created the *Conselho Nacional de Supervisores Financeiros*.
12. *See* the ASF Report on the evolution of insurance activity in 2021 at https://www.asf.com.pt/NR/rdonlyres/73C38463-6F43-49F8-8A84-23009DC16441/0/REAS_1T_2021.pdf.
13. For further reference, *see* https://www.apseguradores.pt/pt/.
14. For further reference, *see* http://www.aprose.pt/public/Home.aspx#.X0g5pS2ZOu4.
15. For further reference, *see* https://deco.pt.
16. For further reference, *see* https://www.acp.pt/institucional/sobre-o-acp.

has acquired a considerable status in the promotion of the interests of drivers, and presently offers a vast array of services to its associates, including roadside assistance and insurance distribution.

29. Unlike what happens in other jurisdictions (e.g., Germany), there are no general insurance contract terms set out by the market's stakeholders, that may serve as a model for contracts covering a certain risk. This can lead the contract terms used by each insurer to differ considerably from each other.

30. By lack of a publicly known model policy for each type of coverage, scholarship can only scrutinise the contract terms that surface in case law. When no specific statutory or regulatory norms apply to the insurance of certain risks, it becomes difficult to know which conditions currently frame their cover.

§2. Historical Background of Insurance and Insurance Legislation

I. Before the Commercial Code

31. The first centuries of evolution of insurance law in Portugal are best understood when one separates insurance contract law from administrative or supervisory insurance law. As it could be expected, they evolved at a different pace, since they mirror different angles of the prevailing conceptions on the role that the State should play in the economy.

32. With regard to the norms on administrative organisation of the supply of insurance, as early as the sixteenth century one can detect the first attempts to establish a public registry of the insurance contracts entered into. The first Registrar, Brás Eanes, was appointed in 1529; as of 1578, the office of Broker was also created, and endowed with a legal monopoly regarding the conclusion of insurance contracts. Since 1573, there are references to a public department encompassing both those offices, the Insurance House (*Casa dos Seguros*).

33. The attributions of this House ranged throughout the centuries.[17] By the beginning of the eighteenth century, it had lost a part of its competences and was again reduced to a mandatory public registry of contracts entered into in Portugal. However, with the approval of new statutes of *Casa dos Seguros* in 1758 (later changed) and their enforcement by royal decree in 1791, authorised insurers came under a new set of duties towards that body, mainly aimed at guaranteeing that the insurers actually paid the promised indemnities.

34. The case is different for insurance private law, aimed at regulating the relation between the contracting parties and third insured parties or beneficiaries. Up until the nineteenth century, the sovereign did not try to enact a consistent body of

17. A. H. Oliveira Marques, Para a história dos seguros em Portugal, Notas e documentos, Arcádia, (1977), 35 and ff., 112 and ff., 179 and ff.

rules (for instance, at the image of the *Ordonnances*) that could govern marine insurance, at this period the most relevant types of insurance. This does not mean that the contract did not receive, from quite early on, attention from the market, from the public powers or from scholarship.

35. Mechanisms akin to insurance were in force since the thirteenth century, protecting merchants against the perils of the sea. A pre-existing mutual fund among the merchants was made compulsory by the monarch, D. Dinis, in 1293; later on, in the end of the fourteenth century, the monarch D. Fernando would himself directly create a guaranty fund (*Companhia das Naus*) to protect against the loss of ships.[18]

36. The taking out of actual ('premium', and not 'mutual') private insurance accompanied, on its hand, the expansion of the sea trade routes. The development of the insurance market was, however, occasionally hindered by greed from both insurers and insureds, especially after the establishment of the maritime way to India. From the insured parties there was a proneness to overly risk-taking behaviour (e.g., acceptance of excessive cargo, or sailing in adverse conditions) and even to insurance fraud.[19] From the insurers, there was a tendency for over-pricing coverage, even bordering usury, which prompted the prohibition of a very widespread contract akin to insurance (risk lending) from 1609 to 1655.[20] From then onwards, the Portuguese market for insurance became growingly dominated by foreign insurers, mostly English; insurers who, it should be added, did not abide their duties to register at *Casa dos Seguros* and consequently did not abide its rules.

37. On its hand, Portuguese scholarship was famously precocious in the construction of insurance as a specific type of contract. In fact, the first treatise on the insurance contract, which was edited in 1552 but is likely to have already been written in the fifteenth century, is attributed to a Portuguese scholar, Pedro de Santarém (Santerna).[21] He is credited with having singled out the feature of insurable interest as the one that distinguishes insurance from a bet, thus concurring in legitimising insurance in the context of the canonic prohibition of usury.[22]

18. The precise date of creation of *Companhia das Naus* is not known; *see* Instituto de Seguros de Portugal, Os seguros em Portugal, da Fundação à Modernidade, Exposição documental da actividade seguradora dos séculos XIII a XIX (2010), https://www.asf.com.pt/isp/catalogo_digital/files/catalogo_exposicao.pdf (accessed 24 Aug. 2020), 10 and ff. On its pioneering role, *see also* Levin Goldschmidt, Universalgeschichte des Handelsrechts, Ferdinand Enke, (1891), 356–357, and A. Oliveira Marques, Para a história …, 22–23, making reference to another mutual fund authorised by D. Dinis. Mention to similar mechanisms can be found throughout the fourteenth and the fifteenth centuries, as displayed by royal orders that were issued by the monarchs called to enforce the payments due to the funds (*see* order issued by D. João I in 1397 and order issued by D. Afonso V in 1459, both in Instituto de Seguros de Portugal, *Os seguros em Portugal* …, 16–19).
19. Eduardo Vera-Cruz Pinto, Os seguros marítimos nas rotas portuguesas do ultramar, uma perspectiva histórico-jurídica, 1, RFDUL, 257 (1998), 269.
20. A. Oliveira Marques, Para a história …, 97 and 112–129; E. Vera-Cruz Pinto, Os seguros …, 280.
21. *See* E. Vera-Cruz Pinto, Os seguros …, 284 and Moses Amzalak, Pedro de Santarém, Notas biográficas (in: Tractatus de assecurationibus et sponsionibus, Instituto de Seguros de Portugal, 9, 2006), 9 and ff.
22. M. Amzalak, Pedro de Santarém, 21–25.

II. The Commercial Codes of the Nineteenth Century

38. It can be said that it was only with the emergence of the Code of Commerce of 1833 that the insurance contract actually attained for the first time a 'regime to call its own' – and even then, it regarded mostly marine insurance law. Although the 1758 statutes of *Casa dos Seguros* did regulate some relevant aspects of the insurance contract,[23] they left out many others. Besides, as mentioned above, foreign insurance was very prevalent in the Portuguese market; therefore, the practical role of those provisions was furthermore limited.

39. The Commercial Code of 1833 was approved on the wake of the liberal revolution (and actually during the Civil war) and intended to grant the country with its first body of commercial law. Ferreira Borges, a liberal lawyer and economist that lived and exiled in London during the preparation of the project, was the author of the text.[24] In his presentation of the Code, the author puts forth many sources of inspiration foreign sources of inspiration – the Commercial Codes of Prussia, Flanders, Spain, the Italian Project, the commercial Law of England and Scotland and the *Ordinances* of Russia and Germany, as well as other older regulations of marine Law. In its features, however, the Code is deemed to have been mainly influenced, like many Commercial Codes of its time, both directly and indirectly, by the *Code de commerce* of 1807.[25]

40. Still, in what concerns insurance, the Code did drift apart from the French solutions. Strikingly, it was not limited to marine insurance, but instead held a general part, whose provisions would apply to all kinds of insurance. Furthermore, the Code allowed for some forms of insurance that were not allowed in France, such as the insurance of expected profits (Articles 1672 and 1720.º).[26] Nevertheless, there were practically no special rules devoted to any of the non-marine kinds of insurance, whereas marine insurance was handled throughout the vast majority of its 140 provisions. The Code followed many of the solutions that had already been put forth by Pedro de Santarém,[27] upholding, for instance, the mandatory reference of the contract to an insurable interest (Article 1675.º). Besides, it displayed considerable concern with the issues arising of moral hazard, setting out a number of imperative provisions in that regard.

---

23. Notably establishing who would be responsible for paying the indemnity; that the indemnity should be paid in money, its deadline, and its proportion to the loss incurred; determining some of the risks insured or excluded from cover; determining the time limit for the communication of the insured event.
24. José Henrique Rodrigues Dias, José Ferreira Borges – Política e economia, Imprensa Nacional – Casa da Moeda, (1988), 56 and ff.
25. For the original text of the Code and its presentation, *see* https://www.fd.unl.pt/Anexos/Investigacao/7510.pdf. *See also* António Menezes Cordeiro, Direito dos seguros, Almedina, 2 Ed (2016), p94 and ff.; Jorge Manuel Coutinho de Abreu, Curso de Direito comercial, I, Introdução, atos de comércio, empresas, sinais distintivos, Almedina (2019), 32–33.
26. Anthoine de Saint-Joseph, Concordance entre les codes de commerce étrangers et le code de commerce français, Videcoq/Delamotte (1844), XXXIX-XLII.
27. Pedro Romano Martinez, Modificações na legislação sobre contrato de seguro, 136, RES, 645 (2008), 645–646.

41. With the advance of the nineteenth century, many of the Code's solutions would however soon face criticism, and it would soon be complemented by a considerable amount of separate statutes. Moreover, with the approval of the first Portuguese Civil Code in 1867, many of the provisions of the Commercial Code became inconsistent with the new general framework of Portuguese private law.[28] This was all the more problematic, since the Civil Code determined that all insurance that did not have a commercial object would be subject to its norms (Article 1540). Those were not any special norms on insurance, which the Civil Code did not entail; they were the general norms on contracts.

42. Hence, a new Commercial Code was approved in 1888, under the auspices of Veiga Beirão, then Minister of Justice, who was also responsible for the project – though the authors of the norms on insurance were José Pereira followed by Frederico Laranjo.[29] The Code now assembled the general provisions on the contract with the special provisions on non-marine insurance (Articles 425.º and ff.) and separately handled marine insurance (Articles 595.º and ff.). Thus, non-marine insurance was now brought to the fore. And, since many of its types that came under special rules did not have a commercial object (e.g., life insurance or harvest insurance), it claimed some of the space that the Civil Code had come to occupy for itself.

43. On the whole, the 1888 Code is a product of liberalism, where there was not yet room for concern with imbalances between the parties. In the role it gives to private autonomy, the 1888 Code strikes yet a more liberal note than its predecessor, establishing that its rules shall only apply when the police does not provide otherwise (Article 427.º). Its overall approach to insurance does not drive significantly apart from the general provisions of the 1833 Code, though it also shows influence from the Belgian Law of Insurance of 1874 and from the Italian Code of Commerce of 1883.[30]

III. Twentieth Century: European Law as a Driving Force for Renewal

44. The twentieth century was, by contrast, a period of relative stagnation in what concerns insurance contract law. The same cannot be said about supervisory law, where the changes were tectonic during this century. In both of these fields, European law was a considerable driving force for renewal.

45. The 1888 Code of Commerce continued as the main source of insurance contract law up until the entry into force of the Regime Jurídico do Contrato de Seguro (RJCS), in 2009. Its norms were thus kept for more than one century; and it should be added that they were barely changed during this long timespan.

---

28. José de Oliveira Ascensão, Direito Comercial, I, Parte Geral, s. ed., (1986–1987), 15.
29. A. Menezes Cordeiro, Seguros, 2. Ed., 100.
30. P. Romano Martinez, Modificações … , 645–648.

46. Eventually, its norms were supplemented by separate statutes that regulate specific issues of the insurance contract. Payment of the premium was the object of three different statutes in succession (Decree-Law 162/84, of 18 May 1984; Decree-Law 105/94, of 23 April 1994; Decree-Law 142/2000, of 15 July). The general trend of these changes was to simplify termination of the contract in case of default on the payment of the premium. In 1995, a statute on 'transparency and rules on the insurance contracts' was also enacted (Decree-Law 176/95, of 26 July). Its provisions, though not many in number (twenty-seven articles), were particularly miscellaneous in content. The statute set out a range of information duties and held an extensive list of definitions of insurance law concepts (taking a role which normally belongs to scholarship, and not to the legislative powers). It also regulated a variety of aspects of different species of insurance contracts that had developed after the approval of the Code of Commerce (e.g., health insurance, legal protection insurance, credit and caution insurance). As it states on its preamble, the statute should play a transitory role while a new general law on the insurance contract did not come to light. More than a decade was yet to come before that moment.

47. This relative inertia should not be credited to the ability of the norms to overcome the test of time. On the contrary, as said above, they were norms of their time, marked by the liberalism of the nineteenth century. Their sparseness and lack of accuracy gave rise to growing doubts on the discipline of the insurance contract throughout the twentieth century – doubts that were increased by the approval of a new Civil Code, in 1966. The long permanence of the regime seems rather to have been driven by a relative absence of interest in insurance from the legislator, accompanied by a relative lack of interest of scholarship to its issues.[31] The number of writings specifically carrying out a thorough analysis of insurance was strikingly small. In this context, the extensive comparative law monograph of Justice Moitinho de Almeida stands out, reassessing the existing insurance law and presenting its own project of a new legal statute.[32] Having been published in 1971, it still remains the reference for Portuguese insurance contract law under the 1888 Commercial Code.

48. Change came, first of all, from the norms on compulsory insurance. Compulsory insurance should be singled out from the general context of insurance contract. It pursues goals of distributive justice – it is sometimes referred to as 'social insurance' – and is therefore more sensitive to changes in public perception about the allocation of wealth and risks. This feature is especially salient in regard to compulsory insurance with a broad social reach, such as work-person's compensation and occupational disease insurance or motor insurance. The first emerged in 1913, in the context of the progressive measures adopted by the First Portuguese Republic. The latter was first adopted in 1979 and was from the onset carved by international norms, initially following the recommendations of the *European Convention on Compulsory Insurance against Civil Liability in respect of Motor Vehicles*, and

31. Francisco Guerra da Mota, O contrato de seguro terrestre, I, Athena, (s/d), 87–88.
32. José Carlos Moitinho de Almeida, O contrato de seguro no direito português e comparado, Livraria Sá da Costa (1971).

latter transposing the European Directives on the matter, which brought a considerable heightening of the national standards of protection of the victims of road traffic accidents – all the more important since Portugal had by the 70s/80s extremely high levels of severe road accidents.[33]

49. A second factor of change came from the norms on the protection of a weaker party – namely, consumer law, and the Law on contracts of adhesion, that in Portugal also applies to contracts between professional parties. European law was naturally key for the heightening of consumer protection standards. However, the most importance statute for the protection of policyholders has been the Law on contracts of adhesion, from 1985, that precedes by far the 1993 Directive on unfair contract terms. This Law has been the main basis for enforcement of the duties of the insurer to inform on the policy; and it has also been abundantly applied by the courts in order to nullify disproportionately imbalanced clauses.

50. Lastly, reference should also be made to the insurance Directives. Although mainly directed at harmonising administrative law, they also entailed provisions on the insurance contract. This was mainly a consequence of the liberalisation of the insurance market as enacted by the Third Insurance Directives, that prohibited the procedures of previous control and approval of the insurance policies by the national supervising authorities.[34] The suppression of this source of scrutiny was compensated by setting out a number of information duties from the insurer towards the policyholder. This new set of information duties was transposed together with the other norms of the Directives and had therefore a quite incongruous seat in the statutes on access to the insurance market and insurance supervision enacted in 1994 and in 1998 (*see below*).

51. The situation was very different in the field of supervisory law. During this century, a proper supervision system was created and it was reshaped several times.

52. The first statute creating an actual system of insurance supervision was the Decree of 21 October 1907, approved still under the Monarchy. It is interesting pointing out how much its underpinnings contrasted those of the Commercial Code which was then in force. As stated in the preamble of the Decree, the view of State neutrality towards the economy was no longer deemed acceptable. As private parties were not in position to carry out the necessary scrutiny of the insurance providers, this task should be undertaken by the public power. Therefore, the Decree

33. *See* https://www.pordata.pt/Portugal/Acidentes+de+viação+com+v%C3%ADtimas++feridos+e+mortos+++Continente-326; for a comparison, *see* World Health Organization, *European Status Report on Road Safety: Towards Safer Roads and Healthier Transport Choices, Copenhagen*, WHO Regional Office for Europe, 2009 (available at https://www.euro.who.int/__data/assets/pdf_file/0015/43314/E92789.pdf, retrieved on 24 Sept. 2021).

34. Council Directive 92/96/EEC of 10 November 1992 (Third Life Insurance Directive), Art. 5., changing Art. 8., 3, of the First Directive on Life Insurance and Art. 31; Council Directive 92/49/EEC of 18 June 1992 (Third Non-life Insurance Directive), Art. 6., changing Art. 8., 3, of the First Directive on Non-life Insurance and Art. 31.

created a supervising authority, *Conselho de Seguros* ('Insurance Council'), and established rules on the matters of authorisation of insurance companies, capital requirements and insolvency proceedings.

53. This structure survived till the end of the Monarchy (1910) and was kept with minor changes during the first Republic (1910–1926). This was also a period of considerable dynamism in the Portuguese insurance market.[35]

54. This framework proved, however, very lax in practice. The period after World War I witnessed several cases of insolvency in the insurance sector. With the *coup d'État* of 1926 and the ensuing instauration of an autocratic regime (*Estado Novo*), the moment was ripe for a tightening of the existing norms.

55. In 1929, the existing *Conselho de Seguros* was replaced by a new supervising entity, *Inspecção de Seguros* ('Insurance Inspection'), integrated in the Ministry of Finance (the Law 17556, of 5 November 1929). On the same date, the capital requirements of insurance companies were updated by another Decree-Law (No. 17555). The new supervising entity, which was reorganised by Decree-Law 21977, of 13 December 1932 is deemed to have efficiently used its inspecting powers. From 1949 onwards, after Decree-Law 37470, of 6 July, the supervision of both the insurance sector and the banking sector was placed under the same department of State, *Inspecção-Geral de Crédito e Seguros* ('General Inspection of Credit and Insurance'). Notwithstanding the formal integration of the supervising activities, they were in fact divided by different services within the General Inspection and continued being exerted separately.

56. The Portuguese Dictatorship was both *dirigiste* and corporatist, which had consequences for the insurance market. It reflected first of all in the very limited emergence of new insurance companies throughout this period. Second, after Decree-Law 26484 of 31 March 1936, it led to the mandatory integration of all insurance companies in an employers' union (*Grémio das Seguradoras*), that collaborated closely with the supervisor.

57. Deep changes came once again with the Carnation Revolution and the fall of Dictatorship (1974). In 1975, ensuing the revolution, the Portuguese banks and insurance companies were nationalised (Decree-Law 132-A/75 and Decree-Law 135-A/75, of 15 March). With particular regard to the insurance market, this meant that the companies controlling most of the market share now belonged to the State – a fact which naturally placed the question of supervision under a different light. By Decree-Law 301/75, of 20 June 1975, the former *Inspecção-Geral de Crédito e Seguros* was abolished; the 'Insurance Inspection' (*Inspecção de Seguros*) simply resumed its activity under the Ministry of Finance. And by Decree-Law 11-B/76, of 13 January 1976, the former corporatist insurers union (*Grémio das Seguradoras*) was replaced by the National Insurance Institute (*Instituto Nacional dos Seguros*),

35. On all this topic, *see* Margarida Mateus, Modelo institucional da supervisão de seguros em Portugal no período 1907–2007, 24, Fórum, 41 (2007), 41–52.

which was made responsible for all the technical coordination of the insurance activity, all well as its overall financial management, and the organisation of risk prevention and reinsurance procurement.

58. The Constitution of 1976 confirmed the principles of democracy and rule of law and created the framework for an economy where three sectors of production could coexist: the public sector, the private sector, and the cooperative sector. In the ensuing years, the private sector gained space and the path to bring the principles of market economy to some of the sectors that had been nationalised, such as that of insurance, began to come into shape. This process would reach a decisive point in 1983, when, by Law 11/83 of 16 August, the Parliament authorised the reopening of the insurance market to private companies. It would later culminate in the approval of the Constitutional Law 1/89, of 8 July 1989, that changed the Constitution in order to allow for the privatisation of the companies that had previously been nationalised.

59. With the reopening of the insurance market, its oversight would not be able to rely on the direct management of its main companies by the State; it demanded the creation of an authority with clear supervisory powers instead.

60. The answer was the creation, by Decree-Law 513-B1/79, of 27 December 1979, of a 'General Inspection of Insurance' (*Inspecção Geral de Seguros*), endowed with more resources and a larger structure than that of its predecessor, the Insurance Inspection, but still integrated in the central government. In 1982, by Decree-Law 302/82, of 30 July 1982, the General Inspection of Insurance was abolished, and the supervising authority gained a new status. It became the *Instituto de Seguros de Portugal* (Portuguese Insurance Institute; hereinafter 'ISP'), an autonomous body with legal personality, endowed with its own budget and with decision-making power. The same act abolished the National Insurance Institute (*Instituto Nacional dos Seguros*). In its place, the Portuguese Association of Insurers (*Associação Portuguesa de Seguradores*) emerged, as a private association set to represent the interest of its associates, the insurance companies authorised to operate in the Portuguese market.

61. In this period, it is also worth pointing out the approval of the first statute on Insurance Mediation, in 1979 (Decree-Law 145/79, of 23 May).

62. The last years of the twentieth century should also be looked at in the light of the accession to the European Economy Community. The prospect of membership determined the revision of the national laws on capital requirements of the insurance companies, in order to bring them in line with the European standards; this was carried out by Decree-Law 98/82, of 7 April 1982. With the opening of the insurance market, a new general law on insurance supervision and the conditions of access to the insurance market was approved (Decree-Law 182/84, of 5 July 1984). The general law was altered in 1986, after accession to the EEC, in order to fully adapt it to the European law then in force (Decree-Law 85/86, of 7 May, Decree-Law 125/86, of 2 June and Decree-Law 155/86, of 23 June).

63. Before the century ended, the general law on access to the insurance market and insurance supervision would still be replaced twice. It was replaced by Decree-Law 102/94, of 20 April 1994 that transposed the third life and non-life insurance Directives. In turn, this statute was replaced by Decree-Law 94-B/98, of 17 April, which brought insurance supervision in line both with other aspects of the Portuguese law (e.g., the new general law on administrative offences), as with the liberal stance and openness towards financial innovation that characterised that period.

IV. The Twenty-First Century: The RJCS and the Continuing Role of European Law

64. The twenty-first century certainly brought a new dynamic to Portuguese Insurance Law.

65. On the side of private insurance law, a new general law on the insurance contract was finally approved in 2008. Its provisions shall be analysed throughout this work. Overall, the Act has received some harsh criticism,[36] and it is fair to say that it does tend to favour the insurer in several aspects where the policyholder would need special protection.

66. That is notably the case with the rules on the applicant's pre-contractual information duty. Following an opposite direction to that followed by other contemporary legislations, it generally set out a duty to spontaneously inform the insurer, rather than merely answer the questions posed by him.[37] That was also the case with the rules on default on premium payment. The RJCS followed a very strict 'no premium, no risk approach', which runs totally contrary to the general norms on payment default, where there is a period of delay before the contract is terminated.[38] That is furthermore the case (just to give a last example) in what concerns insurer's delay. Against the general concerns with the consequences of late payment from the insurer and the risks of moral hazard that can be identified in this regard, the RJCS did not set a time limit for the settlement of claims, nor did it entitle the insured party with a right to provisional payment.[39]

---

36. José Carlos Moitinho de Almeida, O novo regime jurídico do contrato de seguro, Beves considerações sobre a protecção dos segurados (in: J. C. Moitinho de Almeida (ed.) Contrato de seguro, Estudos, Coimbra Editora, 11, 2009), passim; Maria Inês de Oliveira Martins, El derecho de contrato de seguro en Portugal. Un régimen en la encrucijada (in: Pablo Girgado Perandones (ed.) El contrato de seguro y su distribución en la encrucijada, Aranzadi/ Thomson Reuters, 2018), passim; António Santos Abrantes Geraldes, 'O novo regime do contrato de seguro, Antigas e novas questões', 2010, disponível em http://www.trl.mj.pt/PDF/REGIME.pdf (consultado pela última vez a 15 Jan. 2015), nos 4 ff.
37. *See* Part II, Ch. 4, §2, I, Pre-contractual Duty of Disclosure.
38. *See* Part II, Ch. 4, §1, Payment of Premium.
39. *See* Part II, Ch. 5, §1, I, Paying Out the Insurance Money or Performing the Services Promised.

67. Nonetheless, any legal practitioner or scholar would most likely agree that the RJCS brought a much-needed systematisation and transparency to insurance law, and that the field is overall much better with it than without it.

68. The RJCS has been altered once since its establishment, by Law 147/2015, of 9 September 2015. The intervention was limited to specific issues (namely regarding the end of bearer insurance policies, the rules on non-discrimination, the limiting of subrogation in personal insurance and the creation of new information duties in life insurance), and not of transformative nature.

69. In 2015, the supervising authority had its name changed to ASF (Authority for Supervision of Insurance and Pension Funds); its internal rules were also modified.[40]

70. Other key changes were brought about by European law.

71. That was the case at the prudential level. Solvency II Directive was transposed by Law 147/2015, of 9 September 2015, that established a new regime on the taking-up and pursuit of the business of insurance and reinsurance – LBIR – and repealed the previous act in force (apart from some of its provisions). Recent changes in European law – Markets in Financial Instruments II Directive (MIFID II) legislative package, the Directive on insurance distribution and the Directive on pension funds – have caused the LBIR to be altered several times in accordance.

72. The legislative package around MIFID II was also of direct significance to the life insurance branch, since it entailed Regulation (EU) 1286/2014 on key information documents for packaged retail and insurance-based investment products (PRIIPs),[41] and the acts supplementing it. The Regulation was supplemented internally by Law 35/2018, of 20 July 2018.

73. European law was critical in the shaping of insurance distribution law. In 2006, a new law on insurance and reinsurance mediation had been approved by Decree-Law 144/2006, of 31 July, transposing Directive 2002/92/EC on insurance mediation.[42] In 2019, Insurance distribution Directive[43] was transposed by RDS, which repealed the previous statute.

74. Finally, at a life insurance branch level, European law has deeply influenced the regime of pension funds and pension plans, most recently through Directive 2014/50/EU and Directive 2016/2341. The latter was transposed by Law 27/2020, of 23 July, which created a new legal framework for pension funds.

---

40. Decree-Law 1/2015, of 6 January.
41. Regulation (EU) No. 1286/2014 of the European Parliament and of the Council of 26 November 2014 on key information documents for packaged retail and insurance-based investment products (PRIIPs).
42. Directive 2002/92/EC of the European Parliament and of the Council of 9 December 2002.
43. Directive (EU) 2016/97 of the European Parliament and of the Council of 20 January 2016 on insurance distribution.

75. The number of studies on insurance law has been increasing at a fast pace. Several recent PhD and master theses were devoted to different aspects of the insurance contract and nowadays there are different books, as well as a growing number of articles on the matter. Many of them will be quoted along the text.

§3. Sources of Insurance Law

76. In order to understand the dynamics of Portuguese Contract Law, especially after the twentieth century, one should never lose sight of the decisive role that comparative law plays in our legal system. It has been noted by a foreign scholar deeply acquainted with Portuguese private law that legal comparatism is imprinted in its DNA.[44] Since the beginning of the twentieth century, private law scholarship has studied closely the legal solutions adopted by other legal systems, especially those belonging to the Romano-Germanic family, and has kept a particularly close dialogue with German law and scholarship.[45] This legal-comparative approach underpinned the most important changes to Portuguese law; the Portuguese Civil Code, which emerged after decades of legal-comparative work, is a primary example of that. This methodology also supported the preparation of the text of the RJCS in 2008, as well as of other statutes that are particularly relevant here, such as the Decree-Law 446/85, of 25 October, on standard contract terms (LSCT). Moreover, the comparative method influences the interpretation of the existing norms performed by the courts, since their decisions frequently take into account the opinions expressed by scholarship.

I. Legislation

A. International Law

77. In what concerns international conventions that directly provide on insurance matters, Portugal is part of the Montreal Convention for the unification of certain rules for international carriage by air of 1999.

B. European Law

78. The European legislators have been regulating insurance law, mostly in its supervisory matters, for the past fifty years. The bulk of European insurance law is

---

44. Erik Jayme, Luis Cabral de Moncada (1888–1974) e as suas relações com a Alemanha, BFDUC, (1993), 258.
45. In English, *see* Marta Santos Silva, *The Draft Common Frame of Reference as a 'Toolbox' for Domestic Courts, A Solution to the Pure Economic Loss Problem from a Comparative Perspective*, 14–19 and 28–29 (Springer 2017).

nowadays set out by three Directives, that shall be mentioned just below. As of September 2020, all of them have been transposed to internal law. In any event, 'whenever the provisions of a directive appear, as far as their subject-matter is concerned, to be unconditional and sufficiently precise, those provisions may be relied on by individuals against the State where that State fails to implement the directive in national law within the prescribed period or where it fails to implement it correctly'.[46]

79. First of all, there is Solvency II, which provides on the taking-up and pursuit of the business of insurance and reinsurance. Besides setting out new prudential rules, the Directive includes a re-codification of fourteen existing directives in the areas of life and non-life insurance, reinsurance, insurance groups and liquidation. Solvency II is a framework directive adopted by way of the Lamfalussy process, with detailed specifications then provided by a directly applicable EU Regulation, Commission Delegated Regulation (EU) 2015/35 of 10 October 2014. Technical areas are specified using legally binding technical standards developed by the European Insurance and Occupational Pensions Authority (EIOPA) and adopted by the European Commission. All areas of supervisory law can be explained by legally non-binding guidelines from EIOPA.

80. Second, the Motor Insurance Directive. Its provisions, as well as those of its predecessors, cannot be fully understood without reference to the body of case law that ECJ has developed in their regard, through the mechanism of reference for a preliminary ruling.

81. Third, Directive (EU) 2016/97 of the European Parliament and of the Council of 20 January 2016 on insurance distribution (IDD). A number of implementing and delegated acts have been adopted in its regard.

82. In what regards pension plans and pension funds, the current reference is Directive 2016/2341 of the European Parliament and of the Council of 14 December 2016 on the activities and supervision of institutions for occupational retirement provisions.

83. The aforementioned Directives mostly regard supervisory law. There is yet no harmonised general framework for insurance contract law at a European level. There is, however, a set of model rules drawn up by a group of scholars from different jurisdictions, the Principles of European Insurance Contract Law (PEICL). The PEICL have been designed as an optional instrument of insurance contract law, that applies together with other instruments – namely, the Principles of European

46. ECJ, 4 March 1999, Case C-258/97 (*Hospital Ingenieure Krankenhaustechnik Planungs-Gesellschaft mbH (HI)*), no. 34.

Contract Law (PECL). Once opted into, the PEICL therefore entirely replace the reference to national laws, and function in parallel with them (*see* Articles 1:102, 1:104 and 1:105).[47]

84. The PEICL have not, so far, left the academic realm. They have, however, the potential to become European law. In fact, as of 2010 and 2011 both the European Economic and Social Committee and the European Parliament had stated the importance of creating model rules for the insurance contract that could apply by choice of the parties, similar to the PECL.[48] In 2013, the European Commission set up an Expert Group on European insurance contract law to examine barriers to cross-border trade in insurance law across Member States. In February 2014, the Group of Experts made its final report public. It found that differences in contract laws do impede the cross-border supply of insurance products – particularly, in the sector of life insurance and liability and motor insurance. If the issue becomes a political priority, the European Commission may accordingly propose the adoption of a set of model rules.[49] As the Group of Experts is mostly coincident with the group of scholars that authored the PEICL, it is likely that the PEICL are taken as the basis for the model rules.

85. For the time being, the PEICL serve as a reference both for law reforms[50] and *de iure condito*, for scholarship carrying out comparative law. The latter is the case in the Portuguese system; as shall be seen, it is not devoid of practical effects.

C. National Law

86. Portugal has a written Constitution, which is parametric of all other norms. Additionally, the Constitution entails a catalogue of fundamental rights, and establishes that they are directly applicable and binding not only for public entities, but also for private entities (Article 18(1)). There is controversy as to the implications of this last segment, but it can be said that authors tend to favour intermediate or differentiated approaches, according to which fundamental rights function first and foremost as a criterion for the interpretation of private law (especially in what

47. Project Group Restatement of European Insurance Contract Law, Principles of European insurance contract law, Sellier (2015), 7 and ff.
48. Opinion of the European Economic and Social Committee on 'The 28th Regime – An Alternative Allowing less Lawmaking at Community Level' (2011/C 21/05); European Parliament resolution of 8 June 2011 on policy options for progress towards a European Contract Law for consumers and businesses (2011/2013(INI)).
49. *See* https://ec.europa.eu/info/business-economy-euro/doing-business-eu/contract-rules/insurance-contracts/expert-group-european-insurance-contract-law_en. Jürgen Basedow, Der gemeinsame Referenzrahmen und das Versicherungsvertragsrecht, 1, ZEuP, 280 (2007), 280–281; Helmut Heiss, Optionales europaöisches Versicherungsvertragsrecht, 76, RabelsZ, 316 (2012), 317–320.
50. Olavi-Jüri Luik, *The Application of Principles of European Insurance Contract Law to Policyholders of the Baltic States: A Measure for the Protection of Policyholders*, University of Tartu Press, 2016, available at https://dspace.ut.ee/bitstream/handle/10062/52132/luik_olavi_jyri.pdf?sequence=1&isAllowed=y (retrieved on 03 Nov. 2016), 17–46.

regards its open-ended concepts), and should only be directly applied to relationships between private parties in a limited number of cases. For example, where there is a deep imbalance in the relationship, with a de facto social power of one party towards the other (e.g., worker-employee relations), or, according to other authors, where the essential core of a fundamental right is at stake (e.g., racial discrimination on business premises open to the public).[51]

87. At an infra-constitutional level and in what regards insurance contract law, the central piece of regulation is the RJCS. As private insurance law is part of private law, the Civil Code is also applicable at a more general level (e.g., determining the general norms on the conclusion of contracts, legal capacity, ancillary duties, non-performance). The same can be said, *mutatis mutandis*, for prudential law, which pivots around LBIR; or for insurance distribution law, which pivots around RDS. Their provisions need to be complemented by other acts, such as the Administrative Procedure Code, the Act on administrative offences, in the case of LBIR, Commercial Companies Law, or in the case of RDS, the Civil Code.[52]

88. Other than these, there are also statutes regulating insurance at a more specific level. That is the case of the Compulsory Motor Insurance Act (CMIA), which is of great practical significance. That is also the case of Articles 595–615 of the (1888) Commercial Code, which regulate marine insurance. For the life insurance branch, that is the case of Decree-Law 384/2007, of 19 November 2007, which creates a central registry of all life insurance and capital redemption operations that set out a beneficiary for the case of death. As is the case of Decree-Law 229/2009, of 11 November, that sets out measures to protect the consumers taking out life insurance contracts in connection with mortgage; or, more recently, of Law 35/2018, of 20 July 2018, that supplements the European norms on PRIIPS.

89. On the subject of pension funds, the relevant statute is the PFA. As shall be explained later, life insurance branch comprises a further mechanism for long-term savings, the Savings for Education or Retirement Plan (*Plano de Poupança Reforma* – PPR – *or Plano de Poupança Reforma-Educação*, PPR-E), regulated by Decree-Law 158/2002, of 2 July. The underlying funds can be managed as life insurance funds, as pension funds or as investment funds; the respective norms apply to either case. The first two cases pertain to the life insurance branch.

90. Reference should also be made to statutes aimed at the protection of certain vulnerable parties, and that although they are not specific to insurance, they are particularly relevant in this context.

---

51. Paulo Mota Pinto, A influência dos direitos fundamentais sobre o direito privado português (in: Direitos de personalidade e direitos fundamentais, Estudos, Gestlegal, 299, 2018), 308 and ff., himself favouring the latter approach.
52. Respectively, Decree-Law 4/2015, of 7 January; Decree-Law 433/82, of 27 October; Decree-Law 262/86, of 2 September.

91. First, there are the norms that protect consumers, primarily the Law on the protection of consumers, Law 24/96, of 31 July, that provides the general framework in this regard. Reference should also be made Decree-Law 57/2008, of 26 March 2008, concerning unfair business-to-consumer commercial practices before, during and after a commercial transaction in relation to a good or service, that specifically provides for insurance. Also of importance are Decree-Law 95/2006, of 29 May, concerning the distance marketing of consumer financial services, and Decree-Law 24/2014, of 14 February, on the protection of consumers in respect of distance contracts or of contracts negotiated away from business premises, which is also partially applicable to financial services.

92. Second, there is the statute on contracts of adhesion (LSCT), which applies not only to business-to-consumer contracts but also to business-to-business contracts.

93. The statutes on discrimination also belong in this realm. Reference should be made to Law 46/2006, of 28 August, which forbids and sanctions discrimination on the grounds of impairment or existence of an aggravated health risk (*see* especially Article 4(a) and (c)), and to Law 14/2008, of 12 March 2008, which prohibits any discrimination on the grounds of sex in regard to the access to goods and services and their supply (*see* especially Article 6).[53]

94. A further source of protection, applying both the contracts with consumers and with professional parties, is Law 7/2004 of 7 January on electronic commerce in the internal market and on the processing of personal data.

95. For its role in the protection of privacy and prevention of discrimination, Law 12/2005, of 26 January, on personal genetic information and health information, is also worth of mention.

96. Finally, in the specific context of the COVID-19 disease pandemic, Decree-Law 20-F/2020, of 12 May, established an exceptional and temporary scheme concerning the payment of the insurance premium and the effects of temporary reduction of risk in insurance contracts arising from significant reduction or suspension of activity.

II. Governmental Regulations and Regulation by Governmental Agencies

97. The issuing of infra-legal norms on insurance has been generally undertaken by the insurance supervisor, ASF, and not by the Government.[54] The ASF issues two

53. Law 9/2015, of 11 February.

54. Under Portuguese Law, regulatory bodies have the power to issue infra-legal acts, when granted by their statutes Art. 3(2)(e) and Art. 40(2) of Framework Law 67/2013, of 28 August, on regulatory bodies. That is the case for ASF, according to Art. 7(1)(a) of its statutes (Decree-Law 1/2015, of 6 January).

kinds of normative acts: binding regulatory frameworks (*normas*), and non-binding general communications (*circulares*). The ASF's binding regulatory frameworks are key in many areas – e.g., in quantifying the capital requirements laid down by LBIR, in setting out uniform contract terms of compulsory insurance, in specifying how the supervised entities should comply with their duties. They exist in a considerable number and shall be referred to throughout this piece of work. Non-binding general communications are used to make recommendations to the insurance companies, and sometimes to present them with questionnaires on their activity. When relevant, they shall also be referred.

III. Private International Law

A. *Jurisdiction*

98. Regarding international jurisdiction, the special provisions of Articles 10–16 of the Regulation (EU) No. 1215/2012 of the European Parliament and of the Council of 12 December 2012 on jurisdiction and the recognition and enforcement of judgments in civil and commercial matters (hereinafter 'Brussels Ia') and the parallel provisions of the Lugano Convention) must be observed, in each case subject to jurisdiction for consumer matters.

99. Article 8(1) Brussels Ia does not apply (e.g., in the case of direct action against the motor vehicle liability insurer), as Article 10 Brussels Ia does not provide for this. As a rule, the Brussels Ia only applies if the defendant has its seat in the EU (Articles 10 and 6 Brussels Ia). Only private insurances are covered, not public law or social insurances, nor reinsurance contracts or recourse. In most cases, the jurisdiction of domicile under Article 11(1a) Brussels Ia (with the extension of Article 11(2) Brussels Ia) applies relatively easily to actions against an insurer. According to Article 63(1) Brussels Ia, the domicile of companies and legal persons is where their registered office, central administration or principal place of business is located.

100. In principle, actions against an insurer under Article 11(1) Brussels Ia (= Article 9(1) Lugano Convention) may be brought before the courts of its State of domicile (point (a)), the court of the district where the policyholder, the insured or the beneficiary is domiciled (point (b)) or, in the case of co-insurance, before the court of a Contracting State where the lead insurer is sued (point (c)). Furthermore, actions may also be brought in the Contracting State in which a branch, agency or other establishment is located (Article 11(2) in conjunction with Article 7(5) Brussels Ia (= Article 8 in conjunction with Article 5(5) Lugano Convention)).

101. In the case of liability insurance or insurance of immovable property, the insurer may be sued in the place where the harmful event occurred (Article 12(1) Brussels Ia (= Article 10(1) Lugano Convention)), in addition to the jurisdiction provided for in Article 11 Brussels Ia (= Article 9 Lugano Convention). Furthermore, the insurer may be summoned to appear before the court before which the action of the injured party against the insured is pending through a proceeding if this is permitted under autonomous law. The Brussels Ia Regulation's jurisdiction rules apply to the injured party's direct action against the insurer (Article 13(2) Brussels Ia (= Article 11(2) Lugano Convention)). There is also international jurisdiction for the assertion of the direct claim against the liability insurer at the domicile of the injured party. Furthermore, if the law governing the direct action provides notice of the dispute against the policyholder or the insured, the same court also has jurisdiction over these persons (Article 13(3) Brussels Ia (= Article 11(3) Lugano Convention)). Otherwise, the insurer may only sue in the courts of the Contracting State in which the defendant is domiciled, regardless of whether the defendant is the policyholder, the insured or the beneficiary (Article 14(1) Brussels Ia (= Article 12(1) Lugano Convention)).

102. Concerning the agreement on jurisdiction, Article 15 Brussels Ia restricts the admissibility of agreements on jurisdiction for insurance matters quite extensively compared to the general norm of Article 25 Brussels Ia; further-reaching agreements on jurisdiction are invalid (Article 23(5) Brussels Ia). Jurisdictional agreements under Article 25 Brussels Ia (Article 23 Lugano Convention) may only modify the statutory order of jurisdiction to a limited extent. It may only be deviated from for agreements after the dispute has arisen (Article 15(1) Brussels Ia (= Article 13(1) Lugano Convention)), in favour of the policyholder (paragraph 2), in favour of the jurisdiction of the courts of the common State of domicile or residence (paragraph 3), in agreements with policyholders from non-Contracting States (paragraph. 4) and for marine and aviation insurance (paragraph 5). Agreements that contradict these rules are invalid.

103. Nevertheless, they are admissible according to Article 23(3) Brussels Ia if and because policyholder and insurer have their registered office or head office in the same state (Article 60(1) Brussels Ia). The courts of this State have jurisdiction even if the damaging event occurs abroad. However, this derogation of the *forum delicti commissi* presupposes that such an agreement is also permissible under that State's law. In addition, there is the possibility that in the case of general liability insurance of significant risks according to Articles 15(5) Brussels Ia and 16(5) Brussels Ia, a jurisdiction agreement is generally permissible.

B. Conflict-of-Law Rules

1. The Succession of Laws and Their Application in Time

104. The legal regime of the insurance contract (hereinafter 'RJCS') approved by Law 72/2008, of 16-04, which came into force on 01 January 2009 (Article 7), provided for a set of conflict rules to govern the insurance contact in Articles 5–10 RJCS. These rules which replaced the regime provided in the Civil Code (Articles 35, 36, 41, 42 of the Civil Code) for insurance contracts covering risks of Member

States (Article 1(3) and (4) of the Rome Convention (1980)[55]). In turn, on 17 December 2009, Regulation (EC) No. 593/2008 on the law applicable to contractual obligations (Rome I) came into force, replacing the Rome Convention[56] and, with regard to insurance contracts, replacing the conflict rules prescribed in the RJCS.[57]

105. Thus, in terms of succession in time of instruments regulating insurance contracts, it is necessary to delimit the scope of application of each conflict rule. In terms of application of the law over time, the relevant fact is the date of conclusion of the contract to ascertain which conflict rules are to be applicable.

106. In fact, for insurance contracts concluded before the entry into force of Rome I, whatever their configuration,[58] as well as for legal acts and transactions excluded from the scope of the Rome Convention (Article 1), the Civil Code rules will remain applicable. The rules set out in Articles 5–10 of the RJCS only apply to insurance contracts concluded between 01 January 2009 and 16 September 2009 that are not covered by the Rome Convention rules. That is, insurance contracts covering risks located outside the Union and European Economic Area (EEA) and reinsurance contracts are excluded from the scope of application of those rules, Article 1(3) and (4). However, the interpretation and application of the conflict rules provided for in domestic law are subject to interpretation in conformity with European law, insofar as the solutions adopted result from the act transposing Articles 7 and 8 of Directive 88/357/EEC and 32 of Directive 2002/83/EC. The rules set by these Directives have since been repealed by Article 310 of the Solvency II Directive.

2. Definition of the Insurance Contract

107. As a conflict rule, its structure is threefold: *object*, connecting factor and consequence. By delimiting the object (scope of matters) subject to the jurisdiction of the law in the connection, the framework concept refers to any insurance contract. The first challenge is the definition of the concept of the insurance contract. The sole purpose of this provision is to consolidate the conflict rules contained in the Insurance Directives. More specifically, on the one hand, it covers insurance contracts covering large risks, irrespective of the location of the risk, and, on the other hand, all other insurance contracts insofar as the risk covered is within the territory of the Community. Therefore, it is necessary to look into the Union's secondary law to determine what insurance contract is meant. Some areas are partially

55. Approved for ratification by Resolution of the Assembly of the Republic No. 3/94; ratified by Decree of the President of the Republic No. 1/94 and entered into force on 01 Sept. 1994.

56. For the purposes of determining which States are bound by Rome I, it should be understood that the reference to 'Member State' means all Member States of the Union except Denmark, to which Arts 3(4) and 7 apply (i.e., for these provisions Denmark is considered a Member State), Art. 1(4).

57. Luís de Lima Pinheiro, Sobre a lei aplicável ao contrato de seguro perante o Regulamento Roma I, in Estudos Em Homenagem A Miguel Galvão Teles (2012): 681–702, 682–683.

58. It should be noted that, for the purposes of determining whether a transaction is unilateral or a unilateral contract, the law designated by the Rome Convention must first be applied.

harmonised via directives, although not exhaustively regulated, which rules out the possibility of speaking of an autonomous category of European insurance contract law. As an interpretative guideline, we can refer to the concept defined in the Common Frame of Reference and the secondary law of the European insurance contract.

108. Article 7 concerns almost all insurance contracts. Article 1 of the Rome I Regulation is decisive for its scope of application. According to this, the Regulation applies to all contractual obligations under civil and commercial law that have a connection with the law of different states. This means that all insurance contracts are covered. The concept of insurance is to be defined autonomously. What is required is that one party undertakes to cover a particular risk in return for a premium payment. It is characteristic that the conclusion of many similar contracts forms a risk pool. Insurance mediation is not part of this, as only direct insurance (primary insurance) is regulated.

109. In contrast to reinsurance, this includes accident and damage insurance branches, including transport goods and general liability insurance. Life insurance is also mentioned, which is to be understood in the same way. However, a separate regulation for group insurance is missing.

110. Social insurance and other insurance relationships under public law are excluded based on the general provision of Article 1(1) sentence 2.

111. The distinction between the location of risk in the EU (or EEA) and outside the EU has been maintained as a critical connecting factor of the special rule set in Article 7. The distinction between large risks and reinsurance on the one hand and mass risks on the other has also been maintained.

3. Civil Code (Until 31 December 2008)

112. The conflict rules of the Civil Code apply to all insurance contracts concluded before the entry into force of the Rome Convention. After that date, they will keep applying to insurance contracts that present a risk within the Union and EEA until Articles 5–10 RJCS (31 December 2008) entered into force.

113. The codification of the Portuguese conflict rules through the Civil Code, which was the product of a piece of work not very aware of the criticism that was already being made to the classic conflict method at the time, adopted a unitary or synthetic perspective in the definition of the law that regulates obligations, ignoring that each contract has an internal economy that may justify the adoption of its own solutions in conflict terms, besides tending towards a cautious position concerning the exercise of autonomy and not foreseeing any clauses of flexibility or materialisation of the conflict solutions.

114. Article 41 establishes, as a rule, the application of the law that the parties have expressly designated or had in mind (by implied intention). It provides, however, that this law must be connected with one of the elements of the legal transaction which fall within the scope of private international law (subjects, declaration, object, performance, sanction) or correspond to a serious interest of the parties (however, it is usual to say that this serious interest may refer to the search for the substantial validity of the transaction or to submission to a law that is more precise), so that, even with the limitations provided, the use of fraud against the law in contractual matters under the aegis of the application of the Civil Code rules is highly questionable, except when the choice is based on purely capricious reasons).

115. As a subsidiary criterion, in the absence of a choice of law, Article 42 provides that for unilateral legal transactions (e.g., public promise, a promise of performance and acknowledgement of debt, will), the law of the habitual residence of the declarant is applicable. For contracts, the law of the habitual residence of the parties is applicable. In the absence of the latter, Article 42(2) states that the law of the place of conclusion for contracts for consideration and the law of the person's habitual residence granting the benefit should be applied in the alternative for free contracts (donation), free loan, etc.

116. The content of Article 7 goes back to the conflict-of-law directive of the European Community, which issued provisions for the harmonisation of the international insurance contract law of the Member States in the Second Non-life Insurance Directive and the (consolidated) Life Insurance Directive 4 and repealed them with effect from 1 January 2016 by Article 310 of the Solvency II Directive.

4. Rome Convention (From 01 September 1994 to 16 December 2009)

117. Article 1(3) excluded from the scope of the Rome Convention insurance contracts covering risks situated in a Member State to ensure regulation as intended by the directives under discussion at the time. The conflict rules of the Insurance Directives is that if the insurer was established in the Community or to the national conflict rules if he was not so established (which was de facto almost impossible since the Insurance Directives limit access to the insurance service to providers based in the Community or having elected domicile there). However, contracts covering risks located in third countries are subject to the Rome Convention, including Article 5 on the law applicable to consumer contracts if the conditions are met. Reinsurance contracts are covered by the ordinary rules of Articles 3 and 4 of the Rome Convention: these are complex financial transactions that do not follow a purpose of insurance as such, and are concluded between professionals for whom the possible need for protection through the conflict-of-law rule does not arise.[59]

---

59. Paul Lagarde & Aline Tenenbaum, *De la convention de Rome au règlement Rome I*, Revue critique de droit international privé. (2008), n. 33.

5. RJCS (From 01 January 2009 until 16 December 2009)

118. The set of conflict rules provided for in the RJCS establishes a legal framework based on the prevalence of provisions of international and European law, following the provisions of Article 8 of the Constitution (Article 5): 'The general rules of private international law in matters of contractual obligations apply to insurance contracts, in particular, those arising from international conventions and community acts that are binding upon the Portuguese State, with the specificities set out in the following Articles.'

119. The structuring of the conflict rule starts from recognising the parties' conflict autonomy as the primary connection. The parties are recognised as having the power to choose the same law or different laws to govern all or part of the contract (Article 6(4)). For the exercise of the autonomy, it is enough that there is an implicit manifestation of the intention to submit the contract to a specific law, either by express manifestation of a will or in an implicit form (tacit) from the clauses of the contract (Article 6(3)). However, the recognition of such autonomy depends on a connection with the Portuguese legal order. Whether for a spatial link of the risks with the Portuguese territory or because the policyholder, in the case of personal insurance, has their habitual residence in Portugal or the establishment to which the contract refers, depending on whether they are a natural or a corporate person (Article 6(1)). This means that the choice of law by the parties is dependent on the verification of a close connection with the Portuguese legal system (Article 7): 'The choice of law referred to in the previous Article may only apply to laws of which applicability corresponds to a substantial interest of the claimants or is connected with some of the elements of the insurance contract which are relevant in the context of private international law.'

120. Once this has been verified, the parties may refer to any law provided there is a close connection between it and the contract or the parties. This means that one or more elements chosen law must be related to the contract (objective interest) or that it is based on a serious interest of the parties (subjective interest) in the submission of the contract to a different law established by the objective connection (Article 8).

121. In the absence of a choice of law by the parties, Article 8 determines which law is competent or a limit to the conflict autonomy as a putative law. As a bilateral conflict rule except for paragraph 2, it elects as objective connections the connection that establishes the strongest connection with the State where the legal relationship finds its 'seat' (Article 8 paragraph 1 RJCS), it is the exception of paragraph 2.

122. Despite reflecting flexibility in private international law since it allows the conflict solution to be adapted to the type of insurance contract in question, the general rule set out in Article 8 paragraph 1, is nonetheless given in the subsequent paragraphs use of the cascade connections method, similar to the construction of Article 4(1) and (5) of the Rome Convention. It establishes a two-tier form laying in the presumption, referring either to damage insurance ('the legal order of the

State in which the risks are situated') or to personal insurance ('the residence of the victim of the accident or of the situation to which the victim is subject').

123. The order of preference is based on the location of the risk or the policyholder's residence, which is determined by the regime for access to and exercise of insurance activity. Besides the flexibility and bilateral nature of the conflict rule, it is prevalent for the Portuguese law in Article 8(2) (unilateral connection) when Portugal is the place of the risk situation or where the policyholder, in the case of insurance of persons, has their habitual residence or the establishment to which the contract relates in Portugal.

124. For the other cases, paragraph 3 establishes that an insurance contract shall be presumed to be more closely connected with the legal system of the State in which the risk is located. In contrast, in the case of insurance of persons, the closer connection shall result from the habitual residence of the policyholder or the establishment to which the contract pertains, depending on whether it is a natural person or a legal person. Thus, as in the case of two or more risks located in Portugal and another State, concerning the activities of the policyholder and where they carry out a commercial, industrial or liberal profession, the applicable law will be of the States in which the risks are located or, in the case of insurance of persons, the law of the State in which the policyholder has their usual residence, if a natural person, or his main administration, if a legal person.

125. Aligned with the conflict solutions presented by the Rome Convention (Article 7 'Mandatory Rules'[60]), the Portuguese legislator provided for the express regulation of mandatory rules (rules of necessary and immediate application). These rules are of substantive nature that aim to protect fundamental and imperative interests of specific legal order and operate prior (regardless) of the conflict rule, having its own unilateral connection (either by the connection expressly provided for or by interpretation of its purpose). This means that this rule has an overriding nature that arises as *ius cogens* of an international character in a way that the rule asserts itself against a foreign rule that would otherwise be applied to the conflict-of-law rule.

126. Mandatory rules relating to insurance contracts and protecting the public interest, those of consumers or third parties, override the contractual situation, whatever law is applicable, even when their applicability arises from a choice made by the parties. This provision fulfils a positive function of defining the concept of mandatory rules that have a nature and function to derogate from the *lex causae*, ruling

---

60. '1. When applying under this Convention the law of a country, effect may be given to the mandatory rules of the law of another country with which the situation has a close connection, if and in so far as, under the law of the latter country, those rules must be applied whatever the law applicable to the contract. In considering whether to give effect to these mandatory rules, regard shall be had to their nature and purpose and to the consequences of their application or non-application.

    2. Nothing in this Convention shall restrict the application of the rules of the law of the forum in a situation where they are mandatory irrespective of the law otherwise applicable to the contract.'

out the application of the conflict-of-law rule. Paragraph 2 establishes the unilateral spatial connection concerning the prevalence of Portuguese substantive rules over the *lex causae* whenever the insurance contract covers risks situated within Portuguese territory or, in the case of personal insurance, whenever the policyholder has their habitual residence or the establishment to which the contract refers, in Portugal. Thus, a personal connection (residence or establishment) or connection of the object of the contract (risks located in Portuguese territory) is required.

127. The protection of the public interests chosen by the Portuguese legislator, there is an option for the specialisation of the competent law, which determines the distribution of competence according to the location of the risks in more than one State. Jurisdiction is distributed according to the subject matter: *issue-to-issue*. This distributive connection presupposes the existence of mandatory rules in the different legal systems with a connection. It follows that despite the unilateral nature of the mandatory rule defined in paragraph 2, foreign mandatory rules are considered if, in the case of another jurisdiction where one of the risks covered by the insurance contract is located, the connection provided for in paragraph 2 (through the bilateralisation of the connection) is verified. Article 9 only justifies the departure from the *lex causae* when public interests require the substantive rules of a particular State to prevail, considering the principles and purposes of the conflict rules. If there are no such interests, the competent law indicated by the conflict rules should continue to govern the contract. In a certain way, this distributive application follows the protection of Portuguese interests and by analogy those of the third States. By this understanding, Article 10 prescribes the application of Portuguese law to compulsory insurance contracts without affecting the distributive application provided for in Article 9(3)). The rule on compulsory insurance must be interpreted in the light of the object which regulates it and the consequent connection often associated with the activity performed by the insured where the connection is limited to the establishment, registration, or enrolment with a professional association, or to the location of the risk (e.g., compulsory insurance in buildings set up as horizontal property has an implicit *lex rei sitae* connection).

128. Lastly, Article 9(4) establishes a rule of substantive private international law by determining the ineffectiveness of insurance contracts of an international nature that relate to the risks provided for in Article 14.[61] Thus, there is a substantive regulation for contracts, irrespective of the applicable law, whenever the effects of such a contract are invoked in Portugal.

---

61. Article 14 (prohibited insurance):

> 1 – Without prejudice to the general rules about the licitness of the negotiating terms, it is prohibited to enter into an insurance contract covering the following risks
> a) Criminal, misdemeanour or disciplinary liability;
> b) Abduction, kidnapping and other crimes against personal liberty;
> c) Possession or transportation of narcotics or drugs of which consumption is forbidden;
> d) Death of children under the age of 14 years or of those who due to psychic anomaly or any other cause are incapable of controlling their own person.
>
> 2 – The prohibition referred to in paragraph a) of the preceding number shall not extend to any associated civil liability.

6. Rome I Regulation (From 17 December.2009 until Now)

129. As mentioned above, the scope of the application of national law is narrowed, except for the temporal application of the law described above. From 17 December 2009, the relevant conflict rules are those prescribed in the rules set by Rome I, in particular, Article 7. Articles 5–10 RJCS have a very residual application, as we shall see.

130. After the initial approach of the European integration process based on the harmonisation of legal systems through the provision of conflict rules in directives and their exclusion from the Convention, a uniform regulation was enacted through Article 7 of Rome I that is a conflict rule. The purpose of these provisions is to bring together the scattered conflict-of-law rules in a single instrument: Article 23 of Rome I provides that 'With the exception of Article 7, this Regulation shall not prejudice the application of provisions of Community law which, about particular matters, lay down conflict-of-law rules relating to contractual obligations.' The singularity of the source of the conflict rules in matters of insurance contracts follows from this. As noted by Lagarde and Tenenbaum, Article 7 of Rome I, which was introduced at the last minute, is not, however, a copy of the conflicting rules of the above-mentioned directives in a single provision. On the contrary, it has made substantial and complex changes to the latter, intended to apply exclusively to Article 6 of Rome I on consumer contracts.[62]

131. The scope of application of the law governing the insurance contract, which follows from the provisions of Articles 10(1), 12 and 182(1) Rome I, covers, among other things: formation and substantive validity (Article 10(1)); interpretation (Article 12(1)(a)); the performance of obligations arising out of it (Article 12(1)(b)); within the limits of the powers conferred on the court by its procedural law, the consequences of the total or partial non-performance of such obligations, including the assessment of damage, to the extent that this assessment is governed by the competent law (Article 12(1)(c)); the various causes of termination of obligations (Article 12(1)(d)); the consequences of a void contract (Article 12(1)(e)); legal presumptions and the allocation of the burden of proof (Article 18(1)).

132. Rome I also has conflict rules for specific partial questions, notably on the formal validity of contracts (Article 11), performance methods and the measures to be taken by the creditor in the event of non-performance (Article 12(2)). Specific questions will have to be determined by the law designated by the *lex fori* conflict rules, such as capacity (Article 1(2)(a)) and the subrogation of the insurer against

3 – The prohibition referred to in paragraphs 1(b) and 1(d) shall not cover the payment of strictly compensatory benefits.

4 – The coverage of the risk of death by accident of children under 14 years of age shall not be prohibited as long as it is contracted by schools, sports or similar institutions that are not beneficiaries.

62. Paul Lagarde; Aline Tenenbaum, *De la convention de Rome*, n. 34.

third parties liable for damage to the insured (Article 19 Regulation (EC) No. 864/2007 of the European Parliament and of the Council, of 11 July 2007, on the law applicable to non-contractual obligations (Rome II)). Regarding the possibility of the injured party suing the insurer directly, Article 18 of Rome II stipulates 'The person having suffered damage may bring his or her claim directly against the insurer of the person liable to provide compensation if the law applicable to the non-contractual obligation or the law applicable to the insurance contract so provides.'

133. The direct claim of the injured party against the liability insurer of the tortfeasor is an essential subject of private insurance law. Therefore, in terms of conflict of laws, the legal system which determines whether a person entitled to damages can directly address the liability insurer of his debtor in deviation from the relativity of the contractual relationship 'insurance contract', must be decided. According to the Rome II Regulation, this question is answered by way of an alternative connection according to the tort law determined as specified by to Articles 4–9 and 14 (Article 18, first phrase Rome II) or the law applicable to the insurance contract (insurance law, Article 18, second phrase Rome II).

134. Article 18 Rome II Regulation complement the application of the tort law in the interest of a quick and secure compensation of the injured party: The victim of a tort is favoured by being able to claim directly against the insurer of the liable party either from the tort statute or the insurance statute. The connection serves to protect the injured party and strengthens the procedural economy. The insurer does not suffer any disadvantage from the pro-injury alternative connection insofar as he has to expect the authoritative nature of the insurance statute to apply in any case. There is a connection between Article 18 and the Rome I insofar as the insurance statute invoked in Article 18, second phrase may have to be determined under Article 7 Rome I. Article 18 must be seen in connection with Article 13(2) of the Brussels Ia, according to which the jurisdictions of Articles 10–12 of the Brussels Ia apply to direct action against the insurer of the responsible party. The ECJ ruled that in the case of liability insurance, the court of the injured party's domicile also has jurisdiction to rule on the direct claim (Article 13(2) Brussels Ia in conjunction with Article 11(1)(b) Brussels Ia).[63] In another ruling, the ECJ added that this jurisdiction, which serves to protect the weaker party, is only open to the injured party (e.g., the injured accident victim), but not to the social security institution, acting as the statutory assignee of the rights of the directly injured party in a motor accident.[64]

135. Article 7 of Rome I covers the most common insurance contracts. While it has the merit of having brought together and partially adapted the rules of private

63. C-463/06, FBTO Schadeverzekeringen (ECLI:EU:C:2007:792): 'The reference in Art. 11(2) of Council Regulation (EC) No. 44/2001 of 22 December 2000 on jurisdiction and the recognition and enforcement of judgments in civil and commercial matters to Art. 9(1)(b) of that regulation is to be interpreted as meaning that the injured party may bring an action directly against the insurer before the courts for the place in a Member State where that injured party is domiciled, provided that such a direct action is permitted and the insurer is domiciled in a Member State.'
64. C-347/08, Vorarlberger Gebietskrankenkasse (ECLI:EU:C:2009:561).

international law scattered throughout the directives, the provisions show a certain simplification,[65] but at the same time lays down complex conflict-of-law rules. Not all insurance contracts are subject to Rome I. Contracts relating to mass risks not located in a Member State are excluded from Article 7. On the other hand, the system of rules that has been put in place is primarily inspired by directives, even though the latter had a different objective from that of the conflict-of-law rule. As Jean Bigot has already noted in connection with the parallel systems put in place by secondary law and the Rome Convention, 'a single market involving the free movement of services within that market implies a free choice of law, including the law of the insurer distributing his products within the EEC under a single law. The concern for consumer protection implies allowing the consumer to claim the benefit of his law, which is deemed to be the most protective' and, a little higher up: 'Community law tends to apply exclusively the law of the place of establishment (home country control) whereas the conflict rules tend to give jurisdiction to the law of the State where the risk is situated or where the policyholder resides.'[66]

136. The structure of Article 7 of Rome I follows a scheme of narrowing possibilities of a choice of law by the contracting parties from the beginning to the end and accordingly places individual sub-cases of the insurance contract in the order of an exclusion scheme, starting with reinsurance contracts (greatest freedom of choice Article 7(1)), via large risk contracts (Article 7(2)), mass risks (Article 7(3)), to the compulsory insurance contracts, for which the least freedom of choice tends to exist (or can exist – Article 7(4)). Paragraph 5 deals with the case of multiple risk locations, and paragraph 6 defines the central connecting element of risk location.[67]

a. Mandatory Insurances

137. As seen above, Article 10 RJCS submits the contracts of which legal obligation results from its legislation to Portuguese law, without prejudice to the distributive application of various laws depending on the distribution of risks (Article 9(3) RJCS). However, according to Article 7(4) of Rome I, additional rules apply to insurance contracts for which a Member State imposes an insurance obligation. Such protection is primarily in the public interest, which also finds expression in conflict of laws. This covers contracts on large risks (paragraph 2) and mass risks (paragraph 3). Here, first, there is a provision for the sufficiency of the insurance obligation in point a. The provision on insurance is also found in Article 7(4)(b)); this provision, furthermore, states that a Member State may, by way of derogation from paragraphs 2 and 3, order that the law applicable to the insurance contract shall be that of the Member State imposing the obligation to insure. Thus, this regulation may contain general conflict-of-law rules.

65. *See* in this sense: Louise Merrett, *Choice of Law in Insurance Contracts under the Rome I Regulation*, 1, Journal of Private International Law, 2009), 49–68.
66. Paul Lagarde; Aline Tenenbaum, *De la convention de Rome* ..., n. 34.
67. Domenik Henning Wendt (in: Rauscher (ed.), Europäisches Zivilprozess- und Kollisionsrecht, 4. Ed., Otto Schmidt 2016), Versicherungsverträge, Rn. 2.

138. However, the reference to the law of the issuing state is subject to the provision that the Member State concerned also wants its own law to be applied; that is the case. If there is no corresponding provision for compulsory insurance, the connection according to Article 7(2) and (3) remains applicable.

b. Objective Connection

139. Article 7 of Rome I excludes reinsurance contracts, which remain subject to the general provisions of Articles 3 and 4. Instead, it lays down rules common to all contracts within its scope. The conflict-of-law rule distinguishes two categories of contracts, defined by employing a double criterion, material and spatial. The first category consists of insurance contracts covering large risks within the meaning of the First Council Directive 73/239/EEC of 24 July 1973 on the coordination of laws, regulations and administrative provisions relating to the taking-up and pursuit of the business of direct insurance other than life assurance, irrespective of where the risk is situated; the second category includes all other contracts covering only risks located within the territory of the Member States. The distinction between these two categories leads to a differentiated scope of freedom of choice: widely recognised for insurance contracts covering large risks, it is regulated for other contracts.

140. Article 7 is stratified according to the type of risk, which is the object of the insurance contract. This implies the recognition of greater or lesser autonomy in the choice of the applicable law. It depends on the type of risk, which conditions the adequacy of the connection chosen to govern the contract: large risk, mass risk, reinsurance, and the location of the risk. Thus, the possibility of a choice of law is granted to varying degrees. The objective connection also follows different approaches.

141. According to paragraph 1, Article 7 of Rome I only covers:

- Direct insurance contracts covering large risks (paragraph 2), irrespective of whether the insured risk is in a Member State or not. Article 7 applies to contracts under paragraph 2 regardless of whether the risk covered is situated in a Member State. The determination of the location of the risk is based on paragraph 6.
- Direct insurance contracts on 'mass risks' (as opposed to large risks; paragraph 3) when located in a Member State.

142. In contrast, the general provisions set in Articles 3, 4 and 6 of Rome I apply to the connection:

- all reinsurance contracts, irrespective of the location of the risk (paragraphs 1 and 2); and
- direct insurance contracts on mass risks for risks not located in a Member State. If the risk is not situated in a Member State, the conflict rules to be used are Articles 3 and 4, the former in the context of conflict autonomy and the latter in

the context of objective connection, without prejudice to the application of consumer protection conferred by Article 6.

143. In terms of multiple risk location, first, we need to consider the spatial location of the multiple risks. Suppose they are simultaneously located in the Union, the EEA or third States, verifying a distributive connection between applicable laws, even if they concern a single contract. Article 7 applies for risks located in the European area; as for external risks outside the internal market, the rules applied are Articles 3, 4 and 6. The location of the risk is determined by paragraph 6. Rome I does not explicitly state which rules are to apply to the connection.

144. For mass contracts, the location of the risk is important and is determined following Article 7(6) of Rome I, which applies to all other insurance contracts covering risks situated in the territory of the Member States (paragraph 1, sentence 1, point 2). Recital 33 addresses multiple locations. If an insurance contract not covering a large risk covers more than one risk, of which at least one is situated in a Member State, and at least one in a third State, the rules of the Rome I Regulation for insurance contracts should apply only to the risks situated in the Member State(s) concerned. This results in a split of the statutes.

145. As for the reinsurance contracts (according to Article 7(1), sentence 2 of Rome I), the conflict rule applied is Article 4. Since reinsurance contracts do not require special protection of the policyholder, they are to be connected in the same way as other contracts. Therefore, the general contract law provisions of Articles 3 et seq. apply to them. Express and tacit choice of law are permissible (Article 3). The choice of law is free and not subject to any restrictions.

146. Regarding the objective connection, the question of classification in the system of Article 4 arises first. The classification of the reinsurance contract as a service contract according to Article 4(1)(b)) RJCS leads to the habitual residence of the reinsurer (probably the majority opinion). Alternatively, one invokes the characteristic performance (Article 4(2)) or the closest connection (Article 4(4)). The insurance contract tends to be classified as a service within the meaning of Article 4(1) point (b), which leads to the insurer's habitual residence . The same result is reached via Article 4(2). However, Article 6 on consumer contracts also applies. For the subjective connection, the favourability principle of Article 6 then applies. Thus, the law of the policyholder's habitual residence can be the *lex causae*. When choosing a third state law, the choice-of-law restrictions of the consumer law directives can also come into play (Article 7 RJCS).

c. Compulsory Insurance

i. Insurance Contracts Covering Risks for which a Member State Imposes an Obligation to Take Out Insurance

147. Common to all insurance contracts governed by the Rome I Regulation, the rules are stated in paragraphs 4, 5 and 6 of Article 7. In addition, paragraph 4 provides additional rules that give the Member States the option of having their own law prevail when it obliges to take out insurance for the risk concerned against the law designated by the preceding paragraphs of Article 7(5) and (6) relate to the determination of the location of the risk.

148. The contract will have to comply with the specific stipulations laid down by the law of the Member State, which mandates insurance. The latter prevails in case of contradiction with the law of the Member State in whose territory the risk is situated. Moreover, by derogation from the rules laid down in Article 7(2) and (3) of Rome I, a State may designate the law of the Member State, which imposes an obligation to take out insurance.

149. According to paragraph 4, additional rules apply to insurance contracts for which a Member State imposes compulsory insurance. Such protection is primarily in the public interest, which also finds its expression in conflict of laws. This covers contracts for large risks (paragraph 2) and mass risks (paragraph 3). Here, first, there is a provision for the sufficiency of compulsory insurance in point a. The provision for compulsory insurance in Article 7(4)(b) is also included. Furthermore, this provision states that a Member State may, by way of derogation from paragraphs 2 and 3, order that the law applicable to the insurance contract shall be that of the Member State imposing the obligation to insure.

150. First, the predominance of the law of compulsory insurance seems to be the result of a particular method, close to the method of overriding mandatory rules. The law of the place where the risk is situated is to be compared with the law of compulsory insurance, which will prevail in the event of contradiction.[68] The substantive solution prevails over the adequacy judgment formulated by the conflict rule about the spatial connection, imposing an analogous assessment of the substantive regulation at issue. The existence of overriding mandatory provisions corresponds to a regulatory intervention as a manifestation of the pursuit of the interests of a given community to the detriment of the individuality of the parties to the situation and the interests undertaken for the *lex causae*. The growth of this regulatory power raises the question of the paradigm shift and whether the determination of the applicable law is no more than the allocation of the regulatory authority between states.[69]

---

68. Paul Lagarde & Aline Tenenbaum, *De la convention de Rome au règlement Rome I*. Revue critique de droit international privé, (2008) n. 37.
69. Jan-Jaap Kuipers, *EU Law and Private International Law. The Interrelationship in Contractual Obligations*, 4 (Nijhoff 2012).

151. Only the law of the Member State imposing compulsory insurance is taken into consideration. Its application depends on the content of the law of the Member State where the risk is situated. The law of the Member State of the place of the risk is the only other term of comparison: the text does not indicate on what basis this law applies. For contracts covering large risks, the law of the place where the risk is situated will not always be that of a Member State since, as we shall see, Article 7(1) of Rome I determines the law applicable to such contracts irrespective of where the risk is situated. Moreover, for contracts covering major risks, the law of the place where the risk is located need not apply systematically, either in terms of the law chosen by the parties or the designation of the applicable law in the absence of choice.

152. Consequently, imposing a comparison between the law of compulsory insurance and the law of the place of the risk if the risk is situated in a Member State seems at the very least unforeseeable for the parties. Moreover, for contracts covering other risks, the interference of the law where the risk is situated also seems inadequate. The parties can choose this law from a predetermined range of other laws; in the absence of choice, the law of the risk is designated by the Rome I Regulation as the objectively applicable law. The result is that, even if the parties have chosen a law other than the law of the place where the risk is situated, the law of the place where the risk is located must nevertheless be considered rigidly, to the exclusion of all others.

ii. Insurance Excluded from the Scope of Rome I

153. Article 7 of Rome I does not apply to the insurance contracts of Article 1(2)(j). This concerns insurance contracts from transactions carried out by institutions other than the undertakings referred to in Article 2 of Directive 2002/83/EC, old version. However, the Life Assurance Directive has since been repealed and replaced by the Solvency II Directive. The reference is, therefore, now to Article 9(2) of the Solvency II Directive. Article 2 of the Solvency II Directive regulates the scope of application. It covers the taking up and pursuing the self-employed activity of direct insurance by undertakings established in a Member State or wishing to establish themselves there. It also mentions individual transactions. Article 9 of the Solvency II Directive concerns exceptions, such as occupational pensions. The exclusion in Article 1(2)(j) is based on a Swedish proposal that the other Member States did not actively support.

d. Conflict Autonomy

154. To the extent that a choice of law is permitted, the general requirements of Article 3 of Rome I must be met. A partial choice of law is allowed. A choice of law under the conflict of laws is only permitted for state law. This also applies to the principles of European insurance law. Article 3(3) and (4) of Rome I must be observed. For the existence of the grounds for a limited choice of law, it is the time of the conclusion of the contract that matters so that subsequent changes have no effect. However, since a subsequent choice of law is permissible (Article 3(1) and (2)) their occurrence can open the way to a new agreement. The parties' choice is also subject to Article 3(4) allowing for the application European law, which cannot be derogated from by contract when all other elements are in one or more Member States.

i. Mass Risks Insurance Contracts (Paragraph 3)

155. Insurance contracts that are not referred to in paragraph 2 are named mass risk insurance. The law does not define or list mass risk insurance contracts; they are simply identified as those not qualifying as large risk insurance contracts.

156. There are restrictions on the choice of law for these contracts, without prejudice from the provisions on mandatory insurance (paragraph (4) point (b) and Article 10 RJCS). In principle, the parties may only choose between the laws listed in Article 7(3), sub-paragraph (1). These legal systems, with which there is a personal or factual relationship, are listed in detail in points (a)–(e). It depends on the respective type of contract and on its content. The individual permissive elements stand side by side as alternatives. Recital 32 explains that because of the unique nature of insurance contracts, special provisions should ensure an appropriate level of protection for policyholders.

157. Article 7(3) has thus combined the provisions of the life and non-life insurance directives, the main objective of ensuring the effective exercise of the freedom to provide insurance services. Regarding conflict of laws, and given the lack of uniformity of national legislation, this objective had to be reflected in the autonomy of will, which was regulated to distort competition between insurance companies. However, the objectives assigned to the conflict-of-law rule, and in part taken over from secondary legislation, are not clearly and coherently defined. First, the criteria chosen do not all seem to meet the objective of protecting the policyholder, even though this is recalled in Article 7(3), which has thus combined the provisions of the life and non-life insurance directives, the sees its main objective as that of ensuring the effective exercise of the freedom to provide insurance services.

158. The criteria chosen do not all seem to meet the objective of protecting the policyholder, even though this is recalled in Recital 32: if such an objective is the main aim of the conflict rule, then the criterion of the habitual residence of the policyholder is undoubtedly the most appropriate and should even be made into a rigid connecting factor. Moreover, the general aim of legal certainty set out in Recital 16 also seems to be undermined: the choices offered to the parties do not lead to a 'high degree of predictability' of the law applicable to insurance contracts since, at the same time, the interference of overriding mandatory rules under Article 9 could, to a much greater extent than in the directives mentioned above, displace the law chosen by the parties.

159. Article 7(3) has thus combined the provisions of the life and non-life insurance directives, the main aim of ensuring the effective exercise of the freedom to provide insurance services. In terms of conflict of law, and given the lack of uniformity of national legislation, this objective had to be reflected as the auto-determination of the will, which was regulated so as not to distort competition between insurance companies. In the life and non-life insurance directives, the parties' choice of applicable law is presented in a complex three-tier system, after the mandatory connection to the law of the place where the risk is situated for non-life insurance and to the law of the place of the commitment for life insurance.

ii. Individual Cases of Paragraph 3 Sub-paragraph 1

160. Paragraph 3 contains the connecting rules for insurance contracts that do not cover large risks. In this respect, Article 7(3) sub-paragraph 1 allows for a choice of law. However, this is only a limited party autonomy; the selectable rights are mentioned in point (a)–(e). Paragraph 2 assumes, however, that in some instances, national, international insurance law may contain a more far-reaching or different provision. This opening clause extends the freedom of choice of law and thus leads to a 'choice of law by reference' or 'block reference'.[70]

(a) Risk Location (Paragraph 3 Sub-paragraph 1 Point (a))

161. The law of the Member State in which the risk is situated at the time of conclusion of the contract can be chosen (paragraph 3, sentence 1, point (a)). The location of the risk is also determined here according to paragraph 6. This choice of law is unproblematic – admittedly also functionless – as it corresponds to the legal connection anyway.

(b) Ordinary Residence of the Insured (Paragraph 3 Sub-paragraph 1 Point (b))

162. According to paragraph 3 sub-paragraph 1 point (b), the state law under which the policyholder has his/her habitual residence may also be chosen. The habitual residence is determined according to Article 19. The habitual residence is often the place where the risk is located, but it is precisely when the risk and the habitual residence differ. The habitual residence can also be in a non-Member State.

(c) Nationality of the Insured (Paragraph 3 Sub-paragraph 1 Point (c))

163. In principle, Article 7 covers all insurance contracts and determines the degree of freedom of choice of law for them. In the case of life insurance, the law of the Member State of which the insured is a national may be chosen (paragraph

70. Martin Fricke, *Das Internationale Privatrecht der Versicherungsverträge nach Inkrafttreten der Rom-I-Verordnung*, VersR (2008), 448.

3 sub-paragraph 1 point (c)). In these cases, the policyholder often still has a relationship with their home state. Thus, the law of the policyholder's habitual residence cannot be invoked against the chosen law, just as the nationality of the insured person is irrelevant. The decisive factor is the time of the choice of law.

164. If, in the cases of paragraph 3 sub-paragraph 1 point (a) (location of risk), point (b) (habitual residence of the insured) or point € (several risks), the Member States mentioned offer greater freedom of choice regarding the law applicable to the insurance contract. The parties may use this freedom (paragraph 3 sub-paragraph 2). The individual options can be used side by side, i.e., alternatively. What matters is whether the legal systems of the respective Member States offer greater freedom of choice regarding the law applicable to the insurance contract. For these regulatory options, it depends on the national legislation. However, this does not constitute a complete overall reference to the law of the Member States. This reference follows the Directive (Article 7(1)(d) Directive 88/357/EEC). Since the other Member States must respect the choice of law, there is no risk of a fragmentation of law, thereby promoting the liberalisation of the European internal insurance market. Member States following a more liberal international insurance law are free to grant greater freedom of choice of law. This is in the tradition of previous Directive law to allow extended freedom of choice of law. In the Portuguese case, autonomy is conditioned by Articles 6 and 7 RJCS (*supra*).

(d) External Damage (Paragraph 3 Sub-paragraph 1 Point (d))

165. According to paragraph 3 sub-paragraph **1** point (d), the law of the Member State in which the risk is located may be chosen for insurance contracts in which the risks covered are limited to cases of damage that may occur in a Member State other than the Member State in which the risk is situated. Here, a lesser need for protection under a conflict of laws is assumed. Therefore, for a liability insurance policy, the parties may choose, for example, the law of the state in which the damage is likely to occur. The location of the risk is governed by paragraph 6. If the damage can only occur in a non-Member State, the choice of law does not exist.

(e) Multiple Risks (Paragraph 3 Sub-paragraph 1 Point (e))

166. In the case of professional or liberal professional activity, the multiple locations of risks also open the possibility of a choice of law according to paragraph 3. If the insured pursues commercial or industrial activity or a liberal profession and if the insurance contract covers two or more risks that relate to this activity and are in different Member States, the law of a Member State concerned or the law of the state in which the habitual residence of the insured is located may be chosen (paragraph 3 sub-paragraph 1 point (e)). The second alternative of point (e) is admittedly only a repetition of the possibility already existing under point b. However, habitual residence in a non-Member State is also sufficient. The determination of the activity is made autonomously by regulation. The choice of law also applies to life insurance. This choice of law does not exist for contracts with consumers. The insured risk must therefore be related to one of the mentioned activities.

IV. Jurisdiction and Role of Scholarship

167. Portugal is a civil law jurisdiction, and therefore the creation of law is based on statutes. Case law is not a source of binding (general) norms, but rather of binding decisions that strike singular cases. In this sense, it is not a source of law – it is hence absent from the list of sources of law laid down in Articles 1–4 of the Civil Code.

168. Moreover, there is no system of binding precedents. Each court may in principle differ from pre-existing decisions, as long as it gives its grounds for differing. A principle of freedom of judgment is mentioned in this regard.[71] Nonetheless, the principle of equality before the law, as well as the principle of protection of legitimate expectations, does require some harmonisation in case law.[72]

169. Such harmonisation derives, first of all, from the exercise of the right of appeal to a higher court: if a higher court overturns the decision of a lower court, the latter must comply with the ruling (Article 152 of the Code of Civil Procedure). Furthermore, there are forms of appeal to the Supreme Court that actually have the harmonisation of case law as a purpose. That is the case of the exceptional appeal based on the contradiction of the decisions of high courts (*revista excecional*), and of the appeal for the unification of case law (*recurso para uniformização de jurisprudência*), both addressed to the Supreme Court. That is also the case of the extended appeal judgment (*julgamento ampliado de revista*), which also takes place in the Supreme Court, in case of contradiction or risk of contradiction in its case law affecting issues deemed important.[73]

---

71. Francisco Ferreira de Almeida, Direito processual civil, II, Almedina, (2015), 557.
72. F. Ferreira de Almeida, Direito processual II, 556. Although the provisions of criminal procedure law, or administrative procedure law, are not analysed in this text, the same principles apply to them – *see supra*, 561 and ff.
73. Under Art. 672 of the Code of Civil Procedure, an exceptional appeal (*revista excecional*) can be presented to the Supreme Court when three requirements are met: the matter under discussion is of such relevance, that its appreciation is clearly necessary for a better application of law; interests of particular social relevance are at stake; the ruling of the second instance court contradicts a previous ruling of another second instance court or by the Supreme Court, that has acquired the authority of a final decision and that concerns the same fundamental question of law, under the same applicable norms, unless the former conforms with a ruling on unification of case law by the Supreme Court (Art. 672(1)). Under the extended appeal judgment, set out in Arts 686 and 687, the President of the Supreme Court can request the question to be judged by the *plenum* of the civil chambers of the Court when they deems necessary or convenient to ensure the uniformity of case law. The judges of the case have the duty to propose this form of judgment when they see that the ruling issued for the case possibly contradicts uniform case law in regard to the same fundamental question of law and under the same applicable norms. Under the appeal for unification of case law, set out in Arts 688–695, an appeal may be presented to the *plenum* of the civil chambers of the Supreme Court when it has issued a ruling that contradicts a previous ruling by the same Court in regard to the same

170. Both the extended appeal judgment and the appeal for the unification of case law are decided by the *plenum* of the Civil Chamber of the Supreme Court, and in both cases the conclusions of the decision take the form of an abstract rule of interpretation of the applicable norms, which is published in the Official Journal (Articles 687(5) and 695 of the Civil Procedure Code). Nonetheless, this rule is *not binding in a proper sense* – there is no binding precedent, but a persuasive precedent endowed with *auctoritas.*[74] Lower courts may differ from it; although, they risk seeing their decision overturned by a higher court (either at second instance or by the Supreme Court). Even the Supreme Court may differ from the uniform rule it adopted – though it risks triggering the procedure of extended appeal judgment, delivering the decision of the case to the *plenum* of the civil chambers (Article 686(1) and (3)). This very procedure may, however, lead to a change in the uniform rule.

171. Moreover, a court may naturally differ from any previous ruling without risk of being overturned, as long as it shows in the grounds for the decision that the facts of the case are different from those which were taken into account in the previous rulings.

172. All this reflects the view that the case law should preserve its coherence, but nonetheless be able to account for any particular features of the case that justify a different treatment, and even be able to change and evolve, as long as there are sufficient grounds for it.[75] This view has been highlighted since the norms that allowed for the issuing of binding rules of interpretation by the Supreme Court – the 'assentos' – were deemed unconstitutional due to infringement of the principle of separation of powers and therefore revoked.[76]

173. The courts are bound to decide the case under the statutory norms that regulate the case in dispute. However, it would not be correct to say that they merely 'apply' the existing norms. The abstract nature of the norms, and the broad existence of open-ended legal concepts gives them room to consider the particular features of the case, and it can be said that they tend to actively co-define and expand the terms of existing law.[77] This stance is reflected in the style of the courts' decisions, which tend to expose their reasons in length, and to be underpinned with previous case law and scholarship.

---

fundamental question of law and under the same applicable norms. *See also* Art. 671(2) and (3), on the appeal against second instance decisions that regard procedural matters.

74. Armindo Ribeiro Mendes, Recursos em processo civil, Reforma de 2007, Coimbra Editora, (2009), 170–171; Fernando Amâncio Ferreira, Manual dos recursos em processo civil, Almedina, (2009), 123–124; 321–322; F. Ferreira de Almeida, Direito processual II, 557.
75. António Santos Abrantes Geraldes, Recursos no novo Código de Processo Civil, Almedina, (2016); 423–424; F. Amâncio Ferreira, Manual dos recursos ..., 123–124; F. Ferreira de Almeida, Direito processual II, 556–557.
76. Constitutional Court, 7 December 1993, 474/88, Ruling 810/93 (Monteiro Diniz); on the matter, *see* António Castanheira Neves, *O problema da constitucionalidade dos assentos (Comentário ao acórdão n.º 810/93 do Tribunal Constitucional)* (in: *Digesta III, 1 Ed (reimp)*, 337, 2010), passim.
77. For further reference, *see* M. Santos Silva, *The Draft Common ...*, 32 and 35–36.

174. Scholarship is not a source of binding law. However, it does have a marked influence upon 'law-in-action'. On the one hand, it has an impact upon law-making, since it is frequent that expert commissions preparing draft laws are presided over – or at least integrated by – scholars. On the other hand, it has a considerable impact upon case law. This has to do to with the style of Portuguese court rulings, which extensively draw upon existing scholarship (and previous case law) to provide the grounds for their reasoning.[78] Conversely, scholarship tends to have a practical slant, and to attach great importance to discussing the best approach to tackle hypothetical or real cases.

§4. Dispute Settlement and Arbitration

175. An aggrieved policyholder, insured, beneficiary or injured party can first and foremost bring a complaint before the insurer. Insurers are obliged to have a complaints management department made up of unbiased and qualified personnel, which should answer the claim within a maximum of twenty days, extensible to thirty days in cases of special complexity (Articles 157(2), (3), (4) of LBIR and 6–11 of the Regulatory Framework 10/2009, of 25 June, on concerning the market policy of the insurance company).

176. In case the insurer fails to provide an answer, or its outcome is not as expected, the aggrieved party may then present its claim to a Costumer Ombudsperson appointed by the insurer. The Customer Ombudsperson should be chosen by the insurance company from among natural persons that have acknowledged prestige, competence, good repute and independency. The Ombudsperson will review the complaint within thirty calendar days of receipt, or forty-five calendar days in cases of special complexity, and issue a recommendation accordingly (Articles 158 of LBIR and 12–15 of Regulatory Framework 10/2009).

177. This procedure is free of charge for the claimant.

178. An aggrieved policyholder, insured, beneficiary or injured party can also bring a complaint directly before the supervisory authority, ASF (Article 157(1) of LBIR). The ASF, nonetheless, recommends that the complaint is brought before the insurer in first place.[79]

179. Although judicial litigation is still the most searched for sort of dispute resolution, there is a growing interest for out-of-court redress mechanisms. With regard to consumer disputes, this has to do with the fact that some alternative dispute resolution (ADR) mechanisms are considerably less costly than judicial courts, besides being swifter. In what regards disputes between professional parties, a

---

78. For further reference, *see* M. Santos Silva, *The Draft Common ...*, 35–37.
79. *See* https://www.asf.com.pt/isp/PortalConsumidor/Reclamacoes.

growing interest for arbitration may be justified by the length of the judicial proceedings, as well as by a preference for having the case adjudicated by experts, even though this may imply considerable costs.

180. The Portuguese law has general acts on mediation and arbitration, as well as on the Justices of peace (on the latter, *see above* §1, I, Political System). Resorting to any of these mechanisms is generally voluntary; cases in which it is compulsive are exceptional.

181. Law 63/2011 of 14 December 2011 is the general law on voluntary arbitration; it applies both to commercial and to consumer relationships.[80] According to Article 1(1) of Law 63/2011, any dispute involving economic interests may be submitted to voluntary arbitration, unless it is exclusively subject by a special law to the state courts or to compulsory arbitration. These last caveats do not apply to insurance disputes (although contracts with consumers do have some special features, that shall be mentioned below), which are therefore arbitrable. The submission of a dispute to arbitration depends on a written agreement, which can pertain either to a current dispute or, instead, to disputes that might arise from certain contractual or non-contractual obligations between the parties.

182. There are very few limits to the parties' autonomy to select arbitrators. The arbitrators must be physical persons and have full legal capacity; they must also be independent and impartial (Article 9).

183. The tribunal decides according to the applicable law, unless the parties agree that it decides *ex aequo et bono* (Article 39). In arbitrations with more than one arbitrator, the award issued by the arbitral tribunal is taken by majority. However, if a decision by majority is not attained, the award is rendered by the president of the arbitral tribunal (Article 40(1)).

184. Unless otherwise agreed by the parties, the award shall determine the proportions in which they shall bear the costs directly resulting from the arbitration. If the tribunal deems it fair and appropriate, it may also decide that one or some of the parties shall compensate the other(s) for the whole or part of the reasonable costs and expenses that they can prove to have borne due to their participation in the arbitration (Article 42(5)).

185. Except if otherwise agreed, the parties are not entitled to appeal on the merits of an arbitral award; the possibility is excluded if the case was ended through settlement or if it was decided *ex aequo et bono* (Article 39(3)). In international

80. On all these and other points, *see* Miguel de Almada/Frederico Bettencourt Ferreira/Miguel Pereira da Silva/Afonso Moucho Diogo, Commercial arbitration: Portugal (in: Commercial arbitration, 2021), https://globalarbitrationreview.com/insight/know-how/commercial-arbitration/report/portugal (accessed 15 Sept. 2021), which are closely followed above; in general, *see* M. França Gouveia, Curso ..., 119 and ff.

arbitrations seated in Portugal, an appeal is only possible to another arbitral tribunal, if the parties regulate the terms of said appeal. In general, an award may only be challenged before a state court through an application for setting aside, for which there is a very limited set of grounds (Article 46).

186. Mediation is regulated by Law 29/2013, of 19 April, which also has a general scope of application in private law, comprising commercial and consumer relationships.[81] The law does not define mediation; it is defined, in line with the Directive on mediation, as a process whereby two or more parties in a dispute voluntarily attempt to reach an agreement on the settlement of their dispute on their own, with the assistance of a mediator (Article 2(a) of Law 29/2013).

187. Mediation is a strictly voluntary procedure: it is not a necessary step in dispute resolution, but instead, it depends on the agreement of the parties, which can moreover be withdrawn at any time (Article 4). In order to promote the willingness of the parties to negotiate, mediation is subject to a strict principle of confidentiality (Article 5). Moreover, the agreement reached through mediation can have direct executory force, once the legal requirements for the mediation to take place are met (capacity of the parts, compliance with public order, the fact that the interests at stake are at the parties' disposal, general compliance with any legal requirements for mediation) and the mediator is mentioned in the public list of mediators kept by the Ministry of Justice (Article 9).

188. Mediation can be carried out either privately, or through public mediation services, which organise lists of mediators and provide all the logistic support for mediation. This is the case for family mediation, labour mediation and criminal mediation, and also for the service of mediation provided by justices of the peace.[82]

189. In case of public mediation, mediators can only be chosen from the lists provided by the service at stake; they are subject to specific requirements laid down by the law and they are recruited by competitive examination. That is not the case for private mediation, where the mediator can be freely chosen by the parties; he or she may have had specific training for mediation, but that is not mandatory. However, specific training seems to be a requirement for the mediator to be in the general list of mediators kept by the Ministry of Justice.[83] The fact of being named on this list is of considerable importance, since it is a requirement for the agreement reached through mediation to have executory force.

---

81. *See* Dulce Lopes/Afonso Patrão, Lei da mediação comentada, Almedina, (2016), 13–21.
82. Afonso Patrão, Portugal (in: Carlos Esplugues/José Luis Iglesias/Guillermo Palao (ed.) Civil and commercial mediation in Europe, National mediation rules and procedures, I Intersentia, 327, 2013), 333–334; D. Lopes/A. Patrão, Lei da mediação comentada, 17–18.
83. *See* D. Lopes/A. Patrão, Lei da mediação comentada, 61.

190. In any case, mediators are bound to treat the parties with impartiality and carry out his or her competence with independence (Article 7). In case of infringement of their duties towards the parties, the mediator is liable for any damage caused (Article 8).

191. These general norms are flanked by a special regime regarding ADR in consumer disputes, created by Law 144/2015,[84] which applies to arbitration, mediation or conciliation procedures. The main feature of the regime is the regulation of consumer ADR entities, networks and procedures, in order to foster the enforcement of consumers' rights. The Law created a national register of all entities competent to resolve consumer disputes in Portugal; the pre-existing consumer arbitration centres were also given the opportunity to be included in the register (Articles 15–17).[85] These entities are now subject to certain quality requirements (e.g., regarding accessibility, fairness, transparency and provision of the service free of charge or at least at a very low cost – Articles 6 and ff., which transpose Articles 5 and ff. of the Consumer ADR Directive). The Act further sets out the qualifications of the natural persons in charge of the processes at ADR entities, who should be able to prove that they possess expertise and qualifications in the field of consumer dispute resolution, as well as have a general understanding of law. Every ADR entity is obliged to provide training for its employees in these matters and ensure that their training remains up to date (Article 7 of the law, which transposes Article 6 of the Directive). This contrasts with the general provisions applicable to arbitration and mediation, where no special requirement is made in regard to arbitrators or mediators acting outside public mediation systems.[86]

192. It is not mandatory to engage a lawyer, regardless of the value of the dispute; nonetheless, consumers have a right to be represented by third parties in any stage of ADR proceedings (Article 10(2)).

193. In general, resort to ADR is dependent upon on the agreement of the parties, which may be entered upon before or after the dispute has materialised. When it is entered upon before the dispute has materialised – as frequently happens, due to the ADR clause being included in the traders' standard contract terms (SCT) –, it cannot have the effect of depriving the consumer of their right to bring an action before the courts for the settlement of the dispute (Article 13).

194. Such an agreement can also be achieved by a two-step procedure: the trader may issue a public statement, binding itself to resort to one or several ADR centres in case a dispute arises ('statement of adherence', usually issued by means of a

84. The Law transposes Directive 2013/11/UE, of 21 May 2013, on alternative dispute resolution for consumer disputes.
85. On the situation that pre-existed the Law, *see* Cátia Marques Cebola, *The Implementation of the Consumer ADR Directive in Portugal. Necessary Reform or Missed Opportunity?*, in *The New Regulatory Framework for Consumer Dispute Resolution*, 251–263 (Pablo Cortés ed., Oxford University Press 2016).
86. João Pedro Pinto-Ferreira & Joana Campos Carvalho, *Consumer ADR in Portugal*, 89 EuCML 90 (2018).

poster hanging in the trader 's premises); if the consumer later brings a dispute to one of those ADR centres, then they are deemed to have accepted the binding offer of the trader.[87]

195. Moreover, after an amendment of the Consumer Protection Act in 2019, there are special rules for disputes of low value, which are defined as a value not exceeding that of the threshold for appealing a decision of a first instance court (Article 14(3) of Consumer Protection Act). Presently, it amounts to EUR 5,000 (Article 44(1) of the Law on the Organisation of the Judicial System). In these cases, the consumer has the right to refer to an authorised consumer ADR entity centre and submit the case to mediation or arbitration, without the trader having the right to refuse it (Article 14(2)). Judicial fees are only owed by the consumer by the end of the procedure (Article 14(5)). Furthermore, the consumer has the right to be informed at the beginning of the procedure that they may be represented by a lawyer or legal clerk ('solicitador') and that, in case they lack economic resources, they have the right to legal aid (Article 14(4)).

196. There are several ADR entities in Portugal, both with general competence and specialised in consumer disputes.[88] In what directly concerns the insurance branch, a special reference should be made to the Insurance Information, Mediation, Ombudsman and Arbitration Centre (CIMPAS). CIMPAS is competent both for consumer and non-consumer disputes. Its Regulation sets out a three step procedure, comprising a phase of information, a second phase of mediation, and a third phase of arbitration. In any case, the dispute should be solved within a maximum of ninety days counting from the date in which the claim is submitted with all its elements to the Centre.[89]

§5. Protection of Vulnerable Parties (In General and in Regard to Insurance)

I. Mass Risks Versus Large Risks

197. Following suit from Solvency II (Article 3(27)), LBIR separates between insurance covering large risks, and another insurance, named mass risk insurance (Article 5(2) and (3)). Large risks are identified by three different criteria.

198. First, by the nature of the risk. Article 5(2)(a) refers to the risks concerned by the insurance branches mentioned in Article 8(d)–(f), (g), (k) and (l). That is, the risk of damage to railway rolling stock (Article 8(d)); the risk of damage to aircraft

87. C. Marques Cebola, The implementation ..., 257–258, on the first point; on the second, *see* J. P. Pinto-Ferreira & J. Campos Carvalho, *Consumer ADR* ..., 90.

88. The leading arbitral institution in Portugal is the Arbitration Centre of the Portuguese Chamber of Commerce and Industry, which may also act as an appointing authority if agreed by the parties. For consumer disputes, *see* https://www.consumidor.gov.pt/parceiros/sistema-de-defesa-do-consumidor/entidades-de-resolucao-alternativa-de-litigios-de-consumo/ral-mapa-e-lista-de-entidades.aspx.

89. *See* https://www.cimpas.pt/.

(Article 8(e)); the risk of damage to ships, comprising sea, lake and river and canal vessels (Article 8(f)); the risk of damage to merchandise, or baggage or other goods in transit, irrespective of the form of transport (Article 8(g)); the risk of all liability arising out of the use of aircraft, including carrier's liability (Article 8(k)); the risk of all liability arising out of the use of ships, vessels or boats on the sea, lakes, rivers or canals, including carrier's liability (Article 8(l)).

199. Second, by the nature of the risk combined with the professional character of the policyholder's activity. Article 5(2)(b) refers to the risks concerned by the insurance branches mentioned in Article 8(n) and (o), where the policyholder is engaged professionally in an industrial or commercial activity or in one of the liberal professions and the risks relate to such activity. That is, credit insurance, comprising the risks of insolvency (general), export credit, instalment credit, mortgages, agricultural credit (Article 8(n)) and suretyship, both direct and indirect (Article 8(o)).

200. Third, by the nature of the risk combined with the size of the policyholder. Article 5(2)(c) refers to the risks concerned by the insurance branches mentioned in Article 8(c), (h), (i), (j), (m) and (p), as long as the policyholder exceeds the limits of at least two of the following criteria: (1) a balance sheet total of EUR 6.2 million; (2) a net turnover, within the meaning of Decree-Law 158/2009 of EUR 12.8 million; (3) an average number of 250 employees during the financial year.[90] In other words, the risk of damage to land vehicles other than railway rolling stock, comprising land motor vehicles and land vehicles other than motor vehicles (Article 8(c)); the risk of damage to property, other than the property included in Article 8(c)–(g), due to fire, explosion, storm, natural forces other than storm, nuclear energy or land subsidence (Article 8(h)); the risk of damage to property, other than the property included in Article 8(c)–(g), when caused by any event distinct from those mentioned in Article 8(h) (Article 8(i)); the risk of liability arising out of the use of motor vehicles operating on the land, including carrier's liability (Article 8(j)); general liability, referring to all liability other than those referred to Article 8(j)–(l) (Article 8(m)); miscellaneous financial loss, comprising employment risks, insufficiency of income, bad weather, loss of benefits, continuing general expenses, unforeseen trading expenses, loss of market value, loss of rent or revenue, other indirect trading loss, other non-trading financial loss, other forms of financial loss (Article 8(p)).

201. As said, this division is also key in the RJCS.

202. The parties can generally contract out of the provisions of the RJCS. A very limited number of its provisions, as listed in Article 12, are absolutely mandatory – strictly speaking, the contract cannot derogate from them either in detriment of the

90. If the policyholder belongs to a group of undertakings for which consolidated accounts are drawn up, the criteria set out in point (c) of No. 2 shall be applied on the basis of the consolidated accounts.

policyholder, insured and beneficiary, or in their favour. Though many of the provisions listed in Article 12 have to do with public policy concerns, the rationale underlying the list is not fully understandable. It establishes, for instance, the duty of non-disclosure of the insurer to be absolutely imperative. The policyholder's privacy sphere is, however, clearly not a matter of public policy; it is, much on the contrary, typically a private matter, where the principle of private autonomy is the norm. The norms that set out a strict 'no premium, no risk' regime are also deemed absolutely imperative (except for large risks); but there are no clear public policy reasons to forbid, e.g., that the parties apply the general norms on delay. On the other hand, the norm leaves out provisions that make direct reference to the limits posed by public policy (in the sense of *ordre public de direction*), which is by nature mandatory (for instance, Article 46, or Articles 192 and 193[91]). That is no less deprived of rationality.

203. Article 13(1) lists another set of provisions as semi-mandatory, in the sense that the contract cannot derogate from them in detriment of the policyholder, the insured or beneficiary. These provisions are mainly connected to the protection of the policyholder, insured or beneficiary (*ordre public de protection*). The list is however again not fully congruous – for instance, it includes the general provision on the minimum content of the policy (Article 37) but excludes the special provision on minimum content of life insurance policies (Article 187). According to Article 13(2), this does not apply to large risks: there are no semi-mandatory provisions in their regard.

204. Much to the contrary of what their wording might convey, Articles 12(1) and 13(1) are not deemed exhaustive, as it is acknowledged that several norms, in spite of being non-listed, should in view of their rationale be considered (semi or fully) mandatory.[92] The option for including two rather long, yet non-exhaustive lists of mandatory norms seems rather questionable in terms of legislative technique, since it casts doubt onto the possibility of recognising further mandatory provisions.

II. Consumer Protection

205. The core consumers' rights are enshrined in the Constitution. Under Article 69(1), of the CPR, consumers have the right to good quality of goods and services, to training and information, to the protection of health, safety and their economic interests, and to obtain compensation for damages.

91. Maria Inês de Oliveira Martins, Contrato de seguro e conduta dos sujeitos ligados ao risco, Almedina, (2018), 324.
92. That is the case, for example, of Arts 46, 182 or 190. As to the non-exhaustive character, *see* Pedro Romano Martínez, Art. 12, Imperatividade absoluta (in: Lei do Contrato de Seguro anotada, Almedina, 2020), 69–70, and P. Romano Martínez, Art. 13, Imperatividade relativa, 71–72).

206. The general framework for that protection is given by the Consumer Protection Act.[93] It defines the consumer as someone who receives goods, services or rights of any kind from a person that professionally undertakes an economic activity in order to obtain benefits (Article 2(1)).

207. The consumer is granted the following rights: the right to goods and services of good quality; the right to the protection of their health and safety; the right to education in regard to consumption; the right to information; the right to protection of their economic interests; the right to prevention and compensation of any material or non-material damage arising from offence to their individual or collective rights or interests; the right to affordable and prompt redress; the right to participate through their representatives in the legal or administrative definition of their rights and interests (Article 3).

208. Some of those rights may have particular relevance for insurance. That is the case of the right to goods and services of good quality, further defined as the right to goods and services fit for their purpose and apt to cause the effects they should produce according to the applicable norms or, in lack thereof, according to the reasonable expectations of the consumers (Article 4). Article 8 lays down the right of the consumer to clear, objective and adequate information, both during the negotiation and the conclusion of the contract, regarding several of its aspects. Article 9, which regards the right to protection of economic interests of consumers, is also worthy of mention. Apart from reaffirming the duty of good faith and fair dealing in regard to consumers (Article 9(1)), and the application of the LSCT in regard to non-negotiated terms (Article 9(2)), the norm particularly protects the economic freedom of consumers. It establishes that consumers shall be exempted from the obligation to provide any consideration in cases of unsolicited supply, as well as in cases of supply based on a contract which is not valid; they are also not responsible for any costs of return or compensation (Article 9(4)). Traders are furthermore barred from making the access to a good or service dependent on the purchase of other goods or services (Article 9(6)).

209. In what concerns the adjective aspects of consumer protection, reference was made above (§4) to the right to resort to ADR mechanisms. It should also be mentioned that consumers, consumer associations, the Public Prosecutors Office and the General Directorate for Consumers (Article 13) have a right to inhibitory action, with the purpose of preventing, correcting or terminating practices that infringe consumers rights set out in the Consumer Protection Act (Article 10(1)). Without prejudice to the consumer's right to damages, the court may also apply a periodic penalty payment (Article 10(2)).

210. There are other statutes endowing the consumer with further protection against specific sources of danger to their interests, and that are particularly relevant to insurance law. That is the case of the Act on unfair business-to-consumer commercial practices before, during and after a commercial transaction in relation

93. Law 24/96, 31 July 1996.

to a good or service.[94] That is also the case of the Act on distance marketing of consumer financial services.[95] This Act sets out enhanced information duties for the benefit of the consumer (Articles 11–18), as well as a right of withdrawal from the contract without penalty and without giving any reason, within a period of fourteen days, except for the case of life insurance or individual adhesion to open pension funds, where that period is extended to 30 calendar days (Articles 19–25).

211. One should highlight that the concept of 'consumer' adopted by the Consumer Protection Act is not identical to the concept of consumer adopted in the latter two statutes.[96] Most strikingly, whereas a legal person may be deemed a consumer for the purposes of the Consumer Protection Act, the same is not true for the Act on unfair business-to-consumer commercial practices (Article 3(a)) or for the Act on distance marketing of consumer financial services (Article 2(e)), where only natural persons can be treated as consumers.

III. Contracts of Adhesion

212. Insurance is generally a contract of adhesion, and it moreover tends to be composed by SCT.

213. As far as we are aware of, this tends to happen along all segments of the insurance market. Only the amount of premium, the applicable deductibles, and, eventually, in case of insurance of professional risks, the inclusion of risks connected with specific contingencies of the insured (but not the terms of that inclusion) tend to be individually negotiated. Industrial insurance that covers very large risks in specific sectors can eventually be tailor-made; but, even here, the purchase of the necessary reinsurance cover will normally demand that the insurance contract uses the clauses defined by the reinsurers. Consequently, even in those segments, the contract will tend to be a contract of adhesion, though some of its main terms are not SCT.

214. In fact, this contract procedure is particularly suitable for insurance. Because the insurance company undertakes to perform under certain particular future conditions, the description of those conditions is central to the contract –

94. Decree-Law 57/2008, of 26 March 2008, which transposes Directive 2005/29/EC of the European Parliament and of the Council of 11 May 2005, concerning unfair business-to-consumer commercial practices in the internal market.
95. Decree-Law 95/2006, of 29 May 2006, which transposes Directive 2002/65/EC of the European Parliament and of the Council of 23 September 2002 concerning the distance marketing of consumer financial services.
96. On the concept endorsed by the Consumer Protection Act, *see* Jorge Morais Carvalho, Os contratos de consumo, Reflexão sobre a autonomia privada no Direito do consumo, Almedina, (2012), 25 and ff.

insurance is a 'legal product'.[97] Therefore, the unilateral pre-definition of those conditions is a very effective instrument for the enforcement of the business strategy pursued by the insurance company, and for the management of the risk it accepts. However, the unilateral definition of the contract terms by one of the parties carries the serious risk that the party drafting the contract unbalances it in its favour, distributing the rights and duties unevenly between itself and the non-drafting party.

215. These issues are dealt with by the rules on contracts of adhesion, which have a long-standing tradition in policing the insurance contract. In Portugal, these rules are set out by the LSCT. Initially (as the name conveys) the statute only referred to SCT – that is, terms that are not only unilaterally drafted in advance and imposed by one of the parties but that are also pre-formulated for general use in several contracts, frequently an indeterminate number.[98] After having been modified in order to comply with the Directive on Unfair Contract Terms, the statute now encompasses all non-negotiated contracts (contracts of adhesion) and non-negotiated terms – that is, contracts or terms that are unilaterally drafted in advance and imposed by one of the parties on the other.

216. The LSCT applies to all non-negotiated terms, independent of being part of a contract between a consumer and professional party, between two professional parties, or between two consumers. However, different rules apply.

217. First, contracts with consumers are subject to a stricter control than contracts between professionals.[99] As shall be seen below, the LSCT forbids non-negotiated terms that are contrary to good faith (Articles 15 and 16), and illustrates the reach of that prohibition by four lists of forbidden prohibited terms, from which two rely heavily on open-ended terms (relative prohibitions / 'grey list' versus lists of absolute prohibitions / 'black lists'). Two lists (grey and black) containing the most serious offences and breaches to of good faith are applicable both to contracts between a consumer and professional party, and to contracts between two professional parties; the remaining grey and black list are in principle only applicable in contracts between a professional party and a consumer. (Article 20).

218. Additionally, the international scope of application of these lists varies, given that consumers benefit from a mandatory protection under Article 23 LSCT, which in turn is not applicable to businesses.

219. Furthermore, there is some discussion as to whether the provisions of the LSCT regarding contracts between professional parties should only apply when

97. For this expression, *see* Meinrad Dreher, Die Versicherung als Rechtsprodukt, Die Privatversicherung und ihre rechtliche Gestaltung, J. C. B. Mohr (Paul Siebeck), (1991), passim.

98. António Pinto Monteiro, The impact of the Directive on unfair contract terms in consumer contracts on Portuguese Law, 3, ERPL, 231 (1995) 236; António Pinto Monteiro, O novo regime jurídico dos contratos de adesão/ cláusulas contratuais gerais, 1, ROA, (2002), no. 3.

99. Although the LSCT would literally also apply the stricter regime to contracts between consumers, it would seem inadequate to apply it outside the realm of contracts between professional parties and consumers.

actual SCT are at stake, and not merely non-negotiated terms (an argument for this would be the fact that the Unfair Contract Terms Directive, while applying to all non-negotiated terms, applies only to contracts with consumers). Scholarship has taken different positions in this regard, whereas the courts seem to find the legislation applicable to business-to-business contracts in any case.[100]

220. Now, the LSCT has its own definition of consumer and professional party. Contracts between professional parties are defined as contracts between entrepreneurs, members of legal professions, and between one and the other, when each of the parties acts (1) strictly within that status and (2) within their specific activity (Article 17). The party that does not fulfil these requirements will be treated as a consumer.

221. There is doubt on how this norm should apply. Under a literal interpretation, any professional party entering into a contract in a field outside its expertise would qualify as a consumer. This would have implications for insurance, since, except where the party acquiring coverage was also an insurer (e.g., in reinsurance), it would not have expertise in insurance contracts and would therefore be treated as a consumer. In fact, some authors seem to favour this approach, whereas there is case law departing from the assumption that the status of consumer does not apply if the contract is entered into in a commercial context.[101]

222. The LSCT acts in three different fronts: it determines that the drafting party must comply with special duties of information towards the non-drafting party (*see* Part II, Chapter 1, §5, II, A, Information Duties and Exclusion of SCT); it sets out special rules for the interpretation of the contract (*see* Part II, Chapter 1, §2, Rules on Interpretation of Insurance Contracts); and it directly polices the content of the contract (*see* Part II, Chapter 1, §5, II, B, Voidness and Prohibition of SCT). The statute has played a central role in the development of insurance case law in Portugal alongside the norms of the Commercial Code, and plays no less of an important role alongside the RJCS.

---

100. Favourable to the application of those provisions in any case, Joaquim de Sousa Ribeiro, O regime dos contratos de adesão: algumas questões decorrentes da transposição da Directiva sobre as cláusulas abusivas (in: Comemorações dos 35 anos do Código Civil e dos 25 anos da reforma de 1977, Volume III, Direito das obrigações, Coimbra Editora, 209, 2007), 219–220; Ana Prata, Contratos de adesão e cláusulas contratuais gerais, Almedina, (2010), 43, 82–84, 90 and ff.; against, Almeno de Sá, Lei das cláusulas contratuais gerais e Directiva sobre cláusula abusivas (in: Cláusulas contratuais gerais e Directiva sobre cláusulas abusivas, Almedina, 9, 2001), 59 and ff. On case law, *see, for instance,* TRP 27 September 2017, 1897/14.2T2AGD-A.P1 (Inês Moura).

101. In scholarship, *see* A. Prata, Contratos …, 94, 343–345, 476–477, and Luís A. Carvalho Fernandes, Teoria geral do Direito civl, II, Fontes, conteúdo e garantia da relação jurídica, Universidade Católica Portuguesa, (2010), 118–199. For the contrary stance in case law, *see* for instance STJ 4 May 2017, 1961/13.5TVLSB.L1.S1 STJ (Lopes do Rego), stating that the provisions on the black list for terms in contracts between professional parties and consumers do not apply to a swap contract entered into by a construction company, since it pertains to the exercise of its economic activity.

IV. Protection Against Discrimination

223. Article 15(1) of the RJCS establishes that any practice adopted in the conclusion, enforcement, or termination of the insurance contract, which is deemed discriminatory in view of the principle of equality set out in Article 13 of the Constitution, shall be forbidden.

224. The principles of equality and non-discrimination are enshrined in Article 13 of the Portuguese Constitution,[102] as well as in Articles 20–26 of the Charter of Fundamental Rights of the EU.

225. However, the principles of equality and non-discrimination cannot be linearly enforced in relationships between private parties, whose personal freedom is also worthy of legal protection.[103] Statutory law is thus paramount in setting out the conditions under which non-discrimination can be enforced in this setting.

226. In fact, several statutes prohibiting discrimination on different grounds have been enacted in recent years.

227. With particular relevance to the insurance contract, Law 44/2006, of 28 August, forbids discrimination based on disability or on increased health risk. According to Article 4, the practices are considered discriminatory whenever they, wilfully or at least negligently, by means of action or omission, infringe the principle of equality on the ground of disability (or increased health risk). Discrimination can either be direct or indirect (Article 3(a) and (b)).[104]

228. Besides, it specifically lists the refusal or aggravation of the conditions of insurance contracts among the practices that may be considered discriminatory (Article 4(c)[105]).

---

102. Article 13(1) of the PRC states that all citizens are endowed with the same social dignity and are equal before the law. Under Art. 13(2), no one may be privileged, favoured, prejudiced, deprived of any right or exempted from any duty for reasons of ancestry, sex, race, language, territory of origin, religion, political or ideological beliefs, education, economic situation, social circumstances, or sexual orientation. Besides the Charter of Fundamental Rights of the EU, there is a significant number of other instruments of international law relevant to the matter of non-discrimination – *see* Maria Inês de Oliveira Martins, Sobre a discriminação dos portadores de VIH/sida na contratação de seguros de vida, 2, BFDUC, 749 (2013), 760 and ff.

103. *See, for instance*, Paulo Mota Pinto, Autonomia privada e discriminação, Algumas notas (in: Tribunal Constitucional (ed.) Estudos em Homenagem ao Conselheiro José Manuel Cardoso da Costa, Vol. II, Coimbra Editora, 313, 2005), 333 and ff.

104. In the sense of Art. 2(2) of Directive 2000/43/EC or Art. 2(a) and (b) of Directive 2004/113/CE, *mutatis mutandis*.

105. In fact, Art. 4(c) lists as discriminatory 'the refusal or conditioning of the sale, lease or sublease of immovable property, or of credit for house purchase, as well as the refusal or aggravation of the conditions of insurance contracts'. In view of this context, some scholarship has considered that the norms refer only to insurance taken out in connection with house purchase (João Calvão da Silva, Apólice 'Vida Risco – Crédito Habitação': as pessoas com deficiência ou risco agravado de saúde e o princípio da igualdade na Lei n.º 46/2006, RLJ, 158 (2007), 160 and 164). However, as, on the one hand, the list in Art. 4 is not exhaustive, and on the other hand Art. 4(a) refers to the

229. The wording of Article 15(2) RJCS is very similar to that of the norm just quoted. It establishes that the practices are deemed discriminatory whenever they, wilfully or at least negligently, by means of action or omission, infringe the principle of equality on the ground of disability or increased health risk, thus treating the persons affected less favourably than they would treat another person in a comparable position.

230. Furthermore, Law 18/2008, of 12 March, forbids and sanctions discrimination based on sex in access to and supply of goods and services.[106] This Law was altered in 2015, as a consequence of *Test-Achats* case. Presently, Article 6(1) states that use of sex as a factor in the calculation of premiums and benefits cannot result in differences in individual premiums and benefits.[107]

231. In 2017, the former Law that forbade discrimination on the grounds of race, colour, nationality or ethnic origin[108] was replaced by Law 93/2017, of 23 of August, which prevents, combats and forbids (direct or indirect) discrimination on the ground of racial or ethnic origin, colour, nationality, descent or place of birth. Law 38/2018, of 18 August, that safeguards the right to self-determination as to gender identity and the protection of sexual characters of each person, should also be mentioned, since it bars any discrimination on these grounds (Article 2).

232. With regard to discrimination in insurance contracts, the present setting can therefore be synthesised as follows: individual differences in treatment directly based on sex are forbidden (*see also* Article 15(9) RJCS); apart from this special case, discrimination, which may be direct or indirect, should be assessed in light of the principle of equality (Articles 15(1) and (2) RJCS and 4 of Law 44/2006 are explicit in this regard).

---

refusal to supply goods or services, or the hindering of their enjoyment, insurance, as a financial service, could be said to be included anyway. It should also be said that the Law on subsidised credit for house purchase by persons with disabilities (Law 64/2014, of 26 August) establishes that the granting of subsidised credit cannot be made conditional upon the taking out of life insurance by the disabled person (Art. 5(2)). *See* M. I. Oliveira Martins, Sobre a discriminação …, 722–723.

106. This Law transposes Directive 2004/113/CE, of 13 December.

107. According to Art. 6(5), the norm applies to private insurance and private pensions which are voluntary and independent of an employment relationship. Under Art. 6(6), the supervisory authority should inform on the categories of life and health insurance underwriting practices deemed admissible in light of Council Directive 2004/113/EC of 13 December 2004 and of the applicable Guidelines from European Union, for instance those mentioned in the 'Guidelines on the application of Council Directive 2004/113/EC to insurance, in the light of the judgment of the Court of Justice of the European Union in Case C-236/09 (Test-Achats)'. However, to our knowledge, neither the ASF nor its predecessor has provided such information.

108. Law 134/99, of 28August. The present Law transposes Directive 2000/43/EC of 29 June 2000 implementing the principle of equal treatment between persons irrespective of racial or ethnic origin.

233. Now, a mere difference of treatment is not per se an unlawful discrimination, contrary to the principle of equality; if there is a legitimate ground for the difference of treatment, then there will be no unlawful breach of the principles of equality and non-discrimination.[109]

234. This is particularly relevant for insurance. Since the insurance industry evolved into a professional activity based on the principles of statistics, it greatly came to precisely rely upon the discrimination of insureds according to their individual risks – that is, it has come to rely upon the classification of the insureds. According to their characteristics, insureds will be placed in a certain category, which corresponds to a certain expected loss. Therefore, this differentiation of treatment – that is, this segmentation of the pool of insureds – defines whether or not they are granted cover, and under which conditions.

235. Therefore, determining whether there was an infringement of the principle of non-discrimination requires that one determines the extent up to which the insurers can proceed in this differentiation, and whether they should make proof of its rationale. Article 15(3) provides for such a criterion, whereas Article 15(4)–(6) sets out a procedure to ascertain whether such a criterion was met.

236. Under Article 15(3), the requirements that the practices and techniques of risk selection and acceptance used in the conclusion, enforcement, or termination of the insurance contract should meet in order not to be forbidden are set out. They should have objective grounds and be based upon statistical and actuarial data which is accurate and considered relevant according to the principles of the insurance technique.

237. It is quite clear that an insured who is not an actuary will not be able to ascertain whether the refusal to contract, or certain terms proposed by the insurer, are or not objective and rational according to the principles of insurance technique. There is marked asymmetry of information on this regard, which hampers the effectiveness of non-discrimination rules.

238. The RJCS has tried to correct this since its beginning. The original system was abandoned in 2015, after having received considerable criticism.[110] Presently, Article 15(4) establishes that in case the insurer refuses to enter into the contract, or aggravates its premium on grounds of the disability of the candidate/insured, or of their aggravated health risk, it should, based on the data that legitimises its decision, as mentioned in Article 15(3), inform the candidate on the ratio between their risk factors and the risk factors regarding a person in a comparable situation, yet not affected by such disability or aggravated health risk. This information must be provided according to Article 178(3)–(6), which fundamentally implies that it

109. *See, for instance*, P. Mota Pinto, Autonomia privada ..., 357–358, stating that the difference of treatment should be deemed lawful when there is a real and substantial reason that justifies it.

110. *See* Francisco Luís Alves, A discriminação e a avaliação do risco nos seguros, 3–4, RDES, 213 (2011), 251; M. I. Oliveira Martins, Sobre a discriminação ..., 784–785.

should be provided by a doctor, and that the insurer must also, upon request, provide the insured or person at risk with all the information it gathered regarding their health.[111] The insurer shall also inform the candidate/insured of the possibility to present a claim to the ASF, as set out in Article 15(5).

239. In case the insurer does not comply with its duty to inform, as well as when the candidate or insured is dissatisfied or disagrees with the decision to refuse the cover, or with the aggravated terms of the offer, they can present a claim to the ASF, which shall verify whether the insurer complied with the applicable norms (Article 15(5)).

240. The system seems therefore to function as follows: whenever there is a case of refusal, or of aggravation of the terms offered by the insurer, it shall inform the insured, independent of a request on this regard, on the ratio between their risk factors and the risk factors regarding a person in a comparable situation, yet not affected by such disability or aggravated health risk. It seems decisive that this must be carried out independent of request, since the insured might otherwise not even realise that he had been treated differently from other insureds or candidates. This information should be provided by a doctor. In fact, the insurer is not obliged to provide information on the grounds for the treatment – it does not have to explain how it accounts for that risk factor (i.e., its modelling and underlying sources), but merely to inform on the ratio. It is information that a doctor has competence to provide, together with the information on the medical examinations and their consequences for the decision of the insurer, that is requested from them under Article 178(3)–(6).

241. In case the information is not provided, or is deemed unsatisfactory, the insured can then present a claim to the ASF. The ASF shall then verify whether the difference of treatment is legitimate – that is, whether it relies on objective grounds and is based upon statistical and actuarial data which is accurate and considered relevant according to the principles of the insurance technique.[112] The ASF is provided with the necessary actuarial expertise to scrutinise the insurer's modelling and sources and can require further explanations from the insured – naturally remaining bound to duties of confidentiality on the process. In fact, there is a balance to strike in this regard, between the right of defence against discrimination from the insured, and the commercial secrets from the insurer, regarding how it sets the price and conditions of its service.

242. In general terms, in order to comply with the principle of equality and non-discrimination, a differentiated treatment should be proportionate to the reason that justifies it. That is, a legitimate discrimination must comply with the principle of

111. *See* Part II, Ch. 3, §1, Pre-contractual Phase.

112. On these requirements, *see* M. I. Oliveira Martins, Sobre a discriminação ..., 779 ff.; *see also* the report of ASF's predecessor on regulation and market conduct supervision regarding the year of 2010, Instituto de Seguros de Portugal, Relatório de regulação e supervisão da conduta de mercado, 2010, available at https://www.asf.com.pt/NR/rdonlyres/A6C32BE2-3E00-4075-ADE4-7B794B410E3C/0/RRSCM2010.pdf (retrieved on 12 Sept. 2021).

proportionality. The principle of proportionality has three dimensions: it requires that the measure undertaken is *appropriate* to safeguard legitimate interests of the party adopting it; that it is *necessary* for those purposes; and that it is proportionate *stricto sensu* – namely, the costs of its adoption (in view of the interests sacrificed) do not outweigh the benefits.[113] It is debated whether the insurer is bound by the dimension of necessity when making distinctions between the candidates or insureds. Namely, if it is bound to treat the candidates or insureds featuring certain characteristics that aggravate their risk as similar to other candidates or insureds as possible, keeping the distinction to the minimum possible. The RJCS does not refer to this requirement, which would nonetheless derive from the general approach to the principle of equality and non-discrimination. Although the extent of the duty not to discriminate is controversial when only private persons are involved, supervising authority, the courts and scholarship seems to agree to apply the test of necessity to discriminatory treatment applied by insurers to the candidates or insureds.[114]

243. One might also question whether a difference of treatment should be justified only by comparison with the case were there are no aggravated risk factors, or whether there should be comparison with the treatment given to other groups that have aggravated risk factors. In this latter case, discrimination would be seen as unlawful when a certain group with aggravated risk factors was given a more disadvantageous treatment than that provided to another group also characterised by aggravated risk factors. Case law has adopted this approach in at least one case, where the contract set out a significant reduction of life insurance benefits only for cases of suicide or death due to AIDS.[115] The courts sustained that the discrimination of HIV/AIDS patients in regard to persons carrying other serious diseases (e.g., cancer) was not justified and considered the clause unlawfully discriminatory.

244. When there is an unlawful discrimination, the insurer should revert its decision and comply with the principle of equality (that is even expressly stated in Article 10(3) of Law 18/2008). Proof of discrimination is facilitated – e.g., for discrimination on the grounds of disability or aggravated health risk (Article 6(1) of Law 46/2006), for discrimination on the grounds of sex (Article 9 of Law 18/2008) and arguably for the factors of unlawful discrimination set out in Article 13(2) of CPR – and in the case of discrimination on the grounds of race, colour, nationality or ethnic origin, the burden of proof is actually placed upon the defendant (Article 14 of Law 93/2017).

113. José Joaquim Gomes Canotilho, Direito constitucional e teoria da Constituição, Almedina, (2003), 266–270.

114. *See* the act ('Ofício') of ASF's predecessor 301/CDI/2007, quoted in the Recommendation 3/B/2008, of 10 March, of the Ombudsperson; in case law, TRL 16 June 2012, 1269/09.0TVLSB.L1-7 (Pimentel Marcos) and STJ 11 April 2013, 1269/09.0TVLSB.L1.S1, (Paulo Sá); in scholarship, J. Calvão da Silva, Apólice ..., 164–166 and M. I. Oliveira Martins, Sobre a discriminação ..., 789 and ff.

115. TRL 16 June 2012, proc. 1269/09.0TVLSB.L1-7; STJ 11 April 2013, proc. 1269/09.0TVLSB.L1.S1.

245. The victim is entitled to damages under the general norms on civil liability, since discrimination is an unlawful act; some of the statutes on non-discrimination expressly refer to that right (Articles 7(1) and (2) of Law 46/2006; 10(1) of Law 18/2008; 15(1) and (2) of Law 93/2017; 14 of Law 38/2018). The decision that sentences the defendant to pay damages is given wide publicity (Articles 7(3) of Law 46/2006; 10(5) of Law 18/2008; 15(4) of Law 93/2017).

246. In case the insurer persists in its refusal to enter into a contract, the insured is also arguably granted a right to specific execution of the contract.[116]

247. In case of discrimination on the grounds of sex (Articles 12 and ff. of Law 18/2008), disability or aggravated health risk or race (Articles 9 and ff. of Law 46/2006), colour, nationality or ethnic origin (Articles 16 and ff. of Law 93/2017), administrative penalties shall apply.

248. Finally, it should be said that there is a draft law setting out the framework for an agreement between the insurance industry and the State, that could grant persons that have overcome severe health issues a right to 'have those issues forgotten' after a certain number of years.[117]

§6. Compulsory Insurance

249. There is a considerable number of statutes setting out special duties to take out insurance. An approximate list of those cases (unfortunately, not fully up to date) can be found at the supervisor's website.[118] Although there are instances of mandatory insurance throughout different insurance branches, those instances are especially numerous in what comes to liability insurance.

250. Mandatory insurance is governed by general insurance law (RJCS), unless there are special norms providing otherwise. That is distinctly the case for compulsory motor liability insurance, which is endowed with a special statute. In some other cases, compulsory insurance has its general contract terms set out by administrative regulation (e g., mandatory workers compensation insurance, or mandatory fire insurance).[119] Commonly, however, when existent, those special norms touch upon very limited aspects of the regime (very frequently, they establish the minimal amount of cover).

251. The RJCS contains special rules only for compulsory liability insurance (Articles 146–148), and not for compulsory insurance as a whole. The purpose of

116. P. Mota Pinto, Autonomia privada …, 360–361.
117. Draft law 691/XIV/2.ª, presented by the Socialist Party (retrieved at https://www.parlamento.pt/ActividadeParlamentar/Paginas/DetalheIniciativa.aspx?BID=110342).
118. https://www.asf.com.pt/NR/exeres/121FAB2D-E3DB-4517-A4E1-1F63774D8DFC.htm.
119. *See* respectively Government Regulation (*Portaria*) No. 256/2011, of 5 July 2011 and Regulatory Framework of the ASF (*Norma regulamentar do Instituto de Seguros de Portugal*) No. 16/2008-R, 8 January 2009.

those special rules is quite straightforward in enhancing the protection of the victims.[120] In accordance, the victims are endowed with a direct claim against the insurer; their insurance indemnity is determined under the norms on liability; and they keep their right to indemnity even if the insured acted wilfully. Furthermore, the insurer is only entitled to invoke against them defences pertaining to facts that occurred before the insured event. This general regime of mandatory liability insurance is, however, very thin, considering how few the norms that set out mandatory insurance actually are.

120. *See* Júlio Manuel Vieira Gomes, Seguro de acidentes de trabalho, Para uma interpretação restritiva – ou mesmo a revisão – do Acórdão Uniformizador de Jurisprudência n.º 10/2001 de 21 de Novembro de 2001, 116, RMP, 5 (2008), 8–10; Maria Inês de Oliveira Martins, Seguro de responsabilidade civil dos profissionais de saúde: Entre a autonomia privada e a protecção social (in: Responsabilidade civil em saúde, Diálogo com o Prof. Doutor Jorge Sinde Monteiro, Instituto Jurídico – Faculdade de Direito da Universidade de Coimbra, 291, 2021), 296–308.

Part I. The Insurance Company

Chapter 1. The Insurance Company: Its Form

Joana Neto Anjos

§1. Mutual Insurance, Premium Insurance and Other

252. The Decree-Law 102/94, of 20 April 1994, reformulated the essential aspects of Portuguese legislation in terms of access and exercise of the insurance and reinsurance activity. This Decree-Law had two essential purposes in mind: the 'codification' of dispersed legislation regarding access to and exercise of the insurance and reinsurance activity and the transposition into Portuguese law of the third-generation directives, relating to the creation of the 'single market' in the insurance sector – Directive 92/49/EEC, of 18 June, for 'Non-Life' insurance, and Directive 92/96/EEC, of 10 November, for 'Life' insurance.

253. However, in its regulation scope this statute did not cover the sanctioning regime of the insurance activity, regulated by Decree-Law 91/82, of 22 March 1982 (amended by Decree-Law 133/86, of 12 June 1986), and by Decree-Law 107/88, of 31 March 1988. In fact, it had not yet been adapted to the new conceptions of criminal policy resulting from the approval and entry into force of Decree-Law 433/82, of 27 October 1982, which approved the general regime of administrative offences, and the requirements resulting from the new forms of access and exercise of activity, resulting from the transposition into the national legal system of the Community directives that came to establish the single market in the insurance sector.

254. In addition, Decree-Law 102/94, of 20 April 1994, also did not touch the sensitive matter related to the indebtedness of insurance and reinsurance companies, which is one of the main gaps in the legal system applicable to the insurance activity, due to the maladjustment of the legal rules that discipline it and that date back to 1907 and 1971.

255. Thus, in 1998, the Government, acting under the legislative authorisation granted by Law 93/97, of 16 August 1997, approved Decree-Law 94-B/98, of 17 April 1998, which aimed to review the Decree-Law 102/94, of 20 April 1994, regarding access and exercise of the insurance and reinsurance activity, integrated the new sanctioning regime of the insurance activity and of the pension fund management activity within its respective scope.

256. Subsequently, Decree-Law 2/2009, of 5 January 2009, was approved, which amends and republishes Decree-Law 94-B/98, of 17 April 1998. This Decree-Law 2/2009 carried out the transposition of Directive 2005/68/EC, of the European Parliament and of the Council, of 16 November 2005, on reinsurance, safeguarding the harmonisation of the rules for access and exercise of reinsurance activity, necessary for the mutual recognition of authorisations and the system of prudential supervision. The purpose was to establish a system of 'single authorisation' valid throughout the EU and the application of the principle of supervision by the Member State of origin.

257. Currently, Law 147/2015, of 9 September 2015, is in force, which approved the legal regime for access and exercise of the insurance and reinsurance activity ('LBIR'), as well as the procedural regime applicable to the special crimes of the insurance sector and pension funds and administrative offences of which processing is the responsibility of the Insurance and Pension Funds Supervisory Authority, transposing Directive 2009/138/EC, of the European Parliament and of the Council, of 25 November 2009. This statute was recently amended by the Decree-Law 84/2020, of 12 October 2020.

258. According to this legal text, an insurance company (also called insurer) is considered to be 'any company that has received administrative authorisation to carry out insurance business' (Article 5(1,a)).

259. Under the terms of its Article 3, the insurance or reinsurance activity in Portugal can only be carried out by: (a) insurance companies limited by shares (*sociedades anónimas*); (b) mutual insurance or reinsurance companies (*mútuas de seguros*); (c) branch offices of insurance or reinsurance companies headquartered in another Member State, provided that the mandatory requirements are fulfilled; (d) branch offices of insurance or reinsurance companies established in a third country (outside of the EU territory), authorised under the terms of the present regime; (e) insurance companies or public or publicly owned reinsurance companies, created under the terms of Portuguese law, provided that they carry out insurance or reinsurance operations under conditions equivalent to those of private law companies.

260. The insurance companies limited by shares (*sociedades anónimas*) are regulated by the present regime and, subsidiarily, by the Commercial Companies Code and other complementary legislation in everything that does not contradict the LBIR or any other legal provisions specific to the insurance or reinsurance activity.

261. Mutual insurance or reinsurance companies (*mútuas de seguros*) take the legal form of a limited liability cooperative, constituted by a private document, unless a more solemn form is required for the transfer of the assets that represent their initial capital, governed by the provisions of the present regime and, subsidiarily, by the provided for in the Cooperative Code and other complementary legislation in everything that does not contradict the LBIR or other specific provisions of the insurance or reinsurance activity.

§2. Public or Private Nature

262. With the exception of insurance companies or public or publicly owned reinsurance companies, the insurance activity is carried out by private entities. However, this activity is regulated by the ASF,[121] in accordance with the provisions of Decree-Law 1/2015, of 6 January 2015.

§3. Factual Data

263. In the year of 2019, according to the data published by the ASF, a total of 666 insurance company carried out insurance business in Portugal – 39 of which were created under Portuguese law as SAs (insurance companies limited by shares) and 1 as mutual company; 31 were branch offices of foreign companies (all of them have their head office in the EU); and 595 of which operate under freedom of services (FOS; rendering services in Portugal). Furthermore, in 2019, 40 insurance companies or branch offices carried out non-life insurance and 17 carried out life insurance.[122]

264. At the end of 2019, according to the statistics published by the ASF, the number of workers (average) in insurance companies carrying out business in Portugal was 9,814.[123]

265. According to the Evolution Report of the Insurance Activity form the ASF, in the first three months of 2021, the global business volume direct insurance market relating to the activity in Portugal registered an increase of 5.4% compared to the same period of 2020, standing above EUR 2.8 thousand million. Both life and non-life insurances grew by 9.4% and 2.4%, respectively.[124]

---

121. *See below* Ch. 2.
122. For further details, *see* ASF, *Insurance Sector Report and Pension Funds 2019*, https://www.asf.com.pt/NR/rdonlyres/725941E6-3B61-4F16-AD96-C4CBCA43EAE2/0/RSSFP2019_UV.pdf, 40–41.
123. Data only concerns to undertakings under the ASF prudential supervision.
124. For further details, *see* ASF, *Evolution Report of the Insurance Activity (last quarter of 2020)*, https://www.asf.com.pt/NR/rdonlyres/F3BE966B-0D80-4979-9CEE-A94C98932EF4/0/REAS_4T2020.pdf and ASF, *Evolution Report of the Insurance Activity (first quarter of 2021)*, https://www.asf.com.pt/NR/rdonlyres/73C38463-6F43-49F8-8A84-23009DC16441/0/REAS_1T_2021.pdf.

Life Insurance

266. After two years of growth, the direct life insurance business contracted by 12.9% in 2019, which, in absolute terms, represents a decrease of around EUR 1,000 million. This variation is mainly explained by the decrease in the business volume of non-tied deferred capital and non-tied PPR, contrasting with the positive evolution observed in 2018 in relation to these two types of product.

267. This downward trend continued in 2020, according to data from the last three months of the year.

268. In the first three months of 2021, the business volume of direct life insurance increased 9.4%. This was due to the increase in tied life insurance, particularly in PPR (58.6%), which increased their weight in the portfolio from 9.3% to 13.4%. Tied insurance, excluding PPR, also registered an increase of its weight in the portfolio by 6.5 percentage points.

Non-life Insurance

269. In 2019, the direct non-life insurance business generated premium income maintained the growth rate observed in recent years, with an increase of EUR 360.2 million (8.7%), having exceeded EUR 4.5 thousand million. This pattern of behaviour was common to the main branches and modalities, reflecting the growing of the national economy observed throughout this year.

270. At the end of 2020, the business volume of non-life insurance business exceeded EUR 5.370 million, about 161 million more than in the same period of the previous year. Noteworthy is the 8.5% growth in the health insurance branch, whose relative weight in business volume became 17.7% at the end of the period. The fire and other damage insurance, the motor vehicle insurance as well as the work accidents insurance, also increased by 4.5%, 2.3% and 1.2%, respectively.

271. In the first quarter of 2021, the direct non-life insurance business produced more than 1 EUR 558 million in the total market, about EUR 36 million more than in the same period of the previous year. Mention should be made of an 8.9% growth in the health insurance branch, whose relative weight in business volume became 21.1% at the end of the period. The fire and other damage insurance also grew by 6%. The motor vehicle insurance business decreased 1.6%, while the work accidents insurance business remained practically unchanged.

Chapter 2. Access to Business: Authorisation – Requirements and Procedures

§1. General

272. In each country, the insurance activity is subject to special regulation and supervision by the respective authorities, which aim to control its correct functioning at a legal, technical and financial level, with the purpose of ensuring the due protection of policyholders and beneficiaries of insurance contracts. The aim is, therefore, to protect policyholders against the insolvency risk of insurance companies and to ensure that all contractual commitments by them assumed are respected, as well as to guarantee the existence of conditions for healthy competition between companies in the sector.

273. In Portugal, this supervision was carried out systematically by a specialised body, the ISP – public institute under the tutelage of the Minister of Finance – which assumed the role of supervisory authority for the insurance sector and related activities, as well as mediation insurance. Under the terms set out in its statutes, approved by Decree-Law 302/82, of 30 July 1982, the ISP would be competent 'to coordinate and regulate, in accordance with national economic and financial policies, the operation of the insurance sector and reinsurance and its mediation, as well as complementary activities in that sector or any sector related to it'.

274. Through Decree-Law 251/97, of 26 September 1997, and due to the process of privatisation and progressive liberalisation of the market, accession to the European Community and the opening and internationalisation of the economy, the context of the ISP's performance, as a supervisory authority, had to change and adapt to the 'profound transformations in Portuguese society that do not exclude the economic and financial domains'. Therefore, the basic definitions of its competences were updated, certain aspects of the organic structure and management procedures were rationalised, and rules for transparency and prevention of conflict of interests were expressly enshrined. This diploma was revoked in 2001 with Decree-Law 289/2001, of 13 November 2001, due to the 'need to update to a new context marked by the privatisation process, by the single insurance market – the main responsible for the progressive liberalisation and deregulation of activity – and, also, by the proliferation of new products, with a special focus on the institutionalisation of pension funds'.

275. With the approval of Law 67/2013, of 28 August 2013, the ISP's statutes were subject to new changes, in order to adapt to the regime provided in that framework legislation. Under the terms of its Article 3(3,a), the ISP is recognised as a 'currently existing regulatory entity', whose statutes 'must be adapted by decree-law to the provisions of the framework law, attached to this law, within ninety days after the entry into force of this law and enter into force on the first day of the month following that of its publication' (Article 3(1)).

276. Thus, Decree-Law 1/2015, of 6 January 2015, was approved, which defines the new statutes of the Insurance and Pension Funds Supervision Authority (ASF), new name of the Insurance Institute of Portugal. This statutory amendment has the main purpose of 'adapting the supervisor's contract to the framework law of the regulatory entities, which came into force in 2013', and to reinforce its organic, operational and financial independence.

277. According to Article 6 of Decree-Law 1/2015, of 6 January 2015, the ASF's mission is to ensure the regular functioning of the insurance market and pension funds, by promoting the stability and financial solidity of the entities under its supervision, as well as ensuring the maintenance of high standards of conduct by them, with view of the main objective of protecting policyholders, underwriters, participants, beneficiaries and injured parties.

§2. Authorisation: Requirements and Procedures

278. According to Article 47 of the LBIR, insurance companies are financial companies whose exclusive object is the exercise of insurance activity, as well as the operations directly arising from it, excluding any other commercial activity; on the other hand, reinsurance companies are financial companies whose exclusive purpose is to exercise reinsurance and related operations, including the exercise of management functions for shareholdings related to activities in the financial sector.

279. Pursuant to Article 48(1) of the aforementioned law, authorisation for the exercise of insurance and reinsurance activity is granted by the ASF, in relation to insurance company limited by shares; mutual insurance or reinsurance companies, branches of insurance and reinsurance companies of a third country and also insurance companies or public or publicly owned reinsurance companies, created under the terms of Portuguese law, provided that their object is to carry out insurance or reinsurance operations under conditions equivalent to those of companies governed by private law. Insurance and reinsurance business by branch offices established in the territory of EU are not dependent on this authorisation, provided that the legal requirements are complied with (Articles 48(2) and 3(1)).

I. Insurance Company Limited by Shares

280. The constitution of an insurance company limited by shares depends on prior authorisation from the ASF (Article 51 of the LBIR).

281. Authorisation depends on the fulfilment of several conditions and criteria set up by Article 52, in particular: the commitment by the shareholders to constitute a company under the legal company format limited by shares and that the company must have as its exclusive object the insurance or reinsurance activity and a minimum amount of capital, depending on the branch or branches to be operated in by the insurer. In fact, the minimum amount of capital required for the constitution of an insurance company limited by shares varies: EUR 2,500,000, when only health, legal protection or assistance are the areas of business activities; EUR 7,500,000 when more than one of the aforementioned branches or any other non-life area are its areas of activity; EUR 7,500,000 when only life insurance branch is the area of activity; and EUR 15,000,000 when life insurance and non-life insurance are both the areas of activity. Besides the minimum amount of capital required, the law imposes that the shares representing the capital of an insurance company limited by shares must be nominative (Article 61).

282. Moreover, other criteria must be fulfilled, according to Article 52: the suitability of the shareholders of a qualifying holding to guarantee sound and prudent management of the company; the location of the central management of the company is in Portugal; the company presents a programme of activities (Article 54) and the company has sufficient eligible basic own funds available to respect the absolute lower limit of the minimum capital requirement provided for in Article 147(3). As well as this, it must be demonstrated that: the company is in a position to hold sufficient eligible own funds to satisfy the solvency capital requirement provided for in Article 116; that the company is in a position to become the holder of base capital sufficient to meet the minimum capital requirement provided for in Article 146; and that the company is in a position to have a governance system that respects the requirements set out in Chapter I of title III. A claims representative in each of the EU Member States, must also be appointed when the insurance company intends to operate in the non-life area of 'Civil liability of motor vehicle except liability for transportation'. Finally, whenever there are close relationships between the company and other physical or legal persons, there should be no obstacles to the exercise of the supervisory function.

283. In order to obtain authorisation for the constitution of an insurance company limited by shares, an application must be submitted to the ASF. Such application must be accompanied by the following items and documents: minutes of the meeting where the constitution of the company was decided; draft of the company contract or of the statutes of the company; identification of the initial shareholders, holders of direct or indirect holdings, whether natural or legal persons, specifying the share capital and voting rights corresponding to each holding, as well as the elements and information established pursuant to Article 162(3); detailed description of the governance system; the name and address of the claims representative appointed; detailed information that demonstrate that there are no obstacles to the exercise of the supervisory function, in case of close relationships between the company and other physical or legal persons; and, finally, identification of the person responsible for the authorisation process.

284. In addition, the application to be submitted to the ASF must be accompanied by a programme of activities of the company to be authorised. According to Article 54(1), this programme will include the following elements as a minimum: the nature of the risks to be covered or the commitments to be assumed, with the indication of the areas, modalities, insurances or operations to be explored; the type of reinsurance agreements that the reinsurance company proposes to enter into with ceding companies; the guiding principles on reinsurance and retrocession; the elements of core capital that constitute the absolute lower limit of the minimum capital requirement; the forecast of the installation expenses of administrative services and the commercial network, as well as the necessary financial means and the means available to the company to provide assistance.

285. The activity programme must also include, for each of the first three exercises: the provisional balance sheet, with separate information, at least for the headings of original own funds, investments and technical reserves for direct insurance, accepted reinsurance and ceded reinsurance; the forecast of the solvency capital requirement based on the aforementioned forecast balance sheet, as well as the method used to calculate this forecast; the provision of the minimum capital requirement based on the forecast balance sheet, as well as the method used to calculate this forecast; the forecast of the financial means destined to cover the technical provisions, the minimum capital requirement and the solvency capital requirement; in relation to non-life insurance and reinsurance accepted and ceded, the forecast for management expenses that do not correspond to installation expenses, namely current general expenses and commissions, as well as an estimate of premiums and claims per business class; and in relation to life insurance, a plan containing detailed forecasts relating to income and expenses (Article 54(2)). The assumptions on which the elaboration of the projections included in the programme of activities is based must be specifically substantiated, including adverse scenarios (Article 54(3)).

286. According to Article 55(1, 2), if the application is not filed in accordance with the provisions of the aforementioned articles, the ASF informs, within a maximum period of one month, the applicant's representative of the irregularities detected, who then has a period of one month to remedy them, under penalty of expiry and filing of the request. In addition, the ASF may request any clarifications or additional elements that it deems useful or necessary for the analysis of the process, as well as carry out any investigations it considers necessary.

287. The decision on the compliance of the application must be issued by the ASF within a maximum period of three months from the date on which it is correctly and completely instructed. In this decision, the ASF must pronounce itself, namely, on the adequacy of the information elements contained in the application with the activity that the company proposes to carry out (Article 54(3, 4)).

288. The decision is notified to interested parties within six months after receiving the application or, if applicable, after receiving the additional information requested from the applicants, but not later than twelve months after the date of initial submission of the application. Failure to notify within the aforementioned periods constitutes a presumption of tacit rejection (Article 56).

289. The authorisation granted by the ASF expires if the insurance or reinsurance company does not formally constitute itself within six months or if the insurance or reinsurance company does not start its activity within twelve months from the date of authorisation (Article 57(1)).

290. If the authorisation expires or is revoked, the ASF must take the necessary measures to safeguard the interests of policyholders and beneficiaries, namely by promoting the closure of the company's establishments, imposing restrictions on the free disposal of company assets and informing the supervisory authorities of the other Member States so that the insurance or reinsurance undertaking is prevented from starting new operations in its territory.

II. Mutual Insurance Company

291. Insurance or reinsurance mutuals take the form of a limited liability cooperative, constituted by a private document, unless a more solemn form is required for the transfer of assets that represent their initial capital. These companies are governed by the provisions of the LBIR, and, subsidiarily, by the provisions of the Cooperative Code and other complementary legislation.

292. The constitution of a mutual insurance company also depends on previous authorisation (license) by ASF. The authorisation procedure follows, with some adaptations, the authorisation procedure laid down for an insurance company limited by shares (Articles 58 and 59).

293. One difference is that, according to Article 59, in the initial application to the ASF, it is only necessary to identify the 10 founding members who will subscribe the largest number of equity securities. Insurance or reinsurance mutuals, as long as authorised by the ASF, can become an insurance company limited by shares.

III. Insurance and Reinsurance Business by Branch Offices Established in the Territory of EU

294. Access to insurance and reinsurance business by branch offices established in the territory of EU, does not depend on authorisation by the Portuguese supervisory authority.

295. As envisaged in Article 200, an insurance company established in other Member State that wishes to carry out insurance business in Portugal through a branch office must inform the supervisory authority in its home Member State, which communicates this intention to the ASF. After this communication, the ASF informs that authority, within two months, of the conditions to which the exercise of insurance activity by that branch must comply. The branch office can be established and start its activities upon receipt by the supervisory authority of the Member State of origin of the ASF information; or, in the absence of this information, two months after the ASF received the communication (Article 201).

296. In case of a change in the content of the elements communicated by the supervisory authority of the Member State to the ASF, the insurance company must notify in writing the supervisory authority of the Member State and ASF at least one month before making such change (Article 202).

297. According to Article 203, EU insurance companies established in Portugal through a branch office must be members of and contribute to any regime aimed at guaranteeing the payment of indemnities to the policyholder or to third injured parties, namely concerning motor vehicle liability insurance and workmen's compensation insurance, meaning that EU insurance companies must pay financial contributions to the Workmen's Compensation Fund (*Fundo de Acidentes de Trabalho* – FAT) as well as to the Motor Insurance Guarantee Fund (*Fundo de Garantia Automóvel* – FGA).

298. The insurance company headquartered in another Member State that operates in Portugal through a branch must, within the scope of this activity, submit the documents requested by it in the exercise of its supervisory powers to the ASF (Article 205(1)).

299. The supervisory authority of the home Member State of the insurance company operating in Portugal through a branch may, after informing the ASF, carry out, directly or through authorised persons, inspections at the premises of that branch, for the purposes of financial supervision. The ASF can participate in these inspection actions (Article 205(3, 4)).

IV. Insurance and Reinsurance Business by Branch Offices Established Outside of the Territory of EU

300. Access to insurance and reinsurance business by branch offices established outside the territory of EU, that is, non-EU insurance companies, also depends on authorisation given by the ASF, as envisaged in Article 214.

301. Authorisation depends on the fulfilment of several conditions and criteria set up by Article 215, in particular: be entitled, in accordance with its national law, to exercise insurance or reinsurance activity for more than five years; have as its exclusive object the exercise of the insurance or reinsurance activity, pursuant to Article 47; undertake to establish an accounting adequate to the activity that it carries out there, as well as to keep all records relating to the business entered into; appoint a general representative who fulfils the requirements and conditions set out in Article 222; have assets of an amount at least equal to half of the absolute lower limit set in Article 147(3) for the minimum capital requirement available in Portugal, and deposit a quarter of this limit as collateral; and commit to meeting the solvency capital requirement and the minimum capital requirement. There must also be a claims representative appointed in each of the EU Member States when the insurance company intends to operate in the non-life area of 'Civil liability of motor vehicle except liability for transportation'.

302. In addition, the application to be submitted to the ASF must be accompanied by a programme of activities of the company to be authorised. According to Article 217(1), this programme will include the following elements as a minimum: the nature of the risks to be covered or the commitments to be assumed, with the indication of the areas, modalities, insurances or operations to be explored; the type of reinsurance agreements that the reinsurance company proposes to enter into with ceding companies; the guiding principles on reinsurance and retrocession; the elements of core capital that constitute the absolute lower limit of the minimum capital requirement; the forecast of the installation expenses of administrative services and the commercial network, as well as the necessary financial means and the means available to the company to provide assistance.

303. The activity programme must also include, for each of the first three exercises: the provisional balance sheet, with separate information, at least for the headings of original own funds, investments and technical reserves for direct insurance, accepted reinsurance and ceded reinsurance; the forecast of the solvency capital requirement based on the aforementioned forecast balance sheet, as well as the method used to calculate this forecast; the provision of the minimum capital requirement based on the forecast balance sheet, as well as the method used to calculate this forecast; the forecast of the financial means destined to cover the technical provisions, the minimum capital requirement and the solvency capital requirement; in relation to non-life insurance and reinsurance accepted and ceded, the forecast for management expenses that do not correspond to installation expenses, namely current general expenses and commissions, as well as an estimate of premiums and claims per business class; and in relation to life insurance, a plan containing detailed forecasts relating to income and expenses (Article 217(2)). The assumptions on which the elaboration of the projections included in the programme of activities is based must be specifically substantiated, including adverse scenarios (Article 217(3)).

304. Non-EU insurance companies may only be authorised to operate the branches and modalities for which the company is authorised in the country where it has its head office and may not simultaneously carry out insurance activities in the life and non-life branches in Portugal, without prejudice to the provisions in Article 89(1).

305. According to Article 218(1, 2), if the application is not filed in accordance with the provisions of the aforementioned articles, the ASF informs, within a maximum period of one month, the applicant's representative of the irregularities detected, who then has a period of one month to remedy them, under penalty of expiry and filing of the request. In addition, the ASF may request any clarifications or additional elements that it deems useful or necessary for the analysis of the process, as well as carry out any investigations it considers necessary.

306. The decision on the compliance of the application must be issued by the ASF within a maximum period of three months from the date on which it is correctly and completely instructed. In this decision, the ASF must pronounce itself, namely, on the adequacy of the information elements contained in the application with the activity that the company proposes to carry out (Article 218(3, 4)).

307. The decision is notified to interested parties within six months after receiving the application or, if applicable, after receiving the additional information requested from the applicants, but not later than twelve months after the date of initial submission of the application. Failure to notify within the aforementioned periods constitutes a presumption of tacit rejection (Article 219).

308. The authorisation granted by the ASF expires if the insurance or reinsurance company does not formally constitute itself within six months or if the insurance or reinsurance company does not start its activity within twelve months from the date of authorisation (Article 57(1), applicable by reference to Article 220).

309. Pursuant to Article 221(1), the authorisation may be revoked, in whole or in part, at the request of the insurance or reinsurance company, or by the ASF, without prejudice to the sanctions applicable to infringements of the insurance and reinsurance activity or on the inexistence or insufficiency of financial conditions, when one of the following situations occurs: having been obtained through false declarations or other illegal means, regardless of the applicable criminal sanctions; the branch ceases or significantly reduces its activity for a period exceeding six months (according to Article 221(2)); failure to fulfil any of the conditions for accessing and exercising the insurance or reinsurance activity required by this regime; serious irregularities occur in the branch's governance system, accounting organisation or internal control, so as to jeopardise the interests of policyholders or beneficiaries or the normal operating conditions of the insurance market; no communication is made or the designation of a person subject to registration under the terms of Article 43(11) is refused, if they carry out an activity that could jeopardise the healthy and prudent management of the branch; the authorisation on which the activity depends is be revoked by the authorities of the country of the insurance or reinsurance company's headquarters; the branch fails to comply with the minimum capital requirement and the ASF considers that the financing plan presented is manifestly inadequate or the branch does not comply with the approved financing plan within three months from the verification of non-compliance with the minimum capital requirement; the branch fails to comply with the global solvency established by the Member States that have agreed to the request referred to in Article 224; the branch violates the laws or regulations that regulate its activity, in such a way as to jeopardise the interests of policyholders or beneficiaries or the normal operating conditions of the insurance market.

V. Insurance Companies Operating Through Freedom of Services

310. Finally, insurance companies with a head office in an EU Member State can operate either through an establishment (head office or branch office) or through FOS.

311. Pursuant to Article 234, an insurance company headquartered in Portugal that intends to carry out, for the first time, its activities in the free provision of services in the territory of another or other Member States must notify the ASF in advance, indicating the nature of the risks or commitments that it proposes to cover or assume. The ASF communicates, within one month of the date of this notification, the following information to the supervisory authorities of the Member State or Member States in whose territory the insurance company intends to carry out its activities in freedom to provide services: a document certifying that the insurance company complies with the solvency capital requirement and the minimum capital requirement; the lines of insurance that the insurance company is authorised to operate; and the nature of the risks or commitments that the insurance company proposes to cover or assume in the host Member State.

312. The communication is notified by the ASF, at the same time, to the interested insurance company, which may, from that date, start its activity in free provision of services (Articles 235(3) and 237).

313. The Member State where the insurance company intends to carry out its activities in the free provision of services may also require the company to present the following elements: name and address of the representative for claims, responsible for processing and regularising, in the country of residence of the victim, of accidents occurring in a Member State other than the one in which the latter resides; statement attesting that the insurance company has become a member of the national bureau and national guarantee fund of the host Member State (Article 235(2)).

Chapter 3. Supervision

314. As seen above,[125] the supervisory authority for insurance business in Portugal is the ASF, a legal person governed by public law, with the nature of an independent administrative entity, endowed with administrative, financial and management autonomy and its own assets. The statutes of this regulatory agency are enshrined in the Decree-Law 1/2015, of 6 January 2015, which establishes its supervisory powers.

315. The ASF is the competent authority for the supervision of the insurance activities carried out by the insurance (and reinsurance) companies with a head office in Portugal (including their activity carried out in other EU Member States through a branch office or FOS) as well as that carried out in Portugal by branch offices of non-EU insurance and reinsurance companies (Article 2(1) of LBIR).

316. According to Article 7(1) of Decree-Law 1/2015, of 6 January 2015, the supervisory powers given to the ASF include the powers and means to: supervise and regulate the insurance, reinsurance, insurance mediation and pension fund activities, as well as related or complementary activities; participate, under the terms defined by law, in the macro-prudential supervision system for the prevention and mitigation of systemic risks likely to affect financial stability, namely within the scope of the National Council of Financial Supervisors (Decree-Law 228/2000, of 23 September 2000); perform technical support and consultation functions with the Assembly of the Republic and the Government, on matters relating to the sector of activity under supervision, under the terms defined in its statutes; participate in the European System of Financial Supervision; participate, under the terms defined by law, in the audit supervision system, namely within the scope of the National Audit Supervision Council; promote the development of technical knowledge and its dissemination and the strengthening of financial literacy with regard to the insurance sector and pension funds; and manage the funds that are entrusted by law.

§1. Solvency Control

317. The ASF requires insurance companies to comply with certain rules established by law, in order to guarantee their solvency, the so-called financial guarantees. In fact, in an attempt to guarantee the solvency of insurance companies in Portugal, it was through Decree-Law 94-B/98, of 17 April, that Portugal implemented a system of Financial Guarantees, a common practice in the EEC. Financial Guarantees function as controllers and their main objective is to maintain and guarantee the solvency of insurance companies, in order to safeguard the interests of policyholders, beneficiaries and society in general. According to Article 68(1) of

125. *See* Ch. 2, §1, General.

Decree-Law 94-B/98 of 17 April, insurance companies must have three categories of financial guarantees: technical provisions (i.e., technical reserves), a solvency margin, and a guarantee fund.[126]

318. On 1 January 2016, the Solvency II regime began to take effect, representing a comprehensive and in-depth review of the legal framework applicable to insurance and reinsurance activities. The regime at EU level was introduced by the Solvency II Directive (Directive 2009/138/CE), transposed to the Portuguese domestic legal order by the aforementioned LBIR. In the aftermath of the financial crisis, the introduction of this harmonised legal framework sought to strengthen the protection of specific insurance creditors (e.g., policyholders, beneficiaries and injured parties) and financial stability, through the application of a more sensitive model to the risks incurred by operators that promotes a culture of risk-based management in the various functions of companies and that reinforces transparency and market discipline. This new regime also aimed to promote the convergence of supervisory practices, in compliance with the principle of proportionality, and the creation of a level playing field for European operators in order to achieve a true single market in the EU.[127]

319. European legislators decided that the European Commission should review certain matters in 2020 and present legislative proposals to the European Parliament and the Council of the EU, namely, measures relating to long-term guarantees and shareholder risk, the adequacy of methods, assumptions and parameters used in the calculation of the Solvency Capital Requirement standard formula, the rules of Member States and supervisory practices on the calculation of the Minimum Capital Requirement, and the supervision and management of own funds within groups insurance and reinsurance companies.[128]

320. Currently, and pursuant to Article 86(1) of LBIR, insurance and reinsurance companies must establish technical provisions, comply with the solvency capital requirement and the minimum capital requirement, and respect the applicable legal regime for the assessment of assets and liabilities, own funds and investments.

321. Chapter III of LBIR, regarding the financial conditions of insurance and reinsurance companies headquartered in Portugal, is divided as follows: it enshrines

126. For more developments on these categories, *see* Maria José Rangel de Mesquita, Regulação da Atividade Seguradora: Traços Fundamentais, (in Gonçalo Anastácio, Eduardo Paz Ferreira, Luís Silva Morais, *Regulação em Portugal: Novos Tempos, Novo Modelo?*, Almedina, 2009).

127. According to Dirk Horing, *Will Solvency II Market Risk Requirements Bite? The Impact of Solvency II on Insurers' Asset Allocation*, 38, The Geneva Papers, 250 (2012) Solvency II is a new regulatory oversight framework that, for the first time, introduces a method to measure capital requirements adequate to economic risk in the EEA. The Solvency II project also aims to review the current solvency regime applicable to insurance and reinsurance companies operating in the EEA, based on the adoption of economic principles for the valuation of assets and liabilities, in particular technical provisions and requirements based on the risks actually assumed.

128. For further details, *see* ASF, *Regulatory Developments of the Insurance Sector and the Pension Funds Sector 2020*, https://www.asf.com.pt/NR/rdonlyres/2401DC1B-7671-4DEB-95AE-7401AB540629/0/DR_2020_web.pdf.

the method of valuation of assets and liabilities in Article 90 (section II); the provisions relating to technical provisions in Articles 91 et seq. (section III); the regime of own funds in Articles 107 et seq. (section IV); the Solvency Capital Requirement in Articles 116 et seq. (section V); the minimum capital requirement in Articles 146 et seq. (section VI); and, finally, with regard to investments, it enshrines the prudent manager principle in Article 149 (section VII).

§2. Supervision of Tariffs and Insurance Conditions

322. As a general rule, insurance companies are free to fix premiums related to the risks insured and also to draw up insurance conditions. As such, in principle no prior supervision of tariffs or policy conditions exists. However, some exceptions must be considered, namely regarding compulsory insurance.

323. Pursuant to Article 39(1) of LBIR, the ASF may impose, through a regulatory norm, the use of uniform clauses or policies for mandatory insurance lines or modalities. Thus, the insurance company that intends to carry out mandatory insurance must notify the ASF of the general and special conditions of the policy, or any changes to be made, before the start of the respective marketing or within a maximum period of one month from that date (Article 39(2)).

324. The ASF verifies, within a maximum period of three months from the communication, the legal compliance of the general and special conditions communicated, and may, with good reason, request the amendment of the clauses it deems necessary to ensure this compliance (Article 39(3)). This regime extends to insurance that constitutes one of the alternative forms of compliance with a legal obligation (Article 39(6)).

325. Concerning the supervision of other insurance (non-compulsory insurance), the ASF has also been endowed with certain powers in order to ensure compliance with the rules applicable to insurance contracts.

326. In this sense, and in accordance with Article 40(1), the ASF may require insurance and reinsurance companies headquartered in Portugal, branches of insurance and reinsurance companies headquartered in another Member State or in a third country to non-systematic communication of the general and special policy conditions, tariffs, technical bases and forms and other forms that those companies propose to use in their relations with policyholders or with assigning or retroceding companies.

327. The ASF may also require insurance and reinsurance companies headquartered in Portugal and branches of insurance companies in a third country to systematically communicate the technical bases used in the life branch for the calculation of tariffs, benefits, contributions and provisions techniques (Article 40(2)).

328. However, these communications are not a precondition for the exercise of the said insurance activity (Article 40(3)).[129]

129. In accordance with the provisions of Arts 181 and 182 of the Solvency II Directive.

Chapter 4. Technical Reserves and Investments

329. Technical reserves[130] are one of the financial guarantees that must be ensured by insurance companies.[131]

330. Technical provisions are one of the most important items in the liabilities of insurance companies, and their amount must be sufficient to enable the insurance company to fulfil, to the extent foreseen, the commitments arising from the insurance contracts. Technical provisions are, therefore, economic, legal and mandatory provisions that insurers must make to meet their future obligations arising from their insurance operations, which exist at all times and which, therefore, must be reflected in the accounting of the insurers.[132]

331. The classification and requirements concerning the calculation of each type of technical reserves are laid down in Articles 91 et seq. (section III of Chapter III) of LBIR.

332. Pursuant to Article 90(1), insurance and reinsurance undertakings must set up technical provisions in relation to all of their insurance or reinsurance obligations. The amount of the technical provisions must correspond to the current amount that the insurance or reinsurance undertaking would have to pay if it immediately transferred its insurance and reinsurance obligations to another insurance or reinsurance company (Article 90(2)).

333. In the calculation of technical provisions, the information provided by the financial markets and the available elements on the specific insurance risks must be used, and consistency with such information and elements must be maintained (Article 90(3)).

334. The technical provisions must be calculated with prudence, reliability and objectivity, respecting the rules of Articles 92–103 of this law.[133]

335. Rules regarding market conduct are provided for in Chapter IV of LBIR. According to this Chapter, insurance companies must act diligently, equitably and

130. Although the LBIR only refers to technical provisions, several ASF documents (namely regulation standards, reports, etc.) speak of technical reserves, hence the duplication of designation.

131. According to Carlos Baptista da Costa, *Auditoria Financeira – Teoria e Prática*, Rei dos Livros (2014), 657, prudence is the inclusion of a degree of precaution in the exercise of the necessary judgment when making the necessary estimates in conditions of uncertainty, so that assets or income are not overvalued and liabilities or expenses are not understated. Thus, the exercise of prudence does not allow for the constitution of hidden reserves or excessive provisions, as well as the deliberate manipulation (overvaluation or undervaluation) of assets, liabilities, income or expenses.

132. *See* José Gonçalves dos Santos, *Contabilidade dos Seguros*, Quid Iuris (2004), 253. In the author's words, 'The calculation of technical provisions is based on estimates, obtained based on previous experience, and should therefore be carried out with all possible prudence.'

133. For detailed information on technical provisions in the first quarter of 2021, *see* ASF, *Technical Provisions and Assets Report – Quarterly*, https://www.asf.com.pt/ISP/Estatisticas/seguros/estatisticas_trimestrais/Provis%C3%B5esT%C3%A9cnicas_Ativos_Trimestral.pdf.

transparently in their relationship with policyholders, beneficiaries and injured third parties (Article 153(1)); the ASF may prohibit or prevent the sale of insurance products that harm or may harm the interests of policyholders or beneficiaries, namely because they are inappropriate to the respective profile or because they clearly induce or contribute to aggravate situations of conflict with their interests (Article 153(5)); insurance companies must define a policy for the treatment of policyholders, beneficiaries and injured third parties, ensuring that it is disseminated throughout the company and made public (Article 154(1)); conventions, protocols or other agreements entered into between insurance companies that may have an impact on the respective relationship with policyholders, beneficiaries and injured third parties must be communicated to the ASF, namely, in terms of the settlement of claims (Article 155); in the assessment of complaints, the ASF takes the necessary steps to verify compliance with the rules of which observance it is responsible for ensuring and adopts the appropriate measures to obtain the remedy of non-compliance, without prejudice to the opening of administrative proceedings whenever the conduct of the defendant entities, namely by gravity or reiteration so justifies (Article 157(1)); and insurance companies must designate, from among natural persons of recognised prestige, qualification, suitability and independence, the *ombudsman* for the client, to which policyholders, beneficiaries and injured third parties may file complaints regarding acts or omissions of those companies (Article 158(1)).

Chapter 5. Accountancy

336. In terms of the accounting rules, Regulatory Framework 4/2007-R, of 27 April, established an accounting regime applicable to insurance companies subject to ASF supervision based on international accounting standards (IAS). In this context, all IAS were adopted, with the exception of the IFRS 4, of which only the classification principles of the type of contracts entered into by insurance and disclosure companies were adopted.

337. On the other hand, Council Directive 91/674/EEC of 19 December 1991, on the annual accounts and consolidated accounts of insurance companies, established, among other aspects, harmonised rules on recognition and measurement of technical provisions. These rules, which were laid down in Decree-Law 94-B/98, of 17 April, and in the Chart of Accounts for Insurance Companies, constituted the basis for the accounting regime for insurance companies for liabilities arising from insurance contracts.

338. With the entry into force of the new legal regime for accessing and exercising the insurance and reinsurance activity, approved by LBIR, and consequent revocation of Decree-Law 94-B/98, it became necessary to incorporate the rules relating to the recognition and measurement of the technical provisions contained in the aforementioned legal diploma into the Chart of Accounts for Insurance Companies.

339. Thus, Regulatory Framework 8/2016-R, of 16 August, came to regulate the provision of information by the supervised entities to the ASF for the purposes of exercising the supervisory powers that are legally entrusted to them, organising, complementing and operationalising the provision of information based on the Solvency II regime, as well as the provision of accounting, statistical and behavioural information in accordance with LBIR.

340. The aforementioned regulatory standard was, however, amended by Regulatory Framework 1/2018-R, of 11 January, with the main objective of adjusting the regime for providing periodic information and additional information for the purposes of financial stability to the EIOPA, to the changes in Implementing Regulation (EU) 2015/2450, of the European Commission, of 2 December, and in the Guidelines issued by EIOPA.

341. The most recent change was carried out by Regulatory Framework 10/2020-R, of 3 November, of which its main objective was to reflect in the national legislation the changes introduced in the Commission's Implementing Regulation (EU) 2015/2450, of 2 December, by Implementing Regulation (EU) 2018/1844, of the Commission, of 23 November 2018, as well as the amendments made by EIOPA on 25 June 2018 to the Guidelines on the provision of information for the purposes of financial stability.

342. Thus, pursuant to Article 16 of the LBIR, the supervisory authority has the power to approve the accountancy rules applicable to the insurance companies that fall under its supervision and to define the items that the insurance companies must present as well as the items that must be made public, in accordance with Regulatory Framework 8/2016-R, of 16 August, republished as an annex to Regulatory Framework 10/2020-R, of 3 November.

Chapter 6. Taxation of the Company

343. In Portugal, insurance companies, like most other companies, are liable to corporate income tax on their profits in accordance with the Tax Code in force (*Código do Imposto sobre o Rendimento das Pessoas Coletivas* – CIRC), approved by Decree-Law 442-B/88 of 30 November, and as amended thereinafter.

344. Corporate income tax is a state tax. Although there are no taxes on profits levied by local or other non-state authorities, the autonomous regions as well as municipalities can benefit from a percentage of the income tax paid by companies. Corporate income tax is levied on all legal persons governed by public or private law with headquarters or effective management in Portuguese territory. The starting point for the definition of subjective incidence was, therefore, the attribute of legal personality.

345. However, entities with head office or effective management in Portuguese territory were also subject to corporate income tax and which, although lacking legal personality, obtain income that is not subject to individual or legal persons who are part of them. Corporate income tax also applies to entities, with or without legal personality, that do not have their registered office or effective management in Portuguese territory but earn income there.

346. Insurance companies are therefore treated for corporate income tax purposes as an ordinary company. Insurance companies with a head office or 'effective management' in Portugal are subject to tax liability concerning all their income, including income obtained abroad (Articles 2(1) and 4(1)). Companies that have their registered office abroad and carry on insurance business in Portugal are also liable to pay tax concerning income obtained in Portugal only (Article 4(2,3)). Rules concerning the calculation of taxable income, based on profit, are laid down by the CIRC (Articles 15 et seq.). The taxable income is in principle calculated based on the annual tax return submitted by the company (Article 16).

347. With specific regard to insurance companies, for tax income purposes, technical provisions for non-collected premiums, which for both domestic insurance companies and branch offices in Portugal of EU insurance companies are subject to the supervisory authority of the ASF, are tax deductible (Article 39(1,c)).

348. Furthermore, Article 50(1) CIRC states that income or expenses resulting from the application of fair value to assets that represent technical provisions for life insurance with profit sharing, or allocated to contracts in which the insurance risk is borne by the policyholder, contribute to the formation of taxable profit of insurance.

Part II. The Insurance Contract: General

Chapter 1. Generalities

Gabriela Assunção Lacerda, Geraldo Rocha Ribeiro, & Maria Inês de Oliveira Martins[134]

§1. Definition of Insurance

349. The RJCS begins with the description of the insurance contract. According to Article 1, 'by entering into the insurance contract, the insurer undertakes to cover a certain risk pertaining to the policyholder or to another person, by assuming an obligation to perform in case an uncertain event set out in the contract occurs, whereas the policyholder undertakes to pay the insurance premium'.

350. As stated in the preamble of the statute (*see* point V), the concept was deliberately left open, so that it could easily accommodate the diversified array of contract arrangements that have been emerging in the insurance market – as has happened most strikingly in the field of life insurance, where savings and investment products that no longer have the uncertainty quality that is typical of insurance have emerged. Much as in §1 of the VVG, which was the source of inspiration for the Portuguese norm, the concept of insurance contract was set out not as a concept, but as a 'type', meaning that a given contract that does not possess all the traits described in Article 1 can still be considered an insurance contract and fall under the rules of the RJCS (though some rules may have to be adapted).[135]

351. The first feature mentioned by Article 1 is that insurance cover is provided by the *insurer*. As stated in Article 16(1), of RJCS, the insurer should have received

134. Gabriela Assunção Lacerda authored Ch. 1, §5, and Ch. 5, §1, II and III; Geraldo Rocha Ribeiro authored Ch. 3, §2–5, and Ch. 7, §2; Maria Inês de Oliveira Martins authored Ch. 1, §1–4; Ch. 2; Ch. 3, §1; Ch. 4; Ch. 5, §1, I, and §2; Chs 6 and 7, §1.

135. Margarida Lima Rego, Contrato de seguro e terceiros, Estudo de Direito civil, Coimbra Editora, (2010), 35–40; Maria Inês de Oliveira Martins, O seguro de vida enquanto tipo contratual legal, Coimbra Editora, (2010), 115–121; Maria Inês de Oliveira Martins, Pensamento tipológico e contrato de seguro – o seguro de vida, em particular (in: Fernando Alves Correia/Jónatas E. M. Machado/João Carlos Loureiro (ed.) Estudos em Homenagem ao Prof. Doutor José Joaquim Gomes Canotilho, I, Responsabilidade: entre passado e futuro, Coimbra Editora, 2012) 1, 496 and ff.

authorisation for the taking-up and pursuit of the business of insurance or reinsurance, as provided by the law – that is, LBIR. The offer of insurance cover without due authorisation is subject to criminal and administrative sanctions under LBIR. However, the lack of authorisation does not set aside the nature of the contract as insurance. The RJCS sets out a special case of nullity for these purposes, that preserves some of the effects of the contract entered into. Under Article 16(2), unless the other party acted with bad faith, the person that offered insurance coverage is bound by the obligation they undertook, and the clauses and provisions that regulate this obligation will still apply.[136] All the other effects of the contract are, on the contrary, not kept – which first and foremost includes the duty to pay out the premium (although the rules on unjustified enrichment might arguably apply).

352. Second, the contract should have as its purpose the *cover of a risk* pertaining to the policyholder or to another person. As used in this norm, the concept of risk is intertwined with the requirement of an insurable *interest*. An interest consists in a relationship between a person and certain goods (broadly conceived), which determines that this person will suffer a disadvantage in case those goods are disturbed. A risk is, therefore, in this sense, the possibility that a specified event occurs, which will bear disadvantage to that person – it refers to the possibility of disturbance of one's interest.[137] The person who is the holder of the interest and therefore affected by the risk is called the *insured*; they can either be the policyholder or another person. The goods exposed to the risk can be *stricto sensu* goods, or a person, or a patrimony (Article 43).

353. The insurance company *covers the risk* in the sense that it undertakes to pay certain sums or deliver certain goods or services to the *insured* in *case the specified event occurs*. Considering that this event has the potential to disturb the insurable interest, the purpose of the insurance contract becomes clear: it has the *purpose of protecting the holder of the interest*, that is, the insured. Since the same event that brings them disadvantages will now determine that they have the right before the insurer, one can say that insurance *transfers the economic consequences of the risk from the insured to the* insurance company – in short, that it *transfers the risk from the insured to the* insurance company.[138]

136. However, many of the provisions that impact the insurer's obligation – e.g., the provisions on the applicant's pre-contractual information duty, or the provisions on aggravation or modification the risk – only make sense in view of a professional and technically organised insurer (*see* José Carlos Moitinho de Almeida, O contrato de seguro, 51, Cadernos de Direito Privado, (2015), 31).

137. In the realm of insurance contract law, the word 'risk' can have different meanings. Sometimes, risk refers simply the uncertain event specified in the contract – in this sense, risk is an event. Risk can also refer the possibility or probability that a certain event occurs – in this sense, risk is a possibility or probability. The sense used in the text stresses the fact of there being an exposure to the possibility of *negative outcomes* (M. I. Oliveira Martins, O seguro de vida … , 261 and ff.; Maria Inês de Oliveira Martins, Contrato de seguro e conduta dos sujeitos ligados ao risco, Almedina, (2018), 29–30).

138. As the terms 'insured' and 'insurer' are very close, for the sake of clarity, in this segment where the role of the insured – and not that of the policyholder – stands out, the text shall refer to the 'insurance company', instead of referring to the 'insurer'.

354. This transfer has value for the insured from the inception of the contract, and not only if and when the insured event occurs. From the onset they can make their economic plans relying on the fact that the insurance company will perform in case the insured event takes place – which is especially critical in case the insurance is contracted to cover entrepreneurial risks. Moreover, the insured will more easily be granted credit if they have insurance cover in regard to certain risks.

355. In brief, the cover of risk corresponds, in *practical terms*, to a transfer of the risk to the insurance company. This *transfer of certain risks* to the insurer therefore identifies the *practical purpose of the insurance contract* – in other words, the kind of actual utility that an insured can expect to derive from it. The concept of what is the *practical purpose of the insurance contract* is fundamental for the interpretation of the contract, as well as for assessment as to whether the contract is unfairly unbalanced for the purposes of the norms on contracts of adhesion.[139]

356. In legal terms, the insurance company which undertakes to cover a risk comes under a *conditional obligation to perform* in case the insured event occurs. In some cases of life insurance, where there is certainty as to the fact that the insurance company will have to perform, its *obligation is time-limited* (in the sense of Article III. – 1:107 of DCFR (Draft Common Frame of Reference)). The status of the insurance company in the period while the event has not occurred is best described as a *liability*.[140]

357. In any case, the insurance contract must always refer to a certain risk, conceived as a possibility of disturbance of the insured's interest. Otherwise, the contract will not qualify as insurance, but as a gambling contract.

358. The contract must also refer to an *uncertain event*, upon which the obligation of the insurance company takes effect. As mentioned above, in some cases of life insurance, the contract refers to an event that is *certain as to its occurrence*, and uncertain only as to *when it will occur*. That is the case of whole life insurance, where the obligation comes to effect by the death of the insured person; and that is also the case of mixed life insurance, which has a strong savings element, where the right to the insurance capital arises either by the death of the insured person, or upon

139. *See* respectively Part II, Ch. 1, §2, Rules on Interpretation of Insurance Contracts, and §5, Inclusion and Content Control of Standard Terms and Conditions of Insurance Contracts.

140. Liability in the sense proposed by Wesley Newcomb Hohfeld, *Some Fundamental Legal Conceptions as Applied in Judicial Reasoning*, 1 Yale L. J. 44–45, at 49–51 and 53–54 (1913); in Portuguese scholarship, this point has been made by M. Lima Rego, Contrato …, 340–344. The same idea is conveyed by the construction of that state as similar to that of someone against who an unilateral power (*direito potestativo, diritto potestativo, Gestaltungsrecht*) can be exercised – albeit, in the case of insurance, the insurance company is not subject to a certain power, but to the fact that the insured event can occur and bring his obligation to take effect. This state of 'subjection' is termed *sujeição* (*soggezione, Gebundenheit*). For this construction, *see* M. I. Oliveira Martins, O seguro de vida …, 41–46.

its survival of a certain date. The certainty as to the occurrence of the event does not alter the qualification of these contracts as insurance contracts; they do not become savings contracts.

359. It is also a feature of the contract that the insurer undertakes the obligation to perform in case the specified event occurs. Payment is generally made in money, but in some insurance branches it will commonly be made in kind (e.g., in the assistance branch, or in the health insurance branch). There has been a growing trend of supplementing the contract with services that are ancillary in the prevention of the insurance risk (e.g., in the branch of health insurance, or cyber insurance). In these cases, the insurer will incur in obligations that arise before the insured event. The contract will preserve its nature in case these features add on to the core obligation to perform when the insured event occurs. If the contract refers only to services aimed at risk prevention, it will no longer be an insurance contract – it will rather be a contract for the performance of services of a certain kind.

360. Finally, insurance is an onerous contract, where the obligations undertaken by the insurance company are offset by the obligation to pay the insurance premium undertaken by the policyholder. A gratuitous contract, under which a person undertook to cover a certain risk without receiving consideration would be a contract analogous to insurance.[141]

§2. Rules on Interpretation of Insurance Contracts

361. Insurance contract is a contract; therefore, it falls under the general rules on contract interpretation, as set out in Article 236 of the Civil Code, entitled 'Normal Meaning of the Declaration'.

362. The central norm states that: 'a declaration of intent has the meaning that a reasonable person in the position of the addressee would give to the conduct of the person making that declaration, except if this person could not reasonably have anticipated such meaning' (Article 236(1)).

363. Under this criterion, the *declaration should be interpreted in objective terms*, according to the meaning that a *reasonable addressee, normally diligent and knowledgeable*, and endowed with *any special information that the particular addressee has access to*, would give to it.[142] Article 236(2) adds that 'When the addressee was aware of the actual intention of the person making the declaration,

141. There would be no logical obstacle to the application of some of the norms of the RJCS in this situation (*see* José Carlos Moitinho de Almeida, O contrato de seguro no direito português e comparado, Livraria Sá da Costa (1971), 30, in regard to the Commercial Code); however, they would most likely prove generally inadequate, since their solutions were conceived for the setting where the insurance provider is a professional party.

142. The last segment of the norm is thought to have very limited practical effect, since it does not refer to the meaning that the person making the declaration could *actually* anticipate, but to the meaning that it should have *reasonably* anticipated. Now, since the meaning accorded by the addressee is

its meaning will be defined according to that intention.' In fact, this rule (*falsa demonstratio non nocet*) does not part from the general criterion. It merely implies that when the *special information* that the addressee has access to comprises *the actual intention of his counter-party*, then the declaration should be interpreted in light of that intention.

364. In order to determine the meaning that a *reasonable addressee* would accord to a declaration, one should consider all the particular circumstances that would be significant to a normally diligent and fair-minded addressee. Those circumstances are not exhaustively described; some of the most relevant ones are those mentioned in Article II. – 8:102 (Relevant matters) of the DCFR. Namely, the circumstances in which the contract was concluded, including the preliminary negotiations; the conduct of the parties, even subsequent to the conclusion of the contract; the meaning attributed to certain words or expressions by the practices established between the parties, or by the branch of activity concerned; usages that are relevant in that sector; the nature and practical purpose of the contract.[143] The meaning of the declaration will then be that which a normally diligent and fair-minded addressee would infer from all those circumstances (contrarily from what stems from the DCFR, good faith and fair dealing is not considered a circumstance to be assessed, but rather a criterion for the assessment). The *practical purpose* of the insurance contract – that is, the *risk that the contract should be reasonably expected to address*, in view of the particular circumstances of the policyholder that the insurer should have been aware of – particularly stands out.[144]

365. The general criterion of Article 236 of the Civil Code seems to be somewhat limited by Article 35 of RJCS (entitled 'Consolidation of the Contract').[145] Under its terms, the policyholder has thirty days from receipt of the policy to invoke any non-conformity between points that were agreed upon but are not reflected on the policy; beyond that date, they can only avail themselves of any non-conformity that can be proved by a written document or by other durable support.

366. This provision therefore forbids invoking any point agreed upon that was not stated in a durable support after thirty days from receipt of the policy. It seems questionable that such a burden is placed upon the policyholder; moreover, taken literally, the provision would directly conflict with the LSCT.[146] It should be underscored that the provision does not limit the liability of the insurance company for

---

also assessed by an objective criterion of reasonableness, it will be very difficult to find cases where the meaning *reasonably attributed* to the declaration should not have been *reasonably anticipated*.

143. Carlos Alberto da Mota Pinto/António Pinto Monteiro/Paulo Mota Pinto, Teoria Geral do Direito Civil, Coimbra Editora, (2005), 446-447.

144. STJ 5 July 2012, 1028/09.0TVLSB.L1.S1 (António Joaquim Piçarra); TRL 9 September 2021, 15426/17.2T8LSB.L1-2 (Laurinda Gemas).

145. Unlike what happened under the Commercial Code, under the RJCS insurance is not deemed a formal contract (Art. 32(1)), and therefore the special rule on the interpretation of formal contracts (Art. 238 of the Civil Code) does not apply.

146. In this sense, Júlio Manuel Vieira Gomes, O dever de informação do (candidato a) tomador do seguro na fase pré-contratual à luz do Decreto-Lei n.º 72/2008, de 16 de Abril (in: Rui Pinto Duarte/

breach of its duty to inform on the terms of the policy. Neither does it limit the relevance of the conduct of the parties in the execution of the contract for the purpose of its interpretation.

367. The LSCT also establishes special rules in this regard. Article 10 establishes that the general rules on contract interpretation apply, in regard to the context of the particular contract. Article 11 establishes that '1. Ambiguous standard terms are to be interpreted according to the meaning that a normal indeterminate contracting party, limited to the subscribing or accepting of those clauses, would give them, when placed in the position of the actual contracting party. 2 Where there is doubt about the meaning of a term, the most interpretation favourable towards the party that did not draft it shall prevail. 3. This rule on interpretation shall not apply in the context of a judicial injunction aimed at forbidding the future use of certain clauses'.

368. Now, as insurance is generally a contract of adhesion (and moreover a contract composed by SCT), those special rules turn out to be the ones generally applicable. It should also be borne in mind that a current practice in the insurance market is that the insurer drafts the contract terms and sends them to the potential policyholder; this does not have the value of an offer, but merely of an 'invitation to present an offer' (*invitatio ad oferendum*). In case the potential policyholder is interested in entering into the contract as defined in the terms presented, they send a proposal containing those terms, which has the value of an offer. However, as the contract terms are drafted by the insurance company, they are interpreted according to the meaning that the policyholder attributes to them; that is, the policyholder is deemed the addressee of the contract for the purpose of its interpretation, although in terms of formation of the contract they will appear as the part presenting the offer.[147] In case the insurance is taken out for the account of a third party, the contract should be interpreted in light of their expectations. In fact, the contract's purpose is to protect their interest, as the insurance company is well aware of. Besides, when the contract is composed by SCT, as it generally is, it cannot be said that insurance company chose the wording of the terms in view of a certain counter-party. There is therefore no reason to protect its expectations in this regard.

369. The LSCT both has rules that apply in the *context of a particular contract* and rules that provide for *injunctive action aimed at prohibiting the future use of a specific term* and therefore affect all future contracts (Articles 25 and ff. of LSCT). Rules of interpretation are different in these two contexts.

370. In the context of an injunctive action, the interpretation is abstract and focuses on preventing risks for contracting parties. Accordingly, under Article 11(3),

José Lebre de Freitas/Assunção Cristas/Marta Tavares de Almeida/Vítor Pereira das Neves (ed.) Estudos em Homenagem ao Professor Doutor Carlos Ferreira de Almeida, II, Almedina, 2011), 400.

147. Maria Inês de Oliveira Martins, Pluralidade subjectiva no contrato de seguro e determinação da qualidade dos intervenientes, Anotação ao acórdão do Supremo Tribunal de Justiça de 13 de Novembro de 2018, Processo n.º 1699/16.1T8PNF.P2.S2 (Cons. Alexandre Reis), 64, Cadernos de Direito Privado, (2018), 83.

the use of the term will be prohibited should any interpretation that could be accorded to it result in a risk of unfairness.

371. In contrast, in regard to a particular contract, the term is construed under the *general norms on contract interpretation*, with respect to the *context of that specific relationship, according to the meaning that the party not drafting the term reasonably accorded to it*. This is the combined result of Articles 10 and 11 LSCT.[148]

372. That implies that the term at stake is interpreted in the context of the whole contract. Special attention is devoted to the actual purpose that its parties – conceived as reasonable and fair-minded persons – aimed to achieve. In the insurance setting, this translates into the granting of special attention to the specific circumstances of the risk that the contract aimed to cover.

373. For example, in a case where the insurance contract covered the risk of disability of the manager of a small-medium enterprise and defined the risk as 'disability for the undertaking of the company's "management"', the STJ considered that this latter concept should not be understood as reporting to managerial functions in general and abstract terms, but as reporting to the socio-economic reality underlying a micro-enterprise in the construction sector, as the one at stake, where 'management' could imply a continuous presence and contact with clients from the manager.[149] In another case where the owner of an automobile repair shop and commercial parking station had taken out property insurance in regard to the parked vehicles, the insurer had argued that only the vehicles belonging to the policyholder were insured: if he had intended to protect third parties' vehicles, he should have taken out liability insurance instead. The court considered that in view of the practical purpose of the insurance contract at stake, where the vehicles covered would without question normally belong to third parties – the parking station and repair shop clients –, the insurance should be construed as regarding such vehicles belonging to third parties.[150]

374. This general criterion intertwines with the rule established when there is doubt as to the meaning of a term, determining that the term is given the most meaning favourable to the non-drafting party (*contra proferentem* rule, stated in Article 11 LSCT). If even this interpretation leads to the conclusion that the clause is disproportionately imbalanced, then it is declared null (Article 12 LSCT).

---

148. *See* Almeno de Sá, Lei das cláusulas contratuais gerais e Directiva sobre cláusula abusivas (in: Cláusulas contratuais gerais e Directiva sobre cláusulas abusivas, Almedina, 9, 2001), 27–29. The last segment of Art. 236(1) of the Civil Code is deemed not to apply in the context of contracts of adhesion. Since the drafting party unilaterally defined the contract terms, they should bear all the risks regarding the formulation of the terms (José Carlos Moitinho de Almeida, A interpretação e integração das lacunas do contrato de seguro (in: J. C. Moitinho de Almeida (ed.) Contrato de seguro, Estudos, Coimbra Editora, 2009), 118).

149. STJ 24 January 2017, 1237/14.0TBSTR.E1.S1 (Júlio Gomes).

150. TRP 3 December 2020, 6688/17.8T8PRT.P1 (Paulo Dias da Silva).

375. Both criteria concur in the *result of preserving challenged terms*, since they push towards an interpretation that aligns them with the expectations of the non-drafting party and thus gives them a fairer meaning.[151]

376. In what concerns the filling in of gaps in the contract, the key provision is Article 239 of the Civil Code, which Article 10 of LSCT deems applicable to contracts of adhesion.

377. Under Article 239 of the Civil Code, when no legal provision can fill in the gap, the declaration of intent shall be supplemented according to the intent that the parties would have had in case they had envisaged the aspect not provided for, or according to the rules of good faith, where they demand a different solution.

378. The two final criteria would literally seem alternative: the judge would determine how the parties would have regulated the aspect at stake, had they been aware of the omission (hypothetical common intention of the parties); and only when this contradicted good faith should the judge directly apply this standard. However, the two criteria are generally applied in tandem, that is, that judge determines how fair-minded persons placed in the position of the contracting parties would have regulated the point at stake.[152]

379. This combined criterion is generally the most relevant for the field of insurance, since there will frequently not exist any (non-mandatory) norm that could fill in the gap.

380. A gap may arise either because the contract was originally incomplete, or because a contract term – particularly, an SCT – was declared null and void. However, it should be added that an SCT that is null and void and detrimental to the policyholder/insured will generally simply be expunged from the contract. Court decisions where a judge-made provision is put forth to fill in the gap are very rare.[153] As the most frequently challenged terms on insurance contracts are clauses that exclude or in any way condition risk coverage, the general result is therefore that the risk will be covered without that limitation.[154] Moreover, as mentioned, the

151. This result is especially visible in a decision concerning a civil liability insurance for damage caused by pets outside the field of business-to-business contracts (STJ 3 May 2016, 613/08.2TBSSB.E1.S1 (Pinto de Almeida)). The policy excluded coverage when the norms setting out duties for pet owners had not been complied with. The disputed term was considered too vague and with potential to devoid cover of any utility; however, instead of declaring its nullity, the STJ corrected it through interpretation, stating that the exclusion could only be of effect when the pet owner had breached his duties *at least with gross negligence*.

152. J. C. Moitinho de Almeida, A interpretação ..., 139–141; Evaristo Mendes/Fernando Sá, Art. 239.º, Integração (in: Luís Carvalho Fernandes/José Carlos Brandão Proença (ed.) Comentário ao Código Civil, Parte Geral, Universidade Católica Portuguesa, 547, 2014), 548(I) and 551(VII).

153. Maria Inês de Oliveira Martins, Tarifas telemáticas no contexto do contrato de seguro (in: Pablo Girgado Perandones/Juan Gonzáles Bustos (ed.) Nuevos retos en el Derecho de Seguro: Hacia un mercado asegurador más transparente y competitivo, Comares, 417, 2021), 438.

154. *See* the case law quoted in Ana Filipa Morais Antunes, Comentário à Lei das cláusulas contratuais gerais, Coimbra Editora, (2013), 188 and ff.

courts make a rather liberal use of the possibilities granted by the *contra proferentem* doctrine, which saves many clauses from being considered unbalanced and being expunged from the contract.

§3. Categories of Insurance

381. The RJCS divides insurance in two main categories: what is literally called 'damages insurance' (Title II, Articles 123 and ff.) and personal insurance (Title III, Article 175 and ff.). 'Damages insurance' is equated by the RJCS to non-personal insurance. In fact, Article 43(2), of RJCS states that in case of 'damages insurance', insurable interest regards the conservation or integrity of the asset, right or patrimony insured; and Article 123 states that 'damages insurance' may regard any assets, non-tangible goods, claims or any other rights with a pecuniary value. However, what 'damages insurance' technically means is that the insurance at stake has the purpose of compensating for the damage suffered by the insured. As it were, in its more straightforward meaning, the expression is a synonym of indemnity insurance. And, in fact, the core of the general rules on 'damages insurance' consists of the rules that define indemnity insurance (Articles 128–136, on the limits and determination of insurance payment, on over-insurance, under-insurance and subrogation), besides the rule on mitigation of damage (Article 126), which makes sense only in connection with indemnity insurance (or at least insurance where the benefits are somewhat indexed to the extent of the damage).

382. Following its own logic, the RJCS should then restrict the rules on indemnity insurance to non-personal insurance and construe all personal insurance as fixed sums insurance – for which there would naturally be no sound material reasons. In fact, the RJCS clarifies that personal insurance can be set out either as indemnity insurance or as insurance of fixed sums (Article 175(2)). Therefore, although the choice of words by the RJCS is not technically correct and does not contribute to the clarity of the system of insurance law,[155] it does not have practical consequences.

383. Insurance can be separated according to how the insurance benefits are determined. Under this criterion, one identifies indemnity insurance as opposed to fixed sums insurance. In the case of indemnity insurance, insurance benefits should compensate the damage caused by the insured event and should not bring an accrual to the patrimony of the insured (indemnity principle). This is the purpose of the norms that applies to indemnity insurance, particularly by setting the amount of damage caused by the insurance as the maximum payable by the insurance (Article 128); by setting out duties to inform in case of cumulative insurance, and forbidding cumulative payments (Article 133), and by entitling the insurance company with a right to subrogate against a third party liable for the loss (Article 136).[156]

---

155. For a critique, M. Lima Rego, Contrato ... , 236 and ff.; M. I. Oliveira Martins, Contrato de seguro e conduta ... , 252–257.

156. *See below* on this Part II, Ch. 5, §1, II, Rules Applicable to Indemnity Insurance.

384. In case of insurance of fixed sums, insurance benefits are determined in advance by the contract, regardless of the actual damage caused by the insured event. This can be understood in view of the fact that this insurance covers the risk of events that *may affect the insured's personal ability to accumulate wealth* – personal incapacity due to health issues or accident, survival upon a certain age threshold or death. Protection against this risk is therefore achieved if the person is ensured access to a certain amount of accumulated wealth – specifically, of savings – in case (or when, in case of death) these events take place.

385. That kind of risk is *characteristic of personal insurance*. Therefore, only *personal insurance, and not* property or liability insurance, can be designed as insurance of fixed sums (Article 175(2), *a contrario*). That is the rule under the RJCS, as it is generally the rule elsewhere (*see, for instance,* Article 13:101 'Insurance of Fixed Sums' of DCFR). In fact, an event that causes damage to property can affect the ability to accumulate wealth *through a certain asset* and can thus only justify a payment that compensates for the *loss of profit* that would *plausibly be obtained through that same asset.* In case of an event that gives rise to a liability, once the *value of the liability is compensated*, then the ability to accumulate wealth would also be restored. That is, the attribution of a fixed amount of capital in these cases would bear no relation to the consequences of the insured event and thus give rise to problems of moral hazard.

386. However, fixed sums insurance is not immune to the problem of moral hazard. This problem is addressed in regard to cumulative insurance, where either the policyholder or the insured must inform the insurance company of any fixed sums or indemnity insurance covering the same risk (Article 180(3)).

387. Insurance can also be separated according to the nature of the object exposed to the insured risk – as it were, the object upon which the insured event will act. Under this criterion, one identifies personal insurance, where the event will act upon the person of the insured, as opposed to property insurance, where the event will act upon a certain asset.[157]

157. In fact, the RJCS uses a narrower term – namely, that of 'coisa', which is a good that can be the subject matter of rights in rem. It has been contested whether it encompasses both tangible and tangible goods (that is the view of Paulo Mota Pinto, Direito das coisas, Relatório sobre o programa, conteúdo e métodos de ensino, s. ed., (2019) at 82–83), or merely the latter (José Alberto Vieira, Direitos reais, Almedina, 2 Ed. (2018), 126–130). Art. 123 of RJCS would seem to follow the latter construction. As it identifies as possible subject matter of indemnity insurance 'coisas', intangible goods, claims and any other rights with a pecuniary value, it would seem to limit the meaning of 'coisa' in this context to tangible goods that that can be the subject matter of rights in rem. There would, however, be no good reason to treat such tangible (e.g., a house) and intangible (e.g., a trademark) goods differently in regard to insurance; the provisions on insurance of goods that can be the subject matter of rights in rem seem adequate to both cases. Therefore, the text will simply refer to those goods as 'assets'. The same lack of accuracy could in fact be pointed to the expression 'property insurance', since it would literally only encompass insurance of the *assets owned* by the insured, leaving out, for instance, other assets upon which they have another right in rem.

388. This leaves out insurance that does not cover risks affecting either an insured person or a certain asset, but rather risks that give rise to new liabilities. This happens either because the insured event gives rise to a duty to compensate third parties – that is the case of liability insurance – or because the insured event creates the need to make expenses – this is the case of health expense insurance, assistance insurance or legal protection insurance. There is not an established umbrella category that encompasses these cases; there may be reference to 'liabilities insurance' or to 'patrimony insurance', in view of the risk of a negative variation of the balance sheet (through the emergence of a liability). In fact, there are no common rules applicable to this set of insurance, whereas there are rules particular to property insurance and to personal insurance.

389. Specific rules applying to property insurance concern the fact that the insured event will affect a certain asset, upon which the insured has an interest. This interest should be valued in order to determine the value of the potential damage (expected loss). Both the sum insured and the insurance premium should be determined in view of this value. This has consequences for the application of the indemnity principle, where the value of the interest upon the asset sets a limit on insurance payment and the rules on over-insurance and under-insurance police the relation between the value of the interest, the sum insured and the insurance premium (*see* Articles 130, 132, 134).

390. Specific rules applying to personal insurance concern the fact that the insured event will affect the physical-psychologic integrity of a certain person – the insured person. Therefore, the evaluation of the insured risk will demand the collection of sensitive data regarding the health of the insured person. Apart from the norms of the General Data Protection Regulation (GDPR) and the Law on personal data, that apply in this regard, the RJCS sets out specific rules on the collection of medical data, and on the access to that data (Articles 177 and 178).

391. Furthermore, as seen above, it is also important to differentiate between voluntary or non-mandatory insurance and compulsory or mandatory insurance, as it is important to differentiate between insurance of large risks and mass risk insurance. Besides the existence of a special set of rules that apply to mandatory liability insurance, mandatory insurance should generally be understood as having the primary purpose of protecting the interest of third parties, whose interests could also be harmed by the insured event. In contrast, voluntary insurance should be interpreted primarily in light of the interest of the insured (but not exclusively, in view of provisions such as Article 741 of the Civil Code, which grants the victims with a security in rem upon the insurance indemnity, as collateral for their right to damages).

392. In what concerns mass risk insurance vis-à-vis large risk insurance, one should be reminded that the semi-mandatory character of some norms of the RJCS (those mentioned in Article 13) only has effect in regard to mass risk insurance.

§4. General Principles

393. As insurance is a contract, the general principles of contract law apply – first and foremost, private autonomy and good faith. However, some remarks should be made in regard to each of those principles.

394. In regard to the principle of private autonomy, one should highlight that, in fact, its role in insurance contract law is more limited than it would seem, since the contract terms are predominantly non-negotiated.

395. Quite on the contrary, the principle of good faith plays a central role in this field. In fact, it is even emphasised by referring to insurance as a contract of utmost good faith (*uberrima bona fides*).[158] This reference has also been met with some criticism. Unlike in English law, where qualifying a contract as a contract of utmost good faith entails the application of special duties to actively inform the other party,[159] in Portugal all contracts fall under a principle of good faith (Articles 227, 236 and 762 of the Civil Code).[160]

396. This principle is the source of duties of conduct and of duties of information once certain general requirements are met. Namely, in what requires the duties to inform, the existence of an asymmetry of information; the fact the party with an informational advantage recognises both their own superiority and the essentiality of this information in a process of decision-taking by the counter-party; and finally, the reasonableness of imposing this duty on the party provided with the information.[161] Those requirements identify the cases in which it is materially justified to demand such a duty from one of the parties, and the issue therefore becomes that of determining if they are met in that particular case. Reference to a category of 'utmost good faith' contracts would therefore entail the risk of rigidly enforcing duties to inform in cases where there would be no effective material justification to do so (e.g., due to lack of an asymmetry of information between the parties).

397. Moreover, that approach creates a risk of unbalance between the contracting parties. In fact, the traditional role of the principle has been to sanction fraudulent behaviour from the policyholder or insured, and not to react to any lack of information or cooperation from the insurer.[162] It is not desirable to import this unbalance to the Portuguese law. In regard to the insurance contract, it has been

---

158. Pedro Romano Martinez, Direito dos seguros, Apontamentos, Principia, (2006), p. 59.
159. Peter MacDonald Eggers/Simon Picken/Patrick Foss, Good faith and insurance contracts, Informa/Routledge, (2018), 1 and ff., remarking at 5 that '[t]he common law in England has preferred to designate certain contracts as contract *uberrimae fidei*, rather than import wholesale the duty of good faith into every contractual relationship'.
160. Arnaldo Pinheiro Torres, Ensaio sôbre o contrato de seguro, s.ed., (1939), p. 46; M. Lima Rego, Contrato …, p. 441; M. I. Oliveira Martins, Contrato de seguro e conduta …, pp. 168–169.
161. Jorge Ferreira Sinde Monteiro, Responsabilidade por conselhos, recomendações ou informações, Almedina, (1989), p. 361.
162. P. M. Eggers & S. Picken, *Good Faith* … 2018, xx and 3, where they remark that 'The duty has been the constant refrain of an insurer singing the breaches of an assured.' Even when the present

stressed that 'good faith is a two-way street',[163] that can point either to the insured, or to the insurer, since each of the parties has an informational advantage regarding different points relevant to the contract. For instance, in what regards the pre-contractual assessment of the insured risk, the insurance company will be the one that can identify the relevant aspects on which it needs to be informed, whereas the insured will be the one that has access to information on those aspects. A sound understanding of good faith is fundamental to assure that the norms imposing duties to inform on the insured are correctly understood.

398. Within this framework, one should highlight that the insurance contract does tend to exist in a context giving rise to enhanced duties of conduct or information. As a frequently long-term contract, it demands cooperation between the parties. Moreover, it does tend to expose each of the parties to risks deriving from an informational advantage from the other party and to their negligence or even opportunistic behaviour (e.g., the insurance company will be exposed to risks deriving from the conduct of the insured towards the object exposed to the risk, and the insured will be exposed to risks deriving from the conduct of the insurance company regarding the settlement of the insurance claim).

399. Some points of insurance law are also referred to as principles – for instance, the regime applicable to indemnity insurance is referred to as the 'indemnity principle' (Title II, Chapter I, section III of RJCS, Articles 128 and ff.); and the rules setting out that the premium should be returned *pro rata temporis* in case the contract is terminated before its term (Article 107) express what has been termed as the 'principle of divisibility of the premium'.

400. These principles are nowadays a mere way of shortly referring to the rules that underlie them. They are not approached as the expression of rigid standards that would embody the very nature of insurance contracts. In fact, the rules that give form to the indemnity principle are nowadays very nuanced (in view, for instance, of Article 131, which allows for valued policies). In its turn, the 'principle of divisibility of the premium' expresses the general rule of *synallagma* (in other words, of 'reciprocity', or 'mutual exchange') in contracts, and appeared in contrast to the 'principle of indivisibility of the premium', which sustained that the proportional return of premium in case of early termination would be technically unfeasible.[164]

---

statutes refer the duty to comply with utmost good faith to both contract parties (s. 14 of the Insurance Act 2015), there is no consequence when it is breached by the insurance company (8–9 of *ibid.*).

163. Júlio Manuel Vieira Gomes, O acidente de trabalho, O acidente in itinere e a sua descaracterização, Coimbra Editora, (2013), p. 265.

164. Critical of the technical arguments with comparative law arguments, J. Moitinho de Almeida, O contrato …, pp. 129 and ff.; taking a more nuanced approach, Arnaldo da Costa Oliveira, Dois exemplos portugueses da resistência material do contrato de seguro ao direito das cláusulas contratuais gerais, 467, BMJ, (1997), pp. 30 and ff. In recent scholarship, identifying traces of divisibility and indivisibility of the premium, Margarida Lima Rego, O prémio (in: Temas de Direito dos seguros, 2.ª Ed, Almedina, 2016), pp. 283 and ff.

The present approach to these general principles therefore seems to be rather pragmatic, and so as not to fall into a certain danger of oversimplification that referencing principles specific to a certain contract can sometimes harbour, by hiding the rationale that underlies the standards.

§5. Inclusion and Content Control of Standard Terms and Condition of Insurance Contracts

I. Insurance Contract and Law on SCT

401. As referenced in the General Introduction, §5, III, 'contracts of adhesion' – a legal term that was notably broadcast in the beginning of the twentieth century through a publication about insurance contracts[165] – are inherently connected to insurance contracts, which tend to be formulated by SCT, typically designed to be used in an undetermined array of situations.

402. Article 3 RJCS references the LSCT, stating that 'the present regime does not preclude the application of laws regarding laws of standard contract terms, consumer protection laws or distance contracts or of contracts negotiated away from business premises, as asserted in said regulations', which is more broadly summoned in RJCS's Chapter II, section II, concerning 'information duties', and section V, about the insurance contract and insurance policy.[166]

403. The current law on SCT in effect in Portugal was approved by Decree-Law 446/85, of 25 October, and subsequently changed by the Decree-Law 220/95 – in order to make the adjustments necessary to implement Directive 93/13/EEC, of 5 April 1993, on unfair terms in consumer contracts –, and Amendment 114-B/95, both from 31 August Decree-Law 249/99, of 7 July; and Decree-Law 323/2001, of 17 December.[167]

404. In line with what was previously stated, Article 1(1) defines 'SCT' as those drafted without previous negotiation and which indeterminate proponents or addressees merely subscribe or accept. According to Article 1(2), the LSCT further applies to any term inserted in an individual contract, where the term has been drafted in advance and the other party has therefore not been able to influence its substance.

405. According to Article 2, all SCT are to be covered by the definition of Article 1, regardless of its means of communication to the public, its extension, or

165. M. I. Oliveira Martins, Contrato de seguro e conduta dos sujeitos ligados ao risco, Almedina, Coimbra, 688, 2018,

166. Criticising the inexistence of specific rules for policyholders that are consumers, *see* J. M. Vieira Gomes, O dever de informação do (candidato a) tomador do seguro na fase pré-contratual à luz da Lei n.º 72/2008, de 16 de Abril, in Estudos de Homenagem ao Professor Doutor Carlos Ferreira de Almeida, Vol. II, coord. Lebre de Freitas, José, et al., Almedina, Coimbra, 400, 2011.

167. For an always up-to-date version, visit www.pgdl.pt.

its expression in the contracts that they are destined to be integrated in; its substance; or even its author being the proponent; the recipient/addressee; or a third party.

II. Protection of Addressees of SCT

406. The LSCT provides different methods to protect addressees, often consumers who are seen as the weaker party. On one hand, it imposes considerable information duties on the user (and severe consequences for its breach), and on the other it shapes SCT formulation and usage, ascertaining its necessary alignment with a good faith principle and prohibiting specific terms.

A. Information Duties and Exclusion of SCT

407. For SCT to be validly considered part of a contract (Article 5) they must be communicated in full to the addressees who merely subscribe or accept them, in an adequate manner and in due time, so that effective and complete knowledge of its terms is possible to the reasonably diligent addressee, considering the importance of the contract and the extent and complexity of its terms.[168]

408. As stated in Article 6, it should be concluded that it is the user's duty to inform the addressee, in harmony with each case circumstances, on every relevant aspect of the used STC that require clarification, as well as to provide all reasonable clarifications requested by the other parties.

409. These obligations have repercussions on the burden of proof since:

(1) provisions that are specifically agreed upon prevail over any STC, even if they are included in forms signed by both parties (Article 7);
(2) it is the responsibility of whoever intends to avail on a certain term to prove that it has been individually negotiated (Article 1(3)); and
(3) it is the responsibility of the user to prove that the terms have been communicated in an adequate and effective manner (Article 5(3)).

410. The LSCT qualifies certain terms used in contracts as 'excluded', a more severe result than its mere invalidity, since its basic premise is the term's non-existence. Article 8 lists the following as being 'excluded terms from contracts' those:

(1) that have not been communicated as prescribed by Article 5;

168. Therefore, enshrining a principle of transparency, in line with a principle of transparency. *See* J. C. Moitinho de Almeida, Contrato de Seguro – Estudos, Coimbra Editora, Coimbra, 83 ff., 2009, 83.

(2) communicated with breach of the duty to inform, so as to make their effective knowledge unlikely (under Article 6);
(3) which, in their respective context, given their heading or outward appearance, would not be noticed by a reasonable contracting party, placed in the position of the actual party – regarded as 'surprise terms'; and
(4) that were included in a form after its signature by any of the parties.

411. Nevertheless, the remainder of the contract remains in effect, and in the parts affected by the exclusion, the contents of the contract are determined by the default statutory norms and, if necessary, by the legal provisions regarding filling in of gaps in contracts (Article 9(1)). The only exception is the possibility of the contract as a whole, without the excluded clauses, representing an unsurmountable indetermination in essential aspects or an imbalance between the duties of the parties that severely contradicts good faith – in this case it is considered void in its entirety.

412. The LSCT is also dedicated to the interpretation of terms and contracts. Cited Article 9 invokes the general rules of interpretation of contracts (*cf.* Articles 236 and ff. of the Portuguese Civil Code), that are also called upon by Article 10 of LSCT, concerning the interpretation and filling in of gaps of STC, which also requires the hermeneutical consideration of the contract's context.

413. As a general principle, Portuguese law (Article 236 of the Civil Code) recognises that a declaration intended to form a legal contract is to be interpreted with the meaning that any regular counterpart/receiver, in the actual circumstances of the real receiver, could draw from the proponent's conduct, except if it would not be possible for the proponent to reasonably consider that interpretation.

414. Concurrently, Article 11 LSCT states that (1) 'ambiguous standard terms are to be interpreted according to the meaning that a normal indeterminate contracting party, limited to the subscription or acceptance of those clauses, would give them when placed in the position of the actual contracting party'. In case of doubt about the meaning of any term, 11(2) enshrines a principle of preference for the most favourable interpretation to the party that did not draft the terms in use – another refraction of a general principle of protection to the weaker party and consumer (*in dubio contra proferentem* or *in dubio contra stipulatorem*).[169,170] The Portuguese Supreme Court of Justice has been instituting a principle under which any

169. Guimarães Court of Appeals decided on 2 Jul. 2013 that it is contrary to any reasonable understanding made by a lay person to interpret, within an insurance contract destined to cover the transportation of goods, the terms in a manner that will only guarantee damages in goods occurring for accidents/clashes with the transportation vehicle itself with another vehicle/object, and not damages to transported goods that clash with other objects while being transported but with no involvement of the transportation vehicle itself – considering it was not laid down as a liability's exclusion circumstance. A common person that enters into an insurance contract to cover the transportation of good expects damages to be covered regardless of the accident specifics. *See* Case TRG 2 July 2013, 1344/11.1TBVCT.G1 (Filipe Caroço), cf. http://www.dgsi.pt/jtrg.nsf/-/93A622D5895A50A980257BB1003A22D5.

170. Also Guimarães Court of Appeals rendered a decision (TRG 17 December 2019, 554/17.2T8VVD.G1 (Margarida Sousa)), where, after determining if an STC in an insurance contract

term/clause that implies different meanings is to be considered ambiguous (*see, e.g.*, STJ 13 March 2008, 08A369, Sebastião Póvoas[171]).

415. There has been considerable discussion in case law regarding who should be under the duty to inform the insureds in case of group insurance – if it should be the insurer, or the policyholder. This topic is handled below, Part II, Chapter 6, IV, III, B, Duty to Inform the Insureds).

B. Voidness and Prohibition of SCT

416. Other than the aforementioned excluded terms, Articles 12 and ff. LSCT establishes legal consequences for the usage of void and forbidden terms.

417. Regarding void terms, the following rules are to be considered:

418. i) STC in breach of provisions of the LSCT Law are declared void (Article 12);

419. ii) If the addressee subscribes or accepts a contract contemplating void standard terms, they may opt for the maintenance of the contract despite the voidness/nullity (Article 13(1));

420. iii) As in Article 9(1), the parts affected by the nullity are replaced by the default statutory norms applicable and, if necessary, with recourse to the provisions on the filling in of gaps in the contract (Article 13(2));

421. iv) Nevertheless, the rules on partial invalidity shall be applicable when the right granted by Article 13 is not exercised or when its exercise leads to an imbalance between the duties of the parties that severely contradicts good faith (Article 14 LSCT) – which invokes Article 292 of the Portuguese Civil Code, stating that 'voidness or partial annulment shall not determine an invalidity statue for the legal transaction in its entirety, except when it is demonstrated that the deal would not have otherwise been celebrated with the invalid part'.

– that covered 'damages caused to the insured goods as a consequence of waterspout or torrential rain, atmospheric precipitation with an intensity superior to ten millimetres in ten minutes on the rain gauge' – was in accordance with good faith. Concluding that the only valid part was the reference to 'torrential rain', the Court analysed how to interpret the ambiguity of the term that excluded the coverage of damages in the case of 'lack of maintenance and preservation' when the damages had derived not by a single cause (lack of maintenance) but by two (plus torrential rain). The Court concluded, in line with the principle *in dubio contra stipulatorem*, that the term should be interpret in the manner more favourable to the addressed/adherent, that is, the insured person. *See* http://www.dgsi.pt/jtrg.nsf/86c25a698e4e7cb7802579ec004d3832/e6504a1effea34e2802584fc00502ad3?OpenDocument.

171. Available at: http://www.dgsi.pt/jstj.nsf/954f0ce6ad9dd8b980256b5f003fa814/41057db123ca91e18025740b004b9854?OpenDocument.

1. Forbidden SCT: A Principle of the Good Faith

422. Chapter V of the LSCT concerns the usage of forbidden terms, the general principle is, Article 15, that 'standard terms contrary to good faith are forbidden'.

423. The consideration of the general clause 'good faith', in line with Article 16 LSCT, is to be made according to the fundamental values of law as reflected in the particular case, and considering: (a) the trust raised in the parties by the global meaning of the standard terms at stake, by the circumstances of its negotiation, by its contents and by any other relevant elements; (b) the purpose that the parties aimed to achieve through the contract, as determined by the type of contract chosen.

424. Acting in accordance with good faith is to proceed – in the context of a contract and even it this is not objectively stipulated – in a manner consistent with providing all the needed information for an informed decision by the counterpart; to safeguard the other party's interests; keep negotiations confidential if needed; stating one's positions with clarity and, overall, being a loyal partner in business, so that their behaviour does not collide with reasonable expectations for a common person.[172]

425. Portuguese Courts have weighed in the materialisation of the 'good faith' clause, interpreting it in the context of the underlying concrete life situations, and therefore providing certain standards that help us better apprehend its meaning, e.g.:[173]

(1) In a decision given on 27 September 2016, the Portuguese Supreme Court of Justice considered that it is contrary to a principle of good faith to use a term that requires the subscriber to resort to the help of others in daily life tasks, in order to benefit from the cover of an insurance contract for the payment of a home loan in case of absolute and permanent disability. The Court categorises such SCT as void because it significantly creates contractual imbalance between parties and drains the value of agreeing to an insurance contract in the first place, as it is enough to consider the setting of absolute and permanent disability, and irrelevant if the affected person requires the constant help of others.[174]
(2) In another case, the Supreme Court of Justice decided, on 21 June 2016, that any term included in a contract that binds a party to variable or indeterminable conditions/obligations – such as 'payment is to be made as it has been done before' – is contrary to good faith, and therefore void, because it creates

172. For more details, *see* J. C. Moitinho de Almeida, Contrato de Seguro … , 88 and ff.
173. Also, regarding banking agreements the Supreme Court of Justice has issued mandatory standardised jurisprudence for Art. 15 LSCT, with Case Law 2/2016, cf. https://dre.pt/web/guest/home/-/dre/73051019/details/maximized?p_auth=9booZZIR.
174. STJ 27 September 2016, 240/11.7TBVRM.G1.S1 (José Rainho). There is abundant case law deeming consonant to good faith the description attainment of the concept of permanent and absolute disability. For example, cf. TRL 15 December 2020, 25873/16.1T8LSB.L1-7 (Carlos Oliveira).

vague and unclear duties and can result in significant loss for the subscriber without any justifiable legitimate interest to the other party.[175]

(3) On 2 June 2015, concerning anticipated contract termination, the Lisbon Court of Appeals considered it to be against a principle of good faith to establish an SCT giving the user the power to automatically invoice any damage payment as the total value of the contract, regardless of its valid termination by the addressee, the lack of compliance by the user/service provider or the equivalence to contractual performance.[176]

2. Contracts Between Businesses or Equivalent Entities and Contracts with Final Consumers

426. The LSCT establishes terms that are prohibited, either absolutely or relatively, in Articles 17–22, both in contracts between businesses or equivalent entities (Articles 17–19), and contracts with final consumers (Articles 20–22). This listing is merely illustrative, as indicated by the usage of the phrase 'by way of example'.

427. First Article 17 clarifies that 'the prohibitions laid down in the previous section (Articles 15 and 16) and in the present one (Articles 18 and 19) are applicable to contracts between entrepreneurs, members of legal professions, and between one and the other, when each of the parties acts strictly within that status and within their specific activity'.

428. Namely, in contracts between businesses or equivalent entities, it is absolutely prohibited to use the following terms (Article 18), those that:

(1) directly or indirectly exclude or limit the liability for death, or for damages caused to the physical or moral integrity or health of a person;
(2) directly or indirectly exclude or limit the liability for non-pecuniary liability in tort, either towards the counter-party or towards third parties;
(3) exclude or limit the liability for other damage arising from an intentional or grossly negligent breach of duty by the drafter;
(4) exclude or limit the liability for other damage arising from an intentional or grossly negligent breach of duty by a legal representative of the drafter or by a person that the drafter availed to perform their obligations;
(5) directly or indirectly give the drafter the exclusive right to interpret any term of the contract;
(6) exclude the right to withhold performance of reciprocal obligation or the right to termination in case of non-performance;
(7) exclude the right of retention;
(8) exclude the right to set-off, when granted by law;
(9) in any way limit the right to obtain discharge from the obligation by depositing its object to the order of the creditor;

175. STJ 21 June 2016, 2683/12.0TJLSB.L1.S1 (Helder Roque).
176. TRL 2 June 2015, 5202/12.4TBLRA.C1 (Henrique Antunes).

(10) establish perpetual obligations, or obligations of which their duration depends solely on the intention of the drafter; and
(11) give the drafter the possibility of assigning the contract, or transferring his obligations under the contract, or to subcontract, without consent of the counter-party, except when the identity of the transferee or subcontracted person is specified in the contract.

429. And it is relatively prohibited to use the following terms (Article 19), namely, those that:

(1) benefit the drafter by setting out excessive deadlines for the acceptance or rejection of offers;
(2) benefit the drafter by setting out excessive deadlines for performance without incurring in the consequences of delay;
(3) set out penalty clauses that are disproportionate in regard to the damage;
(4) create fabrications of receipt, acceptance or other manifestations of intent, based upon facts that are insufficient for those purposes;
(5) without justification, subordinate the guarantee for conformity of the goods or services delivered to the condition of not relying on third parties;
(6) entitle one of the parties to terminate the contract without due notice and without adequate compensation of the counter-party, when they have made considerable investments or expenses in this sense;
(7) establish a competent jurisdiction in detriment of one of the parties, when this is not justified by the interest of the counter-party;
(8) enable the drafting party to modify the promised performance without compensating the counter-party for any loss of value; and
(9) limit the right to demand performance from the other party without justification.

430. In the context of contracts with final consumers, Article 20 explains that the prohibitions set out in the previous sections (Articles 15–19), as well as the ones set out in the following section apply to transactions with consumers and, more generally, to all transactions not encompassed by Article 17.

431. In line with Article 21, it is absolutely prohibited to use the following terms, namely those that:

(1) limit or in any way modify commitments undertaken by the drafting party or their agents;
(2) directly or indirectly give the drafting party the exclusive right to verify and determine whether the goods or services supplied are in conformity with the contract;
(3) allow performance not to correspond with the indications or specifications made or samples shown in the context of negotiation;
(4) exclude the duties of the counter-party in the event of non-performance or inadequate performance or establish predetermined compensation for those events;

(5) establish that the parties are in possession of certain information on legal or material issues regarding the contracts;
(6) alter the rules on the distribution of risk;
(7) modify the rules on the burden of proof or restrict evidence admissible under law; and
(8) exclude or previously limit the right to take legal action in the case of any dispute between the parties, or that determine rules on arbitration that do not comply with the procedural guarantees set out by the law.

432. And it is relatively prohibited to use the following terms (Article 22), namely those that:

(1) set out excessive periods of time for the duration of the contract or for its termination;
(2) allow the drafting party to terminate a long-term contract without due notice or terminate it without reasonable ground, as set out by the law or by the contract;
(3) allow the drafting party to unilaterally alter the terms of the contract without a valid reason specified in the contract – with some reservations in Article 22(2;3;4) regarding suppliers of financial services and contracts of indefinite duration:
(4) provide for the price of goods to be determined at the time of delivery without giving the counter-party the corresponding right to cancel the contract if the final price is too high in relation to the price agreed when the contract was concluded – with some reservations in Article 22(3,4), concerning financial services;
(5) allow for successive increases in the price for goods or services that are to be delivered or rendered within short delays, or that allow for manifest increases in prices beyond this time limit, without prejudice of the rules on change of circumstances;
(6) exclude immediate termination of the contract when it is justified by increase in prices;
(7) without justification, remove rules on inadequate performance or on the delays to make use of the remedies granted in case of non-performance or inadequate performance;
(8) automatically extend a contract of fixed duration where the counter-party does not indicate otherwise, when the deadline fixed for the counter-party to express this desire is unreasonably early;
(9) enable one of the parties to terminate a contract of indeterminate duration without reasonable notice except where there are serious grounds for doing so;
(10) without justification exclude repair services or other goods or services provided by a third party;
(11) require exaggerated anticipations of performance;
(12) require the provision of guarantees that are excessively costly or refer to an amount that is excessively high in regard to the value that shall be guarantee;

(13) establish places, schedules or ways of performing that are unjustified or inconvenient; and
(14) subject the acts performed within the execution of the contract to formalities not required by law, or that condition the exercise of the parties' rights to the adoption of unnecessary conducts.

C. Procedural Mechanisms

433. As any void act in the legal system, the voidness of an SCT can be invoked at all times (Article 24 LSCT), by any interested party, or declared ex officio by the Court (Article 286 of the Portuguese Civil Code).

434. As an independent procedure, void terms elaborated for future use, and contrary to Articles 15, 16, 18, 19, 21, and 22, can be prohibited by a Court despite its inclusion in a concrete contract, if an injunction is brought by, *ex vi* Article 26:

- recognised consumer's associations;
- unions/professional bodies/ or of economic interests, if within its scope; and
- public Prosecutors, ex officio or by indication of the Ombudsman/Public Advocate (Articles 25–30 LSCT).

435. There is also a protective injunction (Article 31 LSCT), which states that if there is a well-founded fear of usage of SCT incompatible with the LSCT, all the entities with legal standing according to Article 26 can provisionally require the prohibition of the terms.

436. If a term is, by legal action, decisively prohibited – as well as all terms that matches it or is equivalent to it – it cannot, as a consequence, be included in any contracts by the user or recommended to be used, according to Article 32, which, in its number (2), summons the referred regime of Article 9 LSCT. The addressee can, at all times, invoke the incidental declaration of the injunction, even if it is regarding another contract, as long as it is the same user, not having to take legal action again with new legal proceedings.

437. After the decisive prohibition of usage, if the defendant continues to use or recommend said term, he or she incurs in a penalty payment of maximum EUR 4987.98 by infraction – implemented by the same court who decided the initial case, after ensuring the right to adversarial proceedings.

438. The amount obtained with the penalty is allocated in 50% to the addressee/petitioner, and in 50% to the Portuguese State.

Chapter 2. Insurable Risk

§1. Risk and Interest

439. As mentioned above, both risk and interest are central features in the concept of insurance.

440. In order to be qualified as insurance, a contract should refer to an interest upon a determined subject matter and to an uncertain event that can disturb that interest. Risk is sometimes identified with this uncertain event – risk as an event –, and sometimes identified with the possibility or probability of that event occurring – risk as a possibility or probability. These notions of risk are not substantially different; they portray mere differences of perspective of a determinate probabilistic process. In case the event at stake ceases to be possible or becomes certain, risk ceases to exist in its regard. However, even if risk has ceased to exist from an objective viewpoint, the law allows for its cover if the policyholder and insured is not aware of that fact – it allows to cover risk that only exists subjectively, as a mental representation (Article 44(1) and (2)).

441. In any case, as the risk relevant to insurance is attached to a disturbance of the insurable interest, it always regards the prospect of negative consequences; it does not regard the prospect of a gain.[177]

442. Interest is a relation between a person who feels a certain need and the (tangible or intangible) good that they need.[178] If that good (a certain asset, a person, the patrimony as a whole) is affected by an uncertain event (e.g., the house is hit by fire, the patrimony is hit by a duty to compensate a victim), then its ability to satisfy those needs may be compromised or new needs may arise in connection with it. The concept of insurable interest refers to an interest which is the reference of an insurance contract – it is the *interest that can be disturbed in case the uncertain event occurs*. The fact that insurance is built around the protection of an insurable interest differentiates it from a bet or gamble.[179]

443. One should also underline that risk concerns an interest upon a certain good, and not the good itself. There can be different relationships of interest upon a certain good – e.g., the same house can be the object of the interest of its owner, of the interest of its usufructuary, of the interest of a mortgaged creditor – and all of them can be the reference of different insurance contracts.

---

177. *See above* Part II, Ch. 1, §1, Definition of Insurance (*supra* n. 137); *see also* M. Lima Rego, Contrato …, 212 and ff. and José A. Engrácia Antunes, Direito dos contratos comerciais, Almedina, (2012), 705.

178. M. Lima Rego, Contrato …, 212–222.

179. M. I. Oliveira Martins, O seguro de vida …, 283 and ff.; M. Lima Rego, Contrato …, 212 and ff.; Margarida Lima Rego, O seguro por conta de outrem (in: M. Lima Rego (ed.) Temas de Direito dos seguros, A propósito da nova Lei do Contrato de Seguro, 2. Ed, Almedina, 245, 2016), 247 and ff.

444. When insurance regards an interest upon an asset, from the onset, one can know the maximum amount of damage that the insurance event can cause the insured: it corresponds to the value of that interest upon the asset (e.g., the value of the property, in case the insured has a position of ownership of the asset; the value of the usufruct, in case the insured is an usufructuary). This value is relevant to determine the sum insured and the insurance premium. The value of the interest at the time of the insurance event is also relevant to determine the amount of the insurance indemnity, as well as for the purposes of the rules on over-insurance and under-insurance (Articles 130, 132, 134).

445. There is some controversy as to whether the interest should be pecuniary, or whether it can be non-pecuniary. The law does not *a priori* limit the nature of the insurable interest. Article 43(1) states that the insurable interest should be worthy of legal protection. This does not preclude insurance regarding non-pecuniary insurance interests; much on the contrary, this norm practically reprises the norm of the Civil Code that expressly allows for obligations of non-pecuniary nature. That is Article 398(2) which states that performance does not need to have a pecuniary value, but the creditor should have an interest worthy of legal protection in it. There is no consensus regarding how this 'worthiness of legal protection' should be construed.[180] Traditionally, it is thought to bar the enforceability of rights concerning interests that are purely futile and capricious. Other scholarship however points out that the parties are free to define, under their private autonomy, the interests that they intend to make the subject matter of their juridical acts; the law should only draw outer limits in this regard, by determining what is unlawful and therefore forbidden.

446. In any case, none of the perspectives adopted in the interpretation of the requirement of 'worthiness of legal protection' would bar the insurance of non-pecuniary interests. However, some authors deny that such a contract should qualify as insurance and consider that insurable interest must be of pecuniary nature. The main arguments presented are that there would be uncertainty in the assessment of a purely personal interest, and that allowing for its coverage could bring the contract close to a bet, and, in case the contract referred to the risk of death of a third party, it could even create risks of moral hazard. Moreover, the economic nature of the interest would best suit the nature of the insurance benefits, which can either consist of a sum of money or of certain goods or services, but should always have a pecuniary value.[181]

180. For a panorama on different stances, *see* Ana Filipa Morais Antunes, Artigo 398.º, Conteúdo da prestação (in: José Carlos Brandão Proença (ed.) Comentário ao Código civil, Direito das obrigações, Das obrigações em geral, Universidade Católica Portuguesa, 2018), 29.

181. M. Lima Rego, Contrato … , 278–282; J. C. Moitinho de Almeida, O contrato … 2015, 29; J. A. Engrácia Antunes, Direito dos contratos, 705–706, 709; a different stance has been taken by M. I. Oliveira Martins, O seguro de vida … , 293 and ff.; António Menezes Cordeiro, Direito dos seguros, Almedina, 2 Ed (2016), 795–797.

447. Nevertheless, it can also be pointed out that although a payment cannot fully restore a non-pecuniary interest, it can at least compensate it; and the risks connected to moral hazard can be addressed by the requirement of consent from the person at risk.

448. In any case, one can find widespread insurance of personal interests in the branch of personal accidents insurance, where the contracts frequently set out that the amount of insurance payment is determined by reference to the Scale of Assessment of Incapacities in Private law.[182] Since this Scale intends to assess the totality of damage determined by a certain incapacity, it takes into account dimensions of the damage that are non-pecuniary. Therefore, insurance payment determined under these rules also covers purely personal damage, which is tantamount to saying that the contracts at stake also protect purely personal interests.

449. The contract should, therefore, in any case refer to a risk that affects an object of the insured's interest, so that it can be identified as insurance. Moreover, the risk and interest at stake should actually exist, so that the contract can be valid and remain in force.[183]

450. Article 43 concerns the insurable interest. Under Article 43(1), which replicates former Article 428(2) of the Commercial Code, if the insured does not have an interest worthy of legal protection in respect to the risk covered by the contract, the contract should be considered void.

451. For the contract to qualify as insurance, it should refer to the protection of an interest threatened by a risk. Moreover, under Article 43(2) for it to be considered a valid insurance contract, the person to which it grants protection should have an actual interest upon the insured 'good' (asset, person, patrimony).[184]

452. In indemnity insurance, the reasoning is pretty straightforward. The person whose damage the contract repairs – be it by giving them a right to indemnity, be it by granting such right to a third party that was victim of their liability – is the insured and should therefore have an interest upon the goods under threat; otherwise, the insured event will not bring them any damage. When they fail to have such interest, then the contract is void.

182. Approved by Decree-Law 352/2007, of 23 October. In scholarship, this has been highlighted by M. I. Oliveira Martins, Contrato de seguro e conduta ..., 292–293 (*see* note); in case law, *see* TRG 12 November 2015, 558/13.4TBBGC.G1 (Maria Purificação Carvalho); TRC 23 January 2018, 4285/15.0T8CBR.C1 (Vítor Amaral).

183. A careful distinction between risk and interest as features relevant in order to qualify the contract as insurance, and as features relevant in order for the contract to be valid was drawn by M. Lima Rego, Contrato ..., for instance at 48 and 57.

184. M. Lima Rego, Contrato ..., 41–46, 688–777; M. Lima Rego, O seguro por conta de outrem, 246–247; M. I. Oliveira Martins, O seguro de vida ..., 293 and ff., M. I. Oliveira Martins, Contrato de seguro e conduta ..., 27–28.

453. The reasoning is somewhat more complex when fixed sums insurance is at stake. Some scholarship has considered that *the insured – the person who should be the holder of the insured interest* – is the person entitled to choose the beneficiaries of the contract. Other scholarship has considered that the insured is the person at risk, whenever the person at risk is the policyholder or in any case holds the main rights set out by the contract (e.g., right to choose the beneficiaries of the contract, or to request the payment of surrender money); this person is obviously interested in their own conservation. In the remaining cases, the beneficiary is to be considered the insured, and should therefore have an interest upon the conservation of the person at risk.[185]

454. Both the present norm and its predecessor have been applied in a number of cases concerning motor liability insurance, where the policyholder and insured was not an owner or driver of the vehicle to which the contract referred to, but rather somebody close to the actual owner or driver, who would pay considerably lower premiums than the latter.[186] The courts have considered that these are not mere cases of fraudulent non-disclosure of the risk, but rather cases where the person for whose account the contract was taken out – the policyholder – had no insurable interest, since they faced no relevant risk of being liable towards third parties in connection with the vehicle at stake. Therefore, the contract should be deemed void.

455. Article 44 handles the cases of inexistence of the risk.

456. Under Article 44(1), unless the law provides otherwise, the contract is deemed void if, upon its conclusion, the insurance company, the policyholder or the insured were aware that the risk had ceased to exist. This may happen, for instance, because the insured event has already happened, and no other events of the same kind can take place (e.g., in case of life insurance, death of the person at risk has occurred) or because the insurance event became impossible, since the object at risk was destroyed by other causes (e.g., in case of theft insurance, the if the object burned down) or is no longer exposed to that risk (e.g., in case the insurance only covered risks in certain foreign countries, the objects no longer find themselves in them). On the other hand, the contract will not be deemed void if it provided retroactive cover and the policyholder became aware that the risk ceased to exist – e.g., due to the occurrence of the insured event – only after they sent their application to the insurance company, but before the company accepted it.[187] Although the policyholder would have been aware that the risk had ceased by the time of the conclusion of the contract – the time of the company's acceptance –, they would not have been aware of it by the time it sent its application.

185. For the first perspective presented, *see* M. Lima Rego, Contrato ... , 41–46, 688–777; M. Lima Rego, O seguro por conta de outrem; for the latter, M. I. Oliveira Martins, O seguro de vida ... , 293 and ff., M. I. Oliveira Martins, Contrato de seguro e conduta ... , 27–28.

186. For Art. 428(2) of the Commercial Code, *see* STJ 20 January 2010, 471/2002.G1.S1 (Alberto Sobrinho) and STJ 9 July 2015, 487/09.6TBOHP.C1.S1 (Maria dos Prazeres Pizarro Beleza); for Art. 43(1), *see* TRP 18 May 2017, 2059/12.9T2AVR.P1 (Judite Pires).

187. Margarida Lima Rego, O risco e as suas vicissitudes (in: Margarida Lima Rego (ed.) Temas de Direito dos seguros, A propósito da nova Lei do Contrato de Seguro, 2. Ed., Almedina, 2016), 392.

457. Article 44(2) determines that the insurance company does not provide cover for insured events that occurred before the contract was concluded, when the policyholder or the insured were aware of those events by that time. The contract is not deemed void in this case: as long as the possibility of other insured events remains, risk does not cease to exist.

458. As mentioned above, one should highlight that the mere objective inexistence of risk does not suffice for the application of Article 44(1) and (2). The RJCS requires the awareness of the policyholder or insurer, thereby allowing for the coverage of risks that exist only according to a subjective criterion.

459. Article 44(3) determines that the contract does not take effect when it concerns a future risk that does not come into existence. This regards the cases in which the contract covers a risk that the insured has not yet been exposed to, and never comes to be exposed to (e.g., a health travel insurance regarding a journey that never took place).

460. In all of these cases, according to Article 44(4) and (5), the policyholder will be entitled to the reimbursement of the premium paid if they acted in good faith. If the insurance company also acted in good faith, it shall have the right to deduct from that value the costs incurred with the conclusion of the contract. If the policyholder acted in bad faith, the insurance company shall be entitled to keep the premium, unless it also acted with bad faith.

461. In insurance for the account of a third party, there is a presumption of bad faith from the policyholder in case the insured is aware, when the contract is entered into, that the insured event took place (Article 44(6)).

§2. Insurable Risks

462. Article 14 provides that, notwithstanding the general norms on unlawfulness of the contents of the juridical act, the coverage of certain risks is specifically forbidden.[188] It is specifically forbidden to cover the risk of criminal or disciplinary liability, or of liability entailing the application of administrative sanctions (Article 14(1)(a)); the risk of being kidnapped, suffering illegal restraint or any other crime against personal freedom (Article 14(1)(b)); the risk of possession or transportation of narcotics or other unlawful substances (Article 14(1)(c)); the risk of death regarding children under 14 or persons that due to a mental condition or other cause are unable to govern themselves.

463. The rationale underlying these prohibitions seems to be quite straightforward, since all of them are connected to the prevention of moral hazard. They all forbid contracts that could incentivise conducts contrary to public order.

188. On this matter, *see* João de Matos Viana, Seguros proibidos (in: Margarida Lima Rego (ed.) Temas de Direito dos seguros, A propósito da nova Lei do Contrato de Seguro, 2. Ed, Almedina, 2016).

464. That would happen, first of all, if the insurance company could undertake to pay the amount of criminal, administrative or disciplinary fines that were applied to the insured (Article 14(1)(a)), since that would deliver the insured of the consequences of the most serious offences to the law and as consequence deprive those sanctions of their effects. Moreover, under the Constitution, criminal liability is strictly personal (Article 30(3)) and therefore its consequences cannot be transferred to a third party. As the norm further clarifies (Article 14(2)) the same reasoning does not apply to the consequences of civil liability that may arise in connection with those offences. Otherwise, the victims of civil liability would be left unprotected. In any case, the disincentive created by the application of criminal, administrative or disciplinary sanctions seems to be deemed enough to prevent those conducts.

465. Article 14(1)(a) has been applied, both by the ASF and by the courts, to cases different from those it provides for. The ASF has considered that, under this norm, the employer is not allowed to contract insurance in order to cover for any losses they incur in as a result of any of their employees being sanctioned with accessory penalty of license disqualification.[189] According to the ASF, considering the authority of the employer upon the employees, they are in a position to influence their behaviour – by which ASF seems to imply that they should be incentivise to make them comply with road traffic rules. According to the ASF, the administrative sanctions would forfeit their dissuasive effect if the employer could protect themselves from those losses; they are not a victim of liability and therefore the exception of Article 14(2) does not apply.

466. I am not aware of whether this opinion has been challenged in courts. However, it seems clear that this reasoning cannot be followed. Both Article 14(1)(a) and Article 14(2) refer to liability insurance, and not to insurance regarding other losses. In addition to this, it is not correct to say that Portuguese criminal or administrative punitive law pursue the maximisation of deterrence at all costs – that would not even be compatible with the Portuguese Constitution.[190] It would be even more indefensible to state that such deterrence should be pursued at the cost of other persons different from the liable party – e.g., their employer or their family.

467. The courts have, in their turn, applied the prohibition to cover the risk of criminal liability in order to ban the coverage of losses incurred by the employer in view of road traffic accidents caused by their employees under the effect of alcohol, above the threshold of blood alcohol concentration set out by criminal norms.[191]

---

189. ASF, *Relatório de Regulação e Supervisão da Conduta de Mercado* – 2017 (at https://www.asf.com.pt/NR/rdonlyres/F9B98548-65B8-4B7A-BA11-A92807E07F6C/0/RRSCM2017.pdf), 46.

190. In view both of the principle of proportionality and human dignity, and of the rule according to which no penalty entails the automatic loss of any civil, professional or political rights (Arts 1, 18, and 30(4) of the Portuguese Constitution).

191. Judgment of STJ 15 January 2008, 07A4318 (Azevedo Ramos); Judgment of TRP 19 December 2012, 1376/10.7TBPFR.P1 (Leonel Serôdio).

468. Both questions should rather have been framed under the compatibility of the contract with public order (*see below*). In what regards the latter instance, the courts do in fact refer to the infringement of public order, but consider that this would be a result of the coverage of criminal liability.

469. Furthermore, the norm forbids insurance that might incentivise any crime against personal freedom in exchange of a ransom. It further clarifies that it is allowed to contract insurance of strict indemnity in connection with those risks (Article 14(3)). What is forbidden is therefore that the insurance covers ransom costs; it is allowed that the insurance covers other damages or expenses caused by those crimes (e.g., medical expenses, expenses due to contracting of experts in hostage situations).[192]

470. The norm also forbids insurance that could incentivise causing the death of persons who are deemed not fully able to protect themselves – minors under 14 and persons that are psychically challenged. Once more, the norm allows for strict indemnity insurance – e.g., insurance covering funerary expenses – in this regard (Article 14(3)). With respect to children under 14, the norm also allows for insurance contracted by education, sports or analogous institutions, as long as these institutions are not designated as beneficiaries of the insurance (Article 14(4)).

471. The norm on insurance regarding the risks of possession or transportation of unlawful substances does not seem entirely clear, since those facts would not per se constitute an insured event. Some authors consider that the scope of the norm is to forbid insurance of any sort of liability arising in connection with those facts.[193] However, the prohibition of cover of criminal or administrative liability would already result from Article 14(1)(a)); and it is difficult to imagine cases where the mere possession or transportation of unlawful substances could give rise to civil liability. The norm would rather seem to forbid insurance protecting interests upon those substances as assets – e.g., covering the risk of their damage or theft.[194] The general norms on (un)lawfulness of the contract would anyway lead to the same conclusion.

472. Besides the prohibitions specifically provided for, Article 14 determines that the general norms on unlawfulness of the contents of the juridical act additionally apply. The relevant provision is Article 280 ('Requirements of the contents of the juridical act') of the Civil Code. Under its terms, '[a] juridical act, the contents of which are physically or legally impossible, contrary to the law or indeterminate, is deemed null' (Article 280(1)); '[a] juridical act that is in breach of public order or good morals is deemed null' (Article 280(2)).

---

192. J. Matos Viana, Seguros …, 129–130; Pedro Romano Martínez, Art. 14.º, Seguros proibidos, Comentários complementares (in: Lei do Contrato de Seguro anotada, Almedina, 2020), 76.
193. P. Romano Martínez, Art. 14.º, 75.
194. J. Matos Viana, Seguros …, 130–132.

473. Public order refers to the core of imperative principles that underpin the legal system. As it is an open concept, the grounds for its application to a specific case should be carefully explained. In what regards its application to insurance contract, public order seems to underlie a set of norms aimed at the prevention of actions that could harm legal interests (in the sense of *bens jurídicos*, *Rechtsgüter*), in view of the misalignment of incentives (moral hazard) that insurance can create.[195] However, it is clear that the insurance law does not strictly forbid any insurance that could pose enhanced risks to legal interests; it allows, for instance, valued policies (Article 131), as well as the insurance of grossly negligent acts (only intentional acts fall in principle outside coverage – Article 46).[196] Therefore, the conclusion as to whether the cover of certain risks is contrary to public order is very rarely straightforward.

474. In what regards the application of public order, there is case law deciding that it would infringe public order to cover the damage suffered by the person driving with a blood alcohol concentration above the threshold defined by criminal norms.[197]

475. A question that has not yet been discussed by the courts, but that has received some discussion in literature, is the question of the lawfulness of cover for defence costs in criminal cases. There is agreement in regard to the lawfulness of that cover – mainly in view of the right to defence, the right to state support in case of lack of resources to fund one's own defence, of the purpose of criminal sanctions (which is reinstatement of the norms infringed, and not maximal deterrence) and of the presumption of innocence.[198] The question remains however as to whether public order demands that the amounts paid are returned to the insurance company in case the defendant is convicted.

476. Finally, the standard of good morals can have a special relevance in regard to the protection of own legal interests of the insured person. Public order would tend not to intervene in this regard, in view of the principle of personal freedom. Good morals would bar insurance that created high incentives to the sacrifice of one's own physical integrity in view of the insurance payment (for instance, the cover of death caused by suicide in the months ensuing the conclusion of the contract).

---

195. For example, the norms on forbidden insurance (Art. 14), the norms demanding the existence of an insurable interest in the subject matter of the contract (Art. 43), the norms on intentional causation of the insured event (Arts 46, 141, 191–193, 211), as well as on mitigation of damage, the norms on the indemnity principle (Art. 128 and ff.).
196. M. I. Oliveira Martins, Contrato de seguro e conduta ..., 207 and ff.
197. Judgment of STJ 8 January 2009, 08B3722 (João Bernardo); Judgment of TRG of 21 May 2013, 5680/08.6TBBRG.G2 (Filipe Caroço).
198. J. Matos Viana, Seguros ..., 121–122; in regard to Brazilian law, but reasoning in terms that apply mutatis mutandis in Portuguese law, Maria Inês de Oliveira Martins, Dolo e seguro D&O (in: VII Fórum de Direito do seguro José Sollero Filho, Lei do contrato de seguro: solidariedade ou exclusão?, IBDS/Roncarati, 2018), 393 and ff.; Margarida Lima Rego, Adiantamento de custos de defesa nos seguros de D&O (in: Colóquio internacional governação das sociedades, responsabilidade civil e proteção dos administradores, Instituto Jurídico, 2018), 78–82.

§3. Deliberate Causation of the Insured Event

477. Under Article 46(1), unless a statutory or administrative norm provides otherwise, or the parties have agreed differently, and that agreement is compatible with public order and with the nature of the contract, the insurance company is discharged from its obligation in case the insured event is deliberately caused by the policyholder or by the insured. Under Article 46(2), the beneficiary who deliberately causes the insured event loses their right to the insurance payment. The norm is semi-mandatory (Article 13(1)).

478. The fact that the norm is qualified as semi-mandatory can give rise to doubt, since it would mean that it would be admissible to expand the coverage beyond the limits set out by Article 46. However, that would unacceptably imply that intentional causation could be covered even when that offended public order or contradicted the nature of the contract. The semi-mandatory character of the norm seems rather to refer to the possibility that the norm itself grants, of specially agreeing on coverage within the limits posed by public order and the nature of the contract.

479. While referring only to intentional causation, the norm leaves out the cases of negligent causation. Therefore, unless the contract legitimately excludes them from coverage, negligently caused insurance events are covered.

480. Literally, the norm would seem to discharge the company in any case of deliberate causation. When there is active causation of the event with direct intent, it will indeed tend to be so.[199] The insurance company will nonetheless be under the duty to cover the loss resulting from a deliberate event in some cases. First of all, when the insured event does not harm any legally protected interest, as happens for instance in the case of assurance on survival to a stipulated date, or in the case of marriage or birth insurance, as well as in insurance covering expenses connected to the prevention of loss (e.g., health insurance covering routine medical check-ups, or legal protection insurance covering preventive counselling). Second, when the insured event does harm legally protected interests, the law allows for its cover, and when the insurance company agrees to it, as happens in the case of suicide (Article 191) as well as in the case of insurance of civil liability (in this case, in connection with a right of recourse against the liable party – Articles 144 and 148).

481. The cases of indirect causation of the insured event, or causation by omission, demand a particularly careful reasoning. Omission in not legally relevant per se, but only when the law requires an action; and indirect causation would encompass actions that were remote in regard to the event. Taking them into account for the purposes of deliberate causation should not excessively broaden the cases of discharge of the insurance company, otherwise the contract would lose its practical purpose. The policyholder or insured should not see the covered conditioned to a

199. *See* M. I. Oliveira Martins, Contrato de seguro e conduta ..., 327 and ff.

general duty to prevent the insured event, since it would amount to them taking on the risk that should have been transferred to the insurance company.

482. No case law was detected in this specific regard. On its turn, scholarship has proposed some criteria for these cases.[200] The norm on deliberate causation should only apply when the policyholder or the insured are actually aware that the insured event has become likely to happen in an immediate timeframe. Furthermore, the normal handling of the subject matter of the risk can in many instances imply voluntary exposure to some degree of risk – e.g., an infectious disease doctor voluntarily accepts a considerable amount of risk to their health, as well as somebody who lives in a neighbourhood with relevant rates of criminality accepts the exposure to a considerable amount of risk to their property when using public transportation. Therefore, the norm on deliberate causation should additionally only apply if the action or omission of the insured or policyholder increase the level of risk beyond what the contract should allow for.

483. This last criterion somehow echoes in a decision of the STJ regarding credit insurance.[201] The insured had granted their debtor payment extensions that went beyond the maximum deadlines stipulated in the insurance contract. Nonetheless, the court considered that their action, undertaken with the purpose of safeguarding the payment of the total amount due, which was more than three times the insured sum, should be seen as a legitimate attempt at mitigating the insured risk, and not as an infringement of the contract.

200. *See* M. I. Oliveira Martins, Contrato de seguro e conduta …, 327 and ff.
201. STJ 29 March 2012, 349/10TVLSB.L1.S1 (Abrantes Geraldes).

Chapter 3. Formation of the Insurance Contract

§1. Pre-contractual Phase

484. The decision of the insurance company to accept or reject a determined candidate relies on the assessment of the risk. This assessment can be more or less thorough – it will typically be more thorough in regard to large risks and less thorough in case of mass risks – and demand information on different aspects, according to what is relevant to the statistic models used by the insurance company, or to its case-by-case analysis. Moreover, the greater the degree of segmentation of the company's customers, the more information the company will need in order to separate them in different classes of risk.[202]

485. This assessment relies on different sources of information. As the RJCS regulates the relation between the persons implicated in the insurance contract, it focuses mainly on the policyholder and insured as sources of information, by setting out a duty to disclose the risk.[203] However, one should not lose sight of other sources of information, which may under the circumstances have much more importance.

486. The insurance company may, for instance, resort to an analysis of the risk by experts, be it by means of an inspection to the risk site (which tends to happen mainly in regard to industrial risks), or by means of a medical examination of the person at risk. It may as well resort to information collected by other insurance companies. Insurance companies can either informally or by an express agreement pool information relevant for risk assessment (e.g., insurance claims data). It may also resort to information collected by insurance agents or brokers in regard to their past experience with a certain insured, as it may resort to other third parties – public registries, healthcare providers, banks – that hold information regarding the risk.

487. Whenever these activities imply the collection of personal data, they will have to comply with the norms on protection of personal data, which will in many cases demand that the data subject consents to the data processing (Articles 6(1)(a) and (1)(b) and 9(2)(a) of GDPR). The collection of information shall naturally also have to comply with the general duties of confidentiality, e.g., in regard to commercial secrets (Articles 313–315 of the Code of Industrial Property).

488. There are also special rules on the collection of data regarding the health of the person at risk for the purposes of entering into an insurance contract. The RJCS establishes that the conclusion of the insurance contract can be made dependent upon a statement on the health condition of the person at risk, as well as upon medical examinations performed to this person (Article 177(1)). However, it is absolutely forbidden to make any use of genetic information in the context of insurance

---

202. *See* Maria Inês de Oliveira Martins, Entre a avaliação inicial do risco e o regime do seu agravamento subsequente, 43, Julgar, (2021), 77–79.
203. *See* Ch. 4, §2, I, Pre-contractual Duty of Disclosure.

(Articles 177(2) of RJCS and 12 of Law 12/2005, on personal genetic information and health information[204]). Genetic information is defined as health information regarding hereditary features of one or more persons, either akin or sharing common features of that kind. The definition does not include information derived from kinship tests or studies on zygotes in twins, genetic profiling for criminal purposes or the study of somatic genetic mutations affecting cancer (Article 6(1) of Law 12/2005).

489. In particular, insurance companies are not allowed to ask for or make use of any kind of genetic information in order to refuse a life insurance or increase its premium (Article 12(1) of Law 12/2005). They are furthermore not allowed to ask their potential insureds to perform genetic tests or to use genetic information previously obtained through genetic testing for the purpose of health or life insurance or for any other purposes (Article 12(2) and (3) of Law 12/2005). Finally, insurance companies cannot demand or use genetic information regarding family history in order to refuse insurance or to increase its premium or for any other purpose (Article 12(4) of Law 12/2005).

490. In case the insurance company requires the performance of medical exams, it must previously inform the candidate on certain aspects, and prove that they have provided such information (Article 178(1) and (2)). It must exhaustively specify the medical exams, tests and analyses that need to be performed. It must furthermore inform on the entities that can perform those exams, clarify who will bear the corresponding costs and, if that is the case, how those costs will be reimbursed, and identify the person or entity to whom the exam results or medical reports should be sent (Article 178(1)). The person at risk has the right to be informed on the results of the exams, if they wish to receive such information, or to demand that they are provided to a person of their choice; this information should be provided by a physician, unless it regards circumstances of which the person at risk was already aware, or, according to common experience, could be supposed to be aware of (Article 178(3), (4)). The person at risk also has the right to any other information in the possession of the insurance company regarding their health; this information should be provided by means which are ethically and humanely adequate (Article 178(6)). The policyholder and insured have, on their part, the right to be informed on the effect of the exam results on the insurance company's decision, particularly in what regards its refusal to insure or its acceptance of coverage under special conditions (Article 178(5)).

491. Another relevant feature of this phase is that it places a vast array of information duties upon the insurer. Such duties, stem from different sources, and partially overlap; they shall be handled below (*see* Part II, Chapter 5, §2, I, The Different Sources of Information Duties).

204. Law 12/2005, of 26 January.

§2. Actual Formation of the Contract

492. As a common practice, insurance contracts are formed from general contractual clauses following a 'form' of the insurer's exclusive responsibility.

493. As a result, acceptance, as a negotiating declaration tending to form a consensus, results from the pre-formulated proposal by the insurer and is subject to adherence by the policyholder. Thus, the declaration of acceptance is of the policyholder's authorship, but the terms it presents are pre-formulated by the insurer. Hence, even if it contains the general and special conditions subscribed by the policyholder, the policy reflects the formulation of the insurance object drawn up by the insurer. As such, the idea of the 'convention' lies in the asymmetry between formulation and control of the clauses and subjection of the addressee to adhesion.

§3. Validity Requirements

494. The insurance contract presupposes that the party obliged to provide the characteristic service that integrates the type of contract is legally authorised to carry out an insurance activity (Article 16 RJCS). The principle of the reservation of the insurance activity to the authorised entities prevails (Articles 3, 5, no. 1, al. a), 48, LBIR), foreseeing the criminalisation or administrative offence of those who exercise the activity without authorisation (Articles 356, 370, al. a) LBIR). The limitation of private autonomy as to the celebration of the insurance contract is rooted in the public interest of the operation of the insurance market, which is grounded on solvency and the consequent guarantee of compliance with the obligations undertaken by the insurer. Therefore, it integrates the type of insurance contract as an essential element.[205]

495. The consequence of a breach of the provisions of paragraph 1 is the atypical nullity of the contract, to the extent that the contract continues to produce effects for the benefit of the policyholder who has the right to claim the primary benefit, without prejudice to any civil liability for damages caused by the null contract (Article 227 CC), to the extent that the nullity may only be invoked by the policyholder, unless they have acted in bad faith. Consideration must also be given to situations in which the contract's validity is called into question through omissions or intentional inaccuracy carried out by the policyholder (Article 25 RJCS); when this happens, the contract is void by notice given by the insurer to the policyholder. If no insured event has occurred, the notice must be sent within three months from the date the non-compliance was acquired. The insurer is entitled to the premium due at the end of the three months mentioned above, unless the insurer or its representative has committed intent or gross negligence (Article 25(3) RJCS), also, if there *dolus* of the policyholder or of the insured in order to obtain an advantage, the premium is due at the end of the contract.

---

205. José Carlos Moitinho de Almeida, O contrato de seguro no direito português e comparado, Livraria Sá da Costa (1971) 20 and ff.

§4. Proof of the Contract

496. For the distribution of the burden of proof between policyholder and insurer, the standard of proof is generally based on Article 342 CC. Insofar as the parties are burdened with proof, they must therefore generally provide full proof. In dubious cases, the judge must be content with a degree of helpful certainty for everyday living standards and allow doubts to be excluded without entirely excluding them. Insofar as the evidence cannot be produced directly, circumstantial evidence must be made. The aim of circumstantial evidence is that the judge, based on a multitude of circumstances, each of which is not entirely conclusive, becomes convinced with sufficient certainty of the existence of the fact in evidence.

497. If the policyholder asserts a claim for insurance benefits, he must prove all facts giving a claim. This includes the conclusion of an insurance contract covering the risk in question.

§5. Insurance Policies

498. The policies or particular conditions that were issued subsequently to the conclusion of the contract must be communicated to the policyholder in advance and known by them, under the condition of being considered excluded, Articles 5 and 8(a) of LSCT, and 21 RJCS.

499. Regarding this, Margarida Lima Rego states that the 'policy is … the written document that expresses an insurance contract' (Article 362(2), of the Civil Code),[206] further stating that the 'conditions of the contract' correspond to the content of the contract in its entirety. As follows: 'Although the insurer is required to inform the prospective policyholder, before the latter issues its negotiating statement, of all the conditions that will make up the insurance contract, at that point there is still no such thing as a "policy". This only appears later, at the time or in the days following the conclusion of the contract. The duties are different: in one case there is a duty to inform, and in the other, there is a duty to provide a document.'[207]

500. The policy as a document intended as proof of the insurance contract may be a 'document constituting an insurance contract' or a 'document reproducing a previously concluded insurance contract'.[208]

501. Therefore, since the policy is the support that provides proof of the existence of an insurance contract, it has to be the reflection of the contract, inasmuch as

206. Margarida Lima Rego, O contrato e a apólice de seguro (in: Margarida Lima Rego (ed.) Temas de Direito dos seguros, A propósito da nova Lei do Contrato de Seguro, Almedina, 15, 2016), 17.
207. M. Lima Rego, O contrato e a apólice …, 23.
208. M. Lima Rego, O contrato e a apólice …, 25.

it is intended to provide proof of the contract by providing information on the contents of the contract and facilitating its performance.[209] The policy is the written instrument that formalises the insurance contract, that is, that entitles the insurance contract between the policyholder and the insurer, which includes the agreed general and special policy conditions (insurance terms) and if they exist, the particular requirements. The policy must be delivered to the policyholder either when the insurance contract is taken out, within fourteen days (mass risk insurance), or upon agreement (large risks insurance).

502. Therefore, Articles 32, 34 and 35 of RJCS make it clear that the policy, as a means of evidence, is bound to conform to the terms of the contract celebrated, and the policy may be consolidated in its content if no non-conformity between what was agreed, and the content of the policy is invoked. The consolidation of terms stated in the policy will be due thirty days from the date the insurance policy is received. Accordingly, the policyholder does not invoke non-conformity between what was agreed with the insurer and the policy contents. Afterwards, the policyholder can only invoke non-conformity arising from a written document or other durable recordable means. In addition, of course, in compliance with the regime of general contractual clauses, as per Article 3 of the LSCT (*see also* Article 19 RJCS).

503. The insurance policy must be written in the Portuguese language in an understandable, concise and rigorous manner, in clearly legible characters, using words and expressions of everyday language whenever the use of legal or technical terms is not absolutely necessary. It is possible to be written in another language if there is a prior agreement between the parties (Article 36(2) RJCS), except in the case of compulsory insurance, where there must be a Portuguese version of the policy which prevails over the version written in another language (Article 36(2) RJCS).

504. The insurance policy may only be nominative (issued in the name of the policyholder) or to order (meaning that the policyholder can expressly transmit the contractual rights, total or partial, if the insurance contract so determines, to a third party). It will be considered as nominative (issued in the name of the policyholder) in the absence of a stipulation by the parties as to the respective modality. One of the cases where there can be a policy 'to order' is the transport insurance policy. Article 158(2) expressly states that the policy may be in bearer form, in which case the contractual rights of the bearer who is the policyholder or insured are transferred unless otherwise agreed upon.

505. The endorsement of a policy on-demand transfers the contractual rights of the endorsing policyholder or insured without prejudice that the insurance contract may authorise partial endorsement. A nominative insurance policy can also be assigned to a third party, and in such a case, the policyholder must provide the policy to that party (Article 38(4)).

209. M. Lima Rego, O contrato e a apólice …, 32.

506. Article 37(3) sets out a special duty to highlight certain terms of the contract, which may specially affect the interests of the insured. That applies to clauses that establish causes for invalidity, extension, suspension or termination of the contract at the initiative of either party; clauses that specify the scope of the covers, namely their exclusion or limitation; clauses that impose on the policyholder or the time-dependent beneficiary duties of notice.

507. In case the insurer infringes its duty, Articles 37(4) gives the policyholder a right to damages, as well as a right to terminate the insurance contract under the conditions set out in Article 23(2).

508. This is the case of co-insurance contracts where there is joint coverage of risk by several insurers, called co-insurers, of which one is the leader, without solidarity between them, through a single insurance contract, with the same guarantees and identical duration period and a global premium (Article 62 RJCS). In this case, there should be one insurance policy issued by the lead insurer indicating the percentage of risk or capital insured by each co-insurer (Article 63 RJCS). Also, in the case of fire insurance, the policy must state the type of property, the construction material and the state it is in, as well as the location of the building and its name or identification number; the destination and use of the property; the nature and use of adjacent buildings, whenever these circumstances may influence the risk; and the place where the movable objects insured against fire are placed or stored (Article 151 RJCS). As for crop insurance and livestock insurance, there are particularities. In relation to crop insurance, the situation, extension and identification of the building of which product is being insured must be stated in the policy; the nature of the product and the normal time of harvest; the identification of the sowing or planting, in case it already exists at the date of conclusion of the contract; the place of deposit or storage, in case the insurance covers products that have already been harvested; and the average value of the insured harvest (Article 154(1) RJCS). As for livestock insurance policy, it must specify the identification of the building where the livestock farm is located or the building where the animals are usually located or spend the night; the type of animal, possibly its breed, the number of animals insured and the destination of the farm, and the value of the animals insured (Article 154(2) RJCS). In the case of goods transportation insurance, the policy must specify the mode of transport used and whether it is public or private; the type of insurance contracted, namely, if it corresponds to a 'single' policy, an 'open' or 'floating' policy, or a 'travel' or 'on time' policy, the date of receipt of the item and the expected date of its delivery; the identity of the carrier or carriers or the entity responsible for determining it; the places where the insured items are to be received and delivered (Article 158 RJÇS). In contracts for long-term personal accident and health insurance, the policy shall apply in particular, where appropriate, set out in bold characters, the extinction of the right to the guarantees; the possible extension of the warranty beyond the term of the contract and the premium evolution and adaptation regime during the duration of the contract (Article 179 RJCS). And finally, for life insurance, there are two sets of rules of which application is determined by the existence of a group insurance or a singular insurance. As for the latter, the policy must specify the conditions, term and periodicity of payment of the premiums; the indisputability clause; the information provided by the pre-contractual information demanded by Article 185 RJCS; the maximum period in which the policyholder may exercise the right to reinstate the insurance contract after its termination or reduction; the conditions for the continuation of the contract by the beneficiaries in case of death, or by the heirs; whether or not the contract gives rise to profit sharing and, in the first case, how the results are calculated and distributed; whether or not the contract gives rise to an autonomous investment of the assets representing the mathematical provisions and, in the first case, an indication of the nature of and rules for the formation of the investment portfolio of such assets (Article 187 RJCS). In the case of group insurance alongside the above-mentioned content demanded for singular insurance, there must also be a specification of the obligations and rights of the insured persons; the transfer of any right to the surrender value to the insured person, at least in part corresponding to his contribution to the premium, in case of contributory insurance; the entry into force of the coverages for each insured person; and the conditions of eligibility, stating the requirements for the insured person candidate to join the group.

Chapter 4. Obligations of the Insured

§1. PAYMENT OF PREMIUM

509. The norms on the duty to pay the premium can be divided in three groups: the norms on the concept and setting of the premium (Articles 51 and 52), the norms on how the premium should be paid (Articles 53–56) and the norms on the consequences of default (Articles 57–61).

I. Concept and Setting of the Premium

510. Article 51(1) defines the premium as consideration given in return for cover, including everything the policyholder undertakes to give the insurance company, for instance the costs of risk cover, the costs of acquisition, management and billing and the charges connected to the issuing of the policy. This concept corresponds to what was formerly termed by law as 'gross premium'.[210] Any tax or levy for which the policyholder is liable in regard to the contract is not deemed to be part of the insurance premium (Article 51(2)).

511. In its turn, Article 52 entitled 'Characteristics', determines that unless statutory law provides differently, the amount of the premium, as well as the rules for its setting, should be defined by the insurance contract, under the principle of freedom to contract (Article 52(1)). When the contract does not provide for these matters, or does not provide sufficiently, then the premium should be set in such way as to be adequate and proportionate to the risks covered, and should be determined in accordance to the principles of insurance technique, without prejudice of attending to features specific to certain categories of insurance, or to the particular risk at stake (Article 52(2)). In this regard, scholarship has stressed that the insurance company does not have full discretion in setting the premium for a particular contract but is rather bound to treat its customers with respect to the principle of equality.[211] Unless otherwise provided, the premium is set for the whole duration of the contract and should be paid for in its entirety (Article 52(3)). Upon agreement of the parties, the premium may also be fractioned (Article 52(4)).

II. Payment of the Premium

512. On what regards the norms on payment of the premium, Article 53(1) determines that unless otherwise provided, the first premium, or its first fraction, falls due upon the conclusion of the contract. The remaining fractions of the first premium, the subsequent premium or its fractions fall due on the dates set out in the contract

210. José Pereira Morgado, Art. 51.º, Noção (in: Lei do Contrato de Seguro anotada, Almedina, 282, 2020), 282.
211. M. Lima Rego, O prémio, 281.

(Article 53(2)). The accrual in premium regarding adjustments in value, or an aggravation of risk, shall become due on the date determined on the corresponding notification (Article 53(3)).

513. Although the norms do not state it directly, each premium is considered to refer to one year of cover – as it were, first premium refers to the first year of the contract, and subsequent premiums refer to each of the subsequent years. Fractions of the premium therefore refer to periods below one year. This results from the fact that the default duration is set to one year (Article 40) and is reflected in the norms that refer subsequent premium to subsequent periods of one year (Article 61(2) and (3)).

514. According to Article 54, insurance premium can only be paid in cash or by other means of transferring money to the insurance company (Article 54(1)–(4)); set-off is also allowed (Article 54(5)). Originally, Article 54(6), would also allow for payment in kind in personal insurance, in view of some traditional practices of paying in gold for life insurance. However, besides the uncertainty surrounding the evaluation of goods (other than money), this practice had long fallen into disuse;[212] therefore, the norm at stake was repealed in 2015.

515. Article 55 regards payment of the premium by a third party. Article 55(1) establishes that the insurance company cannot refuse payment by a third party. This is in line with the general norms on performance, Articles 767–768 of the Civil Code; as Article 55, these norms are non-mandatory. Article 55(2) is a mere nudge to what the contract may stipulate. According to it, the contract can allow a third party, whose rights to the insurance sum it recognises, to pay premium that has already fallen due, as long as no more than thirty days elapse between the due date and payment. Article 55(3) and (4) regard the effects of payment upon the risk coverage, and should therefore be read together with the norms on default on payment of the premium. According to Article 55(3), payment of the premium under Article 55(2) determines the reinstatement of the contract; it can also be stipulated that payment by a third party determines that risk is covered in the period between the date when the premium falls due and the date of payment. 55(4) sets a limit to this last possibility, establishing that the insured event shall not be covered if it occurred during the period between the due date of payment and the beneficiary was aware of its occurrence.

516. According to Article 56, the insurance company should issue a receipt upon payment (Article 56(1)); if the payment is made by account deduction or check, receipt or any other document only prove that the payment occurred if the insurance company receives the actual sum (Article 56(2)).

517. All in all, the norms on the concept, setting and payment of the premium mostly assert the chief role of private autonomy in this regard.

212. José Pereira Morgado, Art. 54.º, Modo de efectuar o pagamento (in: Lei do Contrato de Seguro anotada, Almedina, 2011), 271.

III. Default on Premium Payments

518. The rules on default of the premium need some clarification from the onset. In fact, section IV of the RJCS, titled 'premium', is divided in two subsections: subsection I, titled 'General rules' (Articles 51–57), and subsection II, titled 'Special rules' (Articles 58–61). Subsection II regards default on the premium; delay and default are also handled by Article 57 of subsection I. Therefore, one would think that Article 57 was the general norm on regard of delay and default, whereas Articles 58–61 would provide for special cases. It is, however, the other way round.

519. Under Article 57(1), if premium is not paid upon the due date, the policyholder is deemed to be in delay. In other words, he is not automatically considered to have defaulted the premium. This is reflected in Article 57(3), which establishes that termination of the insurance contract due to non-payment of the premium or its fraction does not discharge the policyholder from the duty to pay the premium regarding the period in which the contract was in force, accrued of interest for late payment. This norm lays down the normal consequences of delay in payments, and rests on the assumption that delayed payment is still due and possible, albeit accrued of interest regarding compensation for late payment (Articles 804 and ff. of the Civil Code).

520. However, Article 57(2), provides that, without prejudice of the general rules – that is, those of the Civil Code –, the consequences of non-payment of premium fallen due are as follows: for the general case, those set out in Articles 59 and 61 (Article 57(2)(a)); for the contracts mentioned in Article 58, those provided for in the contract (Article 57(2)(b)).

521. Under Article 58, unless the parties agree otherwise and such an agreement is not contrary to the nature of the contract, the rules of Subsection II do not apply to life insurance contracts and operations provided for in the RJCS, to crop or livestock insurance, to insurance provided for by mutual undertakings in which premium is paid through the revenue generated, and to large risks insurance. Conversely, the rules of Subsection II do apply to all other types of insurance.

522. In other words, the *special rules are in the end the general rules*; and they are, as shall be underscored, absolutely mandatory outside of the realm of the contracts mentioned in Article 58.

523. In what regards the contracts mentioned in Article 58, the rules regarding delay or default on premium are those provided for in the contract. When the contract does not provide – or does not sufficiently provide – in this regard, then the general rules of the Civil Code apply (Article 57(2)).

524. The patent deficiency of the law's architecture has naturally been object of criticism. The lack of transparency resulting therefrom is furthermore enhanced by the fact that, even in regard to the contracts exempted from the 'special rules', the insurance companies' standard terms tend to reflect these provisions,[213] since they are particularly advantageous to the insurance company.

525. In fact, these rules lay down a strict 'no premium, no risk/no cover' system.[214] Article 59 establishes that the risk cover is conditional upon the previous payment of the premium.

526. Under Article 60, while the contract is in force, the insurer should warn the policyholder in writing on the amount to pay, as well as on the method and place of payment, at least thirty days before the date in which the premium or its fraction fall due (60(1)). The warning should give legible notice on the consequences of default on payment of the premium or its fraction (Article 60(2)). In respect of contracts in which fractions of the premium fall due every three months, or within shorter periods, when the contract documents inform on the successive dates in which the payments fall due, on the amounts to pay and on the consequences of default, the insurance company may choose not to send the warning mentioned in Article 60(1), as long as it proves that the contract documents referred have been issued, accepted and sent to the policyholder (Article 60(3)).

527. Under Article 61(1), in case the first premium, or its first fraction, is not paid when it falls due, the contract is considered automatically terminated from the date of its conclusion. In case subsequent premiums, or their first fractions, are not paid, the contract is considered not to have been prolonged (Article 61(2)).

528. The contract is automatically terminated when if the following payments are not made when they fall due: a fraction of the premium in the course of a year of its duration (Article 61(3)(a)); an amount regarding an adjustment in premium or part of a variable premium (Article 61(3)(b)); additional premium regarding a modification of the contract due to aggravation of the insured risk (Article 61(3)(c)).

529. In case non-payment regards an excess premium agreed as consideration for a modification of the contract, the modification of the contract shall take no effect; in case it is not possible for the contract to subsist under its previous terms, it is automatically terminated from the date when premium fell due (Article 61(4)).

530. In a word: delay equals default, and causes automatic termination or not prolongation, as the case may be, of the contract (with the small exception of Article 61(4)). This absolute intolerance towards delay marks a striking contrast to the general norms of the Civil Code, where not only delay is not equated with default (Articles 804 and ff. of the Civil Code), as also, in the general cases, after the due date, the creditor should grant the debtor an additional period for performance

213. M. Lima Rego, O prémio, 266–268.
214. P. Romano Martínez, Art. 61.º, Falta de pagamento, Comentários complementares, 300; M. Lima Rego, O prémio, 266–270; STJ 30 April 2020, 2710/11.8TBVCD.P1.P1.S1 (Oliveira Abreu).

(Article 808 of the Civil Code). In view of the harshness of these rules, it is all the more startling that the RJCS has counted Articles 59–61 among the small number of norms it deems absolutely mandatory.

531. Scholarship has criticised these norms for creating an unbalanced solution to the disadvantage of the insured, that moreover does not fit in well with the general approach of the Civil Code to non-performance.[215] Against this background, an author has sustained that the special rules do not apply to insurance contracts regulated in special statutes.[216] Other scholarship, as well as some appellate courts, have emphasised the role of the duty to warn under Article 60. Thus, an author has defended that in case the insurance company has failed to give due warning to the policyholder, it should notify the policyholder granting them an additional period of payment, upon which the contract would be automatically terminated in case the policyholder did not pay.[217] Some appellate courts have considered that the written warning is a condition necessary for the insurance company to terminate the contract under Article 61 and that in the want of it, the general rules of the Civil Code on delay and non-performance apply.[218] This leads to a similar result to the one just described, in that it demands the insurance company to grant an additional period of payment before termination (Articles 806 and 808 of the Civil Code). This reasoning has been followed by the STJ in one case, where it considered that this conclusion furthermore resulted from the norms of the LSCT that set out that contract terms that have not been duly communicated to the non-drafting party cannot be invoked against them.[219] In other case, the STJ has considered sufficient that the policyholder was aware of the date in which the premium became due, and nonetheless failed to make the payment, for automatic termination to apply.[220]

532. It has furthermore been noted that the 'special' norms on default on premium grant the policyholder with a right to automatically terminate the contract. This does not fit in well with the *pacta sunt servanda* principle (Article 406 of the Civil Code) and the general rules on right to performance (Articles 798 and ff. of

215. J. C. Moitinho de Almeida, O novo regime jurídico do contrato de seguro, Beves considerações sobre a protecção dos segurados, 17–19; José Carlos Moitinho de Almeida, A protecção do tomador do seguro e dos segurados no novo regime legal do contrato de seguro (s.d.), retrieved 01 Jan. 2021 from https://www.stj.pt/wp-content/uploads/2018/01/moitinhoalmeida_proteccaotomadorseguro.pdf, no. 6; José Luís Bonifácio Ramos, O pagamento do prémio na Lei do Contrato de Seguro, 39, Cadernos de Direito Privado, (2012), 10 and ff.; Maria Inês de Oliveira Martins, El derecho de contrato de seguro en Portugal. Un régimen en la encrucijada (in: Pablo Girgado Perandones (ed.) El contrato de seguro y su distribución en la encrucijada, Aranzadi/ Thomson Reuters, 2018), 2.1. For a different perspective, *see* A. Menezes Cordeiro, Seguros, 2. Ed., 749–750 (and previous pages).
216. J. L. Bonifácio Ramos, O pagamento ..., 10 and ff.
217. J. C. Moitinho de Almeida, A protecção do tomador ..., no. 6, b); the author criticises J. P. Morgado, Art. 60.º, Aviso de pagamento, 268, who deems the insurance company to be merely liable towards the policyholder in this case.
218. TRG 5 November 2015, 2810/13.0TBBCL.G1 (Miguel Baldaia Morais); TRC 14 September 2018, 279/16.6T8CVL.C1 (Ramalho Pinto); for further references in case law, *see* J. P. Morgado, Art. 60.º, 298.
219. STJ 30 April 2020, 2710/11.8TBVCD.P1.P1.S1 (Oliveira Abreu).
220. STJ 3 July 2018, 776/14.8TBCVL.C1.S1 (Olinda Garcia).

the Civil Code) and can also devoid Article 118, on termination of the contract within a cooling-off period, of practical effect.[221]

§2. Other Duties of the Policyholder

I. Pre-contractual Duty of Disclosure

A. Scope of the Pre-contractual Duty of Disclosure

533. Although the information provided by the policyholder is certainly not the only source of information used by the insurance companies in order to decide whether to enter the contract, and under which conditions to do so, the RJCS mainly focuses on this source of information. That should not come as a surprise, since the RJCS regulates the relation between the persons implicated in the insurance contract; it does not intend to regulate the relation of the insurance company with other sources of information.

534. Nonetheless, as mentioned above (Part II, Chapter 3, §1, Pre-contractual Phase), one should keep in mind that the insurance company organises the collection of information by choosing between an array of different potential sources of information, in view of their relative costs and accuracy/reliability.

535. The duty to inform set out by Article 24. Article 24(1) provides that the policyholder or the insured is obliged to declare with exactitude, before entering into the contract, all the circumstances which they are aware of and should reasonably consider relevant to the assessment of the risk by the insurance company.[222] Article 24(2) clarifies that the same applies in regard to circumstances not specifically mentioned in the questionnaire eventually presented by the insurance company.

536. As it is clear, the policyholder or insured face more than a duty to truthfully answer to the questions posed by the insurance company; they are under the duty to spontaneously inform the insurance company on any relevant circumstance.

537. Relying on a duty of disclosure, and not on a simple duty to respond, this system has been met with strong criticism from scholarship.

538. It is deemed inadequate in regard to the different asymmetries of information between the contracting parties. Although the insured is the party that knows

221. J. A. Engrácia Antunes, Direito dos contratos, 714–175.

222. There is considerable discussion as to the nature of policyholder's duties handled in this Part II, Ch. 4, §2, Duties of the Policyholder, which regard the 'management' of the insured risk. For the sake of simplicity, they shall be referred as duties; for a lengthy discussion on the matter, *see* M. I. Oliveira Martins, Contrato de seguro e conduta …, 779 and ff.

the practical circumstances regarding the risk (their personal or entrepreneurial circumstances), the insurance company is the party that knows which circumstances are relevant (the ones it considered for the calculation of the premium), and what their impact is upon the risk. The insured will not normally have the technical skill to determine if and how their personal or entrepreneurial circumstances affect the risk (e.g., the insured may eventually know that their house is thermally insulated through polystyrene foam, without being aware of the implications of this material in regard to the risk of fire). The system relying on a duty to respond would correctly address this distribution of information between the parties, whereas the system adopted by the Portuguese lawmaker does not.[223]

539. Moreover, the system adopted is deemed incompatible with the norms on data protection, and specifically with the principle of data minimisation (Article 5(1)(c)) of GDPR, according to which personal data shall be adequate, relevant and limited to what is necessary in relation to the purposes for which they are processed; *see also* Article 7(4), for consent-based processing). Since the policyholder/insured does not know which information is relevant for the insurance company, in order to avert the consequences of non-disclosure (*see below*), they will be strongly incentivised to communicate as much information as they can, regardless of it being effectively relevant for the insurer.[224]

540. The harsher effects of the norm can be limited by the application of the general standard of good faith. The conduct of the insurer can lead the policyholder/insured to trust that the insurance company has received all the information it deemed relevant, and their legitimate trust should be protected. When the insurance company chooses only to question about a certain set of circumstances, and during the negotiation does not signal any interest in being informed on other circumstances, the policyholder/insured can in principle assume that the company has no interest in such further information.[225] Therefore, when the contract documents state that, only when the insured sum surpasses EUR 125,000.00, should the insured fill out an extended questionnaire, whereas below EUR 125,000.00 it is enough that the insured fills out a statement on his health condition, the insured does not breach their duty when, in a contract below that threshold, they do not inform on circumstances that are not mentioned in this statement.[226]

223. António Santos Abrantes Geraldes, O novo regime do contrato de seguro, Antigas e novas questões (2010), retrieved 15 Jan. 2015 from http://www.trl.mj.pt/PDF/REGIME.pdf, 5.3 and ff.; J. C. Moitinho de Almeida, O novo … , p. 13; Júlio M. V. Gomes, O dever de informação … , 402; A. Menezes Cordeiro, Seguros, 2. Ed., 633; M. I. Oliveira Martins, El derecho de contrato … , 1.1.; M. I. Oliveira Martins, Entre a avaliação … , 82–83. For a different perspective, *see* Luís Poças, O dever de declaração inicial do risco no contrato de seguro, Almedina, (2013), 33 and ff.

224. M. I. Oliveira Martins, El derecho de contrato … , 1.1.

225. Júlio M. V. Gomes, O dever de informação … , 409–411 (referring to a presumption of completeness of the questionnaire presented); Filipe de Albuquerque Matos, Uma outra abordagem em torno das declarações inexactas e reticentes no âmbito do contrato de seguro, Os Arts 24.º a 26.º do Dec.-Lei. n.º 72/2008, de 16 de Abril (in: Manuel da Costa Andrade/Maria João Antunes/Susana Aires de Sousa (ed.) Estudos em homenagem ao Prof. Doutor Jorge de Figueiredo Dias, IV, Coimbra Editora, 2010), 619–620.

226. STJ 29 June 2017, 225/14.1TBTND.C1.S1 (Maria dos Prazeres Pizarro Beleza).

541. Moreover, the RJCS sets out that, once it has accepted the contract, the insurance company cannot avail itself of the breach of the duty to disclose in certain cases in which this breach was apparent. This happens when: one of the questions posed remained unanswered (Article 24(3)(a)); a question posed in generic terms received a vague reply (Article 24(3)(b)); there are evident contradictions or incoherencies in the answers provided (Article 24.º, 3, c)); the insurer's representatives knew, through the conclusion of the contract, that a certain disclosed fact was untrue, or they were aware of a certain fact that remained undisclosed (Article 24(3)(d)); the facts at stake are known to the insurer, for instance because they are public and conspicuous (Article 24(3)(e)).

542. In fact, this list should be seen as a mere explanation of the general prohibition of illegitimate contradiction with one's own previous conduct (*venire contra factum proprium*), as a result of the duty to comply with the standard of good faith (Articles 227, 334, 762 of the Civil code). If the insurer did not diligently verify the information provided and simply let the contract run its course, while collecting the premiums, the rule of *venire contra factum proprium* bars it from availing itself of the infringement of the duty to inform when it is called upon to make the insurance payment.[227] The most striking case law in this regard concerns property insurance, where, as the property at stake was an easily accessible house in a centre of a city, and it could easily be seen from the outside, and even using Google Maps, that it was derelict, the court considered that the insurance company infringed the standard of diligence required when it kept an insurance contract during two years without in any way checking the information presented by the policyholder. The insurer was therefore barred from raising the defence of non-disclosure.[228]

543. However, this limitation does not apply if the duty to disclose was breached intentionally and with the purpose of obtaining an advantage (Article 24(3)); if that was the case, the insurer will still be allowed to raise the defence of non-disclosure. This would have as a result allowing the insurer to benefit from its own negligent conduct, and even from the wilful misconduct of its representatives. The norm has received strong criticism in this regard.[229]

544. One should point out that there is no infringement of the duty to inform regarding facts there were not known to the policyholder or to the insured.[230] Even if the policyholder or the insured should had been aware of those facts, if they were not actually aware of those facts, then they are not deemed to have infringed the duty. Furthermore, the consequences only apply if the policyholder or insured negligently fail to consider certain facts that they are aware of as relevant for the assessment of the risk, or if they deliberately do not disclose facts they deem relevant. No

227. Júlio M. V. Gomes, O dever de informação …, 414–415; A. Abrantes Geraldes, O novo regime …, 5.1.; M. I. Oliveira Martins, El derecho de contrato …, 1.1; M. I. Oliveira Martins, Entre a avaliação …, 84. This was also stated very clearly by TRL 20 October 2016, 647/11.0TBVPV.L1-2 (Ondina Carmo Alves).
228. TRP 15 November 2018, 12886/16.2T8PRT.P1 (Rodrigues Pires).
229. Júlio M. V. Gomes, O dever de informação …, 414–415, 430–431.
230. M. I. Oliveira Martins, Entre a avaliação …, 83–84.

consequences apply in case of innocent non-disclosure. The insurer bears the burden of proof as to whether there was intent or negligence.

B. Consequences of Infringement of the Duty

545. The consequences of the infringement of the duty to disclose are different for the cases of intentional infringement of the duty to inform (Article 25), and for the cases of negligent infringement of the duty (Article 26). In any case, on one hand, infringement can affect the contract itself, and, on the other hand, the right to insurance payment regarding an insured event that meanwhile occurred.

546. In case of intentional infringement, the insurance company can avoid the contract by notice to the policyholder (Article 25(1)). In case the insurance company becomes aware of the infringement of the duty before the insured event occurs, it should give notice of avoidance within three months after becoming aware of that infringement (Article 25(2)).

547. In case an insured event occurs before expiration of that period, the insurance company is discharged from its duty to pay in its regard (Article 25(3)). One should highlight that, in contrast to the cases of mere negligence, this consequence does not depend on the fact that was not duly informed having any influence on the insured event: no causation is required in this regard.

548. Except when negligence from the insurance company or its representative have concurred to the failure to disclose, the insurance company shall have the right to the premiums due until the end of that same period (Article 25(4)). In case the policyholder or the insured breach the duty intentionally and with the purpose of obtaining an advantage, the insurance company shall be entitled to the premiums due until the end of the contract (Article 25(5)).

549. The right to avoidance in case of intentional non-disclosure is seen by the courts as an instantiation of the general right to avoid a contract in case of fraud, as set out by the Civil Code in Articles 253 and 254. Under Article 254, fraud only gives right to avoid the contract in case the avoiding part proves that they would not have entered into the contract if it had not been for the fraud, or, at least, that they would only have accepted the contract in different conditions. The same requirement was set out by the norm on the duty of disclosure laid down the Commercial Code (Article 429). Although Article 25 does not mention it, the courts apply the general rule of the Civil Code and require the same proof from the insurance company.[231]

231. STJ 29 June 2017, 225/14.1TBTND.C1.S1 (Maria dos Prazeres Pizarro Beleza); STJ 8 November 2018, 399/14.1TVLSB.L1.S1 (Oliveira Abreu); STJ 19 June 2019, no. 4702/15.9T8MTS.P1.S1 (Ilídio Sacarrão Martins); TRP 12 July 2017, 1527/13.0TBOAZ.P1 (Alberto Ruço). However, some second instance courts have rejected this requirement: *see* TRC 17 September 2019, 3833/17.5T8LRA.C1 (Fernando Monteiro).

550. It is worthy of mentioning that, unlike what happens under the general norms of the Civil Code, under the RJCS avoidance of the contract is effected by mere notice, and does not need to be determined by a court.[232]

551. Finally, it should be mentioned that Article 25(5), that entitles the insurance company to the premiums stipulated for the whole duration of the contract, has been deemed disproportionately punitive and arbitrary, since the amount of the sanction (amount of premium retained) does not depend on the seriousness of the offence, but rather on the arbitrary fact of how much longer the contract remains in force vis-à-vis the moment when the offence occurs.[233]

552. Differently, in case of negligent infringement, the insurance company is generally entitled to propose a variation of the contract and exceptionally entitled to terminate the contract. In any case, to this end the insurer must give notice of its intention to the policyholder, within three months after becoming aware of the infringement (Article 26(1)). The insurance company is only entitled to terminate the contract in case it proves that it does not in any case take out contracts that cover risks related to the fact that was not duly informed (Article 26(1)(b)). Termination takes effect after thirty days counting from the day the notice is sent (Article 26(2)). Generally, the insurer is only entitled to propose a variation of the contract and must set a deadline not inferior to fourteen days for its acceptance or, in case it admits it, for the expedition of a new proposal Article 26(1)(a). In case the policyholder does not accept the proposed variation, or rejects it, the contract is terminated twenty days after receipt by the policyholder of the proposal sent by the insurance company (Article 26(2)).

553. In any case, if the contract is terminated, the insurance company is entitled to the insurance premium in proportion of the duration of the contract (*pro rata temporis*) (Article 26(3)). One should also add that, unlike avoidance of the contract, termination takes effect for the future.

554. There are also rules for cases when an insured occurs before termination or variation takes effect, but only as long as the insured event is influenced in its occurrence or consequences by the fact that was not duly informed (Article 26(4)). If the insurance company proves it would not in any case have concluded the contract had it known the information concerned, it is discharged from its obligation, but must return the insurance premium paid. In any other case, if knowledge of the information concerned would have led the insurance company to conclude the contract at a higher premium or on different terms, then it should cover the risk proportionately or in accordance with such terms.

555. One should stress that, unlike what happens in case of intentional infringement, the insurance company is bound to cover the risk if there is no causal link

232. STJ 19 June 2019, 4702/15.9T8MTS.P1.S1 (Ilídio Sacarrão Martins).

233. Júlio M. V. Gomes, O dever de informação …, 425; A. Menezes Cordeiro, Seguros, 2. Ed., 637–639.

between the fact which was not properly informed and the insured event or its consequences.[234] The insurer bears the burden of proof as to whether such causal link occurred.

556. In any case, the insurer should elucidate the potential policyholder or insured on their duty to disclose the risk and on the consequences of its infringement. If it fails to do so, it will be liable for damage caused (Article 24(4)).

557. A final question is whether the general norms on mistake, set out in Articles 251 and 252 of the Civil code, concurrently apply in case of non-disclosure. This possibility is currently denied, since the general norms of the Civil Code would give the insurer (the party in error) the right to avoid the contract, independent of there having been any kind of negligence from the insured/policyholder.[235] This would stand in direct contradiction to the rules of the RJCS, that only apply in case of negligence and only give rise to avoidance of the contract in case of intentional breach.

II. Duties During the Contract

A. *Statutory Duties*

1. Communication of the Aggravation of Risk

a. Overview of the Applicable Norms

558. The RJCS establishes that while the contract is in force, the policyholder or insured should notify the insurer on modifications of risk regarding the information provided under the pre-contractual duty of disclosure (Article 91(1)).

559. This duty is instrumental to the regime on modification of risk (*see* Part II, Chapter 7, §1, Modification of the Risk). It is not the only source of information in regard to the changes in risk, but it is doubtlessly a privileged source of information. The insurance company does not perform continuous assessments of the risk while the contract is in force, similar to those it performed on the inception of the contract. It relies mainly on the information provided by its contract party, the policyholder, or by the insured, who remains in contact with the subject matter at risk.

560. The general provision on the duty to inform on risk modifications is sided by a provision specifically regarding aggravations of risk. The policyholder or the insured should, within fourteen days from becoming aware of the fact, notify the

234. In case law, *see, for instance*, TRL 11 October 2018, 3797/17.5T8LSB.L1-6 (António Santos).
235. Júlio M. V. Gomes, O dever de informação …, 397–398; M. I. Oliveira Martins, Entre a avaliação …, 85.

insurance company on any circumstance that aggravates the risk, as long as this circumstance, had it been known by the insurance company at the onset of the contract, could have interfered in its decision to enter into the contract or to do so in certain conditions (Article 93(1)).

561. In order to understand the scope of the duty to notify, and the consequences of its infringement, one should clarify the purpose of the information. The occurrence of an aggravation of the insured risk gives the insurance company a right to propose a modification of the contract and terminate the contract in case it is not accepted, and, in exceptional cases, it gives the company the right to directly terminate the contract.

562. Within thirty days from becoming aware of the aggravation of risk, the insurance company can propose a modification of the contract to the policyholder; the policyholder shall have an equal deadline of thirty days to accept or reject the proposal, which is deemed accepted in case of absence of reply by the policyholder (Article 93(2)(a)). In case the insurance company proves that it does not in any case cover risks with the characteristics of the aggravated risk, it is entitled to terminate the contract within the same deadline of thirty days (Article 93(2)(b)).

563. The fulfilment or infringement of the duty to notify affects the right to obtain coverage for an insured event occurred before the contract is modified or terminated on the grounds of aggravation of risk. In any case, the right to coverage is only affected when the insured event was influenced by the aggravation of risk (Article 94(1)).

564. In case the aggravation was correctly and timely notified, or in case the insured event occurs before the deadline of fourteen days for notification expires, the insurance company must grant coverage as provided by the contract (Article 94(1)(a)).

565. In case the aggravation was not correctly and timely notified, the insurance company has the right to reduce its payment in proportion to the ratio between the premium paid and the premium that it would have set in view of the aggravated circumstances (Article 94(1)(b)).

566. In these two cases, the insurance company is exceptionally entitled to refuse to pay if two conditions are met: the insurance company must prove that it does not in any case insure risks with features such as those resulting from aggravation of risk; and the aggravation must have proceeded from the policyholder or from the insured (Article 94(2)).

567. In case the duty was infringed intentionally and with the purpose of obtaining an advantage, the insurance company is entitled to refuse to pay, while keeping the right to the insurance premium that fell due (Article 94(1)(c)).

568. Articles 91, 93 and 94 are semi-mandatory (Article 13(1)).

569. A few more clarifications are now necessary in order to explain how these rules apply.

570. The rules that sanction the infringement of the duty to notify (Article 94) apply only during a limited period of time. This period starts within fourteen days from when the policyholder or insured became aware of the aggravation of risk (Article 93(1)); before expiry of the deadline of fourteen days, the duty cannot be deemed to have been infringed. The period at stake ends within a maximum of sixty days counting from the date upon which the insurance company became aware of the risk, in case of exercise of a right to modify the contract (Article 93(2)(a)). In the exceptional cases where a right to terminate the contract is at stake, this period would seem to entail a maximum of thirty days counting from the same date, since the effects of termination seem to be automatic (Article 93(2)(b)). However, it is considered that unless there is fraudulent infringement of the duty to notify, the norm on termination of the contract for negligent non-disclosure, which states that termination only takes effect after thirty days counting from the day the notice is sent (Article 26(2)), should apply by analogy.[236] If this is accepted, the rules on infringement of the duty to notify also apply during a maximum of sixty days in case of termination of the contract.

571. After this moment, the right of the insurance company to reduce or deny cover expires.

572. In order to understand the combined result of Articles 93 and 94, one should distinguish two situations.

573. If the policyholder and the insured were themselves not aware of the aggravation, it remains inconsequential: the insured event is covered. The same applies in case the policyholder and the insured had become aware of the aggravation no more than fourteen days before the insured event occurred (Article 94(1)(a)).[237]

574. If the policyholder or the insured had become aware of the aggravation more than fourteen days before the insured event occurred, then the rules applied depend on whether the insurance company was itself also previously aware of the aggravation, having become aware of it through other sources. In case the insurance company was itself previously aware of the aggravation and the period of sixty days (in case of a right to modify the contract) or thirty days (in case of a right to terminate the contract) had expired, the insurance company will have lost its rights. In case the insurance company was aware of the aggravation but the said period had not expired, as well as in case the insurance company was not aware of the aggravation before, then the rules of Article 94 apply.

236. Arnaldo da Costa Oliveira, Art. 93.º, Comunicação do agravamento do risco (in: Lei do contrato de seguro anotada, Almedina, 2020), 367; M. Lima Rego, O risco … , 408.

237. *See also* Júlio Manuel Vieira Gomes, Algumas notas sobre o agravamento e a diminuição do risco no contrato de seguro, 1–3, RDES, (2015), 13.

575. Therefore, these rules will apply to the frequent cases where the insurance company only becomes aware of the aggravation when an insured event occurs, whereas the policyholder or the insured had been aware of the aggravation for more than fourteen days.

b. Scope of the Duty to Communicate the Aggravation of Risk

576. One should now consider the requirements that should be met so that the norms on the duty to inform apply. For the duty to arise, there should be a relevant aggravation of risk, the insured or policyholder should have actual knowledge of the circumstances underlying the aggravation, and those circumstances should be of the kind that was relevant for the initial assessment of the risk. For the breach of duty to have consequences, the aggravation should be causal for the insured and there should be fault from the person failing to notify on the aggravation.

577. In empirical terms, an aggravation of risk consists of an increase in the amount of the expected loss, deriving either from an increase in the probability of the insured event, or from an increase in the amount of loss that an insured event can cause. In any case, an empirical aggravation of risk does not trigger per se the norms on modification or termination of the contract, or those on the duty to disclose the risk. The aggravation should meet certain requirements so that it can be considered relevant for these purposes: it should be actual, foreseeably lasting and significant (*see below* Part II, Chapter 7, §1, Modification of the Risk).[238] For the purposes of the duty to notify, an aggravation is significant when it exceeds the increase in risk that the insured or policyholder should legitimately expect to be included in the cover – in other words, when it surpasses the aggravation attached to the normal evolution of that risk and to the normal 'management' of the object at risk. The rights of the insurance company to modify or terminate the contract, or to reduce the payment in case of an insured event, are also conditioned upon the fact that the aggravation is significant to the company, in view of its underwriting practices.

578. The duty to communicate the aggravation of risk furthermore requires that the policyholder or insured know the facts that underlie the aggravation.[239] There is no duty to communicate facts that they should have been aware of, but were actually not aware of. An exception is made in regard to cases where the insured or the policyholder deliberately choose to ignore certain facts (e.g., not to read a certain inspection report), in order to avoid becoming aware of a potential aggravation. In

238. On these requirements, which were drawn from the experience in German law, *see* M. I. Oliveira Martins, Contrato de seguro e conduta ..., 359 and ff. and M. I. Oliveira Martins, Entre a avaliação ..., 87 and ff.; they were applied by STJ 19 March 2019, 1680/12.0TBGDM.P1.S1 (Maria João Vaz Tomé). For a similar (though not identical) approach, J. Gomes, Algumas notas sobre o agravamento ..., 9–10, 20 and ff.

239. *See also* J. Gomes, Algumas notas sobre o agravamento ..., 14–15.

these cases the insured or policyholder acts with *dolus eventualis* in regard to the infringement of their duty to communicate; they should be treated as cases of infringement.

579. On what concerns the facts that should be communicated to the insurance company, the RJCS establishes that the duty encompasses all the circumstances that cause an aggravation of risk, as long as they could have influenced the insurance company's decision to enter the contract or to do so in certain terms, had they been known by the company at the inception of the contract (Article 93(1)). Such a broadly cut duty would however be a very extensive limitation to the efficacy of the cover, since it would place the burden of correctly identifying the relevant changes in risk upon the insured or policyholder. It would be even more unbalanced than the duty of disclosure at the inception of the contract, since it would not be fixed in time, but it would rather impend upon the insured or policyholder throughout the contract. Therefore, it is highlighted that this norm should be read together with the first norm on this section, according to which, while the contract is in force the policyholder or insured should notify the insurer on the modifications of risk regarding the information provided under the pre-contractual duty of disclosure (Article 91(1)).[240] In other words, in principle the duty to notify only refers to the circumstances that were already signalled as relevant at the inception of the contract. The duty should only extend to other circumstances in exceptional cases, where it would be understandable that those circumstances would only become present after the contract entered into force (e.g., in case it concerns new technology that could not have been anticipated before the conclusion of the contract).

c. Consequences of Infringement of the Duty

580. Now, on what regards the consequences of the breach of duty to notify, one should underline that causation and fault are required in any case. No consequences will apply if the insured event was not influenced by the aggravation, be it in its occurrence or in its consequences (Article 94(1)). In this regard, the fact of hiding the car keys inside a bush while going surfing was not deemed to have caused the insured event – car theft – in a theft insurance, since it was not proved that the action of hiding had been observed by the thief and caused them to carry out the theft.[241]

581. Causation is a requirement even when the duty to notify was fraudulently breached.[242]

240. Sustaining that Art. 93(1) is limited by Art. 91(1), M. Lima Rego, O risco …, 398 and 405.
241. TRP 27 January 2020, 1643/18.1T8PVZ.P1 (Fernanda Almeida). The (questionable) reasoning of the court seems to be that it had not been established whether the thief had already decided to steal the vehicle anyway when they decided to perform the theft.
242. The law is clear on this regard (*see also* J. Gomes, Algumas notas sobre o agravamento …, 34–35); there is nonetheless a different opinion in literature (A. Costa Oliveira, Art. 94.º, Sinistro e agravamento do risco, 372).

582. Furthermore, the right of the insurance company to a proportional reduction of the payment depends on there being at least negligence from the insured or policyholder (Article 94(1)(a)) – although the norm is not very clear in this regard, it is construed as requiring fault.[243] The insurance company is only entitled to refuse its payment in case of qualified wilful breach, strictly speaking, when the duty was breached with the intention of obtaining an advantage. The law totally exempts the insurance company from any payment while retaining the premiums fallen due, thus treating the risk at stake as not being included in the coverage. There is some doubt as to the meaning of the breach being wilful and performed with intention of obtaining an advantage, since any intentional breach of the duty would naturally be connected to an advantage, even if non-pecuniary, of the non-complying party. This requirement is in consequence interpreted as referring to the intention, at least in terms of *dolus eventualis*, to cause damage to the insurance company – in other words, when, according to available information, the insured or policyholder knew or should reasonably have known that due to providing wrong information they could be provided with cover that they would not be entitled to.[244] Thus, for instance, if, in order to speed up the settlement of the claim, or in order to hide a shameful personal detail of their life, the insured or policyholder omitted a circumstance that they did not have reasonable grounds to suppose that would lead to them having undue cover, they should not suffer the harsh consequence of total loss of coverage for that event.

583. As mentioned above, the insurance company is furthermore entitled to refuse payment if two conditions are met: the insurance company must prove that it does not in any case insure risks with features such as those resulting from aggravation of risk; and the aggravation must have proceeded from the policyholder or insured (Article 94(2)). It should be underscored that this norm does not refer to the duty to communicate the aggravation; the correct communication of the risk is irrelevant for these purposes. Neither does it set out a duty not to aggravate the risk; it would not make sense to set such a duty only in regard to the features of risk that the particular insurance company at stake did not cover in any case. In this regard, it is enough that the aggravation is caused by the policyholder or by the insured, independent from any assessment of fault.

d. Interplay with the Rules on Pre-contractual Disclosure of the Risk

584. A final matter concerns the interplay between the rules on the duty to notify on an aggravation of risk and the rules on the pre-contractual duty to disclose the risk. In view of the wording of the provisions on aggravation of risk, which refer to the period while the contract is in force, they are deemed to apply only to the time span starting at the conclusion of the contract.

---

243. M. Lima Rego, O risco ..., 410; A. Costa Oliveira, Art. 94.º, 370–371 and 373.
244. M. I. Oliveira Martins, Contrato de seguro e conduta ..., 598–600.

585. Therefore, any aggravation of risk occurred after the disclosure of risk and before the conclusion of contract is regulated by the norms on disclosure (Articles 24–26). In other words, if before the conclusion of the contract the policyholder or insured become aware of a change in the information they provided to the insurance company, their duty to update that information is regulated by Articles 24–26.[245]

2. Mitigation of the Loss

a. Overview of the Applicable Norms

586. Article 126(1) establishes that in case an insured event occurs, the policyholder or the insured should make use of all the means available to prevent or mitigate the loss. This also applies to whoever becomes aware of the insurance contract in the quality of its beneficiary (Article 126(2)). In case of infringement of this duty, Article 101(1), (2) and (4) apply (Article 126(3)).

587. Article 101 refers to the consequences of the infringement of duty to communicate the insured event. However, the norm itself does not set out the consequences of the infringement; it merely poses limits to the sanctions that the contract may define. Under Article 101(1), the contract may determine the reduction of the insurance payment according to the damage caused by the infringement to the insurance company. Under Article 101(2), the contract may furthermore determine the discharge of the insurance company in case either of failure to comply with the duty or of incorrect compliance, but only when this is done with intent and causes significant damage to the insurer. Article 101(4) determines that in case of compulsory liability insurance, the insurance company cannot raise this defence against the victims, but can subsequently recover the amounts paid from the infringer, within the limits set out in Article 101(1) and (2).

588. The duty to mitigate should be read together with the right to reimbursement of the expenses incurred in connection with mitigation, as set out in Article 127. Under Article 127(1), the insurance company should reimburse the policyholder, insured or beneficiary of the expenses incurred in the fulfilment of the duty of mitigation, as long as these expenses are reasonable and proportionate, and even if the measures adopted have proved ineffective. Those amounts should be paid by the insurance company before the date in which the claim should be settled, as long as the policyholder, insured or beneficiary ask for the reimbursement, the circumstances do not prevent it, and the insured event is covered by the contract (Article

245. Júlio M. V. Gomes, O dever de informação …, 404–405; M. Lima Rego, O risco …, 398; L. Poças, O dever …, 332.

127(2)). The norm further clarifies that, unless the expenses are made in the enactment of specific instructions given by the insurance company, or the contract stipulates the autonomous cover of those expenses, the amount of the reimbursement is deducted from the insured sum that is still available (Article 127(3)).[246]

589. Articles 126, 101 and 127 are semi-mandatory (Article 13(1)).

b. Scope of the Duty to Mitigate

590. Some clarifications are necessary in order to understand the extent of the duty to mitigate. No relevant case law has yet developed in this regard; however, some authors have tried to explain how the norms should be construed.[247]

591. The means used to prevent or mitigate the loss should not go beyond what is expected from a diligent policyholder, insured or beneficiary in view of the degree to which the expenses they incur can be reimbursed. It should be underscored that the expenses incurred are only reimbursed within tight limits: they will only be reimbursed in the extent to which the loss caused by the insured event does not itself exhaust the insured sum. Therefore, the risk regarding the actual extent of costs is taken on by the policyholder, insured or beneficiary, as appropriate. This should be taken into account when ascertaining whether the measures chosen complied with the standard of care.[248]

592. A different question regards the moment in which the duty to mitigate and the right to reimbursement arise. The wording of Article 126(1) is not entirely clear in this regard. On the one hand, it refers to the occurrence of the insured event, which would imply that the duty only arose when the event was actually occurring; on the other hand, it refers to a purpose of preventing the loss, which would imply that the duty arose when the event was merely imminent.[249]

593. First, it should be pointed out that the policyholder, insured and beneficiary are bound by the general duty to act according to good faith while performing the contract. This would not be compatible with them watching passively while an

---

246. The norm also refers to the cases of under-insurance, by setting out that when the insured sum is inferior to the value of the insured interest at the time of the insured event, the expenses incurred in the fulfilment of the duty of mitigation are reimbursed only in the proportion of the value of the covered interest vis-à-vis the value of the interest at risk, unless the expenses are made in the enactment of specific instructions given by the insurance company, or contract sets out the autonomous cover (no. 4). *See* Ch. 5, §1, II.

247. *See* Júlio Manuel Vieira Gomes, Do dever ou ónus de salvamento no novo regime jurídico do contrato de seguro (Decreto-Lei n.º 72/2008, de 16/4), 28, Cadernos de Direito Privado, 3 (2009), 3 and ff. and M. I. Oliveira Martins, Contrato de seguro e conduta …, 442 and ff.

248. M. I. Oliveira Martins, Contrato de seguro e conduta …, 467 and ff.

249. The latter view is defended by M. I. Oliveira Martins, Contrato de seguro e conduta …, 454 and ff. and (less categorically) by J. M. Vieira Gomes, Do dever ou ónus …, 9; for a different construction, *see* Arnaldo da Costa Oliveira, Art. 126.º, Salvamento (in: Lei do Contrato de Seguro anotada, Almedina, 2020), 438–439.

imminent insured event materialised. Nonetheless, one should also emphasise that under the RJCS the insurance company is only discharged from its duty when the insured event was deliberately caused; it is not discharged when the event is caused with negligence – even when gross negligence is at stake. In consequence, the insurance company should only be discharged of its duty when policyholder, insured or beneficiary deliberately – at least with *dolus eventualis* – failed to prevent an imminent insured event.

594. Second, one should also point out that the insurance company undertook to cover the risk and should not be left to reap the benefits of actions of the policyholder, insured or beneficiary that were so effective, that prevented the loss altogether. Therefore, the norm on reimbursement of expenses (Article 127) should also apply to expenses incurred when the insured event was imminent – specifically, when it had not yet started to affect the insured interest, but it was practically certain that it would.

c. Consequences of Infringement

595. As referred, Article 101 does not itself set out consequences for the infringement; it merely limits the consequences that can be set out by contract. Under its terms, there are no consequences for infringement if it did not cause loss to the insurance company (Article 101(1) and (2)). It allows the contract to provide for reduction of insurance payment in case of negligence and for the discharge of the insurance company in case of deliberate infringement. Neither Article 126, nor Article 101, refers to the degree of negligence that is necessary for the reduction of payment to apply.

596. However, it has been underscored that no consequence should apply if the infringement did not entail at least gross negligence.[250] The general standard of simple negligence for civil liability intends to protect people from damage caused to their rights and interests. However, this rationale cannot be transposed to the insured contract, of which purpose is to grant a meaningful protection against risks, against payment of the premium. As these risks may also stem from the conduct of persons connected with the insured interest, the usefulness of cover is deemed to require that the right to cover is not affected unless there is gross negligence in the failure to mitigate. That is equivalent to saying that the insurance company should cover the risk of simple (not gross) negligence of the persons in contact with the insurable interest.

597. Besides being coherent with the general coordinates of insurance contract law, the requirement of gross negligence as a minimum standard for reduction of coverage allows for a better integration with the norm on deliberate causation. The

250. J. M. Vieira Gomes, Do dever ou ónus …, 19; M. I. Oliveira Martins, Contrato de seguro e conduta …, 460–461.

scope of the norm on mitigation is contiguous to the scope of the norm on deliberate causation – which becomes evident in view of the cases of indirect (deliberate) causation. As the RJCS only discharges the insurance company in case of deliberate causation – gross negligence itself is not enough –, it would be contradictory if in very similar cases simple negligence would be enough to affect the right to the insurance payment.

598. In case the contract does not stipulate any consequence for the case of infringement of the duty, the general rules on civil liability should apply. The insurance company should not bear the loss caused by the infringement of the duty. This could be achieved by allowing the company to deduct that amount from its payment. In case (at least) gross negligence is required for the infringement to be sanctioned, it should, of course, also be required in this case.

d. The Right to Reimbursement of Mitigation Expenses

599. In what regards reimbursement of mitigation expenses, the duty to reimburse is not regarded as a mere proxy of the duty to perform in the case of the insured event, but rather as a particular adaptation of the general rules on benevolent intervention in another's affairs. As a consequence, reimbursement regards not only the compensation of expenses incurred due to mitigation measures, as referred in Article 127(1), but also the compensation for any damage caused by the mitigation measures.[251]

600. In order to qualify for reimbursement, the expenses with mitigation should be 'reasonable and proportionate' (Article 127(1)); the RJCS does not require that they are effective or urgent.[252] The parameters should not be construed restrictively, since the insurance company is safeguarded by the limitation of the maximum amount of its total payments to the value of the insured sum (Article 127(3)). The expenses should be considered reasonable when *ex ante* they seem reasonably apt to reduce the losses caused by the insured event; they should be considered proportionate when *ex ante* their amount does not seem to relevantly exceed the amount of the potential damage.

601. The norms on mitigation and reimbursement only apply directly to insurance qualified as indemnity insurance by the RJCS (Articles 123–174) – in other words, to insurance not qualified as personal insurance by the law (Articles 175 and ff.). The provisions are nonetheless applicable to personal accident insurance, as set out by Article 211(2). There is no discernible reason not to establish their application to health insurance. Some literature has considered that the extension of the norms to the realm of health insurance would be redundant, since the person at risk

251. J. M. Vieira Gomes, Do dever ou ónus … , 14–15; M. I. Oliveira Martins, Contrato de seguro e conduta … , 464–465; A. Costa Oliveira, Art. 127.º, Obrigação de reembolso, 443.
252. M. I. Oliveira Martins, Contrato de seguro e conduta … , 469 and ff.

will tend to take care of their own good health, and the contract will generally provide for the reimbursement of the expenses incurred in this regard.[253] Experience shows, however, that this is not always the case; the general duty of good faith, and the general right to reimbursement in case of benevolent intervention in another's affairs may nonetheless underpin the extension of Articles 126 and 127 to health insurance.

3. Communication of the Insured Event

a. Overview of the Applicable Norms

602. Article 100(1) establishes that the occurrence of the insured event should be notified to the insurance company by the policyholder, the insured or the beneficiary within the period of time set out by the contract; if the contract does not set a specific delay, notice should be given within eight days from the date in which the person obliged to give notice became aware of the occurrence of the insured event. Under Article 100(2), the notice should explain the circumstances surrounding the occurrence of the insured event, as well as its potential causes and its consequences. Under Article 100(3), the policyholder, the insured or the beneficiary should also provide the insurance company with all the relevant information it requests regarding the insured event and its consequences. These norms are semi-mandatory (Article 13(1)).

603. Article 101 is also semi-mandatory. However, as mentioned above, it does not itself set out the consequences for non-compliance with this duty; it merely poses limits to the sanctions that the contract may define. Under Article 101(1), the contract may determine the reduction of the insurance payment according to the damage caused by the infringement to the insurance company. Under Article 101(2), the contract may furthermore determine the discharge of the insurance company in case either of failure to comply with the duty or of incorrect compliance, but only when this is done with intent and causes significant damage to the insurer. Under Article 101(3), Article 101(1) and (2) do not apply in case the insurance company becomes aware of the insured event through another source, within the deadline set out by Article 100(1), or in case the person obliged to give notice proves that they could not reasonably have given due notice before the moment it did. Article 101(4) determines that in case of compulsory liability insurance, the insurance company cannot raise this defence against the victims, but can subsequently recover the amounts paid from the infringer, within the limits set out in Article 101(1) and (2).

253. A. Costa Oliveira, Art. 126.º, 439.

b. Scope of the Duty to Communicate the Insured Event

604. First, it should be said that these norms only apply if the insured presents a claim to the insurance company.[254] If the insured fails to notify the company, but also does not present any insurance claim, the whole case is irrelevant to the insurance contract.

605. The duty to notify is dependent on positive knowledge that the circumstances corresponding to an insured event have occurred. Positive knowledge of the circumstances that should be informed is, in fact, a general requirement for duties to inform the insurance company to apply – as has emerged from other parts of this Chapter. As referred in regard to the duty to communicate an aggravation of risk, cases where the insured or the policyholder deliberately choose to ignore certain facts (e.g., not to read a certain inspection report), in order to avoid becoming aware of a potential insured event, thus acting with *dolus eventualis*, should be equated as positive knowledge of those circumstances.

606. As to the duty to inform the insurance company upon request, it is naturally dependent on the terms of the request presented. The insurance company may ask for the information to be provided in a particular form – e.g., in writing –, or to be certified and obtained from certain authorities. In this latter case, one should rather speak of a duty to provide the company with certain documents, as is the case of death or medical certificates.

607. In any case, the company should not use these requests as an expedient to delay due performance, since that could amount to a breach of the duty to act in good faith (Article 762(2), of the Civil Code). In contracts with consumers, that would be considered an aggressive commercial practice, under Article 12(d)) of the Law on unfair commercial practices (*see* Number 27 of Annex I of the Directive on unfair business-to-consumer commercial practices).[255] According to the norm, it is in all circumstances regarded as an aggressive and hence unfair commercial practice to require a consumer who wishes to claim on an insurance policy to produce documents which could not reasonably be considered relevant as to whether the claim was valid, or to fail systematically to respond to pertinent correspondence, in order to dissuade a consumer from exercising their contractual rights. In this case, the insurance company will be deemed liable for any damage caused, besides being subject to administrative sanctions (Articles 15 and 21 of the Law on unfair commercial practices).

608. Moreover, when these practices are reflected in the conditions of the insurance contract, those conditions may be deemed unfair under the LSCT and thus be declared null and void. This applies also to insurance contracts with professional parties. In fact, these cases may be encompassed by one of the items in the list of

254. On this matter, *see* M. I. Oliveira Martins, Contrato de seguro e conduta ..., 418 and ff.
255. *See* respectively Decree-Law 57/2008, of 26 March 2008, and Directive 2005/29/EC, of 11 May 2005.

relatively forbidden clauses (grey list) in contracts with professional parties or consumers, as set out in Article 19 of LSCT.[256] Under Article 19(-b), according to the context of the standard contract, the terms that benefit the drafter by setting out excessive deadlines for performance without incurring in the consequences of delay, can be deemed forbidden.

c. Consequences of Infringement

609. In what concerns the consequences for non-compliance, Article 101 does not define them itself, but sets limits to what the contract can stipulate in this regard. One should be reminded that infringement can result either from totally failing to notify or provide the requested information, as from belated compliance, or from incorrect or incomplete provision of information.

610. In any case, the contract cannot draw consequences from non-compliance unless it causes damage to the insurance company. When non-compliance is not intentional, the extent of the damage suffered by the insurance company defines the extent of the sanctions it can impose – under Article 101(1), it cannot go beyond deducting the amount of damage from the amount it should pay to the insured.

611. Differently, when non-compliance is intentional, causation of damage to the insurance company is a requirement for the – stricter – sanction of total loss of the right to indemnity. In other words, in case of intentional infringement, the extent of the consequence suffered for infringement can go beyond the extent of the damage caused to the insurance company. For this purpose, however, the damage should be significant (Article 101(2)). The assessment of this significance should be made not in absolute terms, but vis-à-vis the sum insured.[257]

612. It is also understood that the contract cannot draw consequences from non-compliance unless there is at least negligence from the person obliged to comply. The contrary would amount to affecting cover even when the policyholder or insured had acted with normal diligence, which would counter the practical purpose of the contract. Moreover, it would not be coherent with the general norms on breach of a contractual duty, which require fault from the debtor (Article 798 of the Civil Code).[258] Article 101(3) does states that Article 101(1) and (2) do not apply in case the person obliged to give notice proves that they could not reasonably have given due notice before the actual moment they did. However, this could be construed as a reference to force majeure, and not to a minimum requirement of negligence.

---

256. A. Costa Oliveira, Art. 100.º, Participação do sinistro, 395.
257. A. Costa Oliveira, Art. 101.º, Falta de participação do sinistro, 398.
258. M. I. Oliveira Martins, Contrato de seguro e conduta ..., pp. 438–439.

613. No consequence applies if the insurance company becomes aware of the insured event through another source, within the deadline set out by Article 100. In this case, the result sought by the duty was reached by other means.

614. There are other remedies available for the insurance company, besides those mentioned in Article 101. As referred, the duty of the insurance company may not even arise while the insured event is not proved by certain documents defined by the contract (as long, of course, as that is compatible with the law on unfair commercial practices, Article 19(b) of LSCT and with the general duty to act in good faith). After that stage, if it is justifiably necessary that the insurance company requests further documents (e.g., to verify the occurrence of an exclusion of risk) and the insured or policyholder fails to provide them, the insurance company can be granted a right to withhold performance (Article 428 of the Civil Code, construed broadly).[259]

615. Besides, it should be considered that non-compliance can cause the insurance company damage that goes beyond the aggravation of the company's duty to perform, and therefore cannot be absorbed by a reduction of or discharge from this duty. That happens when failure to comply causes the company to have extraordinary expenses in the investigation of the insured event. In this case, the insurance company can resort to the general rules on liability in contract, for breach of an ancillary duty (Article 798 and ff. of the Civil Code).

B. Contractual Duties

616. The contract can set out further duties to adopt measures for control of the risk, or to provide certain elements of information to the insurance company. Unlike what happens in other insurance contract frameworks (e.g., §28 of the German Insurance Contract Act, §6 of the Austrian Contract Act, Article 65 of the Belgian Insurance Law, Article 4:101–4:103 of PEICL), the RJCS does not limit the consequences that the contract can set out for non-compliance with those duties. This does not mean that the contract is not subject to any limit in this regard. The main instrument for this control is the LSCT.

617. The LSCT applies both to contracts with consumers and with professional parties. Apart from laying down duties to communicate the contract terms, and to inform on them, the LSCT also provides for how the standard terms should be interpreted, as well as for the control of the fairness of the terms.

618. In what concerns the control of the fairness of the terms, the clauses that set out duties to inform or control the risk may be considered null and void if they lead to a substantially unbalanced distribution of the risks or rights/duties under the

259. *See* TRP 26 March 2015, 551/13.7TVPRT.P1 (Aristides Rodrigues de Almeida) – though the right to withhold performance did not seem to be the correct frame for the insurance company's defence; STJ 29 May 2012, 7615/06.1TBVNG.P1.S1 (Garcia Calejo).

contract, that would disproportionately favour the drafter of the terms – strictly speaking, the insurance company –, such as to infringe the standard of good faith (Articles 15 and 16 of LSCT).[260] For the purposes of this assessment, two general criteria will stand out as particularly relevant. On the one hand, the criterion of the practical purpose of that transaction, considering the reasonable needs that the non-drafting party aimed to satisfy with the contract, and that the drafting party should reasonably be aware of (Article 16(b)), of LSCT). On the other hand, the criterion provided by the norms that regulate the type of contract chosen. When the law lays down default norms regarding the matters provided for by the general contract terms, then a term that diverges from the default rules is presumed to be unbalanced.

619. Currently, the RJCS does not lay down default norms regarding contractual duties to control the risk or to provide information to the insurance company. However, the RJCS does provide for a set of specific duties to provide information – the duty to provide pre-contractual information on the risk, to give notice of an aggravation of risk, or to give notice on the occurrence of the insured event, and to provide the information requested in this connection – and it does set out a duty to act upon the risk – the duty to mitigate the loss. Therefore, the balance stroke by the RJCS while regulating these duties should provide the standard to gauge whether further duties created by contract should be considered disproportionately unbalanced.

620. This should be considered especially when the contract determines that the insurance company is simply discharged from its duty in case of non-compliance with a contractual duty by the insured or policyholder. In fact, this diverges significantly from the provisions of the RJCS, where non-compliance only brings about negative consequences when it is negligent and causes damage to the insured; causation of damage is only dispensed with in case of intentional non-compliance.[261]

621. There is not yet a relevant body of case law regarding contractual duties to provide information or control the risk. Nonetheless, some decisions regarding exclusions of risk are of interest in this matter, since they can materially be very similar to clauses setting out duties to control the risk. One should underline that, when adjudicating in this matter, the courts have not shied away from using the instruments provided by the LSCT, especially resorting to the interpretation of the contract terms in light of the practical purpose of the contract. Thus, for instance, in a credit insurance, the court considered that the fact of the insured extended the time limit for payment of the insured debts beyond what was authorised by the insurance contract could not be considered an infringement of the contract. Under the circumstances, considering that the total amount of outstanding debt was more than three

260. Joaquim de Sousa Ribeiro, O problema do contrato, As cláusulas contratuais gerais e o princípio da liberdade contratual, Almedina, (1999), 570 and ff; Almeno de Sá, Lei …, 33 and ff. In English, *see* Maria Inês de Oliveira Martins & Rui Pereira Dias, *Portugal*, in *Judicial Review of Commercial Contracts*, 238–239 (Hannes Wais/Thomas Pfeiffer (ed., Beck/Hart 2021).

261. For more detail, and for the distinction between different cases, *see* M. I. Oliveira Martins, Contrato de seguro e conduta …, 722 and ff.

times the amount of the insured sum, the extension of the deadline should be seen as a legitimate attempt of the insured to mitigate the insured risk – specifically, the risk of default by his debtor.[262] In other case, concerning civil liability insurance for damage caused by pets, the court has considered that a clause excluding coverage when the damage caused due to failure of the owner to comply with the statutory duties regarding pets was not compatible with the purpose of the contract. As civil liability generally implies unlawfulness, such a clause would practically devoid the insurance contract of any practical interest for the insured. Therefore, it should be corrected through interpretation, so as to imply that cover would be excluded when the owner of the animal had infringed such norms with gross negligence.[263]

262. STJ 29 March 2012, 349/10TVLSB.L1.S1 (Abrantes Geraldes).
263. STJ 3 May 2016, proc. 613/08.2TBSSB.E1.S1 (Pinto de Almeida).

Chapter 5. Obligations of the Insurer

§1. Main Obligations

I. Paying Out the Insurance Money or Performing the Services Promised

A. *Critical Overview of the Norms on Insurers' Performance and Delay*

622. The insured event triggers the insured's right to the insurance money or to the performance of the services promised (Article 99).

623. Articles 102 and 104 determine when the insurance company's obligations fall due.

624. Article 102(1) establishes that the insurance company should pay or perform the services promised after verifying the occurrence of the insured event, its causes, circumstances and consequences. For these purposes, according to the circumstances, the previous quantification of the consequences of the insured event may be necessary (Article 102(2)). Performance may be pecuniary or non-pecuniary (Article 102(3)), that is, it may consist in a certain payment or in the provision of certain services.

625. Under Article 104, the obligation of the insurance company falls due thirty days after the establishment of the facts mentioned in Article 102.

626. These norms deserve considerable criticism.[264] The time of performance of the insurance company is a particularly sensitive matter in the regulation of the insurance contract. The due satisfaction of the interests of the insured party demands a swift settlement and (if accepted) payment of the claim. The insured event causes loss to the insured party, depriving them of certain goods that they may need to have urgently replaced; moreover, the control or repair of damage may become more onerous with the passing of time.

627. Unlike other norms in comparative law, the RJCS seems to have aggravated the vulnerability of the insured party's position vis-à-vis the insurance company. Most strikingly, the RJCS does not set a maximum term upon which the duty of the insurance company falls due. The time of performance is defined by reference to the date of establishment of the insured event and its circumstances, and the establishment of these facts is a competence of the insurance company. Moreover, after the insurance company considers these facts to be established, the RJCS grants them a whole period of thirty days before performance becomes due.

264. M. I. Oliveira Martins, Contrato de seguro e conduta ..., 50–51 and 424–425; M. I. Oliveira Martins, El derecho de contrato ..., 2.2; A. Menezes Cordeiro, Seguros, 2. Ed., 754; *see also* J. C. Moitinho de Almeida, A protecção do tomador ..., at 17.

628. Furthermore, the RJCS does not set out any right to partial performance as soon as a part of the claim becomes quantified. The norm on the right to reimbursement of the expenses incurred in connection with mitigation does provide for an anticipated payment, by setting out that the insurance company should make the reimbursement before the date in which the claim should be settled, as long as the policyholder, insured or beneficiary ask for the reimbursement, the circumstances do not prevent it and the insured event is covered by the contract (Article 127(2)). However, this provision relies on very open-ended concepts, which in practice endow the insurance company with very wide discretion in regard to payment. It is far from straightforward to determine when the circumstances may prevent the reimbursement; moreover, determining whether an insured is covered by the contract would, in a strict approach, require the ascertainment that no exclusions or limitations of cover applied.

629. The position of the insured is further deteriorated by the general norm on late payment – namely, late performance of pecuniary obligations –, Article 806 of the Civil Code. When defining the compensation that the debtor should pay in these cases, the norms refer exclusively to interest on late payment (Article 806(1)). The creditor is only allowed to obtain compensation for other damage in case of late payment of indemnity for strict or tortious liability (Article 806(3)). Regardless of similarities in terminology, indemnity paid by the insurance company is the performance of a contractual obligation, and not a compensation for liability. Therefore, Article 806(3), does not directly apply to the obligation of the insurance company (except arguably in the case of direct action of the victim in compulsory civil liability insurance).

B. Corrective Mechanisms

630. Against this background, both the courts and scholarship have been highlighting that the insurance company should act in good faith in the settlement of the claim and while performing its obligations, and is liable for damage caused when it fails to do so.[265] The insurance company is deemed to delay performance without justification when it invokes an exclusion of cover but does not prove that it actually occurred.

631. The issue of the obligation not becoming due before certain facts are established by the insurance company has been addressed by applying the norm of the Civil Code on non-quantified obligations. According to the Civil Code, an obligation does not fall due before it becomes quantified; however, if the debtor is responsible for the obligation not being quantified, then it will be considered to have become due (Article 805(3)). When the insurance company is seen as unjustifiably

265. In scholarship, this point is stressed by A. Menezes Cordeiro, Seguros, 2. Ed., 754; M. I. Oliveira Martins, Contrato de seguro e conduta …, 425. In case law, *see* STJ 14 December 2016, 2604/13.2TBBCL.G1.S1 (Fernanda Isabel Pereira); STJ 23 November 2017, 4076/15.8T8BRG.G1.S2 (Salazar Casanova); TRP 25 January 2011, 3322/07.6TJVNF.P1 (Vieira e Cunha).

delaying settlement, it should be deemed responsible for delaying the moment in which the obligation should fall due, and the same consequence should apply.[266]

632. In what regards the kind of damage that should be repaired, it has been pointed out that the insured should be entitled to compensation for other damage not recompensed for by interest in delay. This conclusion is self-evident when one sustains by means of a systematic and teleologic interpretation of Article 806 that indemnity for delay is not in any case limited to interest for late payment.[267] Even if one defends that this limited compensation, as set out by Article 806(1), is the general rule, there are good reasons to extend the special rule of Article 803(3) to the main duty of the insurance company.

633. Although insurance does not give rise to a duty to indemnify in the proper sense, the duty of the insurance company has a similar purpose of compensating for damage suffered, thus protecting the creditor from consequential damage. What is more, insurance has the purpose of endowing the insured with resources in case an uncertain even comes to affect them. Therefore, limiting the damage that could be compensated in case of delay would undermine the very purpose of the insurance contract.[268]

634. Besides, finding the insurance company liable for breach of the duty to act in good faith is a way of requalifying the debt as an indemnity *proprio sensu* and thus overcoming the limitations posed by Article 806(1), of the Civil Code, through the application of Article 806(3). In fact, this framing has been used by the courts to grant damage for loss of use of the object at risk when, due to delay of the insurance company, it could not be repaired in due time.[269]

635. Article 127(2), on the reimbursement of mitigation expenses should also be construed so as to give effectiveness to its command, in view of the presumption of a reasonable legislator (Article 9(3), of the Civil Code). Therefore, the right to reimbursement should be granted when prima facie the insured event appears to be covered; in case an exclusion or limitation was actually proved, the amounts should then be returned to the insured.

636. The norms of the RJCS on the insurance company's duty to perform should therefore be corrected in view of the general norms on contract performance. However, this procedure is clearly not the most desirable, since the extent of their rights

---

266. P. Romano Martínez, Direito …, pp. 117–118; M. I. Oliveira Martins, Contrato de seguro e conduta …, 425. In case law, STJ 23 November 2017, 4076/15.8T8BRG.G1.S2 (Salazar Casanova).
267. For a suggestion in this regard, António Pinto Monteiro, Inflação e Direito civil, Separata do n.º especial do BFDUC 'Estudos em Homenagem ao Prof. Doutor António de Arruda Ferrer Correia', (1984), 32, note 1.
268. M. I. Oliveira Martins, Contrato de seguro e conduta …, 425; M. I. Oliveira Martins, El derecho de contrato …, 2.2.
269. *See* STJ 14 December 2016, 2604/13.2TBBCL.G1.S1 (Fernanda Isabel Pereira), STJ 23 November 2017, 4076/15.8T8BRG.G1.S2 (Salazar Casanova) and TRP 25 January 2011, 3322/07.6TJVNF.P1 (Vieira e Cunha), all of them regarding own-damage motor insurance.

will not be transparent for an average insured. Moreover, as the norms of the RJCS are themselves unbalanced, their correction will generally need to be enforced by the courts, which may inhibit insureds from pursuing their rights.

C. Protection of Third Parties' Rights

637. A reference should be made to Article 103, which establishes that payment made with prejudice to the rights of third parties, for instance secured creditors, that the insurance company is aware of, does not discharge it from its obligation. In fact, it is a common practice to take out insurance regarding goods that are given as collateral, and to give the secured creditor preferential rights upon the insurance payment. This practice goes along the lines of Article 692 of the Civil Code, which gives secured creditors preferential rights upon indemnity for damage caused to the goods given as collateral.[270] The third parties mentioned in Article 103 are not necessarily secured creditors; they can also be insurance beneficiaries or other persons with rights upon the insured goods, that the contract makes reference to (e.g., the owner of the goods, when insurance is taken by the lessee).

II. Rules Applicable to Indemnity Insurance

A. Indemnity Principle: Loss as a Limit

638. Non-personal insurance (damages insurance, under the separation made by Portuguese law) is guided by an indemnity principle, according to Articles 128 and following of the RJCS, which means that, as a rule, insurance companies have an obligation to pay as much as was lost, within the maximum amounts of insured capital. Therefore, compensation equals loss (i.e., insured lost interest), within the limits of the insured sum.[271]

639. In civil liability insurance, loss is determined in accordance with the general civil liability rules (Articles 562 and ff. of the Civil Code). This rule is mandatory for compulsory insurance, unless the law provides differently (Article 146(3) RJCS).[272]

270. *See* José Alves de Brito, Art. 103.º, Direitos de terceiros (in: Lei do Contrato de Seguro anotada, Almedina, 401, 2020); in case law, TRG 14 November 2013, 62/12.8TCGMR.G1 (Manso Raínho).
271. For a more detailed analysis on this topic cf., *inter alia*, Francisco Barros Ferreira Rodrigues Rocha, Do princípio indemnizatório no seguro de danos, Almedina, (2015); Francisco Rodrigues Rocha, *Da sub-rogação no contrato de seguro*, (unedited work), 2011, available at: https://www.asf.com.pt/NR/rdonlyres/E0A868B6-B492-413A-AC0C-BA5AE04CBFA2/0/FDULFranciscoRodriguesRochaDaSubrogaçãonoContratodeSeguro.pdf (accessed 25 Feb. 2022); Filipe Albuquerque Matos, Princípio do indemnizatório e seguros de danos: Algumas questões, 43, Julgar, 13 (2021); Maria Inês de Oliveira Martins, Regime jurídico do contrato de seguro em Portugal, 5, Actualidad Jurídica Iberoamericana, 221 (2016), 221 and ff.
272. *See* Art. 138(2), which refers to the 'general law', i.e., the Civil Code.

640. In spite of the terminology, the insurance payment is the performed is that which is due under the insurance contract, and should not be mistaken for indemnity under civil liability rules.[273]

641. Some Portuguese Courts, as argued by legal scholarship,[274] seek to interpret the indemnity principle substantially, giving higher relevance to the amount needed to substitute the insured item and not to its market value at the time (TRL 18 April 2013, 2212/09.2TBACB.L1-2, (Pedro Martins)).

642. The main idea underlying the principle is that an insurance contract is a means to socialise risks and compensate losses, not meant for gambling. It is not a device for the enrichment of the insured, since, if they were to receive a sum larger than the incurred loss, that could potentiate moral hazard.[275] Payment of a premium lower than what is due would furthermore give rise to an unbalanced contract, that could compromise the sustainability of the risk carrier.

643. The extent and rationale of the principle has nonetheless been debated by scholarship. On the one hand, it has been pointed out that not all insurance has a compensatory nature. That would be the case of caution insurance, as it aims to secure compliance/performance, and not to cover any loss. That would also be the case of fixed sums insurance and of insurance with repair or replacement cost cover under the principle of 'new for old', where the value of insurance compensation exceeds the present value of the loss. First-loss insurance is also mentioned in this regard, since it grants a compensation in a value that is non-proportional to the insured sum.[276] On the other hand, under Portuguese law there can be cover for intentional acts, albeit in exceptional cases, such as those set out in Articles 46(1) and 148(2) RJCS, as well as with regard to acts carried out in order to mitigate the loss, under Articles 126 and 127.[277]

644. The law has therefore adopted a nuanced and pragmatic approach regarding the indemnity principle. This is especially patent in relation to Article 131, which allows for valued policies, as long as the stipulated value is not manifestly unfounded. The indemnity principle has thus become a rather flexible rule, and public order the main limit to the autonomy of the parties.

645. With respect to property insurance, compensation is determined by the value of the interest at the time of the insured event. Loss of profit is only compensated if that is specifically stipulated (Article 130).

---

273. From the outset, its limitation by insured capital defines a completely different regime.
274. For example, António Menezes Cordeiro, Direito dos seguros, Almedina, 2 Ed (2016), 803.
275. On this not being the main function of the indemnity principle, *see*, *e.g.*, F. Albuquerque Matos, Princípio do indemnizatório, 17–18; F. Rodrigues Rocha, Do princípio ..., 78 ff.
276. Margarida Lima Rego, Contrato de seguro e terceiros, Estudo de Direito civil, Coimbra Editora, (2010), 249 ff.
277. F. Rodrigues Rocha, Do princípio ..., 77 ff.

646. There is only a *right to salvage* – that is, the right to transfer the property of the damaged goods to the insurer, and hence receive compensation for total loss – when it is stipulated in the contract (Article 129). Differently, where the insured keeps the damaged good within their property, this value is deducted from insurance compensation.

647. In this regard, the Porto Court of Appeal, decided that insurance companies must take a proactive stance in communicating the value they assign to the damaged insured items, so that the insured can make an informed decision on its sale and exercise of any right to salvage. This is a contractual ancillary duty of the insurers, stemming from the principle of good faith.[278]

648. The Court decided that it is an act of bad faith if insurance companies do not disclose their efforts to sell damage goods, and the price offered to them, during inquiry and investigation. If, while being unaware of such efforts, the insured sells the salvaged items for a lower price, the insurance company may only deduct the actual value obtained with the sale, not the value it would have received if it were to sell them first.

B. Multiple Insurance

649. The insured party can, under contractual autonomy, take out multiple insurance contracts for the same risk and interest, at the same time, and with different insurance companies.

650. Yet, they are required to give notice to all insurers, both once they become aware of that multiplicity, and once the insured event occurs and they present the insurance claim. In case of fraudulent breach of this duty,[279] the insurance companies are discharged of their duties to pay insurance indemnity, while retaining the premium (Article 133(1) and (2)).

651. If the insured has fulfilled the above-mentioned duty, they can choose which of their insurers will pay for the verified loss. The loss is then shared between the insurers. All of them are responsible pro rata, in the proportion of the amount each would have had to pay if they were the sole insurer (the same applies if any insurer becomes insolvent, where its share is proportionally shared between the other insureds) (Article 133(4) and (5)).[280]

---

278. TRP 2 February 2017, 842/14.0TJPRT.P1 (Maria Cecília Agante).

279. Identified in a case-by-case basis, and to be understood not only objectively (e.g., making two equal insurance claims), but also subjectively. *See* João Paulo Vasconcelos Raposo, *Pluralidade de Seguros: Conceito, extensão e valência*, April, Julgar online, 1 (2016), 59 ff.

280. The general civil norms on the right of recovery apply to the cases where an insurer pays a sum above its proportional responsibility.

652. Even though there is no express legal reference, scholarship has argued that where there is communication of multiple insurance, insurance companies are aware that they limit their risk accordingly, and premiums should be proportionally reduced, by way of analogy with Article 132 or by applying unjustified enrichment rules.[281] That does not necessarily lead to giving the insured who acted in good faith the right to ask for a proportional reduction of the premium to all implicated insurance companies.[282]

653. There is debate as to whether Article 133 applies equally to multiple insurance that leads to over-insurance (considering the value of the insured interest), and to the case where it does not, but rather each insurance contract complements the others and their insured sums add up to the total value of insured interest. Scholarship is divided in this regard. Some authors argue that the indemnity principle must be protected in both cases, even if it is not tangibly threatened in the second (and consequently apply 133 to both cases). Others authors consider that Article 133 only applies to multiple insurance that can objectively lead to the enrichment of the insured, and not where the contracts merely complement each other.[283]

654. Under Article 13 RJCS, Article 133 is only semi-mandatory.

655. The same rules apply to personal insurance with a compensatory nature (Article 180(2) RJCS); however, there is no duty to communicate multiple insurance in matters of health insurance (Article 215(b)).

C. Subrogation

656. Once the insurer pays the insurance compensation, it becomes automatically[284] subrogated on all the rights the insured has against the third party liable for the insured event (Article 136).[285] There is no right to subrogate, however, against the insured, when they are legally responsible for damage caused by the third party; against the insured person's spouse; civil or de facto partner; and against relatives in the ascendent and descendent line that live with the insured person in a context of shared resources (*economia comum*), unless their action was deliberate or unless it is covered by another insurance contract.

281. *See, e.g.*, A. Menezes Cordeiro, Seguros, 2. Ed., 808.
282. F. Rodrigues Rocha, Do princípio ..., 119 ff.
283. F. Rodrigues Rocha, Do princípio ..., 121–125.
284. Even though Art. 136 suggests that subrogation is automatic, and that it is predominantly accepted, some authors interpret it rather as a unilateral power that takes effect through communication to the third party. *See* F. Rodrigues Rocha, Do princípio ..., 155 ff.
285. *See also* J. M. Vieira Gomes, Da sub-rogação legal do segurador à luz da nova lei do contrato de seguro (Decreto-Lei n.º 72/2008, de 16 de Abril) (in: Paulo Otero/Fernando Araújo/João Taborda da Gama (ed.) Estudos em memória do Prof. Doutor J. L. Saldanha Sanchez, II, Coimbra Editora, 2011), 647 ff.; Francisco Rodrigues Rocha, *Da sub-rogação*.

657. Subrogation can only regard damage that both the third party and the insurer have the duty to compensate.[286]

658. The policyholder, or the insured person, are liable up until the amount paid by the insurer for any act or omission that hinders its right to subrogation (Article 136(2).

659. Partial subrogation does not preclude the rights of the insured in relation to the part of risk that is not covered, when the insured takes concurrent legal action against the liable third party, except if stipulated differently for large risks insurance (Article 136(3)). This norm is construed as implying that if the third party's assets are not sufficient to provide both for the insured's losses that were not covered by the contract and for the subrogation of the insurance company under Article 136(1), the rights of the insured take prevail.

660. The right to subrogate may be waivered by the insurer, either prior to or after the insured event happens.

661. The right set out in Article 136 has the nature of an actual right to subrogate, and not of a right of recourse, and therefore there is an effective transmission of the legal position of the insured, and an emergence of a new right. This has implications on limitation periods and the transferal of guarantees and other connected rights (Articles 594 and 582 of the Civil Code). Furthermore, third parties must be notified so that legal action can be taken against them.

D. *Over-Insurance and Under-Insurance*

1. Over-Insurance

662. As stated above, the guiding idea is that loss limits compensation, but it may happen that, when the insured event occurs, the insured sum is larger than the value of the insured interest, namely, over-insurance.

663. Over-insurance can either be original – contemporary to the negotiation of the contracts – or arise during or after the conclusion of the contract (supervening). When over-insurance is original, Article 132 should be applied, and not Articles 24 and ff. (concerning initial risk disclosure). Article 133(2) should be applied by way of analogy to cases of fraud. Articles 132 and 133 are specific to the issues posed by the inadequacy of the insured sum in regard to the value of the insured interest, and should not be set aside by the general norms of Articles 24 ff.[287]

---

286. J. Vieira Gomes, Da sub-rogação legal …, 460 ff.
287. F. Rodrigues Rocha, Do princípio …, 100–104.

664. In the case of over-insurance, if the insured event occurs, the insurance compensation shall be limited to the loss incurred, under Article 128 and the indemnity principle, and both parties can require the reduction of the contract (Article 132(1)), with *ex nunc* effects.[288] If the policyholder or insured acted in good faith, i.e., in a non-fraudulent way, the insurer should restitute all over-premiums paid during the two preceding years, while proportionally deducing administrative costs (Article 132(2)).[289]

665. Scholarship has criticised the two years limitation, considering it to be arbitrary and punitive.[290] The fact that the insurer bearing the burden of proof of bad faith cannot be seen as a special concession to the policyholder or insured, thus balancing out the regime, since this expresses the general rule on the distribution of the burden of proof.

666. Portuguese Courts have considered over-insurance remedies as a matter of public order, as a way to protect the core of the indemnity principle.[291]

667. Article 132(1) does not mention the policyholder or insured acting in good faith, contrary to cited Article 132(2). Nevertheless, a systematic interpretation of norms, as defended by some authors,[292] may indicate that the legislator also intended to limit contractual reduction mechanisms to parties who acted in good faith (i.e., in a non-fraudulent manner). This would be in line with Article 25 RJCS, which sets out specific consequences for intentional non-compliance with initial risk communication duties, as well as with Article 94, which also sets out specific consequences in case of fraudulent breach of the duty to communicate an aggravation of risk; and, lastly, it would be in line with Article 133(2), regarding fraudulent failure to inform insurance companies of the existence of multiple insurances for the same risks and interests.[293]

668. Even if the policyholder is the most interested part in requesting contractual reduction, the insurer has the duty to enact it on its own initiative, as results from the wording of Article 132(1), which refers to 'both parties', and by way of analogy with Article 92(1), which states the insurer's duty to decrease premiums in parallel with risk reduction.

669. Portuguese Courts tend not to distinguish between parties in this matter. Nonetheless a dissenting opinion issued at a Supreme Court judgment argued that it is the policyholder who should seek contractual reduction of the insured sum, since

288. Considering it to be *ex tunc*, despite Art. 132(2), vide A. Menezes Cordeiro, Seguros, 2. Ed., 806.
289. *See, e.g.*, TRG 8 June 2017, 7333/15.0T8GMR.G1 (João Diogo Rodrigues).
290. *See* A. Menezes Cordeiro, Seguros, 2. Ed., 807.
291. STJ 24 April 2012, 32/10.0T2AVR.C1.S1 (Mário Mendes).
292. *See* F. Rodrigues Rocha, Do princípio …, 100 ff.
293. In regard to the first norm, *see* Part II, Ch. 4, §2, I, Pre-contractual Duty of Disclosure; in regard to the second norm, *see* Part II. Ch. 4, §2, II, A, 1, Communication of the Aggravation of Risk.

the corresponding adjustment of the premium comes in their benefit; insurance companies would not be under a duty to reduce the sum.[294]

670. As Article 133, regarding multiple insurance, Article 132 is also only semi-mandatory under Article 13.

2. Under-Insurance

671. If, conversely, the insured sum is lower than the insured interest (under-insurance), the insurer is only bound to proportionally compensate loss.[295] The insurer does not compensate the loss fully, but only in the proportion of the ratio between the value of the insured interest and insured sum (Article 134). Therefore, unless there is a full loss of the value of the insurable interest,[296] the insurer will never pay the full amount of the insured sum. In other words, the rule of under-insurance only has practical effects in the cases of partial loss.

672. This rule is deemed to ensure the maintenance of reciprocity between the premium and the value the insurer undertakes to pay.[297]

673. Under-insurance can result from the deliberate agreement of the parties, or it can be the result of an increase in the value of the insured interest.

674. Both parties can agree to a ‘first-loss insurance’, a type of partial insurance where both are fully aware that the insured sum is lower than the value of the insured interest and agree that the loss suffered should in any case be compensated up to the value of the insured sum – thus setting aside the proportional rule.

675. Unless otherwise agreed, in home risk insurance there is an automatic update of the value of the insured house (leading to its increase or decrease), according to an index published by the ASF (Article 135(1)).

676. Article 135(2) sets out special information duties for the insurer.[298] In case of infringement, the insurer is then barred from availing themselves from the norm on under-insurance – it cannot apply the proportional rule in the case of the insured event (Article 135(3)).

---

294. STJ 8 June 2017, 7087/15.0T8STB.E1.S1 (Abrantes Geraldes), dissenting opinion by Justice Oliveira Vasconcelos.
295. Connected to the English principle of *payment subject to average. See* José Carlos Moitinho de Almeida, O novo regime jurídico do contrato de seguro, Beves considerações sobre a protecção dos segurados (in: J. C. Moitinho de Almeida (ed.) Contrato de seguro, Estudos, Coimbra Editora, 11, 2009), 23 ff.
296. F. Rodrigues Rocha, Do princípio …, 135 ff.
297. F. Albuquerque Matos, Princípio do indemnizatório, 30.
298. Under Art. 135(2), upon the conclusion of the contractual or subsequent extensions, the insurer has the duty to inform the policyholder (additionally to Arts 18–21) on the content of Art. 135(1), as well as on the value of the house insured that shall be considered in case of total loss, and on the criteria for its automatic update.

677. The rules on under-insurance and over-insurance are only applicable to property insurance, and not to liability or expenses insurance, or to personal insurance (in this last regard, *see* Article 180(2), *a contrario*).

E. Valued Policies

678. The general indemnity principle has become flexible enough to allow for valued policies. Under Article 131(1), the parties can stipulate the value that they attribute to the insured interest, which shall be considered for calculating compensation in case of insured event, as long as such value is not manifestly unfounded (Article 131(1)).

679. Valued policies are a product of private autonomy, and are limited only by the general clause of the agreed value which is not 'manifestly unfounded'. Scholarship has argued that this limitation was the way the legislator found to make sure the indemnity principle was not completely overridden.[299] In case the agreed value is indeed manifestly unfounded, its reduction can be made by courts ex officio, according to some authors.[300]

680. Traditionally seen as a mere burden of proof reversal, today valued policies are a useful mechanism to reduce litigation regarding the value of the interests, establishing it by agreement and making it unchallengeable.[301] They are a practical instrument for circumstances where it is difficult to determine loss, but they can be used in any case, since they are a reflection of private autonomy.

681. Under Article 131(2), in particular the parties can agree on any value for reconstructing or replacing the insured goods, and they can agree to disregard its loss of value due to ageing and deterioration.

682. Article 131(3) clarifies that the stipulation of an agreed value under Article 131(1) and (2) does not preclude the application of the norms on the modification of the risk.

683. The Portuguese Supreme Court of Justice addressed the topic of valued policies in regard to an antique cutlery set, to which the policyholder had attributed a value of EUR 20,000.00 but which actually cost only EUR 2,000.00.[302]

684. It was established that the policyholder's had had the initiative to ask before the conclusion of the contract if an evaluation of the items was needed. This was deemed dispensable by the insurance company, which had accepted the value of EUR 20,000.00, and had for seven years received the premiums accordingly.

---

299. *See* F. Albuquerque Matos, Princípio do indemnizatório, 19.
300. F. Rodrigues Rocha, Do princípio …, 194.
301. F. Rodrigues Rocha, Do princípio …, 186 ff.
302. STJ 8 June 2017, 7087/15.0T8STB.E1.S1 (Abrantes Geraldes).

685. After a house burglary that lead to the theft of the cutlery set, when presented with the insurance claim, the insurance company challenged the value of EUR 20,000.00. However, the Court concluded that, especially considering the item was an antique, and not a commonly traded item, the act of declining an expert evaluation should be construed as conveying a tacit agreement to the value indicated by the policyholder. The Supreme Court considered that a stricter approach to the indemnity principle would leave legitimate expectations unprotected in this case.

686. Therefore, the Supreme Court upheld the decision of the Appellate Court and denied the reduction of compensation to the value of actual loss (EUR 2,000.00). The Supreme Court further considered that since the insurance company had accepted that value and had not questioned it for seven years, it could not be considered 'manifestly unfounded' in itself.

687. Another court decision considered that if a machine had been insured for its value as a used item, as not as a new item, that did not qualify as a case of valued policy, nor as under-insurance. Therefore the insurance company had the duty to pay an amount equivalent to the loss incurred, and could not decrease compensation in proportion to the machine's substitution value.[303]

III. Rules Applicable to Fixed Sums Insurance

688. Unlike non-personal insurance, in personal insurance, compensation can either obey the indemnity principle or be a fixed sum, where a predetermined amount is to be paid, regardless of the concrete loss incurred (Article 175).

689. Fixed sum insurance can be combined both with indemnity insurance and with fixed sum insurance in relation to the same risk. The insurer can accumulate the compensation received under such contracts. This is a case of multiple insurance different from the one mentioned above; however, similar information duties apply, as set out by Article 180(3).

690. According to Article 181(1), in fixed sums insurance the insurer does not have a right to subrogate into the rights of the insured against a third party. In the original version of the provision, the right to subrogation could be stipulated in the contract; after 2015, this is only lawful in regard to personal indemnity insurance.

303. TRG 26 April 2018, 3888/17.2T8GMR.G1 (Alcides Rodrigues).

691. Portuguese Courts have considered that a compulsory sports insurance (regulated by Decree-Law 10/2009, of 12 January), which covers risks of personal accident or disease, and is therefore personal insurance, can be taken out as a fixed sums insurance.[304]

§2. Information Duties

I. Different Sources of Information Duties

692. The most important category of ancillary duties of the insurer is that of the duties to inform in very broad sense, comprising the provision of information, as well as the explanation of certain points.

693. There are nowadays many different sources of the duties to inform, ranging from the LSCT (Articles 5 and 6), to all sorts of provisions on protection of consumers and other weaker parties[305] and to the RJCS and the Insurance Distribution Act (Articles 37(3), and the provisions it refers to). As is the case with norms of which the scope is the protection of a vulnerable party, those norms do not apply alternatively, but rather cumulatively, guarding the contracting party against different sources of danger. The RJCS itself sets out the cumulative application of the different norms, in its Preamble, in Article 3, and, regarding the duties to inform, in Article 19.[306]

694. Moreover, even in the absence of these provisions, the general standard of good faith can function as a source of duties for the insurer to inform the policyholder, in view of the asymmetry of information between the parties. In order for

304. STJ 11 November 2019, 654/16.6T8ABT.E1.S1, (Tomé Gomes); TRE 30 January 2020. 8818/17.9T8STB.E1 (Conceição Ferreira); TRP 12 October 2020. 6075/15.0T8VNG.P1, (Miguel Baldaia de Morais).

305. Apart from the norms mentioned in the text, some other acts are also especially relevant: the Consumer Protection Act (Arts 7 and 8); Decree-Law 57/2008, concerning unfair business-to-consumer commercial practices (Arts 7–10; some misleading commercial practices that consist of misleading actions – and not omissions – are also forbidden in regard to business-to-business transactions); Decree-Law 7/2004 on electronic commerce in the internal market and on the processing of personal data; Decree-Law 95/2006, concerning distance marketing of consumer financial services (Arts 11–18). *See above* General Introduction, §5, Protection of Vulnerable Parties. *See* Joana Galvão Telles, Deveres de informação das partes (in: Margarida Lima Rego (ed.) Temas de Direito dos seguros, A propósito da nova Lei do Contrato de Seguro, Almedina, 2016), 339 and ff; on information duties in case of distance insurance contracts, *see* Alexandre Soveral Martins, Contratação à distância e contrato de seguro, 10, Estudos de Direito do Consumidor, (2016), passim.

306. Article 3 establishes that '[RJCS] provisions are without prejudice of the application to the insurance contract of the norms on standard contract terms, consumer protection and distance contracts, as set out in those norms'. Under Art. 19(1) 'in the case of a distance contract, the information mentioned in [Art. 18] is without prejudice to the one mentioned in special norms that may apply'. Under Art. 19(2), 'in case the policyholder qualifies as consumer as defined by the applicable statutes, the information mentioned in [Art. 18] is without prejudice to the one mentioned in other norms, for example in the Consumer Protection Act.'

these duties to arise, some general requirements must be met: the lack of information by the policyholder should be apparent to the insurer, as should be the critical role of the information for the decision-making of the policyholder, or for the preservation of their person or property, or for the accomplishment of the purpose of the contract; moreover, this only applies if the insurer can be reasonably required to provide the information at stake.[307]

695. Apart from these general norms, other laws create special duties of information for certain types of insurance – primarily, for life insurance, be it in its role of savings instrument (*see* the norms on insurance-based investment products, that will be further mentioned in Part V, Chapter 4, §3, Life Insurance Savings Products) be it in its role of security for a long-term lender (*see* Decree-Law 222/2009, on the protection of consumers that take out life insurance in connection with their home acquisition loan).[308]

696. When insurance qualifies as a distance contract and the policyholder is a consumer, the insurer is furthermore bound by the pre-contractual information duties set out in Decree-Law 95/2006, of 29 May, concerning the distance marketing of consumer financial services.[309] Article 28 of Law 7/2004 of 7 January on electronic commerce in the internal market and on the processing of personal data sets out further information duties for contracts concluded by electronic or digital means. The norm does not apply, however, to contracts concluded by email, or other individual means of communication (Article 30 of the same Law).

697. It comes as no surprise that some of the duties stemming from these different sources tend to overlap.[310]

698. Among the norms setting out information duties of the insurer, the leading role has so far belonged to the LSCT, which is the tool that the courts more readily resort to when it comes to the enforcement of information duties.[311]

699. In fact, the issues of failure to provide the due information typically arise when the insurer tries to avail itself from a contract clause that works to its advantage, and to the disadvantage of the policyholder, and the policyholder claims that they were not duly informed on that point. As explained above (*see* Part II, Chapter

307. In regard to these general requirements, which were in text adapted to the context of insurance contracts, J. Sinde Monteiro, Responsabilidade ... , 361.

308. Decree-Law 222/2009, of 11 November 2009; *see also* the Regulatory Standard 6/2008-R, of 24 April, issued by the ASF, on the rules applicable to life insurance covering the risk or death, incapacity or unemployment in connection with loan agreements, as well as the ASF Communication ('Carta Circular') 2/10, of 25 February 2010.

309. For the definition of 'distance contract', *see* Art. 2(a) of Decree-Law 95/2006, which reproduces Art. 2(a) of Directive 2002/65/EC, of 23 September 2002.

310. Eduarda Ribeiro, Art. 19.º, Remissão (in Lei do Contrato de Seguro anotada, Almedina, 129, 2020), 114.

311. Arnaldo da Costa Oliveira/Eduarda Ribeiro, Art. 22.º, Dever especial de esclarecimento, Comentários complementares (in: Lei do Contrato de Seguro anotada, Almedina, 129, 2020), 131.

1, §5, Inclusion and Content Control of Standard Terms and Conditions of Insurance Contracts), the consequence set out by the LSCT for the cases either of failure to communicate the clause, or of failure to inform on its content, is the *exclusion from the contract of the clause affected* (Article 8 of LSCT).

700. This regime generally leads to results that are considered desirable. First of all, it grants a very effective protection to the weaker party, since it simply expunges the contract from the clause that was contrary to their interests. Additionally, as it is based on simply establishing that a certain clause was not duly informed, it is not particularly demanding on the party that intends to enforce it. It not only dispenses with the complicated requirements that must be established for civil liability, as it also inverts the burden of proof in what regards its own requirements, by placing upon the drafter (the insurer) the burden of proving that the clauses at stake were actually communicated (Article 5(3) of LSCT). The inversion of the burden of proof is deemed to apply likewise to the breach of duty to inform.[312] Furthermore, by simply removing the non-communicated clause that was detrimental to the policyholder, and leaving the remaining clauses as they are, the regime does not attempt to rebalance the contract, thus playing a desirable dissuasive role upon non-compliance. Finally, it should be added that the courts are quite familiar with the LSCT, which has been in force for more than thirty years now.

701. However, the LSCT does leave room for other legal tools that set out and enforce information duties of the insurer. In fact, it only refers to information on contract clauses, and not to information on the functioning of statutory norms. Moreover, there are some rare cases in which the mere expunging of a certain clause is not the most adequate means to protect the policyholder 's interests.

702. We shall now focus on the duties of information (in broad terms) created by the RJCS, since it is a source of duties that are specific to the insurance contract. The limitations of the RJCS became especially clear after the entry into force of the Act on insurance distribution. The duties of the insurer in its role of insurance distributor encompass more than the points mentioned on the provisions of the RJCS, and its duty to actively explain the implications of the contract is more demanding than what results from the RJCS (*see* Articles 30(1)(a), 30(1)(c), 30(1)(f), 31(6) and 37(3) of IDF[313]). However, the RJCS is still the starting point of the regulation of the insurance contract; besides, the Act on insurance distribution cannot apply in regard to the conclusion of contracts that took place before the Act entered into force.[314]

312. STJ 13 September 2016, 1262/14.1T8VCT-B.G1.S1 (Alexandre Reis); STJ 4 May 2017, 1961/13.5TVLSB.L1.S1 (Lopes Rego).

313. Mentioned below in Part VII, Ch. 2, Insurance Intermediaries and the Insurance Contract, in regard to insurance intermediaries.

314. Law 7/2019, of 16 January 2019, which approved IDF, established that its provisions would take effect retroactively, from 1 Oct. 2018, so as to conform to the time limit for the transposition of the IDD (Art. 16(1)). This (questionable) solution is however limited by the general rules on protection

II. In Particular, the RJCS as a Source of Information Duties

A. General Pre-contractual Duties of Information: Scope

703. The general norms on the matter are Articles 18, 20, 21 and 22. They set out pre-contractual duties to inform and to clarify, and provide for the consequences of their infringement. They are supplemented by Article 91, which lays down duties to inform throughout the contract.

704. Article 18(1) establishes that 'without prejudice to the items that should mandatorily be included in the policy, the insurer should make all the necessary clarifications and inform the policyholder on the conditions of the contract, namely on: a) the insurer's name and its legal form; b) the scope of the risk it undertakes to cover; c) the exclusions and limitations of cover; d) the total value of the premium or, in case it is not possible, the method for its calculation, as well as the modalities for payment and the consequences of default; e) the *bonus-malus* system that may apply to the contract, and a description of how it functions; f) the minimum insured capital in compulsory insurance; g) the maximum amount that the insurer undertakes to pay in each contract period; h) the duration of the contract and the rules on renewal, withdrawal from the contract and termination of a contract that is to last for an indefinite period or that is subject to automatic renewal; i) the rules on assignment of the contract; j) the rules on presenting out-of-court complaints, the corresponding redress mechanisms and the competent supervising authority; l) the rules on the law applicable to the contract, as set out by Articles 5–10, mentioning the law that the insurer proposes to be chosen'.

705. Article 20 adds the duty to inform on the place and State where the insurer's head office is located, as well as on its address and, where appropriate, on the branch concluding the contract and on its address.[315]

706. Under Article 21(1), information should be provided in writing, in clear terms and in Portuguese,[316] before the policyholder binds themselves to the contract. The insurance application presented by the policyholder should refer to the information that the insurer must provide, so as to prove that it was duly provided (Article 21(4)). Under Article 21(2), distance contracts are regulated by special statutes.

707. Finally, Article 22 sets out a special duty of clarification. Under Article 22(1), 'when the complexity of the cover and the amount of premium or the insured sum justify such a duty, and the medium of conclusion of the contract enables it,

---

of expectations and of acquired rights, and cannot imply that duties of conduct and the consequences of their infringement, are applied retroactively – *see* Francisco Luís Alves, Art. 16.º, Produção de efeitos (in: Pedro Romano Martínez/Filipe Albuquerque Matos (ed.) Lei da distribuição de seguros anotada, Almedina, 57, 2019), 57.

315. On this norm, *see* J. Galvão Telles, Deveres ..., 335 and ff.

316. Except when the policyholder requests its provision in a different language, and the parties agree to this – *see* Arts 21(4) and 36(2).

before the conclusion of the contract the insurer should inform the policyholder of which modalities of insurance, among those it offers, are suited for the particular cover intended'. Under Article 22(2), 'for the purposes of complying with this duty, the insurer should not only answer all queries placed by the policyholder, but also call their attention to the scope of the cover that was offered, namely to exclusions of cover, limitation periods, and rules on termination of the contract by decision of the insurer; in cases of succession of insurance contracts, or of their modification, the insurer should furthermore call their attention to the risks of interruption of the cover'. Under Article 22(3), when the cover offered refers to different kinds of risk, the insurer should inform, in detail, about the relationship between the different kinds of cover implied. Article 22(4) establishes that this duty does not apply in regard to insurance of large risks, neither in regard to insurance contracts concluded with the intervention of insurance intermediaries, where only the latter are under duties of informing the policyholder, as set out by the IDF.

708. At least one aspect of these provisions should be singled out: namely, the almost imperceptible reference to a duty to 'make all the necessary clarifications', set out in Article 18(1). The duty to clarify is generally construed as a duty to inform that is *not dependent upon request,* with the purpose of *preventing its creditor from acting against their interests.*[317] The norms do not specify the subject matter of this general duty to clarify – it shall regard all matters where clarification is deemed necessary.[318] It seems therefore that the insurer faces a general duty to clarify with a much broader scope than that of the much more densely regulated general duty to inform, or that of the special duty to clarify (Article 22) – since the general duty to clarify is both spontaneous and not limited to specified matters. It should also be said that, although a duty to inform can be strictly construed as a simple duty to communicate certain aspects, some authors construe the duty to inform in broader terms, as a duty of calling the attention to certain points and providing complete information, according to the needs of the customer. Thus construed, the duty to inform can become almost indistinguishable from the duty to clarify.[319]

B. General Pre-contractual Duties of Information: Consequences of Their Infringement

709. The consequences for the infringement of these duties are set out by Article 23. Article 23(1) provides that the insurer is liable for damages in case of infringement of the duties to inform and to clarify. Article 23(2) adds that in case of infringement of the duties to inform, the policyholder is entitled to terminate the contract, unless either such infringement did not reasonably affect the decision to

317. J. Sinde Monteiro, Responsabilidade ..., 359; A. Costa Oliveira/E. Ribeiro, Art. 22.°, Dever especial de esclarecimento, 125.

318. Differently, J. Galvão Telles, Deveres ..., 334–335, seems to limit the duty to clarify to the points mentioned in Art. 18; however, the wording of the provision otherwise points to the interpretation made above.

319. A. Costa Oliveira/E. Ribeiro, Art. 22., 125; A. Costa Oliveira, Art. 22.°, 129–30. Differently, clearly separating the duty to inform from the duty to clarify, J. Galvão Telles, Deveres ..., 353–355.

enter into the contract, or the insurance claim was presented by a third party. Under Article 23(3), the policyholder has a deadline of thirty days from the receipt of the policy to terminate the contract; termination has retroactive effect, giving the policyholder the right to the reimbursement of all the premium paid. Under Article 23(4), the foregoing also applies in case the conditions of the policy do not correspond with the information given before the conclusion of the contract.

710. It stands out that the right to termination is set out in very narrow terms. It is strictly attached to the duty to inform and does not refer to the duty to clarify. It is premised upon the condition that the policyholder, within the given deadline, verifies whether they received any information on the points mentioned by the law, and whether the information received matches the text of the policy. This remedy is clearly not fit to address cases where the insurer did inform the policyholder on certain points, but did not clarify its implications (e.g., in view of the scope of an exclusion clause). The fact that the policyholder was not given the conditions to understand the relevant aspects of the contract will normally only become apparent once they intend to exercise their rights under the contract; the policyholder will not detect it by themselves. Therefore, if one construes the duty to inform as more than a mere duty to communicate, the limitation of the right to terminate to thirty days from receipt of the policy does not seem to have a rationale.

711. Nevertheless, if the breach of the duty to clarify is serious enough so as to compromise the purpose of the contract, it can give rise to a right to termination for a serious cause (Article 116).

712. The central remedy for the breach of information duties in a broader sense is therefore the right to damages, under the general rules on civil liability. The claim of the policyholder depends on the proof of the general requirements of civil liability: unlawfulness, fault, causation, and damage. The requirement of damage raises some interesting questions. The breach of pre-contractual duties to inform generally gives right to reliance damages. The aggrieved party has a right to be put in the position they would have been in, had they not trusted upon having entered into a contract composed of certain terms. This implies that, if the policyholder event has meanwhile occurred and the policyholder proves it, had they been correctly informed, they would have entered into a different contract that would have granted them the desired cover, the insurer should reimburse them for the premium paid (as damage incurred), and for the amount the policyholder would be entitled to under a different insurance contract (as profit lost), deduced from the premium they would have paid for such a contract.[320] However, this places quite a demanding burden of proof upon the policyholder, who must prove that, by the time they concluded the insurance contract, there was an alternative offer in the market that would suit their

320. It is widely accepted in Portuguese scholarship that reliance damages also comprise compensation for loss of profit – as is, in fact, reflected in Arts 899, 900, 909 and 910 of the Civil Code. *See* Paulo Mota Pinto, Interesse contratual negativo e interesse contratual positivo, II, Coimbra Editora, (2008), 1088 and ff.

interests, that their application would plausibly have been accepted, and that such contract would have been in force until the insured event took place.

713. When the policyholder is not able to prove those facts, all they will have access to will be the compensation for the damage incurred, consisting of the reimbursement of the premium paid. Still, this amount does not grant them compensation for loss of profit and its payment does not incentivise the insurer to duly comply with its duty to inform.

714. In this context, scholarship has been debating whether the policyholder should have the right to be placed in the position where they would have been had the duty to inform been duly complied with and had a contract corresponding to their interests been put in place – which would roughly correspond to the granting of expectation damages.[321] By the means of a restoration in kind, this furthermore allows for the expunging of a (limitative) contract term, or even for the attribution of advantages promised to the policyholder at a pre-contractual stage, but which in the end were not mentioned in the policy. This solution is controversial, since it would correspond to the situation that would have existed had the insurer not only duly performed its duty to inform, but furthermore conformed the contract in accordance with the interests of the policyholder – which, in many instances, is not plausible. All in all, this solution therefore implies that the hypothetical will of the insurer is overridden as a consequence of the infringement of its duties, and that the insurer is called upon performing beyond the limits set out by the contract as it was concluded. Although controversial,[322] this solution is favoured by insurance law scholarship,[323] and backed by the fact that Article 87(3) on group insurance grants a similar protection to the insured, since it establishes that the infringement of duties of information does not entail any limitation of the cover that had been promised to them.[324] In fact, this solution is the one that better protects the reliance of the policyholder, considering that their investment in the contract they entered into becomes irreversible once the insured event has occurred. After that moment, the risk at stake cannot be insured somewhere else. Moreover, this solution is in line with Articles 8 and 9 of the LSCT, which set out the simple expunging of non-informed SCT. The

321. The correspondence is not total – *see* P. Mota Pinto, Interesse … , II, 1413.

322. P. Mota Pinto, Interesse … , II, 1412 and ff; J. Galvão Telles, Deveres … , 358–360.

323. Margarida Lima Rego, O contrato e a apólice de seguro (in: Margarida Lima Rego (ed.) Temas de Direito dos seguros, A propósito da nova Lei do Contrato de Seguro, Almedina, 2016), 30–31; Francisco Barros Ferreira Rodrigues Rocha, Do princípio indemnizatório no seguro de danos, Almedina, (2015), 142–143; M. I. Oliveira Martins, El derecho de contrato … , 1.2.; J. Galvão Telles, Deveres … , 359–360. Similarly, Júlio M. V. Gomes, O dever de informação … , 422, construes Art. 24(4) – which establishes that the insurer is liable towards the policyholder in case it does not inform them on the consequences of the infringement of their pre-contractual duty of disclosure – as giving rise to reparation in the amount of the payment due if a valid and enforceable insurance contract granting the cover at stake had been entered into.

324. *See* Part II, Ch. 6, §4, Group Insurance; in scholarship, *see* Nuno Trigo dos Reis, Os deveres de informação no contrato de seguro de grupo, Journal, Start Page (s.d.), retrieved 22 Dec. 2009 from ww.isp.pt/NR/exeres/C07B7A30-CA6F-4C81-975D-46002195D32E.htm, 52.

rationale of the norms of the LSCT, to incentivise the debtor of information to duly comply with its duties, should also apply here.[325]

C. General Ongoing Duties of Information

715. The general norms on pre-contractual duties of information are supplemented by Article 91. According to Article 91(1), the insurer should inform the policyholder on the modifications of the insured risk that affect the subject matter of the information provided under Articles 18–21 and 24. Taken literally, the provision would not really make much sense, since there is not a direct implication between changes on the insured risk and changes in most elements referred to in Articles 18–21 (or vice-versa). Therefore, scholarship has construed this provision as creating a duty of information regarding any change in the elements referred to in Articles 18–21.[326] The norm does not provide for any specific consequence for the breach of this duty. Therefore, the general remedy of civil liability for the damage caused applies.

716. Furthermore, according to Article 91(2), 'the insurer should inform any third party identified in the policy as a beneficiary under an irrevocable designation, or as the holder of a right to the insured sum, on any modification of the contract that works to their disadvantage, as long as the nature of the contract or the nature of the modification do not oppose it'. Article 91(3) clarifies that the foregoing does not apply if a duty of confidentiality was stipulated on the contract.

717. The information provided should abide the general rule set out in Article 120. Namely, it should be provided in writing or by another durable medium (Article 120(1)). The insurer is only obliged to provide such information if their addressee is duly identified in the policy; the information is deemed as having been duly provided once they are sent to the address mentioned in the policy (Article 120(2)).

718. A modification deemed of particular interest in this regard is the circumstance of the policyholder having defaulted on the premium.[327] Nonetheless, as a general rule, a third party is only allowed to keep the contract in force by paying the premium that has been defaulted on by the policyholder when the insurance contract specifically provides on that case (Article 55(2)). Moreover, in life insurance (as well as in any other personal insurance which is a fixed sums insurance), when the third party is a beneficiary under an irrevocable designation, they have the right to be notified by the insurer on the default on the premium (Article 204).

325. M. I. Oliveira Martins, El derecho de contrato ... , 1.2.
326. A. Costa Oliveira, Art. 91.º, Dever de informação, 355–356.
327. A. Costa Oliveira, Art. 91.º, Dever de informação, 357.

D. Special Norms for Personal Insurance

719. The general norms on the duty to inform are flanked by other norms that specifically provide for personal insurance. That is the case of Articles 78 and 87, on group insurance, of Article 135, on home protection insurance, of Article 178, on information on medical examinations in personal insurance, and of Articles 185 and 186, on life insurance. None of these special norms sets out what shall be the consequence for their infringement. Therefore, the general rules on liability for breach of duties of information apply in this regard. In what concerns Article 185, as it provides for pre-contractual duties of information, supplementing Article 18, Article 22 should apply in its regard.

E. Administrative Offence under Supervisory Law

720. Finally, one should add that the infringement of the duties to inform or clarify the general public, the policyholders, the insured or the beneficiaries of insurance contracts or capital redemption operations qualifies as a serious administrative offence under Article 370(aa) of the LBIR. The applicable administrative fine can range between EUR 15,000 and EUR 1,500,000.

Chapter 6. Insurance and Third Parties

§1. Insurance for the Account of a Third Party

721. As stated in Article 47(1), 'whenever the insured interest belongs to the policyholder, then the contract is made for the policyholder's own account'. This concept should be taken with a pinch of salt, as signifying rather that, in this case, the *person identified by the contract as the holder of the insured interest is the policyholder*, who will then be treated as the insured.[328] In fact, this person may or may not actually be the holder of the insured interest; if they do not hold such interest, the contract will be void due to absence of an insured interest (Article 43(1)); it will not be deemed as having been taken for the account of a third party.

722. Differently, in the case of an insurance for the account of a third party, the person whose insurable interest the contract aims to protect is a third party to the contract.

723. As well as defining insurance for the policyholder's own account, Article 47 also sets out criteria regarding when to apply the rules on insurance for the account of a third party and on insurance for the policyholder's own account. According to Article 47(2), 'unless the contrary results from the contract or from its surrounding circumstances, a contract is deemed to have been taken out for the policyholder's own account'.

724. The importance of this norm becomes clear in face of Article 43(1), described in Chapter 2. Under its terms, the contract is deemed void when the insured does not hold an insurable interest that is affected by the risk covered. It is therefore critical to identify the person that the contract qualifies as insured – either the policyholder, or a third party –, so that their actual insurable interest can be ascertained.

725. 'In case the policyholder's interest upon the subject matter of the contract is only partial, and unless the law or the contract provide differently, the contract is deemed to have been taken out for the account both of the policyholder and for the account of all other holders of the insured interest' (Article 47(3)). This is relevant, for instance, in relation to insurance taken out in regard to a jointly owned asset by one of the co-owners – if the insured sum regards the whole value of the asset, the contract is deemed as having been taken out for the account of all the co-owners.[329]

726. Article 48 specifically addresses insurance for the account of a third party. Article 48(1) establishes that 'in insurance for the account of a third party the policyholder acts for the account of the insured, who may be a determined or an undetermined party'. In this case, the contract identifies a third party as the holder of the

328. Emphasising the need to differentiate between the identification of the insured, and the question of actually holding the insured interest, M. Lima Rego, O seguro por conta de outrem, 246–247.
329. M. Lima Rego, O seguro por conta de outrem, 254.

insured interest. The insured will be an undetermined party when the contract is taken out for the account of 'whom it may concern'. In this case, the insured is identified *per relationem*. That is, the insured shall be whoever holds a certain relationship to the subject matter of the risk, and will therefore change accordingly.[330]

727. The ensuing paragraphs of Article 48 provide for the distribution between the policyholder and the insured of the rights and obligations arising from the insurance contract. Under Article 48(6), if the insurance is taken out for the account of 'whom it may concern' or if the contract refers without further specification to the interest of the policyholder and the interest of a third party, then those paragraphs shall apply if it can be concluded from the circumstances that the interest insured is that of a third party.

728. Under Article 48(2), 'the policyholder should fulfil the duties arising from the contract, with the exception of those that can only be fulfilled by the policyholder'. Under Article 48(3), 'except when the contract provides otherwise, with due regard of Article 43 [on insurable interest], the insured shall be entitled to the rights arising from the contract; the policyholder, even in possession of the policy, shall not be entitled to claim those rights without consent from the insured'.

729. By setting out that a third party shall be directly entitled to rights arising from the contract, these norms reflect the general structure of the contracts to the benefit of a third party (Article 443 and following of the Civil Code).[331] Although Portuguese law broadly allows for the direct attribution of rights to persons that were not parties to the contract, it does not allow for the attribution of duties without the consent of the affected persons (who, by expressing their consent, then become parties to the contract). There is no exception to the privity of contracts in this last regard. Therefore, in spite of the wording of Article 48(2), the contract does not create actual duties, that could be enforced against the insured. What it can create are duties which, in case of non-compliance, give rise to the loss of the right to the insurance benefits, or to their reduction. This is even the case for the duty to pay the premium, when the consequences of non-compliance are defined by the incorrectly termed 'special regime' (Articles 58–61 – *see above* Part II, Chapter 4, §1, III, Default on Premium Payments). Duties with this structure are generally qualified as 'onus' or 'charges' by scholarship.[332] In this case, the disadvantage imposed on the insured in case of failure to adopt the conduct prescribed is contained in the advantage attributed to them by the contract.

330. M. Lima Rego, O seguro por conta de outrem, 256–257; in the context of transport insurance, Francisco Rodrigues Rocha, Algumas notas em torno da cláusula CIF e do seguro de transporte de mercadorias (in: Januário da Costa Gomes (ed.) Temas de Direito dos transportes, III, Almedina, 247, 2015), 272.

331. M. I. Oliveira Martins, O seguro de vida …, 61 and ff.; M. Lima Rego, O seguro por conta de outrem, 253 and ff. On case law, *see* TRL 7 March 2019, 7459/16.2T8LSB-A.L1-2 (Tibério Silva).

332. Diogo Leite de Campos, Contrato a favor de terceiro, 2. Ed., Almedina, (1991), 113–119; J. Moitinho de Almeida, O contrato …, 56 e ss.; M. I. Oliveira Martins, O seguro de vida …, 67–69; M. Lima Rego, O seguro por conta de outrem, 257. For a discussion on these categories, *see* M. I. Oliveira Martins, Contrato de seguro e conduta …, 779 and ff.

730. In this regard, one should also point out that the RJCS frequently 'summons' the insured to comply with duties of information and control of the insured risk. That happens, significantly, in regard to the initial duty of disclosure of the risk (Article 24(1)), of the duty to inform on modifications of the risk (Article 93(1)) or to inform on the occurrence of the insured event (Article 100(1)), or of the duty to mitigate the risk (Article 126(1)).[333] Moreover, the insured event caused by the insured is excluded from cover (Article 46). These solutions are well understandable, in view of the normal proximity of the insured to the subject matter of the contract. They are also compatible with the structure of the contract for the benefit of third parties, since non-compliance with those duties can only entail the loss of advantages created by the contract.

731. As set out by Article 48(5), 'unless the law or the contract provide differently, [the insurance company] can raise any exception based upon the insurance contract against the insured, except when these exceptions regard another relationship between the insurance company and the policyholder, different to the insurance contract'. This is in line with the general norms on contracts to the benefit of third parties (Article 449 of the Civil Code). It would imply that the insurance company could invoke against the insured any grounds for avoidance, nullity, modification or termination of the insurance contract, as well as any clause of the insurance contract.

732. This linear approach is, however, questioned in regard to the particular function of some insurance contracts, that typically have the structure of insurance for the account of third parties.

733. That is the case, for instance, of Directors' and Officers' (D&O) insurance, which is entered into by the company for the protection of its directors and officers against risks of liability[334] (and which can arguably be furthermore qualified as group insurance[335]). The insurance cover is generally offered not out of altruism, but rather as a part of the remuneration of the directors and officers, in view of the growing number of sources of liability, and of the considerable defence costs arising from liability claims. Therefore, case law has considered that the insurance company cannot invoke an arbitration clause against the insured, when it does not prove that the insured agreed to it, since, in view of the costs of arbitration, this could amount to denying the possibility of the insured to assert their insurance claim.[336]

---

333. On how to coordinate the intervention of different persons charged with these duties (policyholder, insured, beneficiary), *see* M. I. Oliveira Martins, Contrato de seguro e conduta ..., 481 and ff.

334. Maria Elisabete Gomes Ramos, O seguro de responsabilidade civil dos administradores, Entre a exposição ao risco e a delimitação da cobertura, Almedina, (2010), 415–417.

335. The qualification as group insurance may not be accepted by the authors who consider a necessary feature of group insurance that the risks covered are not strongly correlated, to the extent that such authors deem that the risks of liability of directors and officers of a determinate company/group of companies are strongly correlated. *See below* Part II, Ch. 6, §4, I, Concept of Group Insurance.

336. TRL 7 March 2019, 7459/16.2T8LSB-A.L1-2 (Tibério Silva).

734. Moreover, Articles 111(2) and 48(4) set out some limitations in regard to the possibility to terminate the contract. Article 111(2) establishes that, 'without prejudice to the norms on group insurance and to the specificities of life insurance, when the policyholder is not the person identified in the policy as the insured, then termination of the insurance contract by mutual agreement [between the insurance company and the policyholder] cannot take place without the insured's consent'. In turn, Article 48(4) establishes that 'unless the contract provides differently, the policyholder can oppose the automatic prorogation of the contract and terminate it, even against the will of the insured'. These norms limit the discretionary powers of the policyholder to terminate the insurance contract, so as to grant some stability to the protection of the insured's interest. Those powers are, however, not absolutely suppressed – which is understandable in view of the principle of freedom of contract (i.e., of the freedom not to be perpetually bound by a contract[337]), allied to the fact of the policyholder is the person charged with paying the premiums.

§2. Third-Party Beneficiary Clauses

735. Third-party beneficiary clauses only apply to fixed sums insurance. In indemnity insurance, unless in cases of direct action of the victim in liability insurance, the right to insurance payment can only belong to the insured, since they are the person whose damage is to be repaired.

736. Therefore, third-party beneficiary clauses will be handled in respect of life insurance (below, Part V, Chapter 4, §1, IV, Third-Party Beneficiary Clauses). As life insurance is the paradigm of fixed sums insurance, it is where the norms of the RJCS on third-party beneficiary clauses have their seat.

§3. Direct Action

737. The law only entitles the victim with the right to direct action in the case of liability insurance. The subject shall thus be handled in this setting (below, Part III, Chapter 4, Liability Insurance).

§4. Group Insurance

I. Concept of Group Insurance

738. The RJCS devotes a whole Chapter to this issue: Chapter VII (Articles 76–to 90), titled 'Group insurance'.

739. According to Article 76 group insurance covers the risks of a group or persons that share a certain link to the policyholder, as long as this link differs from the

337. M. Lima Rego, O seguro por conta de outrem, 259–260.

link created by the insurance itself. Article 176(2), regarding personal insurance, further adds to this description, stating that insurance concerning a family unit or a group of persons sharing resources in informal cohabiting relationships is considered individual insurance.

740. In other words, group insurance rests upon a contract between the insurance company and a policyholder; this contract may be the insurance contract itself or a framework contract. However, the insurable interest does not pertain to the policyholder, but to the third parties who are the members of the group – the insureds. Therefore, group insurance is always insurance for the account of third parties.

741. These parties should all share a link of the same nature with the policyholder; this connection defines them as a group. Article 176(2) clarifies that a family or cohabiting relationship does not form a group for the purposes of group insurance. Apart from these cases, that link to the policyholder can be of different nature (e.g., it is quite common that the insureds are clients of the policyholder, or that they are their employees or members); it can be more or less permanent (e.g., the group may only exist for a certain sports event, or journey, as it may regard a set of long-term contracts with the policyholder) and does not have to pre-exist the moment in which the subject acquires the quality of insured (e.g., they can become a client/worker of the policyholder and simultaneously express its adhesion to group insurance). As to the minimal number of insureds necessary to form a group, it may be formed by only two members.[338]

742. The RJCS does not refer to further characteristics of group insurance; however, scholarship and the courts refer to other traits that should be present in order to identify group insurance. First of all, for the reference to the group to have any materiality, risks should be homogeneous – specifically, they should refer to interests of the same kind (e.g., refer to the same kind of civil liability). Furthermore, the risks of the member of the group should be covered cumulatively, and not alternatively, by the insurance company. That is to say, the duty of the insurance company towards one of the insureds should not be determined by facts pertaining to other insured. This distinguishes group insurance from individual insurance that involves several persons due to the fact of the insured risk being defined by conditions referring to different subjects. The most notorious examples concern personal insurance and regard the so-called insurance upon two heads, where the company undertakes a single duty to perform in respect of several parties, where the conditions for performance are defined by events referring to different persons at risk. That is the very frequent case of life and incapacity insurance entered into as collateral for a single bank loan undertaken by more than a borrower (e.g., a

338. STJ 20 June 2017, 1709/13.4TBFLG.P1.S1 (Júlio Gomes) – albeit as obiter dicta; in scholarship, M. Lima Rego, Seguros coletivos e de grupo, 430.

couple, or two persons starting a business), where the insured event is defined as death or incapacity of any of the borrowers (the persons at risk).[339]

743. Some scholarship has considered that the group should also fulfil requirements that allow it to be economically sustainable. Accordingly, group insurance would require that the risks affecting the members of the group did not have a strong positive correlation. This would exclude from qualifying as group insurance, e.g., a contract where the owner of a warehouse featured as policyholder and the risks covered regarded property interests of the owners of the objects stored in the same warehouse.[340] However, these lines do not seem to be as clean cut (e.g., health risks covered by a supplementary health insurance regarding the workers of a same factory might display the same strong correlation, in spite of the fact of this being generally taken as an instance of group insurance). In addition, it has been shown to be problematic to qualify the contract by reference to its financial underpinnings (one needs only to remember the discussion around the requirement that the contract rests upon a mutuality of insureds, or that the insurer runs an enterprise).

744. There are no limits to the kind of insurable risk group insurance can refer to – it can be personal insurance, as it can regard interests in certain goods or the patrimony as a whole.

745. Group insurance no doubt has a relevant presence in the Portuguese market. Although its use is more widespread, it has surfaced in case law especially in regard to personal or property insurance for the protection of professional lenders – with the lender (normally a Bank), acting as policyholder –, as well as in the segment of mandatory professional liability insurance, with a professional association or body acting as policyholder.

II. Modalities of Group Insurance

A. Contributory and Non-contributory Group Insurance

746. The *summa divisio* adopted by the RJCS in regard to group insurance differentiates between contributory and non-contributory group insurance. Besides the general rules on group insurance, set out in section I of Chapter VII (Articles 76–85), that apply to both modalities, section II (Articles 86–90) sets out special rules for contributory group insurance.

747. Group insurance is deemed to be contributory when it results from the contract that the premium is financed by the insureds (Article 77(2)). This does not

339. M. Lima Rego, Seguros coletivos, 428–430; Maria Inês de Oliveira Martins, Seguros de vida contratados como seguros de grupo e crédito à habitação, Anotação ao ac. do TRG de 6 Oct. 2011, Proc. 771/08, 39, Cadernos de Direito Privado, (2012), 57–58.

340. M. Lima Rego, Seguros coletivos, 429–430.

mean that the insureds are responsible for the fulfilment of the duty or condition precedent of paying the premium; generally, the policyholder will be the one who should perform (Article 80(1)). It rather means that the contract reflects that the insureds are the ones endowing the policyholder with means for fulfilling the contract. However, it can also be agreed that the insureds pay the premium directly to the insurance company (Article 77(3)); in this case, they will be directly responsible for fulfilling the duty or condition precedent, as the case may be, of paying the premium (Article 80(1), *a contrario*).

748. In other words, this distinction relies on an economic criterion – the criterion of who finances the premium. However, for the sake of certainty, it is additionally required that this financing is reflected on the contract. Nonetheless, it should be said that the criterion can give rise to doubts – for instance, regarding cases where insurance cover is attributed to employees as a fringe benefit, since the payment of the insurance premium will then be a replacement of their wage in kind.

749. The special norms on contributory insurance regard three different issues: an enhanced right to be informed by the policyholder (Article 87); an adaptation of the general norms on the conclusion of the contract (Articles 88 and 89); and a norm on the right to participate in the insurance company's profits (Article 90).

750. In addition to the general duties of information of the policyholder in group insurance (Article 78; *see below* Part II, Chapter 6, §4, III, B, Duty to Inform the Insureds), under Article 87(1), the policyholder that is also a beneficiary of the insurance contract should also inform the insureds on any amounts they receive in regard to its intervention in the contract, independent of their form and nature, as well as on the relative dimension of the amounts in regard to the total value of the premium. Under Article 87(2), while a contributory group insurance contract is in force, the policyholder should give the insureds all the information that a policyholder on an individual insurance contract would be entitled to in analogous circumstances. In case of infringement of these duties, the policyholder shall bear the payment of premium corresponding to the insured at stake, without any reduction of their insurance cover, until the date of renewal of the contract or until one year has elapsed since this date (Article 87(3)).

751. Article 88 regards the 'adhesion to the contract'. Article 88(1) and (2) are an adaptation of Article 27, which sets out the circumstances in which, regarding individual insurance, silence from the insurance company has the value of acceptance of the policyholder's offer. One should mention that under the Civil Code silence can only be construed as acceptance when this derives from the law, from usages, of from previous agreement from the parties (Article 218). In what regards contributory group insurance, silence of the insurance company is construed as acceptance of the insured's offer whenever the policyholder is simultaneously an insurance intermediary endowed with powers to represent the insurance company and thirty days have elapsed since the policyholder received the insured's offer, without the insurance company having notified the offeror of its refusal or of the need to obtain additional information essential for risk assessment (Article 88(1)).

In case this additional information is requested, silence of the insurance company shall be construed as acceptance after thirty days have elapsed after such information was provided to the company itself or to the policyholder, when they are simultaneously an insurance intermediary endowed with powers to represent the insurance company (Article 88(2)). For these purposes, the insurance company or the policyholder should provide the insured with a copy of their offer, or of documents providing additional information, stating the date of their receipt (Article 88(4)). The policyholder is responsible before the insurance company for the damages caused by failure to deliver any of these documents, or by their late delivery (Article 88(5)).

752. Article 89 establishes that the declaration of adhesion should contain all the elements that in similar circumstances would be present in an individual insurance.

753. It seems clear that Articles 88 and 89 construe the adhesion as declaration of intention to enter into a contract with the insurance company. However, one should note that in practice the term adhesion may be used in contract documents with different meanings. The typical adhesion documents (or bulletins of adhesion) may embody an actual contract proposal, but they may also merely contain information that should be provided to the insurance company. Any conclusion as to the nature of the document at stake can only be arrived at through its interpretation.

754. Finally, Article 90(1), clarifies that the when the contract sets out a right to participate in the insurance company's profits, this right belongs to the insured. In case the insured only pays for part of the premium, then their right shall be proportional to the payment.

B. Single Insurance Contract or Multiple Insurance Contracts

755. As noted, resulting from these norms is the fact that in contributory group insurance the insured tends to be equated to a policyholder in an individual insurance. However, this can be difficult to square with the position of the insured in the structure of the insurance contract.

756. In fact, the criterion adopted by the RJCS to separate different modalities of group insurance does not reflect the legal structure of the contract. A different distinction should be made in this regard.[341]

757. On the one hand, there is group insurance resting upon a sole insurance contract with the nature of a contract to the benefit of third parties. The insurance contract is entered into by the insurance company and the policyholder. The insureds are not parties to the contract, but they derive rights directly from it, without any need for their assent; the general rules regarding contracts to the benefit of third parties (Articles 443 and ff. of the Civil Code) apply together with the RJCS.

341. M. Lima Rego, Seguros coletivos, pp. 433–436.

758. On the other hand, group insurance can rest upon the combination of a preliminary intervention of the policyholder and the conclusion of several insurance contracts with the insureds. The preliminary intervention of the policyholder may consist of entering into a preliminary contract with the insurance company or of merely negotiating with it the ensuing insurance contracts. The latter case is not relevant to the Portuguese market, and therefore the former is frequently the only referred to case.[342] In this case, the insurance company and the policyholder enter into a framework contract, which sets the terms of the actual insurance contracts to be entered into. The actual insurance contracts are then concluded between the members of the group and the insurance company. Each of the insureds will then be a party to the insurance contract that concerns them.

759. As mentioned above, some norms on contributory insurance only make sense if the insured is not a mere third-party beneficiary in regard to an insurance contract entered into by the insurance company and the policyholder. That is the case of Article 88, which refers to the cases where the adhesion of the insured has the value of a contract offer (presented according to the standard forms of the insurance company, as is typical of insurance contracts). The organisation of the RJCS should therefore not be taken at face value in this regard.

760. The structure adopted for a particular contributory group insurance should be neutral in regard to the rights of the insured who finances the premium. More so, the choice of this structure is generally made by the insurance company and is reflected in its standard terms and contract documents.

III. Main Points of Regulation

A. *Modification or Termination of Contracts*

1. Termination (or Lack of Efficacy) due to Default on the Premium

761. Articles 80–85 set out several cases of modification or termination of the contract. However, they do not always refer to the same legal relationship involved in the structure of group insurance. Some norms refer to the relationship established between the insurance company and the policyholder, while others refer to the relationship between the insurance company and the insureds.

762. That is from the onset reflected in Article 80. Article 80(2) regards either non-contributory or contributory group insurance, as long as the insureds do not pay themselves the premium to the insurance company. In this case, default on payment by the policyholder has the consequences set out in Articles 59–61 – namely, a strict 'no premium, no cover' applies to these cases, determining that the cover does not take effect and/or the contract is automatically terminated in case of default. This

342. M. Lima Rego, Contrato … , pp. 812–814; M. I. Oliveira Martins, Seguros de vida contratados … , 54.

implies that the cover granted to all the members of the group is automatically affected. The application of this harsh regime to group insurance, and even to contributory group insurance, when the policyholder fails to pay the premium, would from the onset seem questionable in view of the interests of the insureds; it does not seem balanced that they do not have the chance to keep the contract in force, unless the contract itself provides on this matter (Article 55).

763. However, the whole of the options made by the RJCS in regard to the rules on premium for group insurance make it definitively worthy of criticism. Article 80(3) establishes that, in case of contributory group insurance where the insureds themselves pay the premium directly to the insurance company, in case of default by the insured the consequences set out in Articles 59–61 shall only affect their right to cover (their relationship with the insurance company). As it were, the rights of the other members of the same group remain untouched.

764. Article 12(1) establishes that Article 80(2) and (3) are absolutely imperative.

765. When taken literally, this regime would seem unjustifiably unbalanced. It would extend the strict 'no premium, no cover' rules to all kinds of insurance, even those that are generally exempt from it – that would be the case of life insurance (Article 58), which is probably the field of insurance where group insurance has more practical relevance. Moreover, this extension of the rules would be absolutely imperative – even for large risks. This would be even less justifiable as in practice very often the insured does not really choose between entering into individual insurance or group insurance – he will simply be presented with group insurance, which may even be the only type of cover available for the risk at stake.

766. In life insurance, that would literally amount to sacrificing the possibility of the insured using the surrender value to finance the cover (*see* Article 203 and below Part V, Chapter 4, Life Insurance), as well as the rights attributed to an irrevocable beneficiary of the insurance payment (Article 204). The courts have not, however, taken these rules face value and have applied the special norms on premium set out for life insurance contracts even when they are group insurance.

2. Termination by the Insured, Exclusion of the Insured, Termination by the Policyholder and Maintenance of Cover

767. Under Article 82(1), after the insured is informed of any modification of the group insurance contract, they may terminate their relationship with the insurance company, as resulting from their adhesion to the group insurance, save for the cases when the adhesion was mandatory in light of the relationship between the insured and the policyholder.

768. The termination made in these terms only affects the insured at stake and not any other member of the group (Article 82(2)). It should be made in writing and sent to the policyholder, or, when the contract so provides, to the insurance company, thirty days before taking effect (Article 82(3)).

769. Some scholarship has pointed out that, although this provision would seem to refer to all kinds of group insurance, in fact it can only apply to a limited set of them.[343] Namely, to group insurance that combines a framework contract between the insurance company and the policyholder and an actual insurance contract between the company and the insured, in any case only when it qualifies as non-contributory group insurance. When it qualifies as contributory insurance, the insured should be granted the same degree of protection as is granted to any individual policyholder. Therefore, in this case, the insured can terminate its relationship with the insurance company under the general rules (Articles 116 and ff.).

770. On the other hand, when the insured is a mere third-party beneficiary in an insurance contract between the company and the policyholder, then there is no actual 'relationship' between the insured and the company; the general rules on termination of individual insurance contracts should simply apply to the insurance contract.

3. Exclusion of the Insured

771. Under Article 83(1), the insured can be excluded from group insurance when they terminates their relationship with the policyholder or, in case of contributory group insurance, when they do not provide the policyholder with the amount needed for the premium to be paid. The insured may also be excluded from the group insurance when either they or the beneficiary, with their acknowledgment, performs fraudulent acts with prejudice to the insurance company (Article 83(2)). The contract should define the procedure for the exclusion and for its taking of effect in regard to the affected insured (Article 83(3)).

772. Exclusion regards only the insured to whom it refers to; the other members of the group are not affected. One should also highlight that the list of grounds for exclusion is deemed to be exhaustive. For reasons of equality of treatment between the members of the group, the policyholder should not have discretion in regard to the exclusion of its single members.[344]

4. Termination of the Contract

773. Under Article 84(1), the policyholder may terminate the contract under the general rules of termination by mutual agreement, termination of a contract that is to last for an indefinite period or that is subject to automatic renewal, or termination for a serious cause. The policyholder should inform the insured on the extinction of

343. M. Lima Rego, Seguros coletivos, 439–442.
344. M. Lima Rego, Seguros coletivos, 443–444.

cover resulting from the termination of the contract (Article 84(2)). In the cases of termination by mutual agreement or termination of a contract that is to last for an indefinite period or that is subject to automatic renewal, the insured should be informed at least thirty days before termination (Article 84(3)); the policyholder is liable for damage caused in case the delay is not complied with due to a fault theirs (Article 84(4)).

774. In a nutshell, this norm literally implies that the policyholder may terminate the insurance or framework contract that is the basis of group insurance, as long as it informs the insured with due delay. Scholarship has accepted this result, considering that the norm cannot be construed as providing differently.[345] Moreover, when the contract between the policyholder and the insurance company is of indefinite duration, the policyholder should have the right to terminate the contract, since that is a basic requirement of the principle of freedom to contract.

775. This perspective is, however, not free from doubt, and does not match the perspective followed by case law.

776. On the one hand, it contradicts the rules applicable to insurance for the account of a third party in this regard. This is the case for Article 48(4), which establishes that in insurance on the account of a third party, the policyholder has the faculty not to renew the contract – yet, *a contrario*, they do not seem to have a right to terminate a contract that is to last for a determinate period.[346] That is also the case for Article 111(2), concerning termination by mutual agreement, which establishes that, when the insured identified in the policy is not the policyholder, then the contract cannot be terminated by mutual agreement without the insured's consent. However, Article 111(2) itself mirrors the contradictory approach of the RJCS to this subject, since it states that the mentioned general rule is without prejudice to the rules on group insurance and to the specificities of life insurance.

777. One should remember that *group insurance is always insurance for the account of a third party*. Moreover, as mentioned above, the borders between group insurance and individual insurance for the account of a third party are not always clean-cut, especially for the authors who consider that group insurance is characterised by a lack of positive correlation between the insured risks (an example of insurance that may be difficult to place is D&O Insurance). Therefore, such a difference between the rules applicable to each of the cases seems to be at least questionable.

778. On the other hand, it seems to undermine the purpose of taking out long-term insurance. It should be reminded that contributory group insurance is often presented to the insured as a structure that is equivalent to that of individual insurance. That is the case in the (extremely relevant) instances of life insurance to the benefit

345. M. Lima Rego, Seguros coletivos, 444 and ff.
346. This fact has been pointed out by the same scholarship – *see* M. Lima Rego, Seguros coletivos, 445, fn. 77.

of an entity that has lent money to the insured. In practice, life insurance policies that are offered to borrowers, to be entered into as collateral for their financiers, are generally group life insurance. It would not be compatible with the purpose of these contracts that the policyholder could terminate them before their term – in other words, while there was still outstanding debt. In fact, this has been the reasoning of the Appellate Court of Lisbon, that has argued that an SCT inserted in the contract between the insurance company and the policyholder, which allowed the policyholder to terminate this contract without a reasonable ground (*ad nutum*) was disproportionately imbalanced in regard to the interests of the insureds, which were central to the contract.[347]

779. In another case, also referring to group life insurance for the benefit of the lender, the Supreme Court considered that a modification of cover, agreed between the insurance company and the policyholder (and affecting the whole group of insureds), could not be invoked against the insured, first and foremost because *he had not given his consent to those modifications* (the issue of them not having been communicated did not even merit discussion).[348] The insured was therefore granted the same level of protection as he would be granted under an individual insurance contract – which would not be compatible with a literal interpretation of Article 84.

780. The reasoning of the courts in these cases is moreover strikingly similar to that referred to in regard to (D&O) insurance for the account of a third party.[349]

781. All in all, this matter does not yet seem settled. A possible evolution may be that Article 84 is construed as applying only to non-contributory insurance; further developments are to be expected.

782. It should also be said that the norms that regulate the relationship between the policyholder and the beneficiaries will often not allow the policyholder to terminate its contract with the insurance company at its discretion. That was considered to be the case in regard to the former norms on labour contracts.[350] The same seems to be true in what specifically regards life insurance to the benefit of a credit institution providing housing credit, in light of Decree-Law 222/2009, of 11 November 2009, which provides for the protection of consumers taking out life insurance in connection with housing credit. Article 5(2) sets out the minimum requirements that life insurance required or proposed by the credit institution should meet. It establishes that life insurance cannot take effect before housing credit does and, unless an insured event takes place, it can only cease to have effect in the date of termination of the housing credit contract.

347. TRL 31 March 2011, 3298/07.0TVLSB.L1-2 (Henrique Antunes).
348. STJ 30 March 2017, 4267/12.3TBBRG.G1.S1 (João Trindade).
349. TRL 7 March 2019, 7459/16.2T8LSB-A.L1-2 (Tibério Silva).
350. TRL 24 September 2008, 6574/2008-4 (Leopoldo Soares), regarding former norms on the labour contract.

5. Maintenance of Cover

783. Under Article 85, in the case of exclusion of the insured or termination of the group insurance contract, the insured will be entitled to keep the cover in the same terms if and when the contract provides on this regard.

B. Duty to Inform the Insureds

784. Article 78, titled 'duty to inform', determines that, without prejudice to the general duties to inform set out in Articles 18–21, that apply with the due adaptations, the policyholder should inform the insureds on the extent of the cover hired, on the risk exclusions, on the rights and obligations in case an insured event occurs, as well as on the changes to the contract, in accordance with a specimen document provided by the insurance company (Article 78(1)). In personal insurance, the policyholder should also inform the persons at risk on the rules regarding designation and change of the beneficiary (Article 78(2)). This provision should be read together with Article 81, which establishes that unless otherwise stipulated, in personal insurance the person at risk should designate the beneficiary; the general rules on designation of the beneficiary apply to this case. The burden of proving that the information mentioned in Article 78 was duly provided rests upon the policyholder (Article 78(3)). The contract can also place the duty mentioned in Article 78(1) and (2) upon the insurance company (Article 78(5)).

785. As stated above, this general duty is flanked by special duties placed upon the policyholder in case of contributory group insurance (Article 87).

786. Notwithstanding the foregoing, the insurance company should, upon request of the insureds, also provide all the information necessary for the understanding of the contract (Article 78(4)).

787. Under Article 79, infringement of the duty to inform makes the infringing party liable for damages under the general rules on civil liability.

788. The distribution of the duty to inform between the policyholder and the insurance company has given rise to considerable controversy in case law. Nowadays, this controversy unfolds in regard to Article 78; before the RJCS, it regarded Article 4 of Decree-Law 176/95, which set out rules of transparency for the insurance contracts.[351] Article 4(1), (2) and (4) of this Decree-Law was in practical terms identical to Article 78(1), (3) and (5); Article 4(3), was practically identical to Article 87(3); and Article 4(4), was practically identical to Article 78(4). Therefore, the courts have generally considered that the arguments presented in regard to the former rules are also valid in regard to the RJCS.

351. Decree-Law176/95, of 27 July 1995, that set out transparency rules for the insurance activity and other rules regarding the insurance contract.

789. The RJCS lays down certain pre-contractual duties to inform that the insurance company should comply with (Articles 18–21); Article 78 itself refers to them. Decree-Law 176/95 (Articles 2 and 3), together with the former norms on insurance supervision, proceeded similarly. However, controversy has arisen not in regard to those duties, but rather in regard to the duties to communicate the terms and inform on their content that are set out in the LSCT (Articles 5 and 6). In fact, given that the former norms establishing duties of information for the insurance contract were deemed overly confusing, and insurance contracts are generally (if not always) contracts of adhesion, case law has become used to resorting more to the LSCT to enforce information duties upon the insurance company. A further advantage of the LSCT lies in the sanction it establishes for the infringement of the duty to communicate or to inform. Under Article 8(a) and (b), the clause that was not duly communicated or informed to the insured is expunged from the contract. This sanction is particularly suited to the needs of the insureds in the cases where the insurance company invokes a clause excluding or limiting coverage against the insured – as typically happens in insurance disputes –, since it keeps coverage without limiting it through the clause at stake.

790. Against this background, case law has debated whether the norms that place the duty to inform upon the policyholder set aside Articles 5 and 6 of LSCT, which place similar duties upon the drafter of SCT. That would amount to saying that, whenever group insurance is at stake, the policyholder is the only person responsible for communicating the terms to the insured and informing on their content. If it was proved that the due communication or information had not occurred, then this could not be held against the insurance company. In other words, the terms at stake would not be expunged from the contract – the insurance company would be able to invoke such a limitation or exclusion of cover against the insured. The insured would be limited to turning against the policyholder and suing them for damages under the general rules of civil liability.

791. This view has gathered considerable support in the STJ and is sometimes considered the prevailing one among its judges.[352] It is also defended by some scholarship, on the basis that expunging the term affected could unsettle the balance of the group.[353]

352. *See* STJ 25 June 2013, 24/10.0TBVNG.P1.S1 (Lopes do Rego), and the case law quoted on the decision; in recent case law, *see* STJ 30 May 2019, 532/17.1T8VIS.C1.S1 (Rosa Tching) and STJ 18 February 2021, 418/19.5T8FLG.P1.S1 (Maria dos Prazeres Pizarro Beleza). STJ 20 May 2015, 17/13.5TCGMR.G1.S1 (Tomé Gomes) is sometimes mentioned as having followed a different approach; however, it seems to have reasoned along the same lines as the case law described in the text, with the only *nuance* of having apparently presumed that if the specimen document or the contract's terms had never been delivered to the insureds, then it would have also not been delivered to the policyholder – which implied that the insurance company had breached its duties.

353. A. Menezes Cordeiro, Seguros, 2. Ed., pp. 785–786. M. Lima Rego, Contrato …, 861–862, is also quoted in this regard, and does state that the insurance company is not barred from invoking the modification or termination of the insurance contract against the insured when they were not informed of those facts, since, according to the structure of group insurance, as defined by Arts 78 and 87, the duty to inform is placed upon the policyholder, and not upon the insurance company.

792. This case law has argued that the RJCS makes the policyholder the person responsible for communicating and informing on the clauses and, in doing that, it releases the insurance company from the duties set out in the LSCT. There would be no reason to make the insurance company responsible for the actions of the policyholder. Under the general rules, the insurance company could only be held liable under strict liability if the infringing party was its agent or employee (Article 500 of the Civil Code). As the policyholder is not an agent or employee of the insurance company, to make the insurance company bear the consequences of the infringement of the policyholder's duties would amount to creating a case of strict liability beyond the cases set out by law. That would challenge Article 483(2) of the Civil Code, which sets that there can only be strict liability when established by (statutory) law.

793. The insurance company could only suffer the consequences of the infringement of duties that the law clearly placed under its responsibility. That would happen in two cases: first, when the insurance company failed to provide the policyholder with the specimen document mentioned in Article 78(1), or provided them with a defective document, since it is the base for the policyholder to comply with his/her information duties; second, in regard to the duty to inform the insureds upon their request, as set out by Article 78(4).

794. In the light of the RJCS, this case law considers that its arguments have gained strength, since, apart from the sanction set out for contributory insurance, which was already set out in Decree-Law 176/95, now, the RJCS clearly sanctions the infringement by the policyholder with civil liability and does not make any reference to the exclusion of the clause. Besides, it has been defended that civil liability can have the same practical result for the insured as the exclusion of the clause.

795. Other case law has defended the exactly opposite view.[354] According to this perspective, if the insurance contract is a contract of adhesion, then the insured cannot be deprived of the protection granted by the LSCT. In other words, the norms of the RJCS do not set aside the duties to communicate and to inform that the LSCT places upon the insurance company, in its role of drafting party.

However, this perspective is held regarding duties to inform that are set out by the RJCS, and not the regarding the specific protection that is granted by the LSCT.

354. This was the position of many second instance courts – *see, for instance*, TRP 27 February 2014, 2334/10.7TBGDM.P1 (José Manuel de Araújo Barros) – but also of STJ – *see* STJ 14 April 2015, 294/2002.E1.S1 (Maria Clara Sottomayor); STJ 29 November 2016, proc. 1274/15.8T8GMR.S1 (Fonseca Ramos). In recent case law, *see* STJ 10 May 2018, 261/15.0T8VIS.C1.S2 (Henrique Araújo); STJ 9 March 2021, 1197/16.3T8BRG.G1.S1 (Maria João Vaz Tomé). Scholarship has highlighted in this regard (M. I. Oliveira Martins, Contrato de seguro e conduta …, 717–720) that when the policyholder is a tied insurance intermediary acting for the insurance company at stake (as is very often the case for banks), then there is no reason not to apply the general rules. Besides, the view that simply discharged the insurance company from its duties to inform under the LSCT seems to be particularly ill-suited in regard to the duty to provide individualised information to the insured (6 LSCT), that goes beyond the mere communication of the contract terms (5 LSCT).

796. This case law considers that both the policyholder, and the insurance company are responsible for informing the insureds on the insurance contract. The norms that place the duty to inform upon the policyholder exclusively regard their relationship with the insurance company; they do not affect the rights of the insureds, who cannot in any way influence how the policyholder and insurance company decide to organise their relationship. Some courts have quoted the preamble of Decree-Law 176/95 in this regard, since it mentioned that its purpose was to reduce the potential for conflicts between the insurance company and the policyholder, by clarifying their mutual position. In turn, the preamble of the RJCS has stated that in contributory group insurance the position of the insured is identical to that of a policyholder in individual insurance, and therefore the insured in the first case should be granted the exact same level of protection that is granted to a policyholder in the latter.

797. What is more, at least, in the modalities of group insurance where each of the insureds would have their own insurance contract with the insurance company, the insurance company would be a party of the insurance contract and could not discharge itself of its duties towards its contract party.

798. Moreover, in many cases the insurer and the policyholder are part of the same economic group. That will happen typically when the policyholder is a Bank belonging to the same group as the insurer. In these cases, there could be strategic non-compliance by the policyholder, in order to promote the acceptance of a contract with severe exclusions, and thus acquire new customers for the insurance business belonging to its group.

799. Finally, it is highlighted that the contrary would amount to enforcing a contract against a party that had never been made aware of its content, which would be flagrantly contrary to private autonomy and the basic principles of contract law.

800. Considering the practical importance of these matters, and that under the Civil Procedure Code there is a special process of appeal in case there are conflicting decisions within the Supreme Court regarding the same point of law under the same legal framework (Article 688 of the Civil Procedure Code), it is expected that the Supreme Court will soon be called to clarify its prevailing position.

Chapter 7. Modification and Termination of the Insurance Contract

§1. Modification of the Risk

I. Aggravation of Risk

801. As stated above, the RJCS sets out a right to modify the contract or in exceptional cases to terminate it in case of aggravation of risk. The exercise of this right is conditioned upon the insurance company becoming aware of the aggravation of risk. The duty to communicate the aggravation of risk is instrumental for these purposes and will in many cases be the main source of information for the insurance company. However, it can have notice of the information through other sources – e.g., inspections to the risk site, medical examinations, continuous processing of data generated by the insured, connection to events regarding other insurance contracts with the same insurance company.

802. In any case, within thirty days from becoming aware of the aggravation of risk, the insurance company can propose ta modification of the contract to the policyholder; the policyholder shall have an equal deadline of thirty days to accept or reject the proposal, which is deemed accepted in case of absence of reply by the policyholder (Article 93(2)(a)). In case the insurance company proves that it does not in any case cover risks with the characteristics of the aggravated risk, it is entitled to terminate the contract within the same deadline of thirty days (Article 93(2)(b)). These rules are semi-mandatory (Article 13(1)).

803. In empirical terms, an aggravation of risk consists of an increase in the amount of the expected loss, which can derive either from an increase in the probability of the insured event, or from an increase in the amount of loss that an insured event can cause. In any case, the right to modify or terminate the contract depends on the occurrence of an aggravation of risk for which these consequences are appropriate. As has been highlighted by scholarship and was recently endorsed by the Supreme Court of Justice, an aggravation of risk that is relevant for these purposes should meet certain requirements.[355]

804. In order to be considered relevant, the aggravation should be actual, foreseeably lasting and significant.

805. First of all, the aggravation of risk should be actual – strictly speaking, the risk should have effectively increased since the moment of conclusion of the contract. If the circumstance at stake was already present before conclusion of the contract, then the rules on disclosure of the risk should apply. Moreover, an increase in

355. On these requirements, which were draw from the experience in German law, *see* M. I. Oliveira Martins, Contrato de seguro e conduta ..., 359 and ff. and M. I. Oliveira Martins, Entre a avaliação ..., 87 and ff.; they were applied by STJ 19 March 2019, 1680/12.0TBGDM.P1.S1 (Maria João Vaz Tomé). For a similar (though not identical) approach, J. Gomes, Algumas notas sobre o agravamento ..., 9–10, 20 and ff.

the amount of premium requires that the overall level of risk has also increased. Therefore, there is no application of the consequences of aggravation if the increase of the level of risk in some regards is offset by the decrease of the level of risk in other regards.

806. Second, in order to determine what qualifies as a relevant aggravation of risk, one must consider that its occurrence can give rise to a lasting modification or termination of the contract. Therefore, a relevant aggravation of risk must likewise be foreseeably lasting; a short-term aggravation does not trigger these rules.

807. Third, it is also to be considered that the insurance contract should in principle be stable, as its purpose is to allow for certainty and economic planning regarding uncertain events. If the contract could easily be modified or terminated, this would distort the market price for cover, since it would pay off to present a low price, that could easily be updated after the contract was in force. Nonetheless, if changes in the circumstances of the risk cause the insurance contract to become significantly unbalanced, the insurance company should be given the opportunity to modify or terminate the contract. This allows for the optimisation of the premium, since the insurance company will not have to fix a premium that would offset all the possible aggravations of risk. Therefore, all things considered, in order for an aggravation of risk to trigger the application of these consequences, it should be significant, so that it surpasses the increases in risk that the policyholder should legitimately expect to see encompassed in the cover (e.g., those that correspond to a normal evolution of the risk at stake, and to the normal 'management' of the object at risk).[356]

808. The aggravation should also be significant for the insurance company itself. As stated above, when setting out the duty to communicate the RJCS refers it to the circumstances which could have influenced the insurance company's decision to enter the contract, or to define its conditions in certain terms (Article 93(1); but *see also* 91(1), as mentioned above). Moreover, the company's right to terminate the contract depends on the demonstration that it does not in any case cover risks with the characteristics of the aggravated risk (Article 93(2)(b)). In accordance, the company's right to modify the contract should be conditioned upon the demonstration that according to its underwriting practices, it would have proposed different conditions for a risk with those characteristics. This is also coherent with the requirements for the proportional reduction of payment in case of negligent infringement of the duty to communicate (Article 94(2)(b)).

809. The rules on aggravation of risk do not apply if the change in circumstances does not merely aggravate the risk, but alters its very nature, in such terms that the risk is no longer covered by the contract (e.g., the insured sets up small

356. The opinion of M. Lima Rego, O risco …, 402 (*see* footnote) seems not to differ significantly from the one above.

industry in the house covered by home insurance).[357] In these cases, the contract expires since the risk it referred to no longer exists.

810. The rules on aggravation of risk as set out in Articles 93 and 94 do not apply to life insurance contracts. When changes in the health condition of the person at risk are at stake, those rules also do not apply to personal accidents insurance or to insurance against disability resulting from an accident or illness when it is supplementary to life insurance (Article 190); in the same case, they also do not apply to health insurance (Article 215(a)). Although these norms are not expressly identified as semi-mandatory (Article 13(1)(a) *a contrario*), they are construed as semi-mandatory in view of their rationale of protecting the integrity of coverage.[358]

II. Reduction of Risk

811. The RJCS also provides on reduction of risk. As soon as the insurance company becomes aware of circumstances causing an unquestionable and lasting reduction of risk that impacts the conditions of the contract, it should be reflected in the insurance premium (Article 92(1)). It has been pointed out that the insurer is only bound to consider the circumstances that it takes into account according to its own pricing practices.[359]

812. If the parties do not agree on the reduction of the premium, the policyholder shall be entitled to terminate the contract (Article 92(2)). The norm setting out the duty of the insurance company is semi-mandatory. The norm on the right of the policyholder would prima facie not be (*see* Article 13(1), referring only to Article 92(1)). Nonetheless, this has been considered an example of the need to construe the list of Article 13(1) as non-exhaustive.[360]

813. Unlike the norms on the aggravation of risk, this norm also applies to life insurance and insurance supplementing it, as well as to health insurance (Articles 190 and 215(a), *a contrario*).

III. Modification of General Background Circumstances

814. The norms on aggravation and reduction of risk (Articles 92–94) only reflect the changes in circumstances that are specific to the contract at stake. They do not apply to changes in general background circumstances that may affect the equilibrium of the contract.[361]

357. M. Lima Rego, O risco …, 401; J. Gomes, Algumas notas sobre o agravamento …, 25–26.
358. A. Costa Oliveira, Art. 190.º, Agravamento do risco, 570.
359. A. Costa Oliveira, Art. 92.º, Diminuição do risco, 360.
360. A. Costa Oliveira, Art. 92.º, 362.
361. M. Lima Rego, O risco …, 400; J. Gomes, Algumas notas sobre o agravamento …, 29–30.

815. Unlike some similar statutes in comparative law, the RJCS does not set out special norms on the modification of long-term insurance contracts due to changes in background circumstances (e.g., an increase in general life expectancy, aggravating the insured risk in lifetime annuities). In case such a modification takes place, the insurance company can only resort to the general norms on the change of circumstances (Articles 437–439 of the Civil Code). However, these general norms do not apply if the risk that was affected by the adverse change had been specifically allocated by contract of by law to one of the contracting parties.[362] As the insured risk is specifically allocated to the insurance company by the insurance contract, background changes that affected it will generally fall outside of the norms on the change of circumstances.

§2. General Grounds for Termination of the Insurance Contract

816. Article 105 RJCS states that the insurance contract shall be terminated under the general terms, namely expiry, termination by mutual agreement, termination of a contract that is to last for an indefinite period of time or that is subject to automatic renewal, or termination for a serious cause. Termination of the contract shall extinguish the effective obligations of the parties (Article 106(1) RJCS). However, the insurer must perform the risk coverage, provided that the accident occurred prior to or concurrent with the termination, even if it was the cause of the termination (Article 106(2) RJCS): an example of this is life insurance.

817. Unless agreed otherwise, early termination shall give rise to a premium rebate unless there has been a compensation or refund of the advance payment provision (Article 107(1) RJCS). The rebate is calculated *pro rata temporis* (Article 107(2) RJCS), i.e., proportional to the period during which the insurance cover was in force. In addition, unless otherwise provided by the law, the parties may not stipulate a penalty applicable to the policyholder whenever he exercises a right that determines early termination of the contract (Article 107(4) RJCS). This legal regime is not applied to life insurance, capitalisation operations and long-term care insurance (Article 107(5) RJCS).

818. Third parties are protected in the case of termination of the insurance contract (Article 108(1) RJCS). This means the possibility of third parties being covered for claims after the termination of the contract (Article 108(2) RJCS). However, the insurer must inform the contract's termination to third parties with rights under the contract and to irrevocably named beneficiaries, provided they are

362. According to Art. 437(1) of the Civil Code, if the circumstances on which the parties founded the decision to contract change beyond what is normal, the affected party has the right to termination of contract, or to its adaptation according to equity, provided that the maintenance of his/her obligations severely contradicts the principle of good faith and cannot be said to correspond to the risks that are inherent to that contract. It is this last segment that gives precedence to any special provision on the allocation of risk (*see* Paulo Mota Pinto, O contrato como instrumento de gestão do risco de 'alteração das circunstâncias' (in: Direito civil, Estudos, Gestlegal, 465, 2018), 479–480 and 489 and ff.).

identified in the policy (Article 108(3) RJCS). This obligation shall also apply to the insurer who is different to the policyholder (Article 108(4) RJCS).

819. One of the causes for the termination of the insurance contract is its expiration, namely at the end of the agreed period (Article 109 RJCS). In addition, Article 110 RJCS mentions the following as specific causes of termination: loss of interest, i.e., the relationship between the insured and the sum insured; the extinction of the risk, namely in case of death of the insured person, total loss of the insured property and cessation of the activity insured (Article 110(2) RJCS); the payment of the full sum insured for the duration of the contract, without provision for the reinstatement of that sum.

820. Article 111 RJCS regulates the cases in which the insurance contract terminates by agreement (termination by mutual agreement). Since it is a contract that has an object of ending the insurance, the insurer and the policyholder may, by agreement, terminate the contract at any time (No. 1). Except for group insurance and the specific life insurance requirements, when there is no correspondence between the insured and the policyholder, the contract's termination requires the latter's consent. As a means of termination of the insurance contract by mutual agreement, it is characterised by being voluntary, discretionary and non-retroactive.

821. Article 115 RJCS regulates the notice of termination. These are relatively imperative rules (Article 13(1) RJCS): they may be departed from in pro of more favourable solutions to the policyholder. In particular, a notice of termination must be given in writing to the other party at least thirty days before the date of extension of the contract; if there is no fixed duration or if the initial period is equal to or greater than five years, the minimum notice is ninety days before the date of expiry of the contract (Article 115(2) RJCS). In this case, the contract terminates at the end of the period of notice or, where there was an advance payment of the premium for a certain period, at the end of that period (Article 115(3) RJCS).

822. Article 116 RJCS, entitled 'Just Cause' (*Justa causa*), states that the insurance contract may be terminated by either party at any time, with just cause, under the general terms. The rule refers to the general regime, namely in Article 432 of the Civil Code. The grounds for terminating the contract may result from the law or the contract. This means that the party, however, who, for circumstances not attributable to the other party, is not in a position to return what it has received, does not have the right to terminate the contract.

823. This means that the termination is limited because it is only permissible when founded in law or an agreement and depends on its allegation. Nevertheless, in terms of effects, the resolution possesses retroactive effectiveness.

824. Regarding special regulation of the insurance contract, Article 117 RJCS establishes the terms under which the parties may agree to terminate the contract in situations of a succession of claims. It excludes the possibility of the insurer settling

in life, health, credit and surety insurance, or compulsory third-party liability insurance. Outside these situations, the law presumes a succession of claims when two claims occur within twelve months or, if the contract is annual, during an annuity. In these cases, the resolution's effects are *ex tunc*. However, these limitations do not apply to insurance of large risks.

825. Article 118 allows the policyholder to free the insurance contract when the latter is a natural person.

826. Termination may occur, without the need to invoke just cause, in the following situations: in life, personal accident and health insurance with a duration of six months or more, within thirty days from the receipt of the policy; in structured savings instruments, within thirty days of reception of the policy, and, in the case of distance insurance other than those already referred to, within fourteen days of receipt of the policy.

827. The *dies a quo* will occur on the date of conclusion of the contract, provided that the policyholder has, on that date, all the relevant information contained in the policy on paper or other durable medium (Article 118(2) RJCS).

828. Article 118(3) excludes group insurance policies. In contrast, Article 118(4) RJCS rules out free cancellation for insurance policies concluded at a distance for less than one month and for travel and luggage insurance. Instead, a cancellation notice must be given to the insurer in writing or by any other durable means available and accessible to him (Article 118(5) RJCS).

829. Although the retroactive effect of the contract's termination prevails, it is not total when the insurance contract has not been concluded at a distance, except in the case of termination of the cover before the expiry of the period of thirty days, at the request of the policyholder (Article 118(7) RJCS). Upon termination of the contract by the policyholder, the insurer (Article 118(6) RJCS) is entitled to the premium *pro rata temporis*, to the extent that it bore the risk, until the termination; to compensation for reasonable expenses it has incurred for due to proven medical examinations and to disinvestment costs.

Part III. Property and Liability Insurance

Chapter 1. Fire Insurance

Gabriela Lacerda Assunção, Geraldo Rocha Ribeiro, & Maria Inês de Oliveira Martins[363]

830. Articles 149 et seq. are the provisions of the fire insurance contract. Their object is to cover damage caused by the occurrence of fire to the property identified in the contract.

831. In terms of economic and social significance, this type of insurance contract is significant in the context of horizontal property and condominium relations. The insurance is compulsory (Articles 1429 and 1436 of the Civil Code) and must be updated annually by resolution of the condominium or, in the absence of such a resolution, by the initiative of the management, according to the index published quarterly by the ASF (Article 5 of Decree-Law 168/94, 25-10, last amendment by Decree-Law 81/2020, 02-10, being the last determined by the Regulatory Framework 1/2021-R, 2 March[364]). It must cover each autonomous fraction and the common parts of the building (roof, stairs, lifts, garage, etc.). The insurance must be taken out by the owners of each unit (apartment owners). The obligation of insurance against fire can be fulfilled by taking out an insurance policy of the 'Fire and Natural Elements' type or by including it in a 'Multi-risk' insurance policy.

832. Moreover, fire insurance also covers damage caused by the means used to fight the fire, as well as damage deriving from heat, smoke, steam, or explosion due to the fire and damage related to removal or destruction ordered by the competent authorities or that is necessary to carry out a rescue (Article 150).

833. Fire insurance can be taken out under a separate policy. However, it is usually taken out as a part of a comprehensive policy (multi-risk), which covers other risks related to property such as storm, flood, water damage, burglary or theft, collision, electrical hazards, explosion, lightning, or earthquake (e.g., a building policy

363. Gabriela Lacerda Assunção authored Chs 7 and 11, Geraldo Rocha Ribeiro authored Chs 1, 4 and 6, and Maria Inês de Oliveira Martins authored Chs 2, 3, 8, 9, 10, 12 and 13.
364. Available at https://www.asf.com.pt/NR/exeres/77D6E455-0E45-4090-86E4-45D8A10042AB.htm.

for residential property or householders' policy). Fire risk coverage is included in the multi-risk insurance associated with home loan contracts as a social and economic practice.

834. Article 150 also includes the loss caused by the negligence of the insured themselves in the cover: 'Cover for fire risk includes damage caused by fire, even if there has been negligence on the part of the insured or of a person for whom they are responsible.

835. On the other hand, under the general terms provided in Article 46 and with the provisions prescribed therein, damage resulting from loss caused intentionally by the insured or by the policyholder will be excluded from cover. This means that the risk covered by a fire insurance policy, when defined as accidental combustion, for some jurisprudence 'must constitute an everyday phenomenon that occurs by chance, that is not foreseen; and has, as an antonym, what is premeditated, intended. An act intentionally performed by a third party is not accidental, arising from chance, but from a will tending towards it, which prevents its qualification as accidental combustion. An act should not be qualified as accidental or causal because it is so from the point of view of the insured, who is extraneous to it and could not foresee it if there is nothing in the policy that defines it that makes it possible to subject this concept to a restrictive interpretation, made from the exclusive point of view of the insured. What is defined therein as accidental must be so objectively, in the interpretation of a normal declarant, even if placed in the position of a contracting party of the insurance.'[365]

836. In this sense, the legislature had no particular concern in regulating fire insurance. That is why it is stated in the law's preamble that 'the regulation of fire insurance, given the general provision of damage insurance, is limited to the scope and special mentions in the policy'. This means that it is for the parties to specify the object of the insurance without prejudice to the duties of information imposed on the insurer and to the rules prescribed in the general contractual clauses.

837. This means that the content of the policy mainly establishes the object of the insurance. In addition to what is required under the general regime Article 37 RJCS (and as already mentioned), the fire insurance policy shall specify the type of property, the construction material and its condition, as well as the location of the building and its name or identification number; the destination and use of the property; the nature and use of adjacent buildings, whenever these circumstances may influence the risk; and the place where the movable objects insured against fire are placed or stored (Article 151 RJCS). In general, the comprehensive policy covers not only the building or constituent parts of the building but also provides cover for appliances (e.g., television, deep-freezer, electric cooker, washing machine, and refrigerator) as well as for the contents of the policyholder's private home (e.g., furniture and clothing, books, jewellery, works of art, or objects relating to hobbies). In the latter case, a complete description of such objects is usually required when

365. TRP 13 June 2018, 952/16.9T8PVZ-A.P1 (Rui Moreira).

their value exceeds a certain amount as fixed by the insurer. When the policy covers the contents of the policyholder's private home, the insured must declare their current real or market value in the insurance form. If the insured does not do so, a proportional rule applies when a claim occurs except if a 'first risk' has been agreed between the insured and the insurer.

838. Uniform contractual clauses regarding fire insurance have been approved by ASF.[366] Therefore, when designing a fire insurance policy's general and specific contractual clause, insurers must include such uniform clauses approved. In addition, the model has to specify the data deemed necessary by Articles 37 and 151 RJCS, also acknowledging the specific exclusions the damages that derive, directly or indirectly, from war, whether declared or not, invasion, act of a foreign enemy, hostilities or warlike operations, civil war, insurrection, rebellion or revolution; Military uprising or act of legitimate or usurped military power; confiscation, requisition, destruction or damage to the insured property by order of the government, in law or in fact, or of any instituted authority (except for the removal or destruction); strikes, riots and public disorder, acts of terrorism, vandalism, malicious mischief or sabotage; explosion, heat release and radiation from splitting atoms or radioactive radiation, as well as those resulting from radiation caused by the artificial acceleration of particles; fire resulting from seismic phenomena, earthquakes, volcanic eruptions, tidal waves or underground fire; direct effects of electric current on appliances, electrical installations and their accessories, namely over-voltage and over-current, including those produced by atmospheric electricity, such as that resulting from lightning, and short circuit, even if they result in fire; malicious acts or omissions of the policyholder, the insured or of persons for whom they are civilly responsible; loss of profits or similar loss; loss, theft or robbery of the insured goods, when committed during or as a result of any covered; loss, theft or robbery of the insured goods, when committed during or as a result of any covered insured event.

839. The risk covered by the insurance contract as set by the uniform clauses specify that the determination of the insured capital, at the beginning and during the term of the contract, is always the responsibility of the policyholder, who shall take into consideration, as far as the insured property is concerned, the provisions of the following numbers. The amount of the insured capital for buildings shall correspond to the market cost of the respective reconstruction, taking into account the type of construction or other factors that may influence such cost or to the registered value in the case of buildings for expropriation or demolition. Except for the value of the land, all the elements constituting or incorporated by the owner or by the holder of the insured interest, including the proportional value of the common parts, shall be considered for determining the guaranteed capital referred to in the preceding paragraph.

366. Regulatory Framework 16/2008-R, of 18 December, available at https://www.asf.com.pt/winlib/cgi/winlibimg.exe?key=&doc=17827&img=2659.

840. To determine the compensation, the assessment of the value of the insured property and the damages shall be made between the insured and the insurer, even if the contract produces effects in favour of a third party. However, suppose the insurer and policyholder do not agree on what was otherwise. In that case, any aggravation that may arise in the cost of repair or reconstruction of the insured property due to a change of alignment or modifications to be made in the characteristics of its construction is excluded from the compensation.

Chapter 2. Loss of Benefits Insurance

841. There is no specific legal framework for insurance covering loss of profits, either at a statutory, or at an administrative level. The RJCS does make a reference to loss of benefits insurance, but rather in the context of the rules on the indemnity principle that define the amount of insurance money due in case of an insured event. In regard to property insurance, under Article 130(1), the loss relevant for setting-up the amount due by the insurer is determined by the value of the insured interest at the time of the insured event. Under Article 130(2), such insurance only covers loss of profits in case this is specifically agreed. In other words, there will only be cover for loss of benefits when it is stipulated by the parties.

842. Loss of benefits insurance is mostly agreed upon as a supplementary insurance taken out in addition to commercial property insurance (where it is sometimes termed *seguro de perdas de exploração*, in line with the French tradition). Traditionally, in the Portuguese market, the right to cover for lost benefits seems to depend upon the occurrence of material damage.[367] From what could be gathered from the context of the COVID-19 lockdown measures, business interruption insurance that is not conditional upon such requirement still seems to be rare.[368]

843. Apart from the cases where cover for lost benefits is specially convened, the insurer may have to compensate the loss of profits by the insured when the court considers that it has abusively delayed complying with its duty to settle the claim, in infringement of good faith. In this case, the duty to compensate for lost profits does not arise from the insurance contract, but rather from civil liability due to unlawful breach of duty, and from the rule of full reparation of damage (Article 566 of the Civil Code) that applies in this context.[369]

367. *See* Margarida Silva Santos, Abordagem à temática 'dano', Seguro de perda de lucros, 11, Boletim da Secção Portuguesa da AIDA, 6 (2005), pp. 9 and ff; in case law, *see, for instance*, TRP 11 April 2019, 232/08.3TVPRT.P1 (Aristides Rodrigues de Almeida); STJ 13 July 2017, 5232/13.9TBMTS.P1.S1 (Tomé Gomes); TRG 14 September 2017, 476/07.5TCGMR.G1 (Maria Amália Santos).

368. *See, for instance*, https://www.mlgts.pt/xms/files/COVID-19/Seguros.pdf, VIII.E.

369. For this construction – which, however, was not applied to the case under scrutiny – *see* TRG 14 September 2017, 476/07.5TCGMR.G1 (Maria Amália Santos).

Chapter 3. Transport Insurance

844. Whereas the RJCS provides for insurance regarding the transport of goods in general, maritime transport insurance is still provided for by the 1888 Commercial Code. The RJCS plays a merely supplementary role in this regard. The same approach was adopted in regard to insurance of postal items. This is laid down by Article 155, entitled 'Scope of the Insurance'. According to Article 155(1), transport insurance covers risks concerning the transport of goods by land, river, lake or by air, as set out in the contract. Under Article 155(2), maritime transport insurance and postal items insurance are regulated by special statutes as well as by the ensuing norms on transport insurance that do not contradict such statutes.

845. As transport insurance refers to the *interest upon the goods* in transit, the general, the rules on property insurance are applicable.

846. Article 156(1) establishes that when insurance is taken out by the policyholder for the account of a third party, Article 48 on insurance for the account of a third party applies. According to Article 156(2), the contract should state the quality in which the policyholder takes out insurance. This norm is deemed rather pointless, since it does not add anything significant to what would already derive from Articles 47 and 48.[370] In any case, it can result from the interpretation of the contract that insurance was taken out in the interest of the policyholder as well as in the interest of an identifiable third party – e.g., when the risks regarding the insured goods are transferred from the policyholder to another person, for instance, a buyer, while the cover is in place.[371] Article 95(3) is of interest for these cases. It establishes that, unless the law or contract provide differently, in case an identified insurer transfers the insured goods to a third party, the transferee is deemed to replace them in their quality of insured, without prejudice to the norms on aggravation of risk.[372]

847. Insurance can also be taken out for the account of 'whom it may concern' – e.g., by reference to whoever is the owner of the goods in transit, since their ownership can change several times before arrival.[373]

848. Transport insurance normally protects an insurable interest of a person having rights upon the carried goods. However, according to some scholarship, the provisions on transport insurance also apply to the cases where it protects the interests of a carrier in case the goods are lost or damaged and they have to reimburse the

370. José Alves de Brito, Art. 156.º, Legitimidade (in: Lei do Contrato de Seguro anotada, Almedina, 513, 2020), 513.

371. For a similar case, albeit regarding maritime insurance, *see* Jorge Ferreira Sinde Monteiro, Venda CIF, contrato de transporte marítimo e seguro de carga; sobre a qualidade de segurado, 3971, RLJ, 105 (2011), 123 and ff.

372. Francisco Rodrigues Rocha, Algumas notas em torno da cláusula CIF e do seguro de transporte de mercadorias (in: Januário da Costa Gomes (ed.) Temas de Direito dos transportes, III, Almedina, 247, 2015), 270–272.

373. F. Rodrigues Rocha, Algumas notas …, 272.

owner of the goods for their value.[374] In this case, transport insurance functions similar to a liability insurance, in that it endows the carrier with means to pay the compensation due to the owner of the goods.

849. Articles 157, 159 and 160 set out default rules for the issues of duration of cover, insured sum and combined transport cases.[375] Article 157(1) provides that unless differently stipulated, cover begins with the receipt of the goods by the carrier and ends with their delivery at the end of the transport. According to Article 157(2), the contract can, for instance, establish that cover commences when the goods leave the place of storage or the carrier's house and ends by the delivery of the goods at the place of storage or home of their recipient. These variations are naturally useful when the transport contract is connected to a sales contract regarding the transported goods, and allow for the adjustment of the duration of cover to the terms of transfer of risk under the sales contract.

850. Article 159(1) establishes that unless differently stipulated, the insured sum comprises the value of the insured goods *at the place and time of loading*, accrued by the cost of carriage to its destination. This provision is deemed to also establish the value of the insurance payment (and not only that of the insured sum), thereby departing from the general rule for property insurance which sets the value of the insurance payment by reference to the value of the interest upon the goods at the *time of the insured event* (Article 130(1)). In fact, goods being exchanged between different markets are expected to have different values in different places and times.[376]

851. Article 159(2) establishes that when the contract separately evaluates loss of profit, it is also deemed covered. Article 160 provides for the cases of combined transport, and states that unless differently stipulated, the provisions on transport insurance (Articles 155–160 of RJCS) apply even when the goods are predominantly carried by sea.

852. Finally, Article 158(1) establishes that the policy should clarify a number of aspects: (a) the means of transport used and its public or private nature; (b) the modality of insurance taken out, for instance regarding it being a 'separate' policy, a 'floating' or 'open' policy, a policy concerning a certain journey, or concerning a certain period of time;[377] (c) the time of receipt of the insured goods and the estimated time of their delivery; (d) where applicable, the identification of the carrier or carriers, or of the entity competent to identify them; (e) the locations where the insured goods should be received and delivered. Article 158(2) derogates from Article 38 (which establishes that policies can only be nominative or payable to the

374. J. Alves de Brito, Art. 156.º, 513; differing, Luís Poças, A delimitação do risco coberto no seguro de mercadorias transportadas (in: Januário da Costa Gomes (ed.) Temas de Direito dos transportes, V, Almedina, 495, 2020), 525.

375. For an analysis of the terms of two transport insurance products being offered in the Portuguese market, *see* L. Poças, A delimitação …, 536 and ff.

376. F. Rodrigues Rocha, Algumas notas …, 279 and ff.; L. Poças, A delimitação …, 498.

377. On these modalities, *see* L. Poças, A delimitação …, 556 and ff.

order), and sets out that in case of transport insurance the policy can be issued to the bearer; in this case, the bearer of the policy shall have all the rights of the policyholder and insured, unless differently stipulated.

Chapter 4. Liability Insurance

§1. Introduction and Legal Framework

853. The general rules for liability insurance contracts (other than motor vehicle liability, aircraft liability, or liability for ships) are set in, as general rules, in Articles 137–148 and special rules for compulsory liability insurance in Articles 146–148 RJCS.

854. Through means of liability insurance, the undertaken insurance covers the risk of an obligation by the insured, through its patrimony, to pay compensation to third parties having suffered loss or injury (Article 137 RJCS). The insurance contract is designed to transfer the risk to the insurer for the insured's liability for damage caused to third parties. Through the insurance, the policyholder aims to transfer all or part of the liability arising from their conduct towards third parties, thus safeguarding their assets. Regardless of the mandatory or non-mandatory nature of the insurance, there is a pre-ordination to protect injured third parties. Therefore, the law enshrines a movable privilege granted by Article 741 of the Civil Code to the injured party over the compensation owed by the insurer. If the law considered the liability insurance optional, that is, purely a matter of the parties' interest, there would be no reason to grant this privilege. Note that the law in no way requires that the benefit received to repair one's damage be used to repair that damage; the insured is free to use it for whatever purpose he wishes. But this is not the case when it comes to insurance against damage caused to third parties, precisely because the law is not alien to their protection.

855. Liability insurance is one of the types of property insurance (as opposed to property insurance, both of which are damage insurance), which are aimed at the passive component of the property. Liability insurance policies generally cover claims regarding bodily injury, injury to health and/or death and/or physical loss or damage to property – including loss of profit and other consequential loss arising from such personal injury or property damage claims.

856. If the insurance of intentional acts has not been agreed or is the result of a legal or regulatory provision, the causation of damage shall not be considered intentional if the agent benefits from a ground that justifies the unlawfulness or excludes fault. Article 141 sets out an interpretative rule to be read in the light of the general scheme provided for in Article 46 regarding intentional acts. When a ground justifying unlawfulness or excluding fault exists, the damage is not considered to have been caused intentionally. It is not possible to exonerate the insurer from its liability in the event of a cause justifying unlawfulness (breach of duty, hierarchical obedience, exercise of a right, direct action, legitimate self-defence, state of necessity, consent of the victim) or excluding fault (error as to the assumptions of direct action or legitimate self-defence, excusable error, relevant fear).

857. The policies usually contain limits of liability (insured sum) per claim, per year, or by the injured person (Article 138(1) RJCS), the duty to pay compensation is covered up to such limits as set out in the insurance policy. If several injured persons exist and the total amount of compensation exceeds the insured sum, the rights to compensation are proportionally diminished – if the insurer in good faith pays compensation exceeding such limits, it is not obliged to pay compensation to other injured persons exceeding the insured sum (Article 142 RJCS).

858. Liability insurance policies are based on the loss-occurrence principle or the claims-made principle. According to the general rules concerning liability insurance and unless otherwise agreed, the insurance covers facts that have occurred within the duration of the insurance contract, including the claims presented after the end of the insurance period. Clauses that define the period of coverage are those based on the fact that caused the loss or damage, knowledge of the damage, or the damage claim are accepted. For example, suppose a clause defines the period of coverage based on the date of the claim. In that case, generally, the insurer pays compensation for damage due to unknown events that occurred within the insurance contract period. However, the claim is presented within one year after the duration of the insurance contract (Article 139 RJCS).

859. Article 142 RJCS regulates situations in which the indemnities to which the various victims are entitled to under the insurance contract exceed the sum insured as the maximum amount payable by the insurer per claim or annuity (Article 49(1) RJCS). Suppose the insured is liable to several injured parties, and the total amount of the indemnity exceeds the sum insured. In that case, the claims of these parties shall be proportionally reduced until the sum insured is equal to the sum insured. In good faith and through ignorance of other claims, the insurer who pays more compensation than the amount resulting from the provisions of the preceding number shall be released from any liability to the other victims for the amount over the sum insured. This results in a rule identical to the general rules on the guarantee of obligations (Articles 601 et seq. of the Civil Code), which imposes distribution between creditors. Non-compliance with this rule is only justified in the case of good faith ignorance of the existence of other claims (Article 142(2) RJCS). The reduction of the claims of the various injured parties only makes sense concerning the insurer, since the amount of the insured capital functions as one of the elements delimiting the scope of the insurance (Articles 37(2), and 138(1) RJCS), as the maximum value of the benefit to be paid by the insurer (Article 49(1) RJCS), and not to the insured.[378]

860. The insurer can intervene in any procedure in which the obligation to compensate is being discussed. The insurance contract can envisage that the injured party can act directly against the insurer – alone or jointly with the insured (Article 140(1)(3) RJCS). The direct action of the injured party against the insurer, may occur in the circumstances provided for in Article 140(2)(3) RJCS, strictly speaking, when the insurance contract provides for the right of the injured party to sue the insurer directly, alone or jointly; and when the insurer has informed the injured

378. José Vasques, *Art. 142.º* (in: Lei do Contrato de Seguro anotado. 3 Ed., Almedina, 2016), p. 492.

party of the existence of an insurance contract with the consequent commencement of direct negotiations between the injured party and the insurer.

861. As to the direct action of the injured party against the insurer, José Vasques writes: 'the admissibility of the direct action within the scope of the insurance contract … is part of the general trend of its consecration within a context of greater protection of the injured: this trend was materialised, first, in the subrogation or oblique action (articles 606 and ff.). This trend was first set in the subrogation or oblique action (Articles 606 and ff. of the Civil Code) – in which, although not exercising a right of their own, the injured party was competing with other creditors of the person liable – an *actio pauliana* (Article 610 of the Civil Code) or for unjust enrichment (Articles 473 and ff. of the Civil Code), and in the contract in favour of a third party through which the injured party acquired the right to the benefit (Article 441(1) of the Civil Code); (…) and on the finding that the claim of the victim of an event involving civil liability has priority over the indemnity owed by the insurer for the liability incurred by the injured party (Article 741 of the Civil Code), the insurer not being released by the payment to the insured (Article 692(2), ex vi art. 753 CC).'[379] Article 140 RJCS establishes in its No. 2 that the insurance contract may provide for the right of the injured party to demand a direct claim against the insurer, alone or jointly with the insured. If not agreed in the contract, the injured party may directly demand the insurer if the insured has informed them of the existence of an insurance contract with the consequent start of direct negotiations between the injured party and the insurer.[380] Although the insurer is allowed to be a party in any legal proceedings in which the obligation to compensate for the risk it undertook is discussed (Article 140(1)), its direct demand is, in principle, conditioned on the existence of contractual provision or the start of negotiations established with the injured party. This factor is necessary after the accident that should serve to establish the procedural prerequisite of passive legitimacy.

862. The preamble of the RJCS states that 'in optional third-party liability insurance, in certain situations, the injured party may sue the insurer directly; this right is granted to the injured party in compulsory third-party liability insurance. Therefore, the possibility of the injured party directly suing the insurer is conditioned on whether the civil liability insurance is compulsory or optional. In the former case, the rule is that this right is granted to the injured party since compulsory insurance is established by law to protect the injured party. In optional insurance, the principle of the relativity of contracts is preserved, providing that the injured third party cannot, as a rule, claim compensation from the insurer.' However, the insured may exercise the right of recourse if its liability for the loss is recognised. The insurer's

379. José Vasques, *Art. 142.º*, p. 451.

380. In case TRG 14 June 2018, 5688/17.0T8GMR-C.G1 (António Sobrinho), the court concluded that since the insurer had carried out an expert's report on the subject matter of the claim, with contact, exchange of correspondence and information between the insurer and the injured party, including a meeting, all with a view to the possible assumption of civil liability by the insurer under an optional insurance contract, it allows for the conclusion that it constitutes the concept of the start of direct negotiations for the purposes of the direct action by the injured party against the insurer.

intervention may be achieved through the incident of accessory intervention provoked, under the terms of Articles 330 et seq. Therefore, besides the disadvantages of the solution as to the substantive law, the option for the exceptionality of the direct action leads to an unnecessarily complex legal-procedural regime, which could easily have been overcome if another option had been adopted in which, as a general rule, direct action against the insurer was allowed, with or without a claim by the insured, without prejudice to the intervention of the insured when necessary.[381] The legal solution is different, except when otherwise set forth by special legislation, the insurer waives recourse directly against the policyholder or the insured that caused the damage deliberately or that deliberately caused damage to the insurer after the claim (Article 144(1) RJCS).

863. Whenever the insured and the injured have taken out insurance with the same insurer or a conflict of interests exists, the insurer must inform the parties and the insured, if no agreement is reached, they may entrust their defence to someone of their choice (Article 140(4)(5) RJCS). On the other hand, the acceptance of the right of the injured party by the insured as well as any payment they have made without the insurers' consent cannot be opposed by the latter (Article 140(7) RJCS).

§2. Types of General Liability Insurance

864. There are different types of liability insurance: private liability insurance, professional liability insurance, commercial and products liability insurance (general liability insurance for enterprises), and special liability insurance. Liability insurance can either be taken out as a separate policy or as a comprehensive policy covering several other risks related to the private or the professional activity of the insured as well as of companies.

865. The Portuguese legislator has introduced the duty to insure the civil liability emerging from certain private or business activities and professions. Therefore, the supervisory authority has approved uniform contractual clauses of several types of liability insurance in many cases – the updated list of compulsory liability insurance and uniform contractual provisions can be accessed at the ASF site.[382] As stated in Articles 138(2) and 145 RJCS, general rules regarding tort law set out in the Portuguese Civil Code are applicable (Articles 483–510 of the Civil Code), namely concerning the determination of damage (and therefore of the compensation to be paid to the third party, Articles 562–572, as also Article 496 of the Civil Code) and limitation periods (Articles 498 and 300 et seq. of the Civil Code).

---

381. Case TRG 19 October 2017, 6101/15.3T8BRG.G1 (Eugénia Maria de Moura Marinho da Cunha). In the same interpretation, *see* Case TRP 14 December 2013, 1394/13.3TBMAI-A.P1 (Pedro Martins).

382. https://www.asf.com.pt/NR/exeres/3CB687F3-3230-46EF-BCF4-19E3479E8B80.htm.

866. Liability insurance does not normally cover the payment of compensation for the application of any sureties, fees or fines; damage resulting from acts of terrorism, war, civil war, invasion, hostilities, insurrection or labour disturbances (strikes, riots, etc.); damage resulting from an accident that must be covered by another compulsory insurance, namely occupational accident insurance or motor vehicle liability insurance.

867. Unless otherwise agreed, the insurance covers the insured's liability for events occurring between the beginning and the end of the contract, covering claims made after the end of the contract.

I. Private Liability Insurance

868. Private liability insurance covers private individuals. That is, it provides coverage for individuals in their private capacity. It covers the legal liability which the insured incurs for any bodily injury or property damage. It can be taken out as a separate policy. Still, it is usually taken out as a part of a householders' insurance package covering several other risks (multi-risk), such as fire, theft, or legal aid. When the insurance is taken out as a part of comprehensive householders' insurance, it provides cover not only for the policyholder and insured but also to their household, that is, the family members living with them at home, namely spouse, a person cohabiting with the policyholder in a relationship akin to marriage, children and parents living at home and who are economically dependent on the policyholder.

869. As private liability insurance is not a compulsory insurance, the parties are free to stipulate the extent of coverage. The pre-contractual and information duties are safeguarded and the requirements of proof of the contract and its coverage set by Article 37 RJCS as well as the special responsibilities that arise for the insurer when it uses general contractual clauses, particularly in informing of clauses excluding liability or determining the object of the insurance. Generally, the standard policy conditions for private liability insurance contain a certain number of exclusions according to which the insurance does not provide cover for the liability incurred by the insured even if the insured has incurred legal liability, namely, as a result of their professional or business activity, a contract, animal-owners, hunting, use of motor vehicles, caravans, sail- and motor-ships, ships or aircraft – such liability is usually covered by a separate insurance policy, mainly if a legal obligation to insure liability in such cases exists and uniform contractual clauses have been approved by the supervisory authority.

II. Professional Liability Insurance

870. Professional liability insurance covers liability incurred by the insured persons related to their specific professional activities (negligence, errors, or omissions). This type of insurance, therefore, includes coverage for different professionals, such as doctors, attorneys, judges, engineers, architects, directors and officers, insurance intermediaries, brokers, and auditors, construction, travel agencies, real estate mediators, private security services, limited liability law firms, solicitors and execution agents, notaries, societies of notaries, companies applying plant protection products on land, investment consultants, and aerial work operator.

871. In some professional activities, it is mandatory to have insurance,[383] but even in cases where it is not necessary, it is common for the professional to have insurance for their activity.

872. Professional liability insurance can be taken out as a separate policy, but it is usually taken out as a part of a comprehensive insurance policy covering several other risks related to the profession and to the place where the profession is exercised, specifically, the professional office – such as fire, theft, loss of income, or legal aid. When the insurance is taken out as a part of a comprehensive policy, it can provide cover for the policyholder and the insured and the people in their service. Therefore, the insurance can provide cover for the policyholder when they incur direct liability towards a third party (e.g., a client) and when they incur indirect liability because of being liable for the actions or omissions of their employees. In addition, if agreed, professional liability insurance can cover tort law also as contractual liability.

873. Professional liability insurance is usually based on the claims-made principle. However, claims for damages of a third party to be covered must be notified during the duration of the insurance. One must consider whether the contract recognises the direct action to the injured party or whether the regime of Article 140 RJCS applies. Moreover, professional liability insurance usually considers the standard of a normally competent professional to provide coverage. Depending on the profession involved, the insurance policy can cover personal injury claims and/or property damage.

874. Generally, the contract does not cover liability for activities outside the scope of the insured's profession.

III. Commercial Liability Insurance

875. Commercial liability insurance covers liability incurred by companies (legal persons) and persons acting in the course of business, that is, in connection with carrying out business activities (namely production and distribution of goods or delivering of services) set out in the policy. The policy would give cover if the event giving rise to the insured's liability to third parties occurred in the course of

383. The updated list is available at https://www.asf.com.pt/NR/exeres/6305CEA1-CF8F-4534-A717-4D82BC1C84E7.htm.

business subscribed on the cover note. When the insurance is optional, the parties may agree in insurance that covers legal liability (tort actions) and contractual liability.

876. Coverage is generally taken employing a comprehensive policy providing cover for business liability exposures, including environmental liability, as well as for the products or services in which it deals and other risks (such as fire, theft, or financial loss insurance).

877. The policies are generally based on the loss-occurrence principle, and coverage is provided regarding liability arising out of the insured period. The policies usually contain limits of liability per event and per year.

878. The liability insurance policy usually provides cover not only to the company itself but also to its employees and agents and members of the company's legal organs while acting on behalf of the insured (*see* Articles 396(1)(2), 418-A, 445 of the Commercial Companies Code).

879. There are cases where general liability insurance on several commercial or business activities (related to either products or services) is compulsory, such as industrial activity, collective transportation of children, activities involving environmental risks, travel and tourism agencies, inspection of motor vehicles, concessionaires of activities involving production, transportation, distribution and commercialisation of electricity, gas or natural gas or oil, air transportation, and private health units, Responsible Business Zone management entity, bullfighting show promoter, a caster of articles with precious metals and gemological materials, intermediaries registered with the Portuguese Football Federation, Energy Service Companies, owners of local accommodation management resulting from the exercise of the activity of providing accommodation services, garages that adapt or repair vehicles using LPG or NG, an activity carried out in tanning centres, auction companies.[384]

880. The standard policy conditions for commercial liability insurance generally contain a certain number of exclusions, for instance: environmental liability, in other words, damage resulting from pollution of air, water, or soil (except if otherwise expressly agreed or resulting from a sudden uncertain event); criminal liability; liability through loss, damage, or injury caused deliberately and/or wilfully; cost of replacement of defected products; liability arising out of the use of motor vehicles and aircraft; war risks or damage caused by nuclear explosions.

384. The updated list is available at https://www.asf.com.pt/NR/exeres/6305CEA1-CF8F-4534-A717-4D82BC1C84E7.htm.

IV. Special Liability Insurance

881. Special liability insurance can also exist while related to a particular risk to the private life of the insured, such as hunting[385] or owning of animals; it can also fall outside this realm, as is the case with environmental insurance.

882. The relevance of special liability insurance has been increasing in connection with new forms of compulsory insurance.

883. In what regards compulsory liability insurance for hunting, the insurance does not cover damages due to natural disasters, acts of war, terrorism, civil disturbance and use or transport of radioactive materials; accidents attributable to the injured party themselves, to the extent of such attribution; accidents covered by the law on accidents at work; and payments due as a result of criminal, administrative or disciplinary liability. The parties can agree in the particular conditions that the insurance covers accidents occurring on the way to or from the hunting location are not covered, whatever the means of transport used.

884. As for animal-owners' liability, it is compulsory for owners of dangerous and potentially dangerous animals.[386] In this case, the obligation to enter into the insurance contract does not apply to the keepers of animals used in circus shows. The insurance contract shall not cover the insured animals during their participation in shows, competitions, contests, exhibitions, advertising and similar events. It is excluded from the insurance damages caused to employees, salaried employees or agents of the insured while in the service of the insured, as long as such damages are the result of an accident falling within the scope of the legislation on accidents at work; caused to partners, managers, legal representatives or agents of the legal person whose liability is guaranteed; caused to any persons whose liability is guaranteed by this contract, as well as to the spouse, person living in a common-law marriage with the insured, ascendants and descendants, or persons living with them or in their charge, as well as the keeper, guardian or user of the animal; caused by animals while hunting, which, in accordance with the law, must be subject to a compulsory civil liability insurance policy; due to liability for accidents occurring to vehicles, which, under the terms of the law, must be subject to compulsory civil liability insurance; resulting from costs and any other expenses arising from criminal proceedings, bail, fines, fees or additional charges of the same nature; caused by non-compliance with the legal provisions in force that regulate the keeping of pet animals; caused by the transport of animals in vehicles not appropriate for that purpose, as well as those caused to vehicles transporting animals; caused to other animals of the same species; resulting from failure to observe the hygienic, prophylactic and therapeutic measures recommended in the case of infectious or

385. Law 173/99, 21-09, amended by Decree-Law 2/2011, 06-11, Decree-Law 202/2004, 18-08. Uniform clauses set by Regulatory Framework 20/2008-R of 31 December (https://www.asf.com.pt/Biblioteca/Catalogo/winlibimg.aspx?key=&doc=17845&img=2665).

386. Decree-Law 315/2009, 29-10, Annex II of Law 46/2013, 04-07, and Ministerial Order 585/2004, 29-05.

parasitic diseases; occurring as a result of war, strike, lock-out, riots, civil commotion, assault, sabotage, terrorism, acts of vandalism, civil or military insurrection or decisions by authorities or forces usurping authority, robbery and air piracy.

885. Environmental liability insurance is provided for under the Regime for Liability for Environmental Damage (Decree-Law 147/2008, of 29 July 2008, last amendment Law Decree 13/2016, of 09 March 2016). Article 22 demands that the persons conducting certain activities contract a financial guarantee in regard of the environmental liability that may arise in its connection. Insurance contracts are a means of providing such a guarantee, but other forms of guarantee (bank guarantees, participation in environmental funds, constitution of reserves for the purpose) are also allowed (Article 22(2)).

886. Such guarantees (including insurance) obey the principle of exclusivity. They may not be diverted to another purpose or be the object of any total or partial encumbrance, whether original or supervening. Minimum limits may also be set for constituting mandatory financial guarantees through a decree order to be approved by the members of the Government responsible for the areas of finance, the environment and the economy, namely in relation to the scope of activities covered, the type of risk to be covered, the period of validity of the guarantee, the temporal scope of application of the guarantee, and the minimum value that must be guaranteed. As for the compensation obligation, the legal prerequisites are specially determined in Articles 7 and 8 of the legal regime.

887. Some sources of danger are not included in the scope of environmental liability, and are thus naturally excluded from coverage under the liability insurance contract entered into for this purpose. That is the case of environmental damage or imminent threats of such damage caused by any of the following acts and activities, like acts of armed conflict, hostilities, civil war or insurrection, natural phenomena of a wholly exceptional character that cannot be foreseen or which, though foreseen, are unavoidable, activities the main purpose of which lies in national defence or international security, and activities the sole purpose of which lies in protecting against natural disasters. Also excluded is environmental damage or imminent threats of such damage resulting from incidents in respect of which liability falls within the scope of any of the international conventions, resulting from nuclear risks or caused by the activities covered by the Treaty Establishing the European Atomic Energy Community, or by incidents or activities in respect of which liability or compensation falls within the scope of any of the international instruments.

888. General liability insurance progressively excluded environmental risks from the scope of coverage. Insurance companies tended to design special environmental insurance policies to cover pollution damage, including damage resulting from gradual pollution. Such policies are typically based on the claims-made principle. Article 2 Regime for Liability for Environmental Damage determines the object of environmental liability to environmental damage, as well as to imminent threats of such damage, caused as a result of the exercise of any activity performed within the scope of economic activity, irrespective of its public or private, profit-making or non-profit-making character, abbreviated to occupational activity.

Chapter 5. Motor Vehicle Insurance (*Pro Memoria*)

889. *See* Part IV, below.

Chapter 6. Legal Aid Insurance

890. Legal aid insurance is envisaged in Articles 167–172 RJCS and intends to protect the insured person against financial disadvantages that come upon them in the form of legal costs (lawyer's fees, court costs, etc.) in the event of a legal conflict.

891. Furthermore, besides general rules concerning the insurance contract and general rules regarding damage insurance, there is specific legislation on legal aid insurance according to what is enshrined in Articles 198 et seq. of the Directive 2009/138/EC of the European Parliament and of the Council of 25 November 2009 on the taking-up and pursuit of the business of Insurance and Reinsurance (Solvency II) that repeal the Directive 87/344/EEC of 22 June 1987.

892. This type of insurance differs from situations in which legal aid cover is included in other types of insurance contracts. Unlike these, this is an autonomous and distinct contract of which purpose is to ensure transparency and avoid situations of conflict of interest (Recital 82 and Article 199 Solvency II).

893. The relationship between the policyholder and the lawyer shall rely on the regime established in respect of the conclusion of the mandate, even though this results in a trilateral relationship. The mandate of the lawyer to represent the policyholder's interests raises the question of the extent to which this gives rise to rights or obligations vis-à-vis the insurer. The decisive factor here is that the insurer appoints the lawyer in the name of and on behalf of – i.e., only as a representative of – the policyholder. This excludes legal relations between the insurer and the lawyer from the outset (Article 444 of Civil Code (contract in favour of a third party)). There are also the cases where the policyholder is obliged to pay fees under the mandate agreement with their lawyer and the reimbursement of these fees is the subject of the agreement with the legal expenses insurer, which results in a triangular relationship with an exchange of services based on different rights and obligations between each other.

894. Legal aid insurance covers the costs of legal services, such as defence and legal representation of the insured and costs of legal, judicial, or administrative proceedings (Article 167 RJCS). These insurances may have the following scope, in a logic of alternative systems, claims management by separate personnel; claims management by a legally distinct company; free choice of lawyer (Article 168 RJCS). Legal aid insurance can be taken out either as a separate contract and policy or as an autonomous chapter of a comprehensive policy indicating the scope of the legal aid coverage. Since a conflict of interest can arise if an insured has legal aid insurance and any other insurance with the same multi-branch insurance, insurers must choose one of the alternatives mentioned above to prevent such a conflict.

895. There is particular information to be provided by the insurer and included in the policy, alongside the information prescribed in Article 37 RJCS. Article 170(1) RJCS specifies that the contract shall expressly refer that the insured has the right to resort to the arbitration procedure in the case of a dispute between the insured and their insurer, without prejudice to the insured taking action or lodging an appeal, advised against by the insurer, at their own expense, being reimbursed for the costs incurred to the extent that the arbitral decision or award is more favourable to them than the proposed solution presented by the insurer; to be informed in due time by the insurer, whenever a conflict of interest arises or there is disagreement as to the resolution of the dispute, of the rights referred to in the preceding paragraphs; and to freely choosing a lawyer[387] or, if they prefer, another person with the necessary legal qualification to defend, represent or serve their interests in judicial or administrative proceedings and any other case of conflict of interests.

896. The latter is not mandatory (Article 170(2) RJCS) if the insurance is limited to proceedings arising from the use of road vehicles in national territory; associated with a contract of assistance to be provided in case of accident or breakdown involving a road vehicle, or neither the legal expenses insurer nor the assistance insurer cover classes of civil liability. It is also not necessary to mention if the terms of the contract provide that legal advice and representation of each of the parties to a dispute will be given by a lawyer who had not represented any of the parties in the last year when the said parties are insured under legal expenses insurance with the same insurer or with insurers that are in a group relationship with each other.

897. Legal aid insurance shall be excluded from the object of such insurance and, consequently, from these mandatory rules where it concerns disputes or risks arising out of, or in connection with, the use of sea-going vessels. Also excluded is the activity carried out in the defence or representation of the insured in any legal or administrative proceedings, insofar as this activity is carried out simultaneously and in their own interest under the same cover. Finally, also excluded are situations where the legal expense cover is provided outside the State of habitual residence of the insured and forms part of a contract intended solely to assist persons who get into difficulties while travelling, when away from home or while away from their permanent residence, provided that the contract expressly states both these circumstances and that the legal expenses cover ancillary to the assistance cover (Article 172 RJCS).

387. Before coming into force the Solvency II, the ECJ stated that where a large number of insured persons suffer loss as a result of the same event, the insurer cannot reserve the right to select the legal representative of all the insured persons concerned; C-199/08, Eschig, ECLI:EU:C:2009:538.

Chapter 7. Aviation and Space Insurance

§1. Aviation in General

898. In 1999, the Montreal Convention adopted concerns on the unification of certain rules for international carriage by air.[388] It replaces the Warsaw Convention, signed in 1929, and entered into force in 2003, having 127 Parties, one of which is Portugal since 28 May 1999.

899. Not all International Civil Aviation Organization Contracting States (a United Nations Specialized Agency) are Parties to the Montreal Convention, but, in its Thirty-Ninth Assembly in 2016, it adopted Resolution A39-9, urging Governments to ratify the Montreal Convention.

900. Article 50 of the Montreal Convention regards insurance, stating that 'State Parties shall require their carriers to maintain adequate insurance covering their liability under this Convention. A carrier may be required by the State Party into which it operates to furnish evidence that it maintains adequate insurance covering its liability under this Convention.'

901. As a Member of the EU, Regulation (EC) 785/2004 of the European Parliament and of the Council of 21 April 2004, on insurance requirements for air carriers and aircraft operators, also applies.

902. Decree-Law 321/89, of 25 September (altered by Decree-Law 279/95, of 26 October) institutes compulsory insurance for air transportation activities, concerning all aircrafts – carrying passengers; luggage; cargo; mail or animals – with Portuguese registration, as well as all aircrafts with foreign registration but using Portuguese airports or crossing Portuguese airspace.

903. Complementarily, Government Regulation 893/99, of 20 September, implements minimum capital of civil liability insurance policies relating to airport ground handling activities in some airports (Lisbon, Porto, Faro, Madeira (Funchal), Madeira (Porto Santo), São Miguel (Ponta Delgada), Santa Maria and Faial (Horta) islands).

388. Available at: https://www.iata.org/contentassets/fb1137ff561a4819a2d38f3db7308758/mc99-full-text.pdf.

§2. Unmanned Aircraft Systems

904. Decree-Law 58/2018, of 23 July, instituted in its Article 10 a compulsory civil liability insurance with regard to operating unmanned aircraft system, or Drones, heavier than 900 g (and lighter than 20 kg[389]), if they are not covered by sporting activity insurance.

905. Registration is regulated by the Commission Implementing Regulation (EU) 2019/947 of 24 May 2019, on the rules and procedures for the operation of unmanned aircraft, published after Decree-Law 58/2018.

906. Coverage, minimum capital and conditions are regulated by Government Regulation 2/2021, of 4 January.

389. If heavier than 20 kg, Regulation (EC) 785/2004 of the European Parliament and of the Council of 21 April 2004, on insurance requirements for air carriers and aircraft operators, applies.

Chapter 8. Theft and Embezzlement Insurance

907. There are no special statutory or administrative rules regarding theft and embezzlement insurance. Since the protection of an interest upon certain assets is at stake, the general rules on property insurance apply.

908. Recent case law in this realm has mostly regarded the interpretation of insurance contract clauses that define what is considered theft or embezzlement for the purpose of the cover.[390] It is of interest to notice how a second instance court applied a clause of insurance protecting against car theft, that excluded cover in case the car key had been left inside the vehicle, or on its lock.[391] In the case, the insured had left the key in the ignition of his vehicle while he had come out to open the garage gate; it was established that the vehicle was stolen while the insured was about two meters away from the vehicle. In spite of the behaviour of the insured having corresponded to that of a normally diligent car owner, the court considered that the case was encompassed by the exclusion clause and considered that there was no right to cover.

909. Taking out insurance against theft or embezzlement is mandatory in some cases. For example, regarding the activity of private security ventures providing the services of transport, custody, processing and distribution of cash, values and other objects that due to their value may require special protection and for which such protection is required. In order for a private security activity comprising such services to be licensed, the ventures must take out insurance against theft and embezzlement with the minimum capital of EUR 5,000,000 (Articles 47(3)(f) and 3(1)(d) of Law 34/2013, of 16 May, on the activity of providing private security). It is also mandatory for an entity that promotes the exhibition of works of art to take out theft or embezzlement insurance, as stated in Article 158 of the Code on copyright protection.[392]

390. STJ 18 February 2021, 64/18.0T8BRG.G1.S1 (Oliveira Abreu); STJ 21 October 2020, 22277/17.2T8LSB.L1.S1 (Maria Clara Sottomayor).
391. TRP 17 June 2021, 2578/19.6T8PRD.P1 (Aristides Rodrigues de Almeida).
392. Decree-Law 63/85, of 14 March.

Chapter 9. Agricultural Insurance, Hail Insurance and Livestock Insurance

910. Due to their extended cycles of production and to their dependence on weather conditions, agriculture and livestock are especially prone to uncertainty. This is reflected in the insurance law norms issued in their regard.

911. The uncertainty affecting agriculture prompted the State to create an Integrated System of Protection Against Climate Variables, as early as 1996.[393] The System comprised three mechanisms of protection: agricultural insurance, a guarantee fund that protected farmers in case of calamities and a compensation scheme that reimbursed insurers in case the claims amounts exceeded a percentage of the value of premiums (Article 1 of Decree-Law 20/96). Livestock insurance protection was provided for later, by Decree-Law 137/2001, of 24 April.

912. With the exception of the norms on the guarantee fund, both acts were repealed in 2015 by the Act on the national system of agricultural insurance.[394] As was the case with the old insurance mechanisms, the new insurance mechanism consists of a *system of public subsidisation of insurance premiums.*

913. The scope of the new system is broader than that of the original system. It encompasses harvest, livestock and plants insurance; wine harvest insurance; fruit and vegetables harvest insurance in the context of European funds (Article 2). Agricultural insurances are in principle voluntary, although the right to other public aid may be conditioned upon having taken out agricultural insurance (Article 3(e)); moreover, an obligation to take out insurance can be established under certain requirements (Article 6). Insurance premiums are not regulated, but rather freely set by insurers. However, subsidisation can be denied in case the premium set surpasses a certain threshold of reasonableness, if no objective reasons regarding the degree of risk of the insured are provided (Article 3(d)). The system of subsidised agricultural insurance is managed by a public entity, *Instituto de Financiamento da Agricultura e Pescas, I. P.* (Article 7 of Decree-Law).

914. Agricultural insurance is regulated in detail by Regulation 65/2014[395] and by the Regulatory Framework of the ASF 4/2018-R, which sets out the uniform conditions of the harvest insurance for the Portuguese mainland. Regulation 18/2015[396] provides for further insurance covers that are also part of the system – such as the cover against adverse climatic events, plants or animal plagues or environmental hazards.

393. Set out by Decree-Law 20/96, of 19 March; there had in fact been a previous attempt at creating the system in the previous year.
394. Decree-Law 162/2015, of 14 August.
395. Administrative Regulation ('Portaria') 65/2014, of 12 March.
396. Administrative Regulation ('Portaria') 18/2015, of 2 February.

915. At an insurance contract level, the uncertainty affecting agriculture or livestock can especially cast doubt upon the ascertainment of the amount of loss. The RJCS has tried to address this issue, by setting out criteria for the determination of the amount of loss in either case. Article 152 provides for harvest insurance, described as insurance which gives right to a compensation set in regard of a certain loss in crops (Article 152(1)). Under Article 152(2), the compensation is set according to the value that a normal production would have had by the time of harvest, if the insured event had not occurred; this value is deduced from the costs that were not incurred and from other savings and advantages that came to the insured from the insured event.

916. Article 153 provides for livestock insurance, which it describes as insurance that gives right to a compensation set in regard of a certain loss in certain kind of livestock (Article 153(1)). Livestock insurance does not cover risks regarding individual animals; property insurance, and not livestock insurance, should be used for those purposes.[397] Article 153(2) provides for the case in which the insurance covers the risk of sickness or death of calves. In this case, similar to what happens in agricultural insurance, the compensation is set according to the value that the animals would presumably have had by the time they were sold or slaughtered, if the insured event had not occurred; this value is deduced from the costs that were not incurred and from other savings and advantages that came to the insured from the insured event.

917. Article 154 sets out the elements that the policy should mention, in regard to each of the types of insurance.

397. Pedro Romano Martínez, Art. 153.º, Seguro pecuário (in: P. Romano Martínez (ed.) Lei do Contrato de Seguro anotada, 4 Ed., Almedina, 510, 2020), 510.

Chapter 10. Catastrophe Insurance

§1. General

918. There are no special statutory or administrative rules regarding catastrophe insurance as such.[398] Insurance protection against catastrophes is only provided in the context of agricultural and livestock insurance, as mentioned above (Part III, Chapter 9).

919. There have been several attempts at creating insurance and insurance-like mechanisms of protection against catastrophic – and especially seismic – risks. In 2010, there was a public consultation for a Decree-Law on this matter, but the initiative was abandoned.[399]

920. The APS, the insurance industry association, has also recently tried to foster the creation of a system of protection against catastrophic risks, which would include mandatory coverage of seismic risks, a public guarantee fund and the last resort responsibility of the Portuguese State.[400] No further developments have yet been divulged in regard to this matter.

921. In practice, risks regarding natural (floods, storms, wildfires) or human-caused catastrophes (wildfires, nuclear hazards) are moreover generally excluded from cover by the contract's terms. The parties remain free to stipulate their cover.

§2. Nuclear Risks

922. There are no special statutory or administrative rules regarding insurance of nuclear risks. Such risks are moreover generally excluded from cover by the contract's terms. The parties remain free to stipulate their cover.

§3. Natural Catastrophes

923. Apart from the context of agricultural and livestock insurance (Part III, Chapter 9), there are no special statutory or administrative rules regarding insurance of nuclear risks. Such risks are moreover generally excluded from cover by the contract's terms. The parties remain free to stipulate their cover.

---

398. On this topic, *see* Margarida Lima Rego/Rute Carvalho da Silva, Catástrofes naturais e seguros (in: Carla Amado Gomes/Rute Gil Saraiva (ed.) Actas do Colóquio 'Catástrofes naturais: uma realidade mutidimensional' Instituto de Ciências Jurídico-Políticas, 2012), https://www.icjp.pt/sites/default/files/publicacoes/files/ebook_catastrofes_final1_isbn.pdf (accessed 03 Nov. 2021).

399. https://www.asf.com.pt/NR/rdonlyres/4B871EA8-A16C-4A56-AEBB-0768E589DFA8/0/DocumentodeConsultaPública.pdf.

400. http://www.prociv.pt/bk/Documents/SPRC%20–%20José%20Galamba%20de%20Oliveira.pdf.

Chapter 11. Credit and Caution Insurance

§1. Credit Insurance

924. Credit insurance is a non-compulsory type of insurance contract, which arose from market practices and which is regulated, *inter alia*, by Articles 162–166 RJCS; 8, paragraph (n) and (o); and 12, paragraph (g) LBIR; and by Decree-Law 183/88 of 24 May, establishing the legal framework for credit insurance.[401]

925. Only pecuniary damages are to be compensated (Article 12 of Decree-Law 183/88), and there is no compensation for loss of profit. Promissory insurance agreements can be concluded under Article 13 and stay in force for a maximum period of three months.

926. Other relevant legislations are, for example:

- Decree-Law 295/2011, of 21 November regulating Portuguese foreign direct investment, altered by Decree-Law 51/2006, of 14 March; by Decree-Law 31/2007, of 24 February; and by Decree-Law 94/2018, of 14 November, which creates the Council of Financial Guarantees to Exports and Investment of Portuguese companies;
- Directive 98/29/EC, regarding export credit insurance; and
- Council regulation (EC) 806/2003, of 14 April, adapting to Decision 1999/468/EC the provisions relating to committees which assist the Commission in the exercise of its implementing powers laid down in Council instruments adopted in accordance with the consultation procedure.

927. Credit insurance is usually entered into by traders or businesspeople who are creditors and want protection against events affecting their right to a certain payment. The interest protected by the contract is therefore the interest of a creditor; they have the quality of insured.[402]

928. Under Article 161 RJCS, the insurer undertakes to indemnify the insured for instance in case of lack or delay of payment; due to political/natural/contractual risks that obstruct compliance with a payment obligation; non-recovery of expenses undertaken in view of such credits; variation in exchange rates; abnormal and

401. For a more comprehensive study, *see* J. M. F. Alves de Brito, Seguro-caução: primeiras considerações sobre o seu regime e natureza jurídica, in Estudos em memória do Professor Doutor José Dias Marques, coord. Ruy de Albuquerque, António Menezes Cordeiros, 2007, 385 ff; M. E. Gomes Ramos, Um seguro que substitui a caução dos administradores. Que seguro é este?, in Julgar, 43, 2021, 115 ff.; Ségio Coimbra Henriques, O seguro de crédito à luz do regime jurídico do contrato de seguro, *in* Julgar Online, 2014; Luís Poças, A natureza jurídica do seguro-caução, in RDES, LVI, January-September 2015, 101 ff.

402. *See* TRG 11 September 2012, 756/10.2TBFLG.G1, (Ana Cristina Duarte).

unpredictable raise of production costs; arbitrary suspension or withdrawal of the transaction or termination of the contract by the debtor before the credit emerges.[403]

929. Under Article 5 of Decree-Law 183/88 coverage is limited to a percentage of the credit, except if the State has provided collateral under Article 15 of the same Decree-Law.[404]

930. Considering its nature, credit insurance places special collaboration and information duties upon the insured (Article 10 of Decree-Law 183/88),[405] and insurance companies are granted access to information from official databases that they otherwise would not have, in order to enable a more rigorous risk assessment (Article 21 of Decree-Law 183/88).

931. Article 8 of Decree-Law 183/88 establishes that contracts must mention, e.g., the identity of the policyholder and of the insured person; the credit related to the insured risk; the percentage of insured credit; deadlines for presenting claims and fulfilling the duty to pay out.

932. Once payment is made, the insurer becomes subrogated in the amount paid, in line with Article 136 (referenced in Article 165 RJCS), except if subrogation was only partial, case in which both the insurance company and the insured can exercise their rights pro rata.

§2. Caution Insurance

933. Caution insurance cover risks regarding lack or delay in payment in cases where, either by law or contract, someone is required to provide caution, bailment or surety (personal guarantee). It comprises direct and indirect caution; bailment-insurance and surety-insurance. Contrary to credit insurance, caution insurance is agreed between an insurer and the debtor (direct caution) or the counter-guarantor (indirect caution), and it protects the interest of the creditor (Article 162 of RJCS). In other words, caution insurance is always taken out for the account a third party, the creditor.[406]

934. The limitation of Article 5 of Decree-Law 183/88, does not apply to caution insurance, and therefore it can cover the total insured interest, unlike credit insurance.

403. For other instances insured events, *see* Art. 3 of Decree-Law 183/88. In regard to information duties in this field, *see, e.g.*, TRP 26 March 2015, 551/13.7TVPRT.P1 (Aristides Rodrigues de Almeida). *See* Menezes Cordeiro, António, Direito dos Seguros, Almedina, 834–835.
404. Regarding State's guarantees, *see* Art. 15 of Decree-Law 183/88, May 24.
405. Coimbra Henriques, O seguro de crédito ..., 14 ff.
406. On its trilateral contractual relation, *see* TRL 23 September 2008, 3033/2008-1 (Rui Vouga); on its *intuitu personae* character, *see* TRL 23 March 2021, 13483/16.8T8SNT.L1-7 (Diogo Ravara).

935. Articles 8 and ff. of Decree-Law 183/88, are applicable both to caution and credit insurance.

936. Caution insurance is mentioned in several statutes, such as:

(1) Public Contracts Code, Decree-Law 18/2008, 29 January.
(2) Decree-Law 262/86, 2 September, Commercial Companies Act.
(3) Decree-Law39/2008, 7 March, concerning instalment; exploration and operation of tourism enterprises.
(4) Decree-Law 3/2004, 3 January, concerning licensing for instalment and exploration of dangerous residues elimination centres.
(5) Decree-Law 260/2009, 25 September, regarding agency activity for temporary work.
(6) Decree-Law 195/99, 8 June, regulating supply contracts for essential public goods.
(7) Decree-Law 555/99, 16 December, establishing the legal framework for urbanisation and edification.

937. As in credit insurance, under Article 165(2), once payment is made insurance companies become subrogated in the insured's rights. Caution insurance can, also, contemplate a right to redress for the insurer against the policyholder.

938. The nature of caution insurance is debated by legal scholarship and in the Courts. Some consider it to be (with nuances) a form of guarantee, and not an insurance contract; others consider it a *tertium genus*, between a guarantee and an insurance contract; and others think of it as an insurance contract.[407]

407. For a detailed study, *see* Coimbra Henriques, O seguro de crédito ..., 118 ff.

Chapter 12. Technical Insurance

939. The category of 'technical insurance' is not generally referred to in the Portuguese market. The terminology used in this regard varies quite significantly. Sometime policies draw upon the English terminology and refer to 'machinery breakdown insurance' (*seguro de avaria de máquinas, seguro de quebra de máquinas*), or 'all risk construction insurance' (*seguro de construção – todos os riscos*) and 'erection all risks insurance' (*seguro de montagem – todos os riscos*); but it is also frequent to see the same covers offered under broad commercial property insurance.

940. There are no special statutory or administrative rules regarding technical insurance. This category can encompass different kinds of cover – e.g., it may protect the interest of the insured upon the production assets themselves, as well as their interest in protecting their balance sheet against risks of liability or a loss of profits. According to the nature of the cover, the rules on property insurance, loss of benefits, or liability insurance shall apply.

941. Both named perils coverage and all risks coverage can be present in this segment; ascertaining which is the kind of protection granted is a matter of interpretation of the contract. It should be said that named perils coverage – especially under multi-risk insurance – seems to be the prevailing kind of cover.

Chapter 13. Miscellaneous Insurance

§1. Assistance Insurance

942. Assistance insurance should also be mentioned. It is addressed by Articles 173 and 174 of RJCS, which reproduce segments of Article 2(2) of Solvency II.

943. Article 173 sets out the concept of assistance insurance, as insurance in which the insurer undertakes to provide aid or to make aid available to the insured where that person is in difficulties following the occurrence of a chance event, in the cases and under the conditions set out in the contract. Article 174 clarifies that the assistance activity shall not cover servicing, maintenance, after-sales service or the mere indication or provision of aid as an intermediary.

944. Unlike Solvency II, the RJCS does not state that the aid may comprise the provision of benefits in cash or in kind. However, there are no doubts as to this possibility.[408] Assistance insurance is generally invoked as one of the established precedents in the issue of providing insurance services in kind – a question that has recently acquired much importance in view of the provision of loss prevention services by the insurance industry.

408. Leonor Cunha Torres, Art. 173.º, Noção (in: P. Romano Martínez (ed.) Lei do Contrato de Seguro anotada, 4 Ed., Almedina, 529, 2020), 530.

Part IV. Compulsory Motor Vehicle Insurance

Chapter 1. Applicable Law

Gabriela Lacerda Assunção

945. Motor vehicle insurance has been compulsory under Portuguese law since Decree-Law 408/79, of 25 September was enacted.

946. It is currently regulated by Decree-Law 291/2007, of 21 August,[409] CMIA, which in its original form partially transposed Directive 2005/14/EC, of the European Parliament and of the Council of 11 May 2005, and Directive 2000/26/EC, of the European Parliament and of the Council of 16 May 2000.[410]

947. There is more applicable legislation, such as, for example:

- Governmental Regulation 377/2008, of 26 May, altered by Governmental Regulation 679/2009, of 25 June 25, setting guiding criteria and amounts of reasonable proposals for compensating bodily harm;
- Decree-Law 214/97, of 16 August, concerning transparency in matters of over-insurance in non-compulsory motor vehicle insurance;
- Norm 14/1997, of 9 October 9, altered by Regulatory Norm 8/1998-R, of 15 June, regulating Decree-Law 214/97, of 16 August;
- Regulatory Standard 14/2008-R, of 27 November, approved by the ASF, regarding the 'Standard part of general conditions for an insurance policy for compulsory motor vehicle insurance liability';

409. All provisions mentioned without any reference belong to Decree-Law 291/2007, of 21 August.
For a comprehensive analyses, cf., e.g., Filipe Albuquerque Matos, O contrato de seguro obrigatório de responsabilidade civil automóvel – alguns aspectos do seu regime jurídico, in BFD, 78, 2002, 329 ff; Arnaldo Filipe da Costa Oliveira, Seguro Obrigatório de Responsabilidade Civil Automóvel- síntese das alterações de 2007', Almedina, 2008; António Jorge Rebelo, Acidentes de Viação: a regularização dos danos pelo Seguro, Coimbra Editora, 2013; José Vítor dos Santos Amaral, Contrato de Seguro, responsabilidade automóvel e boa-fé, Almedina, 2017.

410. Both Directives were repealed by Directive 2009/103/EC, of the European Parliament and of the Council of 16 September 2009, relating to insurance against civil liability in respect to the use of motor vehicles, and the enforcement of the obligation to insure against such liability (Motor Insurance Directive).

- Regulatory Standard 16/2007-R, of 20 December, approved by the ASF, altered by Regulatory Standard 7/2009-R, of 14 May, and subsequently altered by Regulatory Standard 17/2010-R, of 18 November, both of the ASF, concerning the regularisation of accidents and motor vehicle's insurance;
- Regulatory Standard 9/2006-R, of 24 October, approved by the former insurance supervising authority, regarding the placement of motor vehicle risks for which mandatory cover has been refused; and
- Government Regulation 234/2020, of 8 October, concerning insurance labels for vehicles.

Chapter 2. Duty to Insure

948. Under Article 4(1), everyone who can be liable to repair bodily or material damages[411] caused to third parties by a land motor vehicle of which use requires a driving license, or by its trailers, that is normally parked in Portugal, has the duty to take out an insurance contract covering such third-party liability in order to use the vehicle.[412]

949. That duty falls, as stated by Article 6(1), on the owner, or, exceptionally, on whoever enjoys the right of usufruct; on the buyer of a vehicle, even if the seller has retention of tittle; and on the tenant of a lease contract. However, the obligation can, according to Article 6(2), be fulfilled by anyone – independent of being the person under the duty or not.

950. With regard to compulsory motor vehicle insurance taken out by a third party – that is, someone with no objective interest upon the vehicle – the Portuguese Supreme Court of Justice decided that, under the cited Article 6(2), and in line with a principle of good faith, insurance companies cannot invoke that as a cause of invalidity, even if the contractual party does not have a driver's license but states it does. It is the company's responsibility to make sure those declarations are true. Moreover, the reason underlying compulsory motor vehicle insurance is to socialise third-party risks, which should be jeopardised by an internal contractual matter, with no external resonance.[413]

951. Nevertheless, some parties are exempt from the duty to insure (Article 9), such as foreign States, under a principle of reciprocity; international organisations of which the Portuguese State is a member of; and the Portuguese State itself, concerning its vehicles, if so decided by ministerial order.

952. Concurrently, Article 150 of the Traffic Code (now regulated by Decree-Law 114/94, of 3 May) states that motor vehicles, and their trailers, can only travel on public roads if their use is covered by civil liability insurance, as provided for by special law. Failing to do so will result in an administrative fine between EUR 500.00 and 2,500.00, in the case of motorcycles and automobiles, and between EUR 250.00 and 1,250.00 if concerning any other mother vehicle.

---

411. In contrast, Decree-Law 522/85, of 31 December, mentioned pecuniary and non-pecuniary loss. Regardless, this new formulation is not interpreted as a way of overruling the compensation of bodily and material damages. For example, Adriano Garção Soares, M. J. Rangel de Mesquita, Regime do Sistema de Seguro Obrigatório de Responsabilidade Civil Automóvel, Coimbra, Almedina, 21–22, 2008.
412. Some exemptions can be found in regard to vehicles running on rails, including underground vehicles (this does not apply if they are electric, as well as where rails intersect with a public road), and the ones not requiring registration plates, or used exclusively for in agriculture and industry, as stated in Art. 4(2) and (3).
413. STJ 3 March 2018, 647/11.0TBVPV.L1.S1 (Távora Víctor).

Chapter 3. Insurance Scope

§1. Material Scope

953. With respect to its material scope, compulsory motor vehicle insurance, as provided for by Article 4, covers:

(1) Compensation derived from civil liability under national law, regarding accidents that occur within the Portuguese territory Article 11(a)).
(2) Compensation derived from the national law of the third country in which the accident occurred, with regard to countries participating in the National Insurance Bureau (Green Card Bureau). If that country is part of the EEA the Portuguese law will always be applicable if it guarantees greater coverage Article 11(b)).
(3) If an accident happens on route between two countries that are part of the EEA, where there is no national insurance scheme, only damages suffered by residents of an EU Member State or residents of countries which signed-in to the National Insurance Bureau will be covered, and in accordance with Portuguese law Article 11(c)).
(4) All damages suffered by pedestrians; cyclists; and drivers of any other non-motorised form of transportation, giving they are covered by the applicable law Article 11(2)).

§2. Territorial Scope

954. Under cited Article 4, and for the length of its validity period, an insurance contract comprises the territory of countries participating in the National Insurance Bureau; routes between two countries that are part of the EEA where there is no national insurance scheme; civil liability arisen from use of a vehicle in countries where there are Insurance Bureaus created according to Recommendation No. 5, adopted on 25 January 1949 by the Road Transport Sub-committee of the Inland Transport Committee of the United Nations Economic Commission for Europe, and there are guarantees of an international certificate of insurance (green card). A list of all countries participating in the National Insurance Bureau can be found on Portugal's Insurance Institute website.

§3. Insured Liability: Coverage and Exclusions

955. Under Article 15, compulsory motor vehicle insurance covers civil liability of:

(1) policyholders (Article 15(1));
(2) whoever has a duty to insure in line with Article 4 (Article 15(1));
(3) legitimate holders or drivers of a motor vehicle (Article 15(1)); and

(4) the civil liability of perpetrators of theft; robbery; vehicle-usage theft; and of all deliberately caused accidents – except if the injured party is the vehicle's owner, usufructuary, buyer with reservation of ownership, or lessee; or even if the injured party is the perpetrator or an accomplice, and of those willingly transported with knowledge of the unlawful possession of the vehicle by the offender (Article 15(2)).

956. Even so, general third-party liability insurance excludes coverage, as contemplated in Article 14, for:

(1) *Bodily harm* suffered by the driver if they are responsible for the accident and resulting damages (Article 14(1)).
(2) *Material damages* caused to (Article 14(2)):
  (a) drivers if they are liable for the accident;
  (b) the policyholder;
  (c) those whose liability is covered by Article 15(1), as well as vehicles' co-owners;
  (d) companies or legal representatives of a legal person liable for the accident, if they are exercising their professional duties;
  (e) spouse, ascendant, descendant, adoptees of those mentioned in lines (a)–(c), as well as other relatives or kinships to the third degree (only if there is cohabitation or economic dependency);
  (f) all those who can collect compensation, under Articles 495, 496 and 499 of the Portuguese Civil Code, due to ties to previously mentioned entities; and
  (g) passengers transported in violation of the Traffic Code.
(3) If the people mentioned in lines (e) and (f) pass away as a consequence of the event/accident, all compensation to the liable individual is to be excluded under Article 14(3).
(4) Damages caused at the insured vehicle itself; to transported goods (during transportation or loading/unloading); caused to third parties during loading or unloading of goods; damages due to explosions, either directly or indirectly; heat release or radiation stemming from atoms' decay and fusion, artificial particle acceleration or radioactivity; damages occurred during sporting events or practices,[414] if not covered by Article 8 (Article 14(4)).

414. Which do not include illegal street races. *See* STJ 12 June 2017, 8/07.5TBSTB.S1 (Sebastião Póvoas).

Chapter 4. Insured Capital

§1. Minimum Insured Sum

957. For general compulsory motor vehicle insurance, according to Article 12(1), the insurance minimum coverage capital is, per accident, EUR 1,200,000.00, for bodily loss, and EUR 600,000.00, for material loss – in the circumstances described in Article 11(1), paragraphs (a) and (c).

958. From 1 December 2009 onwards, those values are to be considered as, respectively, EUR 2,500,000.00 and 750,000.00; and from 1 June 2012 onward, respectively, EUR 5,000,000.00 and 1,000,000.00, per accident, being reviewed thereafter every five years, pursuant to Council Regulation (EC) 2494/95, of 23 October 1995 concerning harmonised indices of consumer prices, nowadays set by Regulation (EU) 2016/792 of the European Parliament and of the Council, of 11 May 2016, on harmonised indices of consumer prices and the house price index, and Commission Implementing Regulation (EU) 2020/1148 of 31 July 2020, laying down the methodological and technical specifications in accordance with Regulation (EU) 2016/792 of the European Parliament and of the Council as regards harmonised indices of consumer prices and the house price index.

959. As to public transportation insurance and insurance for sport events, Article 13 states that the insurance minimum coverage capital is, respectively, two times and eight times the above-mentioned figures, with a cap, per victim, of the aforesaid.

960. From 1 June 2017 onwards, the minimum insured sum is, per accident, EUR 6,070,000.00 for bodily loss and EUR 1,220,000.00 for material damages.[415]

§2. Insufficient Capital

961. If, in view of the plurality of aggrieved parties, the global loss exceeds the total insured sum, the injured parties' legal rights against the insurance company or against the Motor Vehicle Guarantee Fund will be reduce pro rata (Article 24).

415. Cf. Communication from the Commission 2016/C 210/01, concerning the adaptation in line with inflation of minimum amounts laid down in the Motor Insurance Directive.

Chapter 5. Right of Recourse Against the Insured Person/Entity

962. Under Article 27, once compensation is paid, insurance companies have a right of recourse against the insured party in certain cases, namely: when the driver caused the event/accident intentionally; against the perpetrators or accomplices of theft, robbery, vehicle-usage theft, as against any driver causing the accident that was aware or should have been aware of such crimes; against drivers under the influence of alcohol (above the legal limit), drugs or other toxic substances; against drivers without driver's license or that have deserted the accident's location, abandoning the vehicle; against the individuals liable to third parties due to the fall of poorly secured cargo; against garage owners who have not complied with Articles 6(3) and 7; against the person liable for damages to third parties by the usage of vehicles in violation of technical and security requirements, if the accident is caused by such conditions; against the person who has a duty to submit the vehicle to periodical technical inspection, if the accident is due to that failure.

963. The Portuguese Supreme Court of Justice issued a ruling on this regard, under the procedures for unifying case law, stating that insurance companies have the burden of proof regarding the causal link between the influence of alcohol and the accident occurred.[416]

964. Considering the different formulations enshrined by Decree-Law 291/2007 – since Decree-Law 522/85, stated 'acting while under the influence of alcohol'; and the former states 'giving cause to the accident and driving under the influence of alcohol' – courts have deciding in terms that do not conform to the ruling of the Supreme Court. It has been considered that insurers do not have to prove the causal connection between the ingestion of alcohol and the accident occurred, since the existence of such causal derives, in any case, from the rules of logic and general experience (*id quod plerumque accidit*).[417]

416. STJ 28 May 2002, 6/2002 (Simões Freire), at https://dre.pt/dre/detalhe/jurisprudencia/6-2002-206661. *See* Jorge Sinde Monteiro, Seguro automóvel obrigatório: Direito de regresso – Acórdão de Uniformização de Jurisprudência n.º 6/2002, de 28 de Maio, Proc. 3470/01, 2.ª Secção, in Cadernos de Direito Privado, 2, Abril/Junho 2003, 29 ff.

417. *See* TRC 22 June 2020, 516/18.2T8CNT.C1 (Isaías Padua).

Chapter 6. Motor Vehicle Guarantee Fund

965. The Guarantee body was created by Decree-Law 522/85, of 31 December. It is administratively and financially autonomous, and managed by the ASF.

966. It aims to compensate damages caused by unknown offenders; by those under no obligation to insure; or by drivers who infringed their duties to take out insurance (Article 47).

§1. Material Scope

967. Under Article 49, the Fund ensures payment of compensation, up until the minimum insured sum, for:

(1) bodily harm caused by unknown individuals, by those without valid and enforceable insurance contracts, or in the case of the insurance company's insolvency;
(2) material damages, if the liable party is known but does not have a valid or enforceable insurance contract; and
(3) material damages, in the cases where the responsible is unknown, but the Fund should nonetheless pay compensation in view of the occurrence of significant bodily harm (i.e., harm that leads to death; hospitalisation for seven/or plus days; temporary absolute disability for 60 or plus days; or partial permanent disability of 15% or more), as well as in cases where the perpetrator has deserted the accident's location, abandoning the vehicle, without being covered by valid and enforceable insurance, as long as there is a police report confirming the presence of the vehicle at the site of the accident.

968. The Fund's duty to compensate is limited in the cases set out in Article 51. Under Article 52(1), the exclusions of liability under general compulsory motor vehicle insurance contracts set out in Article 14, as described above, also apply.

969. Article 52(2) sets out further exclusions for this case. There is no cover for: material damages caused to persons who failed to comply with the duty to insure; damages caused to passengers who had voluntarily entered the vehicle responsible for the event, although the Fund has the burden of proving that they were aware that the vehicle was not insured; damages suffered by the person who deliberately caused the accident, or by the perpetrator of theft, robbery, or vehicle-usage theft, or by any passenger that was voluntarily transported and was aware of the illegitimate use of the vehicle.

970. It is also the duty of the Fund to reimburse the Green Card Portuguese Bureau for its payments in certain circumstances, as well as other homologous entities created within the EU or international agreements signed by Portugal (Article 55).

§2. SUBROGATION

971. Once compensation is paid, the Fund becomes subrogated in all the aggrieved party's legal rights towards the liable person, and it can legitimately claim default interest and reimbursement for all expenses with the claim process and payment[418] (Article 54) – it is a mechanism not to be mistaken with right of recourse.[419]

972. The mere holder of the vehicle, its owner and the driver who caused the accident are, simultaneously, jointly responsible towards the Fund, even if they were not the ones with a duty to insure the vehicle.

973. Scholarship and case law theorise if this norm should be interpreted as an extension of liability before the Fund even to individuals not liable for the accident, or if it should be restrictively interpreted. The latter seems to be the one with more support, even if the issue is not settled.[420]

974. There is subsidiary liability as well for those who contribute to error or contractual defects leading to its invalidity, hand in hand with the seller failing to honour their duties with regard to insurance.

975. All the aforesaid individuals have right of recourse against any others.

976. The Fund's credit, under Article 54(6), which invokes Article 498(2) of the Portuguese Civil Code, has a limitation period of three years (counting from the last payment date, if payment is split or paid to several aggrieved parties on different dates).[421]

---

418. Portugal's Insurance Institute attests to the Fund's payment of compensations under its power, and that is an authentic document, making full proof of its content. Howbeit, it is not, on its own, an enforceable title since it does not define the liable person/original debtor. *See* TRP 21 February 2008, 1275/14.3T8OAZ-C.P1 (Augusto de Carvalho).
419. *See* TRL 12 November 2015, 1971-08.4TBMFR.L2-6 (Maria Teresa Pardal).
420. *See*, for the first opinion, *inter alia*, STJ 2 March 2004, 3499/03 (Nuno Cameira), and TRL 19 March 2015, 9036-11.5T2SNT.L1-6 (Vítor Amaral); and for the second interpretation, *inter alia*, STJ 8 November 2018, 770/12.3TBSXL.L1.S1 (Abrantes Geraldes); STJ 6 June 2019, 519/14.6TBEVR.E1.S1 (Maria dos Prazeres Pizarro Beleza); and recently STJ 20 April 2021, 440/07.4TBLNH.L1.S1 (António Magalhães). For a comprehensive analysis, cf. M. I. Oliveira Martins, *Subrogation of the Guarantee Fund and Liability of the Persons Failing to Take Out Mandatory Insurance: An Endorsement of the Prevailing Opinion of Portuguese Courts*, 4 Insurance Review 43 ff. (2019); and M. I. Oliveira Martins, Sub-rogação do Fundo de Garantia Automóvel e responsabilidade pela falta de Seguro obrigatório, *in* Revista de Direito Comercial, 2021, 719 ff., also available at https://static1.squarespace.com/static/58596f8a29687fe710cf45cd/t/609e886a9405ed1f86341195/1621002347359/2021-13+-+0719-0766+-+LA-PV.pdf (accessed 25 Feb. 2022).
421. Therefore, Art. 54(6) puts an end to the controversy created under the previous regime (Decree-Law 522/85, 31 December), making it clear that if there is split payment the limitation period is counted from the date of the last instalment. *See*, *e.g.*, TRL 22 April 2021, 352/18.7T8LRS.L1-6 (Ana de Azeredo Coelho).

977. If the liable person against whom the Fund can exercise the injured party's legal rights becomes insolvent, fresh start insolvency mechanisms cannot erase the Fund's credit when it emerges from a wrongful action with malicious intent, but not mere negligence (such as failing to comply with the duty to insure), under Article 245(2) paragraph (b) of the Insolvency Code (Decree-Law 53/2004, of 18 March).[422] Some decisions have taken another route, considering that even if the accident is caused with negligence, there was malicious intent with the failure to comply with insurance duties, and, therefore, the credit cannot be considered in the fresh start mechanism in any circumstance.[423]

422. *See, inter alia,* TRG 11 June 2015, 2916/13.5TJVNF.G1 (Heitor Gonçalves); TRP 17 June 2014, 2573/13.9TBVCD-C.P1 (José Igreja Matos).

423. *See* TRC 28 June 2016, 4372/15.4T8CBR.C1 (Fonte Ramos), and TRG 24 April 2014, 124/12.1TBPCRF-F.G1 (Antero Veiga).

Chapter 7. Procedural Rules and Proceedings

978. Aggrieved parties can take legal action, presenting direct claims for compensation against the insurers, in case the compensation claimed is below the value of minimum insured sum for compulsory motor vehicle (Article 12). Nonetheless, the insurer can call upon the policyholder to intervene as a procedural party, as it can enact its right of recourse within the same action. Victims can also take legal action against both the insurance company and the liable individual (by civil law standards), when claiming damages above the minimum insured capital (Article 64).

979. When there is no valid and enforceable insurance cover, the injured party can directly take legal action against the Fund, as long as they bring the action against the known liable person as well (mandatory *litis consortium*) (Article 62(1)).

980. If the liable person is unknown, legal action is to be taken directly against the Fund (Article 62(2)).

981. In case the victim had taken out insurance that covers the damage caused by the accident, legal action must be jointly brought against the Fund and the victim's insurance company.

Chapter 8. Insuring Other Risks

982. Apart from Decree-Law 291/2007, all kinds of other motor vehicle's risks can be insured under contractual autonomy. It is fairly common to take out a so-called all-risks/comprehensive insurance policy, which is normally a requisite to access most forms of financial products connected with vehicles, such as credit in general, leasing, and renting (Articles 8, 10, 11 and 12, of LBIR).

983. Non-compulsory insurance of motor vehicle risks is, thus, not akin to compulsory motor vehicle insurance, and should not have the same constraints. *See*, regarding compensation and cited Portuguese Supreme Court of Justice standardised opinion, Case Law 6/2002, TRC 25 October 2011, 770/07.5TBGRD.C1 (Jaime Carlos Ferreira).

984. Decree-Law 214/97, of 16 August, implements certain rules for the promotion of transparency in motor vehicle insurance with non-compulsory coverage, focusing on consumer rights and control of SCT.

985. In particular, it establishes a mechanism for the automatic update of the insured vehicle, and therefore of the premiums, taking into account depreciation, with the purpose of mitigating the risks of unintended over-insurance (Article 2).

986. Insurers have special information duties in this regard, both at a pre-contractual and at a contractual level, regarding the premium; the insured vehicle's value and the depreciation index. They should update the information provided yearly.

Part V. Insurance of the Person

Chapter 1. Workmen's Compensation and Occupational Disease

Joana Nunes Vicente & Maria Inês de Oliveira Martins[424]

§1. General

987. The CPR establishes the right to redress damages arising from professional risks – accidents at work and occupational diseases – as a fundamental right which every worker is entitled to (Article 59(1)(f)). The CPR also sets out the right to social security as a universal right which includes social protection in old age, disability, family expenses and unemployment or in any other situation that entails a lack of or reduction in means of subsistence or capacity to work (Article 63(3)). At an infra-constitutional level, general rules about workmen's compensation and occupational disease insurance are laid down in Law 7/2009, of 12 February 2009 (which forms the Labour Code for the private sector[425]), in Law 98/2009, of 4 September 2009 (approving the legal rules for workmen's compensation and occupational diseases), in Decree-Law 352/2007, of 23 October 2007 (which approves the National Table of Incapacities caused by Work Accidents and Occupational Diseases) and in Decree-Law 142/99, of 30 April 1999 (creating the Industrial Accidents Fund[426]). There are, in addition, statutes regulating workmen's compensation at a more specific level. That is the case of the legislation about workmen's compensation concerning independent workers (Decree-Law 159/99, of 11 May 1999[427]) as well as professional sportsmen (Law 27/2011, of 16 June 2011) and accidents in service for public servants (Decree-Law 503/99, of 20 November 1999[428]).

988. Workmen's compensation insurance basically provides cover for industrial injuries and occupational diseases, including accidents which relate to work or working conditions, occupational diseases and harmful exposure. According to current Portuguese law, workers – both employees and independent workers – and their

424. Joana Nunes Vicente authored Ch. 1; Maria Inês de Oliveira Martins authored Chs 2–5.
425. Last amendment: Law 1/2022, of 3 January 2022.
426. Last amendment: Decree-Law 18/2016, of 13 April 2016.
427. Last amendment: Decree-Law 382-A/99, of 22 September 1999.
428. Last amendment: Law 19/2021, of 8 April 2021.

family members[429] have the right to compensation for damage arising from accidents at work or from work-related diseases.

989. Regarding compensation due to accidents at work, the general scheme is established by Law 98/2009, of 4 September 2009. These general rules on workmen's compensation insurance apply both to employees (private sector) and independent workers, although some specific legislation is applicable to independent workers (Decree-Law 159/99, of 11 May 1999). Workmen's compensation insurance is compulsory for employees and independent workers. Employers (or in the case of independent workers, themselves) are responsible for the full financing of protection against this eventuality. Employers are obliged to take out insurance policies with insurance companies to offset liability for damages (Article 79(1) of Law 98/2009, of 4 September 2009). Independent workers must take out their own policies with insurance companies (Article 1(1) of Decree-Law 159/99, of 11 May 1999).

990. According to Article 81(1) of Law 98/2009, of 4 September, the uniform contractual clauses for workmen's compensation, regarding different professions and activities, namely for employees and independent workers, are to be approved by regulation issued by the ministers for finance and labour, following a proposal by the supervisory authority (the ASF). Under the terms of this article, the associations representing insurance companies and the Economic and Social Council should be consulted beforehand.

991. Pursuant to Article 81(2)(3) of the aforementioned law, such uniform contractual clauses must follow the principle that the insurance premium be adequate to the degree of risk of accident, the nature of activity, and the prevention measures put in place, as well as any revision of the insurance premium in the event of a change in the prevention measures put in place. Any additional contractual clauses contrary to the rights and duties envisaged by the uniform contractual clauses are null and void (Article 81(4) of Law 98/2009 of 4 September).

992. The uniform (general and special) contractual clauses for compulsory workmen's compensation, regarding both dependent and independent workers, were approved by Ordinance No. 256/11, of 5 July 2011 and by Regulatory Framework 3/2009-R, of 5 March 2009, respectively. The updated list of the uniform contractual clauses can be consulted at the supervisory authority's website.

993. In accordance with the provision of Article 83 of Law 98/2009, of 4 September, the supervisory authority (the ASF) has approved a regulatory norm – the Regulatory Framework 001-2000, of 14 January 2000 – regarding the coverage of

429. Workers' compensation systems provide dependents with benefits for a specified period of time after an employee's death. Benefits awarded to surviving dependants consist of payment of a percentage of the deceased employee's wages (Arts 59 and 60 of Law 98/2009, of 4 September 2009).

risks under workmen's compensation insurance which are excluded by insurance companies. These rules apply to those with an employment contract but also to independent workers.

994. With respect to compensation due to occupational diseases, general rules are established by Law 98/2009, of 4 September 2009, and cover both subordinate and independent workers (Article 93(1) of Law 98/2009, of 4 September). In contrast to the situation with accidents at work, occupational diseases are included in the public social security system (Articles 283(7) of the Labour Code and 93(1) of Law 98/2009, of 4 September 2009). Employees and independent workers are entitled to receive benefits only if they are enrolled in the public social security system. As regards this employment relationship, both the employer and the employee enrolled in the social security system are required to pay contributions. The self-employed have to pay monthly contributions.

995. In the case of public servants, employees fulfilling public functions are all covered by specific legislation (Decree-Law 503/99, of 20 November 1999), with exception of employees fulfilling functions in entities excluded from the scope of application of such legislation (i.e., to say, public sector employees who fulfil functions in the state corporate sector and regional and local administrations). This special regime provides the right to the same benefits and adopts the same concepts as the general scheme, namely, regarding the definition of an accident at work and the occupational diseases classification. Nevertheless, it does not transfer liabilities to the insurance companies in contrast to the general scheme, except in duly justified situations and only if more advantages and rights are safeguarded in full as guaranteed by the special regime.

996. Concerning professional sportsmen, the legal framework of protection against occupational accidents is established by Law 27/2011 of 16 June 2011.[430] Besides the application of Law 98/2009, of 4 September, Law 27/2011 of 16 June contains specific provisions in several fields, such as: a specific disability table; a pension ceiling wage in the event of death, permanent disability for exercising one's usual occupation and absolute permanent disability; insurance deductibles in case of temporary disability. The registration of the employment contract depends on the conclusion of the insurance contract. In case of accident, the athlete must sign a hospital discharge form to be allowed to return to competition.[431]

430. In fact, Law 54/2017, of 14 July 2017 establishes the legal framework of the employment contract for sports practitioners and sports training, regulating as well the activity of the sports agents. However, this legal act does not provide for the protection against occupational accidents and diseases.

431. This provision has been introduced to avoid conflicts over the limitation period of the right of action. *See* Ana Cristina Ribeiro Costa, *Breves notas sobre o praticante desportivo profissional e a segurança e saúde no trabalho: estará esta fora de jogo?*, 4, Revista de Desporto, 20 (2020), at 29 and ff. On this topic, *see also* Joana Carneiro, Acidentes de trabalho dos jogadores de futebol: algumas considerações, 42, Questões Laborais, 437 (2013), at 446 and ff.

§2. Workmen's Compensation Insurance for Employees

997. The legal framework on the compensation of accidents at work, established by Law 98/2009, of 4 September 2009, apply to subordinate employment – that is, to workers whose employment status is one of subordination or personal dependency. However, Article 4(1) of Law 7/2009, of 12 February (which approves the Labour Code) extends the scope of protection of Law 98/2009 to: (a) persons working not as a subordinate employee but with some form of economic dependency;[432] (b) trainees and apprentices; (c) chief executive officers, directors, managers or equivalent, as long as they are salaried. In addition, Law 98/2009, of 4 September 2009 sets out other extensions. In the same way that foreign workers working in Portugal (and their family members) have the right to same benefits as Portuguese workers (Article 5), the provisions on occupational accidents are also extended to Portuguese workers (or foreign workers resident in Portugal), working abroad, unless foreign law gives them the right to compensation, in which case the worker concerned has a choice of applicable law (Articles 5 and 6).

998. To receive workers' compensation benefits an employee must suffer an occupational accident. According to Article 8(1) of Law 98/2009 of 4 September 2009, an accident at work is basically defined as an accident: (1) that occurs at the place and time of work and; (2) produces direct or indirect injury, functional disorder, resulting in reduction in work capacity or in death or disease.

999. The first element of the definition of occupational accident concerns the circumstances of the accidents covered. According to Article 8(2) of the aforementioned law, the terms 'Working time' and 'work place' should be considered broadly.[433] In addition, some extensions are envisaged by Article 9 of Law 28/2009, of 4 September 2009. An occupational accident is in fact considered to be an accident that occurs: (a) on the way to the place of work or on the journey home; (b)

432. In recent years, there have been many changes to working relationships and arrangements, which have presented difficulties regarding the legal frameworks for determining whether workers are or are not in an employment relationship and thus entitled to a range of protections under labour law. The traditional paradigms of, on the one hand, subordinate employment and, on the other, autonomous self-employment/independent contractors, are less often the norm. 'Economically dependent workers' is the Portuguese legal term to represent workers in this grey area (terms such as 'parasubordinate worker', 'quasi-employee' or 'intermediate worker' have been used in other legal systems). Only some provisions of Portuguese Labour Code apply to this intermediary category, e.g., anti-discrimination law, protection against occupational accidents and diseases, health and safety legislation (Art. 10 of the Labour Code). Art. 3(2) of Law 98/2009 of 4 September sets out a presumption of economic dependency that in jurisprudence is considered a rebuttable presumption – *see* Viriato Reis/Diogo Ravara, *Os acidentes de trabalho e as doenças profissionais – uma introdução*, Acidentes de Trabalho e Doenças Profissionais – Introdução, Centro de Estudos Judiciários (2013), available at: http://www.cej.mj.pt/cej/recursos/ebooks/trabalho/Caderno_Acidentes_trabalho.pdf (accessed 27 Oct. 2021). *See* Judgment of TRP 19 April 2021, proc. 1076/19.2T8VLG.P1 (Jerónimo Freitas).

433. Cf. Luís Menezes Leitão, *Direito do Trabalho*, 7th ed., Almedina (2021), at 441 and ff.; Pedro Romano Martinez, *Direito do Trabalho*, 9th ed., Almedina (2019), at 876 and ff. For instance, working time in this context includes coffee and meal breaks – *see* Judgment of TRP 29 November 2004, proc. 0413696 (Machado da Silva).

during the performance of tasks not requested by the employer, but which may nevertheless bring economic benefits to the employer; (c) at and outside the workplace, as a representative of the employee and to exercise the right of assembly; (d) while participating in training courses which take place at the usual place of work or outside the usual place of employment, their frequency being authorised by their employer; (e) at the place where the payment of the salary is made and during the time when the worker must remain there for the same purpose; (f) in places where the worker is being treated because of a previous work accident; (g) during the period provided for by law to allow the worker to seek a new job; (h) in carrying out activities requested or authorised by his employer, even if they take place outside of the place or time of work.[434]

1000. There is no consensus regarding the interpretation of these extensions.[435] Those who believe that accidents at work can be justified with the theory of economic risk or authority[436] argue that the extensions are exceptions and should be strictly interpreted. Others point out that employer's liability is justified, not by the idea of risk, but by an obligation of solidarity from the employer towards the employee or by an obligation of social assistance[437] or by the link of subordination or personal dependency.[438] According to proponents of this point of view, the extensions support a broader interpretation. In fact, in some extensions provided by Article 9 there is no possibility of control by the employer over the employee's activity and its consideration as an accident at work justified in terms of risk is doubtful. That is the case of an accident that occurs during the period provided for

434. For a more detailed analysis of these legal provisions, *see* Júlio Gomes, *O Acidente de trabalho – O acidente in itinere e a sua descaracterização*, Coimbra Editora (2013), at 95 and ff.

435. For instance, an accident that takes place during an activity organised by the employer, such as a team building activity, a staff party can be considered job-related, and this even if participation in the activity is optional. In a case involving an accident during a tour organised by the employer, the court reached the conclusion that the accident was an occupational accident, even though the tour had been voluntarily accepted by the employee (Judgment of TRP 8 March 2019, proc. 589/15.0Y7PRT.P1 (Fernanda Soares)). The TRE has reached the same conclusion in its judgment of 15 of April 2008, proc. 415/08-2 (António Gonçalves Rocha). The accident occurred when the employee was authorised by his employer to travel briefly and in his vehicle to his son's nursery in order to pick him up and bring him to his workplace where the Christmas party for all the company's employees was taking place. By contrast, in another case, the same court did not classify as an occupational accident an accident that took place during soccer game organised by the employees and authorised by the company (Judgment of TRE 24 September 2019, proc. 564/15.4T8EVR.E1 (Paula do Paço).

436. Pedro Romano Martinez, *Direito do Trabalho*, at 883 and ff.

437. Luís Menezes Leitão, *Acidentes de Trabalho e Responsabilidade Civil (A Natureza Jurídica da Reparação de Danos Emergentes de Acidentes de Trabalho e a Distinção entre as Responsabilidades Obrigacional e Delitual)*, 48, Revista da Ordem dos Advogados, 773 (1998), at 773 and ff.

438. Cf. Júlio Gomes, *Breves reflexões sobre a noção de acidente de trabalho no novo (mas não muito) regime dos acidente de trabalho, Acidentes de trabalho e doenças profissionais - Introdução*, Centro de Estudos Judiciários (2013), available at: http://www.cej.mj.pt/cej/recursos/ebooks/trabalho/Caderno_Acidentes_trabalho.pdf (accessed 27 Oct. 2021).

by law to the worker to seek a new job[439] or the accident on the way to work and on the way home (commuting accidents).[440]

1001. The second element of the definition of occupational accident is the type of damage that results from the accident. Only accidents (a) that directly or indirectly cause physical or psychological damage, functional disturbance, an illness or the death of the worker; (b) and that result in a disability or reduction in the worker's capacity to earn or gain are considered accidents at work. Some authors have criticised the notion of including damage in the concept of accident.[441] In a more technical approach damage is one of the elements of the workers' compensation claim. However, the definition is important in highlighting the fact that worker's compensation was created to compensate employees for occupational injuries, not to compensate employees for all property damage, and it does not pay out for non-pecuniary losses.[442]

1002. The industrial scheme is based on no-fault. This means, first, that neither the employer nor any of his employees has to be shown to be at fault for the claim to succeed; and second, the negligence of the employee himself will not bar entitlement to benefit. However, the employee's at-fault contributory behaviour can have consequences for recognition of the job-related nature of the injury. For instance, intentional fault by the employee[443] in disobeying the health and safety instructions issued by the employer and gross negligence[444] rule out any possibility of recognition (Article 14 of Law 98/2009, of 4 September of 2009) of the accident as coming under this scope.

---

439. Cf. Ana Estela Leandro, *Estudo Comparativo de 2 Regimes Jurídicos de Acidentes de Trabalho: a Lei n.º 2/27 de 21 de Agosto de 1965 e a lei 100/97 de 13 de Setembro*, 58, Prontuário de Direito do Trabalho, 36, 1999, at 36 and ff.; Júlio Gomes, *O Acidente de trabalho*, at 133 and ff.

440. Another controversial jurisprudential issue concerns how to classify an accident that occurs during the period in which the worker is performing functions outside his usual place of work, but in an action from his or her private life. *See* Judgment of STJ 2 April 2008, proc. 08S529 (Pinto Hespanhol) about an accident that occurs during a work trip in the bathroom of a hotel.

441. Rosário Palma Ramalho, *Tratado de Direito do Trabalho – Parte II*, 8th ed., Almedina (2021), at 810 and ff.; Pedro Romano Martinez, *Direito do Trabalho*, at 871 and ff.

442. Except if employer's liability in tort is established (violation of health and safety legislation). In that case employer is required to pay for both pecuniary and non-pecuniary losses resulting from injury or death (Art. 18 of Law 98/2009). However, the subsidiary liability from the insurance company and from the Industrial Accident Fund only covers occupational injuries. For a critical approach, *see* Manuel Rosário Nunes, *Notas sobre revisão das prestações emergentes de acidentes de trabalho: dos limites temporais ao seu exercício*, 1, Prontuário de Direito do Trabalho, 161 (2020), at. 168 and ff.

443. Concerning suicide, there is controversy in Portugal as to whether suicide can be qualified as the intentional fault of the employee. According to Carlos Alegre, *Regime Jurídico dos Acidentes de Trabalho e das Doenças Profissionais*, Almedina (2000), at 60 and ff., suicide is considered an intentional act. By contrast, other authors, such as Ana Cristina Ribeiro Costa, *O Acto Suicida do Trabalhador – A Tutela ao abrigo dos Regimes das Contingências Profissionais*, 40, Questões Laborais, 203 (2012) at. 224 and ff., argue that the exception of Art. 14(1)(a) of Law 98/2009 of 4 September 2009 should be strictly interpreted as covering only cases of employee fraud.

444. Regarding the meaning of 'gross negligence', Portuguese courts usually adopt a restrictive interpretation of the concept in Art. 14(1)(b) of Law 98/2009 of 4 September 2009 – cf. Judgment of STJ 6 November 2021, proc. 1059/13.6TTCBR.C1.S1 (Chamber Mourisco); and Judgment of STJ

1003. Workers' compensation is awarded to replace the lost earnings of employees who are injured. Compensation is awarded according to five categories of disability: temporary total disability; temporary partial disability; partial permanent disability for exercising one's usual occupation; total permanent disability for exercising one's usual occupation; or absolute permanent disability (Article 19 of Law 98/2009, of 4 September 2009). Under the terms of Article 20 of Law 98/2009, of 4 September 2009, the degree of disability is determined according to the national disability table in force on the date of the accident. The Disability National Table for Workmen's Compensation and Occupational Disease has been approved by Decree-Law 352/2007, of 23 October 2007, which has been in force since 21 January 2008. It is according to the aforementioned table that the damage is assessed: the medical appraiser decides on a disability rate according to the injury listed on the national scale, and the rate is used to calculate benefits. Personal characteristics (nature of the infirmity, age, gender, training and job capabilities, potential for rehabilitation) of the victim/employee and socio-economic factors can be taken into account and at most represent a correction, especially when the victim's occupational situation is greatly affected by an injury (Article 21 of Law 98/2009, of 4 September 2009).

1004. In case of death or disability, compensation includes either pecuniary benefits or non-pecuniary benefits (Article 23 of Law 98/2009 of 4 September 2009).[445] Pecuniary benefits include: compensation for total or partial temporary disability; compensation (lump sum payments or pension) for permanent injury/disability corresponding to the decrease in working or earning capacity; compensation in the event of a serious permanent injury/disability; survivor's pension, death grant and reimbursement of funeral expenses; compensation for housing re-modelling; allocation for third party help/supplementary care benefit; compensation for occupational training programmes (Articles 23(b) and 47 of Law 98/2009 of 4 September 2009). Non-pecuniary benefits include: medical treatment, rehabilitation and aids and other required operations of any nature (medical, surgical and pharmaceutical assistance; nursing; hospital stays and thermal treatment; hotel stays; transportation for medical observation, treatment or court hearings; prosthesis and similar; occupational reintegration; medical and functional rehabilitation services; mental health services) which are necessary and adequate in order to improve the state of health of the injured person as well as his/her capacity for work and his/her recovery for active life (Articles 23(a) and 25 of Law 98/2009, of 4 September 2009).

---

14 of June 2021, proc. 507/16.8T8VLG.P1 (Paula Leal de Carvalho). *See also* Jerónimo Freitas, *Acidentes de Trabalho e Doenças Profissionais: A Obrigação de segurança no Trabalho*, 1, Prontuário de Direito do Trabalho, 389 (2020) at 441.

445. The employer is under the obligation to integrate a worker suffering from temporary partial incapacity or from permanent, partial or total incapacity for regular work as a result of an employment injury or an occupational disease. Such workers are also entitled to vocational training, adaptation of the workplace, part-time work and leave for retraining or for finding another job. In addition, they are entitled to a working allowance for attending professional rehabilitation activities, corresponding to the expenses incurred (Arts 154, 155, 156, 157 and 158 of Law 98/2009, of 4 September 2009).

1005. Finally, under Article 79 of Law 98/2009 of 4 September 2009, the employer has a statutory duty to take out insurance covering employees, or in other words, to offset legal liabilities to an insurance company authorised to carry out workers' compensation insurance business.[446] The violation of this obligation by the employer is considered a very serious administrative offence (Article 171(1) of Law 98/2009, of 4 September 2009). The salary of the employees must be fully declared in order to allow for the calculation of the insurance premium. When the salary declared does not correspond to the real salary, the insurer is liable only up the declared salary and the employer will be liable for the difference, as well as proportionally for the costs incurred (hospital bills, medical assistance and transportation) (Article 79(4)(5) of Law 98/2009 of 4 September).

1006. According to uniform contractual clauses in force there are two types of workmen's compensation insurance contracts regarding employees: fixed premium insurance contracts and variable premium insurance contracts. The former is taken out whenever the insurance covers a determined number of workers and their salary is known in advance; the latter is taken out whenever the insurance contract covers a variable number of workers receiving variable salaries and the insurer covers the persons and their respective salaries, who and which are listed periodically (usually monthly) by the employer and communicated to the insurer (Clause 5 of Ordinance no. 256/11, of 5 July 2011).[447]

§3. Workmen's Compensation for Independent Workers

1007. Besides general rules on workmen's compensation insurance established by Law 98/2009, of 4 September 2009, specific provisions are adopted by Decree-Law 159/99, of 11 May 1999 concerning independent workers.

1008. Under Article 1 of Decree-Law 159/99 of 11 May 1999 independent workers have the duty to take out workmen's compensation insurance in order to cover the same benefits regarding employees, and their family members – unless their production is exclusively for self-consumption.[448] Proof of the existence of the insurance contract is by means of a document issued by the insurer identifying the worker and the insurance period – the insurance contract must be taken out for a minimum period of one year (Article 4 of Decree-Law 159/99, of 11 May 1999).

446. However, the insurance contract only covers strict liability. If the employer commits a tort that causes the employee's injuries or infringes health and safety obligations, the insurance company pays the injured employee up to the limit of damages covered by strict liability and can recover the amount from the employer responsible for the damage (Art. 79(3) of Law 98/2009, of 4 September 2009).

447. About this distinction, *see* Júlio Gomes, *Seguro de acidentes de trabalho : para uma interpretação restritiva - ou mesmo a revisão – do acórdão uniformizador de jurisprudência n.º 10/2001 de 21 de Novembro de 2001*, 116, Revista do Ministério Público, 5 (2008), at 5 ff.

448. According to case law, an insurance contract is mandatory even if the service is provided free of charge. *See* Judgment TRG 7 February 2019, proc. 1635/17.8T8VCT.G1 (Vera Sottomayor).

1009. Pursuant to Article 3(1)(2) of Decree-Law 159/99, of 11 May 1999, the territorial scope of insurance includes not only Portugal but also the territory of other EU Member States where the worker exercises his/her activity there for a period of up to fifteen days. An extension for the territory of other EU Member States for a period exceeding fifteen days or for the territory of third-party states can be agreed between the parties.

1010. Regarding the concept of accident at work, Decree-Law 159/99, of 11 May 1999 does not provide a definition of occupational accident. Therefore, it the legal definition from general scheme would seem to apply. However, according to Article 6 of Decree-Law 159/99, of 11 May 1999, the term 'work place' should be considered more restrictively than in Law 98/2009, since the extensions envisaged are weaker than those provided by the general law. In addition, when the accident victim at work is both independent worker and employee, in doubt, it will be assumed, until proven otherwise, that the accident occurred at the service of the employer (Article 7 of Decree-Law 159/99, of 11 May 1999).

1011. In the event that an accident occurs, the injured or the legal beneficiaries must report this to the insurance company as envisaged in the insurance contract's clauses. The insurance company has to communicate to the competent court any accidents that cause permanent disability as well as those that cause the death of any person insured – within, respectively, eight days after the injured person gets out of hospital and immediately (Article 8 of Decree-Law 159/99, of 11 May 1999).

1012. Furthermore, the annual remuneration to be considered, for the purpose of calculating premiums and pecuniary benefits, must correspond, as a minimum, to fourteen times the highest minimum monthly salary, or any other value, at the worker's choice. For any amount higher than the minimum remuneration mentioned above, the insurance company reserves the right to demand proof of income (Article 9 of Decree-Law 159/99, of 11 May 1999).

§4. Workmen's Compensation Fund

1013. Portuguese law provided for the setting-up of a fund – the Industrial Accidents Fund – which is an entity with legal personality and financial and administrative autonomy (Decree-Law 142/99, of 30 April 1999). The Fund functions within the aegis of a supervisory authority (the Insurance and Pension Funds Supervision Authority) which assures its technical and financial management.

1014. The main competences of the Fund are: (1) to guarantee the payment of the benefits due in the event of accident when the entity which is responsible for such payment cannot meet its obligation due to financial difficulties as declared by insolvency proceedings, any equivalent process or by a corporate recovery procedure; (2) to pay the insurance premiums of companies that are not able to do so because they have been engaged in a recovery procedure; (3) to pay back to the insurance companies the amounts envisaged by law; (4) to update pensions due to permanent incapacity of 30% or more or due to death, as well as to update to supplementary provision for third-party assistance; (5) to reinsure and return any risks for which coverage has been declined (Articles 1 of Decree-Law 142/99, of 30 April 1999 and 82(1)(2) of Law 98/2009, of 4 September 2009).

1015. The Fund envisages several types of income: proceeds from fines; financial investments; amounts arising from refused reinsurance contracts; percentages calculated from the salaries declared collected by the insurance companies from the policyholders whenever a workmen's compensation insurance premium is processed (Article 3 of Decree-Law 142/99, of 30 April 1999).

§5. Compensation due to Occupational Diseases

1016. The legal framework on the compensation of occupational diseases, established by Law 98/2009, of 4 September 2009, covers: (1) employees, with the exception of public sector employees; (2) independent workers who contribute to social security; (3) domestic workers providing that they are registered as salaried workers; (4) persons registered for voluntary social insurance, if they have contributed 0.5% for occupational health.

1017. There is no definition of occupational disease in Law 98/2009 of 4 September 2009. However, one can say that occupational disease covers any disease contracted as a result of an exposure to risk factors arising from work activity (working environment, nature of work task performed, situations particularly imposed on the worker).[449] The fact that diseases are usually caused by a process extended over a period of time or series of repetitive actions allows a distinction between diseases and accidents to be made. Usually accidents are unforeseen and occur at a specific time, either for the accident itself or the onset of symptoms in the injured worker.[450]

1018. Regarding the forms of identification and recognition of an occupational disease entitling workers to compensation, Portugal has adopted a 'mixed system'. That is, it combines a 'list system' – prescribing a list of diseases for which there is a presumption that they are of occupational origin – complemented by a general provision ('open clause') that allows the victim to show that the disease is occupational in origin. The list of occupational diseases is organised and updated by the National Committee for the Review of the Occupational Diseases' List, the composition and functions of which are established by Regulatory Decree 3/2019 of 2 December 2019 (Article 94(1) of Law 98/2009, of 4 September 2009). The list of occupational diseases in force has been approved by the Regulatory Decree 6/2001

449. Ana Cristina Ribeiro Costa, *O Acto Suicida do Trabalhador*, at 207 and ff.

450. Viriato Reis/Diogo Ravara, *Os acidentes de trabalho e as doenças profissionais*, at 28 and ff.; Pedro Romano Martinez, *Direito do Trabalho*, at 853 and ff. Although this distinction seems straightforward it is not always the case. The fact that an accident is sudden does not necessarily mean that it has to be instantaneous, but rather concentrated over a period of a few hours or days – cf. Júlio Vieira Gomes, *O Acidente de Trabalho*, at 31 and ff.

of 5 May 2001 and published in the Official Journal (Diário da República) according to Article 283(2) of Labour Code.[451] Other bodily injuries, functional disorders and diseases not included in this list can give rise to compensation as long as it can be proved that the disease was a necessary and direct consequence of the professional activity and did not correspond to normal deterioration of the human body (Articles 283(3) of the Labour Code and 94(2) of Law 98/2009, of 4 September 2009).[452]

1019. The right to receive compensation due to occupational disease exists whenever the two following conditions are met: the worker suffers from the occupational disease and the worker was exposed to the corresponding risk due to the nature of the industry, professional activity or conditions, environment, and usual working procedures (Article 95 of Law 98/2009, of 4 September 2009).

1020. According to Article 96 of Law 98/2009, of 4 September 2009, the service with competences in the area of protection against occupational risks is the entity responsible for evaluating, establishing the degree of the condition and compensation for occupational disease.

1021. Compensation due to occupational diseases includes both pecuniary benefits and non-pecuniary benefits (Articles 102, 103 and 104 of Law 98/2009, of 4 September 2009).

451. Subsequently amended and republished by the Regulatory Decree 76/2007, of 17 July 2007.

452. Until 2017 the recognition of harassment as an occupational accident or occupational disease was controversial (cf. Ana Cristina Ribeiro Costa, *Revisitando o assédio e o caminho para o seu enquadramento no regime dos acidentes de trabalho e doenças profissionais*, 2, Prontuário de Direito do Trabalho, 281 (2017), at 298 and ff. Law 73/2017 of 16 August, which introduced several amendments to the Portuguese Labour Code, in order to reinforce the legal framework for the prevention of work harassment, established that employers are to be held liable for the repairing of any damage from a professional disease caused by work harassment. For this purpose, Social Security shall bear the costs for the repair of the damage, being then entitled to claim reimbursement from the employers, plus interest (Art. 283(8)(9) of Labour Code).

Chapter 2. Bodily Injuries: Personal Accident Insurance

§1. Terminology and Scope of the Regime

I. Bodily Injuries vis-à-vis Personal Accident Insurance

1022. Bodily injuries may result from other sources besides personal accidents – primarily, from health conditions, which may in their turn result from ageing. The RJCS has chosen to specifically regulate insurance of bodily injuries resulting from personal accidents. When bodily injuries result from an underlying health condition, the norms on health insurance (Articles 213–217) apply – albeit with some adjustments.

1023. Moreover, in the case of insurance against personal injury including incapacity for employment (whatever the cause) and insurance against disability resulting from an accident or sickness, where they are underwritten in addition to life insurance, the norms on life insurance are also applicable (Article 184(1)).

1024. As already mentioned, the form of insurance specifically regulated by the RJCS that refers to a bodily injury is that of personal accidents insurance, provided for in Articles 210–212.

1025. It should also be added that there is a considerable number of cases of mandatory personal accidents insurance – e.g., work accidents insurance of the self-employed persons, insurance connected to sports or sports events, insurance of the blood donator, or insurance of children under the care of a child-minder.[453] In each of these cases, the statutes and regulatory standards that set out the duty to take out insurance may also provide for some specific rules.

II. Concept of Personal Accident

1026. Under Article 212, personal accidents insurance covers the risk of occurrence of bodily injury, permanent or temporary incapacity or death of the person at risk, due to a sudden, unpredictable, and external cause.

1027. The interpretation of the term ‘cause’ that seems more fitting to the expectations of a normal policyholder is to see it as the event that caused the bodily

453. *See* respectively Art. 4(2) of the Labour Code and Regulatory Framework 3/2009-R, of 5 March; Decree-Law10/2009, of 12 January on sports insurance, and Law 24/2013 of 20 March on scuba diving and its insurance, and Regulatory Framework 1340/2007, of 11 October, on the same matter; Law 37/2012 of 27 August on blood donators; Decree-Law 115/2015 of 22 June on children under the care of a childminder, and Regulatory Framework 226/2015, of 11 July, on the same matter. The list of mandatory personal accidents insurance provided by the supervisory authority can be retrieved at www.asf.com.pt/NR/rdonlyres/103BE5D9-7438-49C4-A135-3CFEC7E92543/0/2LegislaçãoSegurodeacidentespessoais.pdf.

injury.[454] The event that caused the bodily injury should first of all be external, in the sense that it should not have been a disease. This trait allows for the distinction between personal accidents and health insurance. Thus, if the bodily injury was a heart attack, it may be covered by personal accidents insurance depending on the event that caused it – for instance, whereas the administering of anaesthesia that produced anaphylactic shock is deemed to be an external event, atherosclerosis causing heart attack is not.[455] The fact that the insured person performed his work under hostile weather conditions and in a state of fatigue and stress was also deemed an external cause of the stroke they suffered.[456]

1028. The event should furthermore be sudden[457] – that is, the process of exposure to the source of bodily damage should not be stretched in time. This trait intends to separate personal accidents from diseases, especially occupational diseases. For instance, the prolonged exposure to asbestos, or to stress, is not deemed to be a sudden cause. Naturally, it is not possible to predefine which should be the maximum length of the procedure, since it depends on the agent of the injury (e.g., a car crash may be instantaneous, whereas a gas leakage will not come to cause bodily injury unless it has a certain duration). The process should nonetheless occur within a limited time frame and be continuous within these limits. This trait does not imply that the bodily lesion should occur immediately or that all of its effects should happen in a short period of time. On the contrary, the unfolding of the bodily injury process may be long lasting (just think of a car accident that can lead to a long process of treatment and recovery).

1029. Moreover, the event should be unpredictable. This should not be taken as requiring the event to be objectively unpredictable; it is rather required that the event was not predicted by the person at stake.[458] Otherwise, there would not be cover for events that are known to be dangerous, and for which cover is legitimately expected, and often expressly agreed – such as extreme sports or tasks with dangerous machines.

---

454. And not as the cause of that event. *See* Maria Inês de Oliveira Martins, Contrato de seguro e conduta dos sujeitos ligados ao risco, Almedina, (2018), 264 and ff. This also seems to underlie the reasoning of José Carlos Moitinho de Almeida, O contrato de seguro no direito português e comparado, Livraria Sá da Costa (1971), 398–399.
455. TRC 1 March 2016, 4992/13.1TBLRA.C1 (Maria Catarina Gonçalves): a heart attack caused by anaphylactic shock – reaction to an anaesthesia – is deemed to have an external cause; however, if the court cannot rule out that the heart attack was due to internal causes (obesity or diabetes which affected that particular person), it cannot qualify the cause of the accident as being external. TRE 8 May 2014, 1071/10.7TBSTR.E1 (Mata Ribeiro): a heart attack caused by atherosclerosis is not deemed to be an accident, since its cause is an internal and slowly progressing disease; the fact that physically demanding gardening work may have contributed to the heart attack does not alter this conclusion.
456. STJ 21 April 2009, 09A0449 (Fonseca Ramos); it was not proved that the stroke could be attributed to any pre-existing disease.
457. M. I. Oliveira Martins, Contrato de seguro e conduta …, 276–278.
458. For a more thorough analysis, drawing upon comparative law, M. I. Oliveira Martins, Contrato de seguro e conduta …, 278–279.

1030. Finally, the bodily injury should not have been caused intentionally. It should be stressed that the feature of non-intentionality does not refer to the event causing the bodily injury – many events, such as sports or driving, are voluntarily undertaken –, but to the bodily injury itself. Although Article 212 does not refer to this feature, the fact that intentional accidents are not covered results from Article 46. The interplay between Article 212 and Article 46 determines that the insured does not have to prove the non-intentional nature of the injury; the burden of proving the intentional nature of the accident falls upon the insurance company.

§2. The Personal Accident Insurance Regime

1031. Personal accidents insurance can be taken out either as a fixed sums insurance, or as indemnity insurance, as it can combine benefits of either nature. Personal accidents insurance clearly has the nature of indemnity insurance in regard to the payment of medical or assistance expenses (or of the direct provision of these services). However, whenever a certain sum is paid as a compensation for the consequences of the bodily injury, there may be cases which are doubtful as to the nature of the insurance. For instance, when the contract predefines certain amounts as insurance benefits, yet associates each of them to different degrees of gravity of the bodily injury, there will be room for questioning whether a fixed sums insurance or an indemnity insurance is at stake. These amounts may be regarded as similar to life insurance benefits – that is, as a way of replacing the diminution or loss of the capacity to obtain and accumulate income.

1032. Now, there is a considerable difference as to the norms applicable to each of the cases. As the RJCS separates between 'damages' insurance and personal insurance,[459] the norms on indemnity insurance are not directly applicable to personal accidents insurance.

1033. Articles 180 and 181 set out the rules that strictly separate indemnity insurance (embodying the 'indemnity principle') from fixed sums insurance.

1034. Under Article 180(1), unless otherwise provided for in the contract, fixed sums payments can be cumulated either with other fixed sums payments, or with insurance indemnity granted for the same insured event. Nonetheless, the policyholder or insured should warn the insurer on the existence of other insurance contracts that cover the same risk, even when they also grant fixed sums.

1035. Differently, under Article 180(2), Article 133 is applicable to the case of indemnity insurance. In this case, there is no right to cumulate different insurance benefits in regard to the same risk. When the same risk regarding the same insurable interest is covered by different insurers in regard to the same period, the insured event is then covered by the insurer (or insurers) chosen by the insured, within the limits of the risk one or all of them promised to cover (Article 133(3)). Moreover,

459. *See* Part II, Ch. 1, §3, Categories of Insurance.

the policyholder should inform all of the insurers on the existence of cumulative cover and should remind the insurers when the insured event occurs (Article 133(1)).[460]

1036. In what concerns subrogation, the difference has also become marked after 2015. Before 2015, Article 181 established that, unless the contract provided differently, the insurer had no right to subrogation in the case of fixed sums insurance. *A contrario*, it was inferred that it would always have a right to subrogation in case of indemnity insurance. However, this could counter the expectations of the insured, especially in fixed sums insurance, since it is seen as a way of replacing the reduction or loss of capacity to obtain and accumulate income, which would not contend with the right of the insured to damages. Subrogation may also come as unexpected in indemnity insurance, since, as mentioned above, in personal insurance it may not be clear whether the amounts promised by the insurer have the nature of indemnity, or of a fixed sum that aims to replace the diminution or loss of the capacity to obtain and accumulate income.

1037. These issues seem to have been taken into account, since the terms of Article 181 are very different today. Under Article 181(1), performance by the insurer does not entitle them to subrogate into the rights of the person at risk or the beneficiary against a third party that caused the insured event, unless agreed otherwise in indemnity insurance. Article 181(2) establishes that, for the purposes of the foregoing, insurance (i.e., the benefit at stake) is deemed (a) to have the nature of indemnity when performance by the insurer is due in regard of it being necessary to make good for the damage suffered by the insured; (b) in case of doubt, insurance is only considered to have the nature of indemnity when that is clearly and expressly set out in the policy. Under Article 181(3), the term setting out the right to subrogation should be highlighted in the policy; furthermore, the special duty of clarification set out in Article 22(1) and (2) applies in its regard.

1038. Whether the insurance was taken out as a fixed sums insurance or as indemnity insurance is a matter of interpretation of the contract.[461] In view of Article 181(2)(b), and of the general *contra proferentem* principle, in case of doubt, the contract should be construed as fixed sums insurance, since the norms applicable to it are more favourable to the insured than those applicable to indemnity insurance.[462]

1039. Articles 211 and 212 further summon other norms from different parts of the RJCS.[463] In case a third-party beneficiary is entitled to payment due in case of the insured event, then Articles 192, 193, 198, 199(1)–(3), 200 and 201, set out for

460. On this norm, *see further* Part II, Ch. 5, §1, II, Rules Applicable to Indemnity Insurance.

461. For a well-reasoned interpretation of the contract and of the applicable norms, *see*, against the backdrop of the Commercial Code, STJ 22 February 2011, 667/06.8TBOHP.C2.S1 (Helder Roque).

462. M. I. Oliveira Martins, Contrato de seguro e conduta ..., 293–294.

463. Article 179, enshrined among the general norms applicable to personal insurance, specifically provides for long-term personal accidents and health insurance, by requiring that some special mentions are made in the policies.

life insurance, shall apply (Article 211(1)).[464] Article 212(1) further clarifies that where the contract refers to a third party, in case of doubt, they will be deemed to be a third-party beneficiary. In case the policyholder is also the beneficiary of the contract, and yet they are not the person at risk, then the consent of the person at risk shall be required, as long as they are identified in the contract (Article 212(2)).

1040. Finally, Article 211(2) establishes that the norms on mitigation of the loss and reimbursement of expenses (Articles 126 and 127) apply *mutatis mutandis* to personal accidents insurance. The measures adopted in order to control the consequences of the insured event can in many cases interfere directly in the bodily sphere of the person at risk, and weigh upon their bodily self-determination. Therefore, the standard of reasonableness should be interpreted with special attention to the specific circumstances of the person at risk. In principle, the person at risk will be deemed to have complied with their duty to mitigate if they seek the treatments they would have sought were they not insured.[465]

464. *See* Part V, Ch. 4, §1, IV, Third-Party Beneficiary Clauses.

465. M. I. Oliveira Martins, Contrato de seguro e conduta … , 466–477; *see also* Júlio Manuel Vieira Gomes, Do dever ou ónus de salvamento no novo regime jurídico do contrato de seguro (Decreto-Lei n.º 72/2008, de 16/4), 28, Cadernos de Direito Privado, (2009), 4 and, in the past, Luiz da Cunha Gonçalves, Comentário ao Código Comercial português, II, Edições José Bastos, (1916), 601–602.

Chapter 3. Private Health Insurance

§1. Scope of the Regime

I. Role of Private Health Insurance in Portugal

1041. It is important to explain the role of private health insurance in the access to healthcare in Portugal, since this doubtlessly influences how its regime is interpreted.

1042. Portugal follows a Beveridge model of provision of public healthcare.[466] Universal access to healthcare is granted through a National Health Service, funded mostly through taxation and therefore tending towards free health service (Article 64(2)(a) of the Portuguese Constitution).[467] Private health insurance is generally voluntary[468] and its taking out does not allow for the opting out of the public health system. It functions rather as a complement to the public health system, granting smaller waiting times, higher comfort or a greater variety of therapies.

1043. Therefore, unlike what may happen in countries where private insurance is paramount in the access to quality healthcare, private health insurance shall not be interpreted in Portugal in light of the constitutional right to healthcare and the protection of health. The insured will benefit from the same sources of protection that are relevant in other non-negotiated long-term contracts: mainly, the norms of the LSCT and the principle of good faith and its corollaries, that may determine the protection of the legitimate expectations of the insured.

II. Concept and Possible Forms

1044. Articles 213–217 form the last section of the RJCS, titled 'health insurance'. According to Article 213, in health insurance the insurer covers risks related to the provision of healthcare. This definition does not, of course, prescribe what should be considered health insurance. Private autonomy has the say in this regard,

466. Theodore Tulchinsky, *Case Studies in Public Health*, 142–144 (Academic Press/Elsevier, 2018); Rowena Jacobs & Maria Goddard, *Social Health Insurance Systems in European Countries, The Role of the Insurer in the Health Care System: A Comparative Study of Four European Countries*, 15–16 (Centre for Health Economics, University of York 2000).

467. There are some instances of (public) social health insurance, but they pertain to specific sectors, and are remnants of the system that existed before the Portuguese Constitution, where access to health was based on occupational benefits schemes. That is the case of ADSE, referring to the public servants, or of ADM, referring to member of the military. *See* Pedro Pita Barros, Sara Ribeirinho Machado, & Jorge de Almeida Simões, *Portugal, Health System Review, European Observatory on Health Systems and Policies,*, 16 and 19–30 (World Health Organization 2011).

468. For an exception, *see* the mandatory health insurance of high performance sportspersons, set out in Arts 11 and 17 of Decree-Law 10/2009, of 12 January on sports insurance.

and other contract arrangements are legitimate. The concept provided is nonetheless useful in describing the kind of insurance that Articles 214–217 intend to regulate.

1045. The concept endorsed is clearly broad and does not require the existence of disease. Rightly so, since diagnosis is a complex process, requiring the intervention of experts and not seldom leaving room to doubt. On the other hand, some of the disadvantages associated with disease can be present even when disease is merely possible – that is clearly the case of expenses with diagnosis, as well as with preventive healthcare, which the concept set out in Article 213 does not exclude from the scope of the contract.

1046. The broadness of the concept furthermore becomes apparent when it is compared with the concept of personal accidents insurance. As personal accidents can give rise to the provision of healthcare, any loss caused in this connection can also be covered by health insurance. That is, whereas damage caused by a personal accident is in principle covered by health insurance, the opposite is not true: damage caused by disease, while covered by health insurance, falls outside of the concept of personal accident.

1047. There can be different forms of health insurance. Health insurance is generally thought of as a way of acquiring access to complementary healthcare. The contract can grant the reimbursement of expenses, the direct provision of healthcare or the access to a network of healthcare providers, of which services the insured will pay a lower fare. In this case, there is no doubt that the contract qualifies as indemnity insurance.

1048. Other forms of health insurance rest upon the payment of certain amounts in case of disability (temporary or permanent), eventually varying in accordance to its degree, or to days of hospital stay. As described in regard to personal accidents insurance, doubt may arise in regard to the qualification of each of these insurance benefits as forms of indemnity insurance or fixed sums insurance. The same arguments put forth above recommend that in case of doubt the insurance is deemed as being of fixed sums.[469]

1049. It should again be reminded that the norms on life insurance are applicable to insurance against disability resulting from sickness that is underwritten in addition to life insurance (Article 184(1)).

§2. Regime of Private Health Insurance

1050. The scarce norms on health insurance work in favour of the insured, which is common to them, when compared to the norms that would otherwise apply. The granted protection is, however, rather illusory in some cases.

469. *See* Part V, Ch. 2, §2, The Personal Accident Insurance.

1051. Article 215 establishes that some regimes do not apply to health insurance, namely: the regime on the aggravation of risk, as set out by Articles 93 and 94, in regard to changes in the health condition of the person at risk; the duty to inform on the existence of more than one insurance covering the same risk, as set out by Article 180(2) and (3). In what concerns the exemption from the duty to communicate the existence of more than one insurance covering the same risk, it should be said that this provision is understandable in light of insurance that grants healthcare or the reimbursement of its costs. Voluntary *complementary* health insurance is taken out in this regard precisely to grant the person at risk with a plurality of possible ways to obtain healthcare, which may legitimately be combined, so as to have several opinions or therapies, or cumulated, to obtain coverage for longer treatments. However, this exemption is hard to grasp in regard to health insurance that gives right to certain sums in case of disability. In any case, if the policy does not contract out of Article 215(b), the exemption should also apply to these cases.

1052. Article 216(1) establishes that pre-existing health conditions which the person at risk is aware of upon the conclusion of the contract are included in the cover, but may be excluded by agreement, individually or generically. Article 216(2) establishes that the contract may also set out a waiting period not longer than one year for the cover of pre-existing health conditions.

1053. This seems to clarify that Article 44(1) and (2) – which establishes that the contract is void when, upon its conclusion the risk had ceased to exist, and that previous insured events are not covered – does not apply to health insurance. It does not seem to exempt the person at risk from their duty to correctly disclose the risk when entering the contract, under Articles 24–26. However, the fact that a certain health condition is pre-existing to the contract cannot be equated with the full extinction of the risk, since health conditions are long-lasting and dynamic states, of which consequences are unfolding and can remain to a considerable extent uncertain. Therefore, the clarification provided by Article 216(1) would result from a correct application of Article 44(1) and (2) to the risk at stake. Moreover, the protection granted by the norms is rather modest, since it highlights that pre-existing health conditions can, in any case, be generically excluded from cover. Only in case the insurer does not exclude them, will they have to comply with covering them after a period not longer than one year.

1054. Finally, Article 217(1) provides that in case the contract or the cover at stake is not renewed and the risk is not covered by a subsequent insurance contract, during a period of two years and until the insured sum agreed for the last period while the contract was in force has been totally paid out, the insurer shall not be allowed to refuse cover for disease or another insured event that was covered by the contract, as long as the insured event occurs while the contract is in force. For these purposes, Article 217(2) establishes that the insurer should be informed of the health condition within thirty days after termination of the contract, unless the person at risk was reasonably unable to do so.

1055. In other words, under Article 217, the person at risk keeps the right to insurance protection after termination of the contract, until the insured sum has been fully paid out. However, the protection granted seems quite feeble for cases where the person at risk suffers from a serious health condition. In fact, as the contracts are generally taken out for renewable periods of one year (Article 40),[470] an insurer that realises the person at risk has a serious health condition will normally not renew the contract. In these cases, the person at risk will have trouble finding another insurer willing to cover their aggravated risk, and cannot rely on the previous contract to give her access to the treatments required by a serious disease (e.g., cancer), since they will quickly deplete what would remain of the insured sums.

1056. In fact, health insurance as designed by the general rules of the RJCS does not provide a solid protection for serious diseases that become more likely with the process of ageing – such as cancer or dementia. Insurance coverage may allow for the financing of more innovative treatments in this regard, that are beyond the standard approach of the public health system.

1057. As long as the possibility not to renew the yearly insurance exists, the insurer may always discretionarily choose not to renew the contract. There was an attempt to provide for a long-term health insurance,[471] but the process seems to have been definitively abandoned. Meanwhile, insured persons have the choice of proceeding with private treatments by financing them themselves, or of turning to the public health system.

470. In this regard, Art. 214 establishes that the policy of yearly renewable health insurance should highlight the following mentions: that the insurer only grants the benefits convened, or reimburses the expenses as stipulated, in each of the years when the contract is in force; that the conditions under which there may be a right to insurance benefits in case of non-renewal of the contract, or under which the person at risk may have a right to cover, regard the risk covered by the contract, with respect to Art. 217.

471. It was the preliminary draft for a special regime regarding health insurance with enhanced or lifelong cover. The text can be retrieved at https://www.asf.com.pt/NR/rdonlyres/D170A4B3-B39D-4B59-A9E9-4F30E07D23B2/0/ATP_DL_SSV2.pdf.

Chapter 4. Life Insurance

§1. Individual Life Insurance

I. Concept of Life Insurance Contract and Main Norms Applicable to It

1058. Article 183 establishes that 'in life insurance the insurer covers a risk related to the death or survival of the person at risk'. The norm describes life insurance by connecting the risk it covers to a certain insured event – death or survival of the person at risk –, leaving a broad space for private autonomy. As in other legal systems, this space has been used to provide for different purposes.

1059. In what concerns life insurance where the insured event is the death of the person at risk, there is whole life insurance – mainly aimed at succession planning, but also used to cover funerary expenses – as well as temporary life insurance, with an array of purposes. Temporary life insurance can be used for personal risk management and family protection (e.g., in view of insurance for the period while a dangerous job is exercised), for entrepreneurial risk management (e.g., in case of key person insurance) as well as to provide security for a long-term creditor (e.g., in case of life insurance in connection with home loans). When the insured event is the survival of the person at risk, life insurance is mainly used as a placement for long-term savings, be that at a personal level, or at an entrepreneurial level. Nonetheless, the insurance market for long-term savings has been led by forms of mixed insurance, where there is a right to insurance benefits either in case of death of the person at risk, or in case they survive a certain age. In some cases, the amount corresponds, in either case, to the capitalisation of the premium paid until that moment (so-called capitalisation insurance[472]); in other cases, one of the benefits may be determined through different criteria and may differ considerably from the amount of premium paid.

1060. There is also temporary insurance, where death of the person at risk triggers not the payment of the insured sum, but the release from the duty to pay the premium. In this case, insurance is typically used to provide for a third party, who has a right to the insurance payment after a certain deadline (e.g., after reaching a certain age).

1061. In any case, insurance can be paid in a lump sum or in annuities – annuities are more common in case of life insurance as a long-term savings placement.

1062. Article 184(1) establishes that 'the norms on life insurance also apply to the following contracts: a) supplementary insurance underwritten in addition to life insurance, in particular, insurance against personal injury including incapacity for

472. Luís Poças, Os seguros de capitalização (in: Estudos de direito dos seguros, Almeida e Leitão, 2008), *maxime* 14–15.

employment, insurance against death resulting from an accident and insurance against disability resulting from an accident or sickness; b) annuities insurance; c) marriage insurance; d) birth insurance'.

1063. Although these are not strictly speaking life insurance contracts, they imply the payment of fixed sums, as is typical of life insurance; furthermore, they tend to have the purpose of providing for future pecuniary needs, as is the case with many forms of life insurance.

1064. According to Article 184(2), except for Articles 185 and 186 (on pre-contractual and ongoing information duties), the norms on life insurance apply to insurance linked to investment funds. The rule is as should be expected, since life insurance linked to investment funds is nonetheless life insurance. Differently, the exception is puzzling, since it does not reconcile with Article 185, which explicitly refers to unit-linked policies.

1065. Now, on what concerns the regulation of life insurance at a contract law level, the most important statutory provisions are those of the RJCS. They are flanked by statutes that apply only to some forms of life insurance: the Act on the central registry of life insurance contracts, personal accidents insurance contracts and capital redemption operations that give rights to third-party beneficiaries in case of death of the person at risk;[473] specifically on the matter of insurance-based investment products, the Regulation on key information documents for packaged retail and insurance-based investment products and the acts that implement it ('PRIIPs Regulation'),[474] as well as the Insurance Distribution Act; and the Act that approved the PFR on life insurance-based occupational pension plans.

1066. At an administrative level, three regulatory standards of the ASF are especially relevant for life insurance contracts. The first of them is Regulatory Standard 16/1995 on life insurance.[475] The Regulatory Standard was enacted in 1995. Therefore, many of its provisions, even though not formally repealed by subsequent acts, were contradicted by them or simply became superfluous. Nonetheless, where the Regulatory Standard is compatible with the statutes now in force, it is deemed to be still in force. The second is the Regulatory Standard 6/2008-R, of 24 April, on the rules applicable to life insurance covering the risk or death, incapacity or unemployment in connection with loan agreements. The third is Regulatory Standard

473. Decree-Law 384/2007, of 19 November.

474. Regulation 1286/2014 of 26 November; Commission Delegated Regulation 2017/653 of 8 March 2017, laying down regulatory technical standards with regard to key information documents; at a national level, the Regulation is supplemented by the Rules on PRIIPs, enacted by Law 35/2018, of 20 July, which approved rules on the marketing of financial products and on the organisation of financial intermediaries (Annex II).

475. Regulatory Standard 16/1995 of 12 September on the pursuit of the business of insurance – Life insurance.

14/2010-R on the central registry of life insurance contracts that give rights to third-party beneficiaries in case of death of the person at risk.[476]

II. Special Duties of Information

1067. Article 185(1) sets out a list of information that should be provided to the policyholder before the conclusion of the contract. The norm transposes Article 185 of Solvency II Directive, adding very few items to its list.[477] The provision of the information specified is also required in regard to collective retirement funds (Article 185(2)). Article 185(3) establishes that the supervising authority can issue regulatory standards further specifying the information to be provided when that is considered necessary to allow for a full understanding by the policyholder of the main features of the contract. Article 185(4) establishes that such regulatory powers can be used to require the provision of an informative prospectus, and to define its form and content.

1068. The ASF made use of the regulatory powers granted by the RJCS in regard to insurance connected to home loans, by enacting Regulatory Standard 6/2008-R, mentioned above (*see* especially Article 3). However, with the enactment of Decree-Law 222/2009,[478] on the protection of consumers that take out life insurance in connection with their home acquisition loan, some of these duties acquired legislative (supra-administrative) status. In turn, Regulatory Standard 16/1995 does set out some information duties – yet non-systematically, but in connection with the regulation of different aspects of life insurance (*see, for instance,* Nos 44, 49, 49.1).

1069. Under Article 186(1), throughout the term of the contract, the insurer should inform the policyholder on any change affecting the information provided at

476. Regulatory Standard 14/2010-R, of 14 October 2010, on the central registry of life insurance contracts, personal accidents insurance contracts and capital redemption operations that give rights to third party beneficiaries in the case of the death of the person at risk.

477. Under Art. 185(1), in relation to life insurance, besides the information mentioned in Arts 18–21, the following should be additionally provided: (a) the means of calculation and distribution of bonuses; (b) the definition of each benefit and each option; (c) an indication of surrender and paid-up values and the extent to which they are guaranteed, as well as an indication of the penalties applicable in case of surrender, reduction or transfer of contract; (d) information on the premiums for each benefit, both main benefits and supplementary benefits; (e) indication of the minimum guaranteed return, including information on the applicable interest rate and on the duration of the contract; (f) for unit-linked policies, the definition of the units to which the benefits are linked, as well as the indication of the number of such units; (g) an indication of the nature of the underlying assets for unit-linked policies; (h) general information on the tax arrangements applicable to the type of policy; (i) in contracts with a savings component, the amounts to be paid by the policyholder, the means of payment and the moment in which payment is due; (j) the indication that the person at risk has access to the result of the medical exams performed on them; (k) a concrete reference to the report on the solvency and financial condition as laid down in Art. 83 of LBIR, allowing the policyholder easy access to this information; (l) any specific information which is necessary in order to provide a proper understanding of the risks underlying the contract which are assumed by the policyholder.

478. Decree-Law 222/2009, of 11 September.

the conclusion of the contract and that may influence its performance. Under Article 186(2), upon termination of the contract, the insurer should inform the policyholder on the amount of the benefits they are entitled to, as well as on any documents or procedures necessary for its receipt.

1070. Life insurance as a security for home loans has deserved a special attention from the lawmaker, which was also reflected in the provision of specific information duties – *see* Articles 4 and 9(1), stating that the insurer is liable for the damaged caused by breach of its duties.

1071. Nonetheless, the form of life insurance that deserves a special mention in this regard is that of *insurance which gives rise to the distribution of bonuses.*[479] The distribution of bonuses – namely, of surpluses, connected with profit and valuation reserves – was not made mandatory or dependent on special conditions,[480] but it is surrounded by an array of duties to inform.[481]

1072. Article 185(5) and (6), which were added to the RJCS in 2015 in order to transpose Solvency II, have this form of insurance as their central object. According to Article 185(5), 'where, in connection with an offer for or conclusion of a life insurance contract, the insurer provides figures relating to the amount of potential payments above and beyond the contractually agreed payments, the insurer shall provide the policy holder with a specimen calculation whereby the potential maturity payment is set out applying the basis for the premium calculation using three different rates of interest'. According to Article 185(6), 'the insurer shall inform the policyholder in a clear and comprehensible manner that the specimen calculation is only a model of computation based on notional assumptions, and that the policy holder shall not derive any contractual claims from the specimen calculation'. Article 205(3) was present in the original version of the RJCS, as it transposed a provision from the Life insurance Directive. It establishes that throughout the term of the contract, the insurer should inform the policyholder every year on the amount of the bonuses shared. Article 205(4), which transposes Solvency II, establishes that where the insurer has provided figures about the potential future development of the

479. The terminology used is that of the Portuguese version of Solvency II Directive, which equates the distribution of bonuses with surplus sharing in broad terms and does not differentiate between distribution of bonuses and profit participation (*see* Art. 185(1)(e) and 185(5) of Solvency II Directive).

480. The only aspect of payment of bonuses that is regulated by the RJCS is that of the bonus due when the contract terminates. Under Art. 205(4), in this case, the policyholder, insured or beneficiary, whatever the case, has the right to the share of the bonuses that had already been allocated to them in spite of not having been distributed yet, as well as a right to the share of the bonuses that have not yet been allocated to them, and that is to be determined *pro rata temporis* since the last allocation of bonuses to the policyholder, insured or beneficiary at stake and until termination of the contract.

481. Apart from the RJCS and the norms on insurance-based investment products, Regulatory Standard 16/1995 lays down rules that the insurer should abide with in case it stipulates the distribution of bonuses (*see* s. IV, Nos 39–45). The duties set out are towards the supervisory authority; they are duties of administrative nature, and not contract law duties towards the policyholders.

distribution of bonuses, the insurer shall inform the policyholder of differences between the actual development and the initial data.

1073. Moreover, the norms on insurance-based investment products also apply to *insurance which gives rise to the distribution of bonuses.*[482] Therefore, the insurer should draw up a key information document and publish it on its website under Articles 5 and ff. of the PRIIPS Regulation and should also provide it to the policyholder in case it directly distributes the life insurance product at stake (Articles 13 and 14 of the PRIIPS Regulation). In that case, the insurer should also comply with the duties of information set out in Articles 40–45 of the Insurance Distribution Act (*see* Article 46 of the Insurance Distribution Act).

III. Adaptation of the General Norms

1074. Some norms on life insurance can be considered adaptations of the general norms on the insurance contract to the context of life insurance.

1075. Article 188, with the title 'indisputability' is a limitation to the norms on pre-contractual duty of disclosure. Under Article 188(1), the insurer is barred from invoking the negligent breach of the pre-contractual duty of disclosure after two years have elapsed since the conclusion of the contract, unless a shorter period is stipulated on the contract. Under Article 188(2), the foregoing does not apply to supplementary personal accidents or disability insurance underwritten in addition to life insurance, unless the contract provides otherwise. Article 188(1) is qualified as semi-mandatory by Article 13(1).[483] There is no doubt as to the possibility of establishing a shorter time limitation for the invocation of sanctions set out in Article 26, in regard to negligent non-disclosure. It is also defended that in this case the insurer can renounce their invocation altogether. There is, however, controversy as to whether the contract can introduce a time limit for the invocation of sanctions set out for *intentional non-disclosure*. In view of the wording of the norm, some scholarship considers that this possibility was not intended by the lawmakers. However, there would be no reasons of public order to reject such a stipulation, since the intentional breach of the duty of disclosure only gives the insurer the right to avoid the contract, which it may decide not to make use of; besides, the norm at stake – Article 25 – is only semi-mandatory under Article 13(1).[484] Other scholarship considers that the RJCS grants such a possibility; still, except for very few cases, which should be identified on case-by-case basis, that possibility would generally collide

482. In Portuguese law, *see* Arnaldo da Costa Oliveira, Art. 184.°, Âmbito, Comentários complementares (in: Lei do Contrato de Seguro anotada, Almedina, 2020), 554.

483. It is self-evident that Art. 188(2) can be contracted out only in favour of the policyholder/insured.

484. Júlio Manuel Vieira Gomes, O dever de informação do (candidato a) tomador do seguro na fase pré-contratual à luz do Decreto-Lei n.° 72/2008, de 16 de Abril (in: Rui Pinto Duarte/José Lebre de Freitas/Assunção Cristas/Marta Tavares de Almeida/Vítor Pereira das Neves (ed.) Estudos em Homenagem ao Professor Doutor Carlos Ferreira de Almeida, II, Almedina, 2011), 438–440.

with public order.[485] In any case, no policy existing in the Portuguese market and containing such a stipulation has come to our knowledge.

1076. Article 189 provides for mistake regarding the age of the person at risk. Under Article 189(1), mistake regarding the age of the person at risk gives the insurer a right to avoid the contract if the actual age is below or above the minimum or maximum age threshold that the insurer has established for the type of insurance at stake. Article 189(2) establishes that when the difference between the age declared and the actual age does not give a right to avoid the contract, then the insurance benefits are reduced in the proportion of the premium paid, or else the excess premium is returned, as the case may be. This rule is deemed to attend to the fact that, even though the policyholder or insured will normally be in position to provide accurate information on the age of the person at risk – it is enough to present their ID card –, exactly the same applies to the insurer or its distributors, who may as easily verify the ID card of the person at risk. Therefore, in this regard, the policyholder and insured deserve a higher degree of protection than the one provided by the general rules on pre-contractual disclosure of the risk – namely, Articles 24–26.

1077. There is, nonetheless, doubt as to the interplay between these norms. To some scholarship, Article 189 is a particular case of the regime laid down by Articles 24–26 and should be read in the light of their provisions.[486] Thus, in case the contract is avoided by the insurer, if the mistake was caused by negligence of the policyholder/insured, they will have the right to the reimbursement of the premium; if the policyholder/insured wilfully caused the mistake, unless there was also at least gross negligence from the insurer or from its representatives, the insurer shall be entitled to retain the premium. Other scholarship considers that Article 189 lays down an autonomous regime, that, quite differently, is not dependent on the assessment of the degree of fault by the policyholder/insured and should therefore be free of the punitive elements present in Articles 24–26.[487] Hence, in case of avoidance of the contract by the insurer, it should simply reimburse the premiums paid.

1078. In turn, Article 190 provides for the matter of aggravation of risk. Under its terms, the rules on aggravation of risk set out by Articles 93 and 94 do not apply to life insurance and, when the aggravation of the risk results from the worsening of the health condition of the person at risk, they also do not apply to supplementary insurance against personal injury or against disability underwritten in addition to life insurance. Therefore, in regard to supplementary insurance, the policyholder or insured should for instance inform the insurer of a change in their profession that

485. A. Costa Oliveira, Art. 188, Incontestabilidade, 566.
486. A. Costa Oliveira, Art. 189.º, Erro sobre a idade da pessoa segura, 568.
487. Júlio M. V. Gomes, O dever de informação ..., 441–442.

leads to an aggravation of risk; in regard to life insurance *tout court*, all modifications of risk are deemed irrelevant.[488] Although Article 190 is not mentioned in Article 13(1), it is deemed relatively mandatory in view of its rationale.[489]

1079. Articles 191, 192 and 193 regard the matter of intentional causation of the insured event. Article 191 provides for the case of suicide of the person at risk, setting out in 191(1) that, unless the parties agree otherwise, cover is excluded in case of death caused by suicide, in case it occurs before one year after commencement of the contract. Article 191(2) establishes that the foregoing also applies in case of the increase of the insured sum promised for the event of death, as well as in case the contract is terminated and reinstated; in any case, the exclusion will then only apply to the additional cover arising from those circumstances.

1080. The norm is not mandatory; therefore, the waiting period can be either restricted – even suppressed – or extended by the contract. Unlike the Commercial Code, the RJCS does not differentiate between 'voluntary' and 'involuntary' suicide; it seems to have been the intention of the lawmaker to avoid litigation connected to the qualification of suicide as involuntary (leading to the granting of cover).[490] However, as suicide has the meaning of death voluntarily caused to the self, there is room to question whether the term 'suicide' can even apply to cases where a pathology totally excluded any freedom of decision from the person at risk.[491]

1081. Article 191(2) points to a restrictive interpretation of this exclusion of cover. Against this background, some scholarship considers that in case of life insurance on the life of a person different from the policyholder, the exclusion does not apply (as was expressly laid down in the Commercial Code).[492] This construction rests upon the idea – which can be questioned – that Article 191 intends to prevent cases of premeditation, where life insurance was taken out with the purpose of triggering the insurance payment through suicide.

1082. Articles 192 and 193 concern the cases where a third-party beneficiary has either tried to cause the insured event, or proves to be unworthy of the benefit. Under Article 192, the author, accomplice, instigator, or concealer of murder (intentional homicide) of the person at risk loses the right to insurance benefits; the rules on designation of third party beneficiaries shall apply. Under Article 193, without prejudice to Article 46 (on intentional causation of the insured event) and to the (foregoing) norms, in case the beneficiary intentionally causes a bodily damage to

488. This was already the view of José Carlos Moitinho de Almeida, O contrato de seguro no direito português e comparado, Livraria Sá da Costa (1971), 375.

489. A. Costa Oliveira, Art. 190.°, Agravamento do risco, 570.

490. A. Costa Oliveira, Art. 191.°, Exclusão do suicídio, 571.

491. Pedro Romano Martínez, Art. 191.°, Exclusão do suicídio, Comentários complementares (in: Lei do Contrato de Seguro anotada, Almedina, 2020), 573–574.

492. A. Costa Oliveira, Art. 191.°, 573.

the person at risk, then the person at risk shall become the person entitled to the benefits granted by the contract. That is, Article 193 applies even when attempted murder could not be established and it does not require the criminal conviction of the beneficiary. Article 193 cannot thus be considered a particular case of intentional causation of the insured event, but rather a norm analogous to those on revocation of the donation due to ingratitude of the done.[493]

1083. Finally, Articles 202–204 regard the issue of payment of the premium. As was mentioned above (*see* Part II, Chapter 4, §1, Payment of Premium), life insurance is one of the few realms where the strict rule ‘no premium, no risk’ is not mandatory. According to Article 202(1), the policyholder should pay the insurance premium in the dates and according to the conditions set out in the contract. Under Article 202(2), the insurer should warn the policyholder, in writing, on the amount to pay, as well as on the method and place of payment, at least thirty days before the date in which the premium or its fraction fall due.

1084. According to Article 203(1), the absence of payment by the due date gives the insurer, according to the case and to what the parties have agreed, the right to terminate the contract, accompanied by the payment of the due surrender value, the right to reduce the benefits granted by the contract or the right to convert the contract in a paid-up policy. Under Article 203(2), the policy should set out the deadline for the policyholder to reinstate to its original terms, and without being subject to new medical examinations, the contract that has been terminated or reduced; the deadline should start from the date of termination or reduction.

1085. According to Article 204(1), where the contract gives an irrevocable right to a third-party beneficiary, in case the premium is not paid on the due date, the insurer must notify the beneficiary of the contract, who shall have a deadline of thirty days to pay the premium in the place of the policyholder. Under Article 204(2), the insurer that has not duly notified the beneficiary cannot invoke the consequences of default on premium against them.

1086. There are many different possibilities to address the cases where life insurance premium is not paid. Article 203 takes into account that life insurance is generally a fixed sums insurance contract, often aimed at long-term savings and in many cases attracting a surrender or conversion value. Therefore, the possibility arises of reducing the value of the long-term savings expected – namely, of the insurance benefits promised – by reducing the premium; or even of using the surrender value to finance the maintenance of cover, also with reduction of the insurance benefits.

---

493. Maria Inês de Oliveira Martins, Contrato de seguro e conduta dos sujeitos ligados ao riscó, Almedina, (2018), 325; *see* Arts 974, and 2166–2167 of the Civil Code and Art. IV. H. – 4:201 (‘Ingratitude of the donee’) of the DCFR.

1087. These possibilities are normally not used when life insurance is taken out as a security for a long-term lender. In these cases, the insurance benefit should follow the outstanding amount of debt, which is not compatible with it being reduced. After the RJCS, in the case of the lender being an irrevocable third-party beneficiary in insurance contract, they will then be given the possibility to pay the premium and keep their protection (Article 204). At least in these cases, the policyholder will generally be granted a period of delay in which they can pay the premium and avoid the termination of the contract. However, when there is no irrevocable third-party beneficiary to the contract, the insurer will in principle be free to set out a 'no premium, no risk' regime in the contract – although the LSCT may raise some issues in regard to such contract terms, when they contradict the normal expectations of the policyholder in view of the purpose of the contract.

1088. To fully understand how these rules have been put into practice, one should remember that until the RJCS entered into force, differently from what happened in other types of insurance, in matters of life insurance, default on premium was still regulated by Decree of 21 October 1907. In Article 33(1), the Decree set out that life insurance contracts could only be deemed extinguished due to lack of payment when the insured, after being warned of the fact by registered letter, did not pay the premium fallen due within a deadline of at least eight days, unless the policy stipulated a longer term. It was not rare that the insurer did not notify the policyholder as required, remaining passive instead until the insured event occurred. The contract was then considered to be in force, and the insurer was then called to perform before the beneficiary (it could recover the amount of the premium fallen due from the estate of the deceased).[494]

1089. Along this line, the communications that the insurer should address to the insureds/persons-at-risk, either under Article 202, or under special provisions of the policy, have remained in the focus of case law. In the cases of joint life insurance taken in regard to the life of two spouses or domestic partners – a form of insurance which is very relevant for the market –, the established case law rightly requires that the insurer notifies each of its insureds/persons-at-risk. When each of them is the debtor of a single common and indivisible debt, the notification of one of them, even when espoused to the other, does not replace the notification of the other.[495]

1090. However, on this matter, the STJ has recently decided that, although the contract remains in force in regard to a non-notified debtor, they are not protected

494. *See* STJ 3 October 1998, 98B646 (Nascimento Costa); TRP 16 June 2014, 6260/11.4TBMAI.P1 (Manuel Domingos Fernandes).

495. *See, for instance,* in light of the norms in force before the RJCS, STJ 3 February 2009, p08A3947 (Helder Roque); STJ 3 November 2016, 3248/09.9TBVCD.S1 (Maria da Graça Trigo); after RJCS, *see* STJ 22 February 2018, 10942/14.0T8LSB.L1.S2 (Rosa Tching); STJ 13 November 2018, 1699/16.1T8PNF.P2.S2 (Alexandre Reis). In scholarship, *see* Maria Inês de Oliveira Martins, Pluralidade subjectiva no contrato de seguro e determinação da qualidade dos intervenientes, Anotação ao acórdão do Supremo Tribunal de Justiça de 13 de Novembro de 2018, Processo n.º 1699/16.1T8PNF.P2.S2 (Cons. Alexandre Reis), 64, Cadernos de Direito Privado, (2018), 85–86 and also the previous pages.

against the risk of death of their co-insured/person-at-risk; the survived non-notified debtor would only be protected against the risk of their own death.[496] This case law cannot be followed, since it ignores the fact of the insurance *being joint life insurance* ('insurance upon two heads'), where the risks entailed by each person at risk are cumulatively – and not separately, as would be the case in group insurance – guaranteed.[497] Each insured is protected against the risk of death of the other insured(s). That is the reason why the same case law that the decision drawn upon has – rightly – been considering the duty to pay the premium as being indivisible.

IV. Third-Party Beneficiary Clauses

1091. Life insurance is often the source of rights for third-party beneficiaries. This happens when the policyholder/person at risk intends to manage their patrimony and plan their succession, by granting rights to persons they intends to protect or benefit; but also when life insurance is used to provide security to a long-term lender.

1092. Life insurance contracts to the benefit of third parties are contracts in favour of a third party; therefore, the general norms of the Civil Code on the matter – Articles 443–451 – apply. Under the general norms, the contract party that undertakes to perform in regard of the third party is called the 'promisor', and the contract party to whom this promise is made is called the 'promisee' (Article 443(1)).

1093. Nonetheless, the RJCS makes some adaptations to these norms, and clarifies some doubts that could arise in the interpretation of clauses that grant rights to third party beneficiaries.

1094. According to Article 198(1), the policyholder or the person they appoint shall designate the beneficiary; the designation can be made in the policy, in a written statement sent afterwards to the insurer, or in a will. According to Article 198(2), unless the contract provides differently, in case of death of the person at risk, the insurance benefits shall be paid: (a) to the heirs of the person at risk when a beneficiary has not been designated; (b) to the heirs of the latter when a beneficiary has not been designated,; (c) to the heirs of the beneficiary in case the beneficiary dies before the person at risk, and there was renounce to the revocation of the beneficiary; (d) to the heirs of the beneficiary in case the person at risk and the beneficiary die simultaneously. According to Article 198(3), unless the contract provides differently, in case of insurance for the case of survival to a certain date, the insured benefits shall be paid to the person at risk, either when no beneficiary was designated, or when the beneficiary died before the person at risk.

1095. Article 205 further clarifies how the designation should be interpreted in case of ambiguity, regarding the cases where the contract makes a generic reference

496. STJ 22 February 2018, 10942/14.0T8LSB.L1.S2 (Rosa Tching).
497. M. I. Oliveira Martins, Pluralidade subjectiva … , 77, 85–86.

to the children of the policyholder (Article 205(1)), to their spouse or legal heirs (Article 205(2)), or when it designates several beneficiaries simultaneously (Article 205(3)).

1096. Article 199 provides for the alteration of the beneficiary, and for the revocation of the designation. Under Article 199(1), the person that designates the beneficiary may at any time revoke or change the designation, unless they have expressly renounced that right or, in case of insurance for the case of survival to a certain date, when the beneficiary has manifested their adhesion to the benefit. In these two cases, under Article 199(2), unless the contract provides differently, the policyholder does not have the right to request the payment of the surrender value, to request the reduction of the contract or to request advance payments on the surrender value. Under Article 199(3), the power to change the designation ceases when the beneficiary acquires the right to the payment of the insurance benefits.

1097. In turn, Article 200 establishes that the relationship of the policyholder with persons other than the beneficiary does not affect the designation; that is, the duty to account and restore gifts and legacies, the provisions on hotchpot, or the actions against the infringement of legal rights of creditors, shall only regard the amounts paid by the policyholder, and not the amount of the insurance benefits.

1098. Articles 199(1)–(3) and 200 directly relate to the general norms of the Civil Code on contracts in favour of a third party. In what regards Article 200, Article 450 of the Civil Code similarly establishes that the right of the beneficiary is immune to the rights of creditors of the promisee. As regards Articles 199(1)–(3), Article 448(1) of the Civil Code similarly establishes that, unless the contract provides differently, the benefit to the third party can be revoked at any time before the beneficiary adheres to it, unless the benefit is to be granted after the death of the promisee, since in this case the benefit can be revoked until the death of the promisee. It becomes clear that the law intends to protect the freedom of the promisee, who bestows their assets upon a third party, in view of the extension of the time lapse between the moment where the benefit is attributed, and that in which it is to take effect. That would seem to also be the rationale underlying Article 199(1), in view of the distinction it establishes between insurance for the case of death and insurance for the case of survival of the person at risk. However, when the person at risk is not the policyholder, they will not be the promisee. In these cases, the rationale for tying the freedom to revoke to their death is not apparent.

1099. Articles 199(4) and (5) are directly connected to the requirement that the person at risk give their consent to the insurance contract taken out by another person, as set out in Article 43(3). Under its terms, in life insurance, where the person at risk is not the beneficiary they should provide their consent for the risk to be covered, unless the insurance contract is taken out in order to comply with a command of law or of a collective labour agreement. The law seems to extend the requirement of consent by the person at risk to all forms of life insurance, instead of limiting it to insurance for the case of death. This seems correct when one considers that the purpose of consent is not merely to put a check on moral hazard, but also to grant the person at risk the right to decide on who can profit from their longer or shorter longevity.[498]

1100. Consent should not be a blank check, and it would not be material if the person at risk could not control who stood to profit from the contract. Under Article 199(4), when the person at risk signed the insurance proposal together with the policyholder, and the policy named the beneficiary, or when the person at risk designated the beneficiary, the beneficiary cannot be changed without the consent of the person at risk. When the change of the beneficiary is made by someone different than the person at risk and takes place without their agreement, then the insurer should communicate the alteration to them (Article 199(5)).

1101. A question of chief importance to the effectiveness of the designation is that of the beneficiaries being aware that they have a right to insurance benefits, so that they can present their claims. This concern can nonetheless collide with the wish of confidentiality from the person granting benefits that are to take effect only after their death, and that can normally be revoked until that moment. To reconcile these concerns, Portuguese law has created a central registry of life and personal accidents insurance and capital redemption operations, when they give rise to the attribution of benefits to third parties in case of death of the person at risk or the subscriber. The central registry framework was enacted in 2007, by Decree-Law 384/2007,[499] and substantially reshaped in 2013; it is further regulated by Regulatory Standard 14/2010-R, of ASF. The registry is managed by the ASF.[500]

1102. The information which is nowadays kept in the public registry is that of the existence of insurance or capital redemption contracts that refer to a certain person at risk and designate a beneficiary for the case of death, and of its insurer (Articles 6 and 8 of Decree-Law 384/2007). Any interested party may now ask the registry on the existence of such contracts regarding a certain person, and on the identity of their insurer, as long as they are the person at stake, or else justify their interest in the information and exhibits a death certificate of the person concerned (Article 9). In case there is such a contract, the interested party can then turn to the insurer at stake and, by presenting a certificate issued by the ASF, obtain information as to whether they are designated beneficiary of the contract (Article 9(A)).[501] In case it is so, the insurer should give them all the information necessary to exercise their rights; if not, the insurer merely informs them that they were not designated beneficiary.

498. Margarida Lima Rego, Contrato de seguro e terceiros, Estudo de Direito civil, Coimbra Editora, (2010), esp. 629 and ff.

499. Decree-Law 384/2007, of 19 November.

500. *See* https://www.asf.com.pt/NR/exeres/E5BAD587-383B-4EE9-85CB-771917D88CCF.htm.

501. In fact, even without such a certificate, an interested party can at any time request an insurer to inform them on the fact that they are the beneficiary of any contract in the case of death (Art. 9(A)(2) of Decree-Law 384/2007).

1103. One should note that the insurer should itself inform the persons designated as beneficiaries in the insurance contracts that they have such quality, no later than thirty days after the date in which they became aware of the death of the person at risk or subscriber (Article 3). However, given the fact that the beneficiaries may be designated by will, and also considering that the designation may be ambiguous as to their identification, it seems judicious to grant the faculty of requesting information to the potential beneficiaries themselves.

V. Right to Insurance Benefits, Right to Surrender Value and Other Rights Granted by the Contract

1104. As seen above, the norms of the RJCS on the payment of the insurance benefits – Articles 102 and 104 – are considerably lax and per se do not incentivise the insurer to comply timely with its duties. Apart from general remedies that can be drawn from the Civil Code, when the policyholder – or, arguably, the beneficiary – is a consumer, they may also rely on the Law on unfair commercial practices, which forbids the insurer to demand documents of them that may not reasonably be considered relevant in order to ascertain the validity of their claim (Article 12(d)).

1105. In this regard, the ASF has issued recommendations for the realm of contracts especially tailored for long-term savings – namely, for capitalisation insurance and capital redemption operations (ASF Communication – 'Carta Circular' – 10/2009, of 20 August). The recommendation encompasses both the payment of the insurance benefits, and the payment of the surrender value. For these cases, the ASF specifies the documents that should be required by the insurers for the payment of benefits, and the maximum deadline within which such payments should be granted (Nos 1 and 2). Moreover, in general terms, it recommends that if the insurers demand further documents or extend the deadlines, they do so in terms that are proportionate to the liquidity, complexity and nature of the product (Nos 3 and 4).

1106. Finally, the consequences of the contract attracting a surrender value should also be considered. Not every contract attracts such a value; Regulatory Standard 16/1995 lists several life insurance contracts in which that possibility is excluded (No. 29). The norm is not very clear, since it does not use a straightforward criterion, but rather refers to forms of life insurance by the name that they took under market practices, which can be volatile. It can however *grosso modo* be said that such a possibility is excluded when under the contract the right to receive payments from the insurer is uncertain. Under Regulatory Standard 16/1995 (No. 30), whenever there is a right to the surrender value or to the conversion of the contract, the insurer cannot refuse their exercise as soon as a single premium has been paid, or as soon as three yearly premiums have been paid, as the case may be.

1107. First of all, the contract may grant the right to payment of the surrender value in case an insured event occurs. That is typically the cased in mixed policies, in which if the death does not occur within a certain time frame, the survival beyond that time frame gives right to the surrender value. In what the market has termed 'capitalisation insurance', the value paid either in case of death or in case of survival upon a certain date corresponds in any case to the value generated by the investment of the premiums until that moment with deduction of the costs incurred. That is, the insurance benefits equal in any case the surrender value attracted until the moment of their payment. The fact that the insurance benefits are always proportionate to the amount of the premium paid until that moment has initially given rise to some questioning in regard to the nature of the contract. Due to the uncertainty surrounding the occurrence of the insured event (its 'if' and 'when'), there is normally a disproportion between what each of the contracting parties pays the other – there is no direct correspondence between the amount of premiums paid and the amounts paid by the insurer. Insurance is therefore generally qualified as an aleatory contract. As this is not the case in case in capitalisation insurance, some case law denied the contract the nature of insurance.[502] This rather formalistic approach was criticised by scholarship and meanwhile abandoned; and rightly so.[503] It ignored the fact that the risk of loss or diminution of income covered by life insurance can be aptly hedged by granting the insured the right to a certain amount of savings, there being no reason to forbid this amount to correspond to the capitalisation of the premiums paid.

1108. The value accumulated can also be used to convert the original contract into a paid-up policy or into a contract with a reduced premium (conversion value); in any case, the insurance benefits are reduced. Moreover, as referred to in Article 195, the insurer may also grant advance payments on the surrender value, as set out by the contract. Finally, when the contract is terminated without the insured event having occurred, the insurer shall have the duty to pay the surrender value, after deducing the costs of contract conclusion that have not yet been recovered, and with accrual of the amount of bonuses that would have been paid to the insured, determined *pro rata temporis* (Article 106(3)).

1109. Under Article 194(1), in case the contract allows for the payment of the surrender value, or conversion based on that value, it should allow the person entitled to that value to know its amount at any moment. Under Article 194(2), in contributory group life insurance, the contract should determine who the holder of the right to surrender value is, in view of the contribution of the insured. Whenever the contract assures the right to a minimum value, the insurer should attach a table to the policy, displaying which shall be the surrender and conversion values by the dates of renewal of contract; the policy should refer expressly to this table (Article 194(3) and (4)). The contract should also set the conditions for the exercise of the right to surrender value whenever there is a beneficiary with irrevocable rights to insurance benefits Article 194(5).

---

502. TRL 14 April 2005, 1851/2005-6 (Fátima Galante).

503. L. Poças, Os seguros ..., *maxime* at 101–104; Maria Inês de Oliveira Martins, O seguro de vida enquanto tipo contratual legal, Coimbra Editora, (2010), 259–261. In case law, *see* STJ 12 November 2013, 530/10.6TJPRT.P1.S1 (Gregório da Silva Jesus); TRC 25 June 2019, 1472/17.0T8GRD.C1 (Luís Cravo).

1110. It should also be mentioned that the policyholder who is not the person at risk can assign their rights and duties under the contract to a third party, if the insurer consents to it (Article 197(1) and (2)). The assignment should be notified to the person at risk and should be mentioned in the policy.

§2. Group Life Insurance

1111. Although life insurance is probably the type of insurance which is more relevantly offered as group insurance, there are no special norms on group life insurance. The matter of group life insurance was therefore mostly handled under the general heading 'Group insurance' (*see* Part II, Chapter 6, §4, Group Insurance), together with other types of insurance contract.

1112. There are, however, some provisions which specifically strike group life insurance. Within the RJCS, Article 187(2) sets out some elements that should be mentioned in group life insurance policies. However, more relevant than this provision is the Act that approved the PFR.[504]

1113. Article 3 of the Act determines that some of the norms on professional pension plans organised through pension funds apply to professional retirement plans which are organised through life insurance,[505] and it further provides specifically on the latter. The norms at stake fundamentally transpose Directive 2014/50/EU on the acquisition and preservation of supplementary pension rights[506] – yet expanding the scope of its provisions, which apply not only to cross-border, but also to purely internal matters.

1114. The focus is on retirement plans which give rise to vested rights, that is, rights the participants keep even if they cease their professional relationship with the sponsoring undertaking before becoming eligible for a supplementary pension (Articles 20(1) and 32(1)(a) of the PFR). The PFR further clarifies that in defined contribution plans that do not set out regular contributions from the sponsoring undertaking, the participants have a vested right to the amounts assigned to them by the plan (Article 20(2)).

1115. As required by the Directive, where a vesting period or a waiting period, or both, is applied either by law, or by a collective agreement, the total combined period shall under no circumstances exceed three years for outgoing workers; where a minimum age is stipulated for the vesting of pension rights, that age shall not

504. On this topic, *see* A. Costa Oliveira, Art. 184.°.
505. Namely, Arts 20, 32(1)(a) and (3), 159, 160(1) and (2), 162(5), 162(2) of the PFR.
506. Directive 2014/50/EU of 16 April 2014 on minimum requirements for enhancing worker mobility between Member States by improving the acquisition and preservation of supplementary pension rights.

exceed twenty-one years for outgoing workers (Article 20(3) and (4)). Moreover, some duties of information set out for pension plans also apply to the life insurance at stake.[507]

1116. The provisions applicable to group life insurance further provide for the protection of the persons at risk, by setting out their right to be informed and a rule of equal or at least equitable treatment between the vested rights of the persons at risk who cease their professional relationship with the sponsoring undertaking before becoming eligible for a supplementary pension and the vested rights of the persons at risk that maintain their relationship with the sponsoring undertaking (respectively, Article 3(3) and (4) of the Act that approved the PFR).

§3. Life Insurance Savings Products

I. Insurance-Based Investment Products

1117. As in other Member of the EU, insurance-based investment products have been subject to special rules aimed at the protection of investors. The PRIIPs Regulation [508] provides the most important legal framework in this regard. It is supplemented by other norms, from which mention should be made, at an EU level, to Commission Delegated Regulation 2017/653, which lays down regulatory technical standards with regard to the presentation, content, review and revision of key information documents and the conditions for fulfilling the requirement to provide such documents.[509] At a Portuguese State level, mention should be made to the Framework on PRIIPs, enacted by Law 35/2018.[510] Article 206 of RJCS should also be referred in this regard. Not so much because of the concept of structured investment products that is provided (Article 206(1)), which has lost relevance in view of the enactment of the Regulation on PRIIPS; but especially because it sets out some elements that should be mentioned in the policy (Article 206(3)).

1118. Insurance-based investment products encompass a considerable array of insurance products, ranging from unit-link insurance to equity-linked insurance and

507. Articles 159, 160(1) and (2), 162(5), 162(2) of the PFR.

508. Regulation 1286/2014 of the European Parliament and of the Council of 26 November 2014, on key information documents for packaged retail and insurance-based investment products (PRIIPs); Commission Delegated Regulation 2017/653 of 8 March 2017, supplementing Regulation 1286/2014 of the European Parliament and of the Council on key information documents for packaged retail and insurance-based investment products (PRIIPs) by laying down regulatory technical standards with regard to the presentation, content, review and revision of key information documents and the conditions for fulfilling the requirement to provide such documents.

509. For a more detailed approach, *see* Paulo Câmara, Art. 40.º, Deveres de informação em especial (in: Pedro Romano Martínez/Filipe Albuquerque Matos (ed.) Lei da distribuição de seguros anotada, Almedina, 332, 2019), 332–333.

510. Law 35/2018, of 20 July.

to capitalisation insurance or insurance based savings plans, as long as their maturity or surrender value is wholly or partially exposed, directly or indirectly, to market fluctuations (Article 4(2) of the Regulation on PRIIPS). That may happen, for instance, when their surrender value is indexed to a variable interest rate.

1119. After the transposition of the MIFID[511] in 2007 (by Decree-Law 357-A/2007), insurance-based investment products were placed under the supervision of the Financial markets authority (CMVM). This decision was reversed in 2015, in the context of the transposition of the MIFID II in 2018 (by Law 35/2018), and insurance-based investment products are now again placed under the competence of the ASF.[512] This had as a consequence that insurance-based investment products became less regulated than other package retail investment products, since, whereas the CMVM has enacted regulatory standards regarding package retail investment products,[513] the ASF has not done likewise.

II. Capital Redemption Operations

1120. As clarified by Solvency II Directive, capital redemption operations are contracts based on actuarial calculation whereby, in return for single or periodic payments agreed in advance, commitments of specified duration and amount are undertaken (Article 2(3)(b)(ii)).

1121. Different to insurance contracts, the right to benefits does not depend on the occurrence of uncertain events; instead, it is acquired at the end of a certain term.

1122. Although capital redemption operations are not insurance contracts, they are regulated by the RJCS, which in Article 207 establishes that the general provisions on insurance contracts, and the special provisions on life insurance are applicable to capital redemption operations. Apart from this reference to other norms, the RJCS does devote some norms specifically to capital redemption operations. Article 208 sets out some mentions that should mandatorily be made in the contract terms. On its turn, Article 209 clarifies that in case of death of the subscriber their position under the contract is simply transmitted to their heirs; the contract shall be in force until the right to benefits falls due. The distance to life insurance – where the death of the person at risk triggers either the right to insurance benefits, or the automatic termination of the contracts – becomes thus clear.

511. Directive 2004/39/EC, of 21 April.

512. Eduarda Ribeiro, Art. 206.°, Instrumentos de captação de aforro estruturados (in: Lei do Contrato de Seguro anotada, Coimbra, 2020), 619–620.

513. Regulatory Standard 8/2018, of 5 December 2018, on information and marketing duties regarding PRIIPs; before it was enacted, the standard applicable to the matter was Regulatory Standard 2/2012, of 25 October 2012, on complex financial products and marketing of insurance contracts and operations linked to investment funds.

Chapter 5. Pension Funds

§1. PENSION FUNDS

1123. Pension Funds were object of the recent act that approved the PFR. The act transposed Directive 2016/2341 of 14 December 2016 on the activities and supervision of institutions for occupational retirement provision and follows much of its terminology. To this moment, the ASF has only issued one regulatory framework in regard to the provisions of the PFR – Regulatory Framework 11/2020-R, of 3 November 2020, which sets out how the fund managers should comply with their information duties in regard to the ASF. In any case, the regulatory frameworks previously issued by the ASF remain in force to the extent that they are compatible with the new provisions (Article 10 of the Act that approved the PFR).[514]

1124. Pension funds finance both pension plans and health benefits plans (Article 4(a) and (b) PFR), and they can also finance equivalent mechanisms as alternative mechanisms to the Work Compensation Fund (that protects workers in case of termination of their contracts), as defined in Law 70/2013, of 30 August (Article 4(c) and (d) PFR).

1125. A pension plan can be a contract, a set of rules, and, in case of cross-border activities, an agreement or a trust deed, stipulating which retirement benefits are granted and under which conditions (Article 4(a) PFR). Retirement benefits means benefits paid by reference to reaching retirement or, where they are supplementary to those benefits and provided on an ancillary basis, benefits paid in the form of payments on death, disability, or cessation of employment; in case of cross-border activity, it also means benefits in the form of support payments or services in case of sickness, indigence or death (Article 4(e) PFR).

1126. Health benefits plans are contracts or sets of rules that define the conditions for payment or reimbursement of health expenses that the sponsoring undertaking (in the wording of the PFR, the 'associate') has bound to assure for the case of an involuntary change in the health condition of the member, that takes place after retirement due to age or disability, survival, early retirement or anticipated retirement (Article 4(b) PFR).

1127. The PFR refers to both closed pension funds and open pension funds (Article 8(1)). Closed pension funds concern one single sponsoring undertaking, or several undertakings that have entrepreneurial, associate, professional or social links. In the case of open pension funds, no relationship between the contributors to the pension fund is required, and membership only depends on the acceptance by the managing company.

---

514. *See* https://www.asf.com.pt/NR/exeres/D4E856C8-0825-42DF-99D0-9CEBC83EE52A.htm for a list.

1128. Pension funds can either underpin the attribution of benefits in a collective basis, organised by a sponsoring undertaking, or the acquisition of benefits through individual membership.

1129. The *attribution of benefits in a collective basis* relies either on *closed pension funds* or on acts of *collective adhesion to open pension funds* (Article 12(1)). The pension plans concerned may be defined contribution plans, benefit plans or mixed plans. They may further be contributory plans, when the members make contributions to the plan, or non-contributory plans, when the plan is exclusively financed by the sponsoring undertaking (Article 12(3)). The rules on non-contributory plans also apply to defined benefit plans where the contributions made by the members are mandatory under the law or under a collective agreement (Article 12(4)). The attribution of benefits in a collective basis is also the exclusive realm of health benefits plans (Article 14).

1130. The attribution of benefits through *closed pension funds* or through acts of *collective adhesion to open pension funds* is specially provided for in Articles 17–20.

1131. Article 17 clarifies the circumstances which may give rise to the attribution of benefits, in a way that does seem to be fully coherent with the definitions provided for in Article 4(e) and (b). Under Article 17(1), such rights may arise, as set out in the plan, from retirement due to old age or incapacity, early retirement, anticipated retirement or survival. Under Article 17(2), the plan may also give rise to benefits in the case of death, where they are supplementary to the benefits referred to in Article 17(1) and provided on an ancillary basis. Under Article 17(3), the plan may grant other retirement or health benefits that are not financed by the pension funds; it may also extend the whole or part of the benefits to family members (as defined in the Act on Savings for Education or Retirement Plans[515]) of the member of the plan. Contributory plans may furthermore set out the right to benefits in case of unemployment, serious disease or long-term incapacity for work, as defined in the Act on Savings for Education or Retirement Plans[516] (Article 17(4)).

1132. As a special governance feature, the attribution of benefits through closed pension funds or through collective adhesion to open pension funds requires the constitution of a consultative committee that should verify that the pension plan is duly executed and the pension fund is duly managed. The committee should include representatives from the sponsor and from the members and beneficiaries and, after the new PFR, it should also include a representative of the works council and one representative from each of the two most important trade unions in the applicable economic sector (Article 138).

515. Decree-Law 158/2002, of 2 July, and Regulation 1453/2002 of 11 November. *See below* §2 in this chapter.

516. Decree-Law 158/2002, of 2 July, and Regulation 1453/2002 of 11 November. *See below* §2 in this chapter.

1133. The acquisition of benefits through individual membership relies on an individual adhesion to an open pension fund. This case only gives rise to defined contribution plans (Article 12(2)). It is especially provided for in Articles 21 and 22. Under Article 21(1), the circumstances that may give rise to benefits, as defined in the plan, are all those mentioned in Article 17(4).

1134. The new legal framework on pension funds is considerably more extensive than the former. Besides the questions mentioned above, some of the features deemed more relevant in the new rules concern the reinforcement of transparency from the managing company, which now faces an extensive set of duties of information towards members, potential members and beneficiaries of the plans (Articles 153–171). Furthermore, managing companies must now post a statement of the fund's investment principles on the manager's site. The statement must be revised at least every three years and after any significant investment policy change and must disclose the investment risk measurement methods; risk management processes and the strategy followed in regard of asset allocation; and how environmental, social and governance factors are taken into account (Article 157).

1135. Another very relevant change concerns the application of the norms on insurance distribution to entities distributing pension plans, which may only be their managing companies or insurance mediators (Article 172).

1136. At a governance level, it should be highlighted that presently the managing company should appoint an actuary not only in case of defined benefit plans, but also in the case of defined contribution plans where the funds pay pension benefits directly to beneficiaries (Article 133).[517]

§2. Savings for Education or Retirement Plans

1137. Reference should also be made to Savings for Education or Retirement Plans, particularly in view of the considerable practical importance of Savings for Retirement and Savings for Education or Retirements Plans. Due to a special regime of tax benefits, they have been a preferential long-term placement for individual savings. In fact, under Article 21 of the Statute on Tax Benefits,[518] the subscriber has the right to a tax deduction in regard to part of the amount of their contributions; besides, part of the value of the benefits paid is exempt from tax, and the remaining is subject to a special tax rate.

1138. Savings for Retirements Plans, Savings for Education Plans and Savings for Education or Retirements Plans are regulated by Decree-Law 158/2002, of 2

517. On funds that pay pension benefits directly to beneficiaries, *see* the ASF Regulatory Framework 8/2018-R, of 28 December.
518. Enacted by Decree-Law 215/89, of 1 July 1989.

July. The underlying funds can be managed as life insurance funds, as pension funds or as investment funds; the respective norms apply to either case (Articles 1(3) and 3).

1139. Under Decree-Law 158/2002, the plans allow for the payment of benefits only under a specific set of circumstances. It is not forbidden for the plan to allow for the payment of benefits under different circumstances. However, in those cases no tax benefit is applicable to the amount of benefits paid, and the tax deduction applied to the contribution must be returned, accrued of a penalty (Articles 21(4) and (5) of the Statute on Tax Benefits and 4(5) of Decree-Law 158/2002). This affects only Savings for Retirements Plans and Savings for Education or Retirements Plans, which are the cases where tax benefits apply.

1140. Under Article 4(1) of Decree-Law 158/2002, Savings for Education or Retirements Plans can give rise to the payment of benefits in the following circumstances: (a) retirement due to old age of the plan participant; (b) long-term unemployment of the participant, or of any of their family members; (c) permanent incapacity for work, regarding the participant or any of their family members, whichever the cause; (d) serious disease of the participant or of any of their family members; (e) after the participant turns 60; (f) in case the participant or of any of their family members enrols or takes part in a university or technical course, when that gives rise to expenses in the year at stake; and (g) when the amount is used to pay amounts due under mortgaged loans entered into in order to finance the acquisition of the participants permanent home. Article 4(8) specifies the types of loan agreements encompassed by Article 4(1)(g). Regulation ('Portaria') 1453/2002 of 11 November specifies when these circumstances are considered to be met, and how they should prove Article 4(8).

1141. In case of the circumstances mentioned in Article 4(1)(a), (e), (f) and (g), the participant may only claim the amount of benefits corresponding to each of the contributions made if at least five years have passed since that contribution was made (Article 4(2)). They may claim the whole amount of benefits accrued if five years have passed since the first contribution and the total amount of contributions made in the first half of the duration of the contract corresponds at least to 35% of the whole amount applied (Article 4(3)). These two provisions also apply to the circumstances described in Article 4(1)(b)–(d) if, in the moment in which each of the contributions was made, such circumstances already occurred (Article 4(4)).

1142. Under Article 4(9), the mentioned provisions apply to Savings for Education or Retirements Plans, with the exception of all that regards Article 4(1)(f). The mentioned provisions also apply to Savings for Education Plans, with the exception of all that regards Article 4(1)(a) and (e). However, there is no tax benefit applied to Savings for Education Plans.

Part VI. Private Insurance: Social Security

Maria Inês de Oliveira Martins

1143. Article 63(1) of CPR grants every citizen the right to social security. It is the responsibility of the State to organise, articulate and subsidise a system of social security which is unitary, decentralised and participative (Article 63(2)).[519]

1144. The Portuguese system of public social security comprises three subsystems: the citizenship social protection system, the 'insurance system' and the supplementary system (Article 23 of the Social security framework law[520]).[521] The reference to 'insurance system' is not present in the Portuguese law; it is merely an attempt at translating the expression *sistema previdencial* and should be taken with caution. In fact, the system is not insurance-based – *hoc sensu*, it not based on the provision of benefits by social or private insurers. It relies rather on the direct provision of social security benefits by the State and cannot be opted-out. Whereas the citizenship social protection system is mainly financed by taxes, the 'insurance system' is mainly financed by the contributions made by workers and their employers, and also by self-employed persons (Article 54). There is not, however, a strict correlation between the contributions paid and benefits granted (Articles 61 and ff.) – the Portuguese system is still fundamentally a pay-as-you-go system, and not a capitalisation one.[522]

1145. Differently, private insurance plays a central a role in the supplementary system of social security. This subsystem is strictly voluntary (Articles 82–84). It is composed, on the one hand, by a public capital redemption fund (Article 82); on the other hand, it is composed by private mechanisms, which can be individual or collective (Articles 83 and 84). These private mechanisms consist of individual or group life insurance and operations (e.g., life insurance, pension plans, PPR). All that has been said above (Part V, Chapters 4 and 5) in this regard therefore applies.

519. *See* José Joaquim Gomes Canotilho/Vital Moreira, Constituição da República Portuguesa Anotada, Volume I, Coimbra Editora, 4 Ed. (2007), 811 and ff.

520. Law 4/2007, of 16 January. All Articles quoted in Part VI refer to this Law.

521. *See* https://ec.europa.eu/employment_social/empl_portal/SSRinEU/Your%20social%20security%20rights%20in%20Portugal_en.pdf

522. José Casalta Nabais/Maria Matilde Lavouras, O financiamento da Segurança Social, 4028, RLJ, 238 (2021), at 254–256.

Part VII. Insurance Intermediaries

Joana Neto Anjos & Maria Inês de Oliveira Martins[523]

1146. The Portuguese framework on insurance intermediaries, IDF, was approved by Law 7/2019, of 16 January, which transposed the IDD. This law amended the LBIR and revoked Decree-Law 144/2006, of 31 July, on insurance intermediation.[524]

1147. Specific provisions concerning insurance intermediaries are also laid down in the RJCS.[525]

1148. The supervisory authority regarding the activity of insurance (and reinsurance) mediation is the ASF, which is authorised to adopt the necessary regulatory standards, in accordance with Article 13 of Law 7/2019. In conformity, the ASF issued the Regulatory Standard 13/2020-R, of 30 December.

523. Joana Neto Anjos authored Ch. 1; Maria Inês de Oliveira Martins authored Ch. 2.
524. On the topic of insurance intermediation in general, *see* Pedro Romano Martinez, Filipe Albuquerque Matos (eds.), *Lei da Distribuição de Seguros Anotada*, Almedina (2019).
525. *See below* on this Part VII, Ch. 2, §2.

Chapter 1. Law of Establishment and Supervision

§1. General Introduction

1149. The IDD succeeded Directive 2002/92/EC of the European Parliament and of the Council, of 9 December 2002, regarding insurance mediation. Directive 2002/92/EC was intended to harmonise national regimes for the distribution of insurance and reinsurance across the EU. However, it only regulated the insurance mediation activity. The IDD, on the other hand, extended the scope of the desired harmonisation to the entire distribution of insurance, in order to ensure that the same level of protection is applied regardless of the channel through which customers purchase an insurance product (directly with an insurance company or indirectly through an intermediary). This new regime aimed to provide insurance customers with a single protection standard, regardless of their access route to insurance products.[526]

1150. The vast majority of the provisions of this new Directive were transposed, in the Portuguese legal system, to the new insurance distribution regime, that is, to the IDF. This regime also replaced the previous Portuguese legislation on insurance and reinsurance mediation, contained in Decree-Law 144/2006, of 31 July.

1151. In fact, insurance contracts are usually taken out with the intervention of insurance intermediaries. According to Article 9(1) of the IDF, natural or legal persons can act as insurance intermediaries and carry out the insurance distribution activity in one of the following categories: insurance agents (*agente de seguro*), category in which a person carries out the insurance distribution activity in the name and on behalf of one or more insurance companies or other insurance intermediaries, in accordance with the terms of the contract or contracts that it enters into with those entities; and brokers (*corretor de seguros*), a category in which a person carries out insurance distribution independently from insurance companies.

1152. In addition, pursuant to Article 9(2), natural or legal persons may register as an ancillary insurance intermediary and carry out the activity of insurance distribution in the name and on behalf of one or more insurance companies or insurance intermediaries, in accordance with the terms of the contracts they enter into with these entities.

§2. Registration

1153. According to Article 11(1) of the IDF, only natural persons residing in Portugal who fulfil the following conditions may be registered in the register of insurance, reinsurance and ancillary insurance intermediaries. Namely, they should:

526. For further developments on the subject, *see* Margarida Lima Rego, Influência da regulação institucional na contratação de seguros: O impacto do novo regime da distribuição na responsabilidade pré-contratual do distribuidor, 43, Julgar, 151 (2021).

(a) be of legal age or emancipated; (b) have the legal capacity to perform commercial acts; (c) have adequate qualifications in view of the specific distribution activity they intend to carry out, under the terms of Article 13; (d) be of good repute for the exercise of the distribution activity, not finding themselves, namely, in the situations provided for in Article 14; (e) not be in one of the situations of incompatibility provided for in Article 15; (f) declare the identity of people with whom they have close relationships and that these relationships do not impede the exercise of the supervisory functions of the ASF; (g) there should further be no obstacles to the exercise of supervision by the ASF based on the existence or imposition of compliance with laws, regulations or administrative provisions of a third country to which one or more natural or legal persons with whom the insurance or reinsurance intermediary or the ancillary insurance intermediary has close relationships; (h) any persons directly involved in the activity of distributing insurance or reinsurance should fulfil the conditions set out in subparagraphs (a)–(e).

1154. The specific conditions for becoming an authorised insurance agent are worth mentioning. For this purpose, pursuant to Article 16, the natural or legal person must enter into a written contract with each of the insurance companies that they will represent. The contract should set out the terms under which the insurance company mandates the agent to carry out insurance distribution in its name and on its behalf. The agent must have their own technical, commercial, administrative and accounting organisation and economical/financial structure, which must be appropriate to the size and nature of their activity. This agent also needs to demonstrate that they hold, or will hold by the time of beginning of their activity, a professional civil liability insurance covering the entire territory of the EU.

1155. With regard to registration as an insurance agent, it is the responsibility of the insurance company that has entered into the contract with the agent to verify that the applicant has duly completed their application with all the necessary elements and to send it to the ASF for registration. The ASF is responsible for verifying the fulfilment of the requirements by the candidate, and may request any clarifications or elements that it deems useful or necessary for the analysis of the process, either directly from the candidate or through the proponent insurance company (Article 17).

1156. Regarding the specific conditions for becoming an authorised insurance broker, the natural or legal person must have their own technical, commercial, administrative and accounting organisation and economic and financial structure, which must be appropriate to the exercise of the activity, and must demonstrate that they hold, or will hold by the time of beginning of their activity, a professional civil liability insurance covering the entire territory of the EU. The insurance broker must also prove that they hold or will hold by the date of beginning of their activity, a bank guarantee or surety insurance that covers the payment of any claims from policyholders or beneficiaries against the broker. In addition, in the case of a natural person, they must not carry out any profession that could limit their independence in the activity of insurance distribution; in the case of a legal person, it must have as its exclusive corporate purpose activities included in the financial sector (Article 18(1)).

1157. In order to register as an insurance broker, according to Article 19, the applicant is responsible for duly completing their application and submitting it to the ASF, which is done through its website. The ASF is responsible for verifying the fulfilment of the requirements by the candidate. The ASF may request any clarifications or elements that it deems useful or necessary for the analysis of the process. The insurance broker is allowed to begin their activity as soon as it is notified by the ASF of the respective registration.

1158. Finally, for the purposes of registration as an ancillary insurance intermediary, the natural or legal person must enter into a written contract with each of the insurance companies that they will represent. The contract sets out the terms under which the insurance company mandates the agent to carry out insurance distribution in their name and on their behalf. The ancillary insurance intermediary must have their own technical, commercial, administrative and accounting organisation and economic and financial structure, which should be appropriate to the size and nature of their activity. They should also prove that they hold, or will hold by the time of beginning of their activity, a professional civil liability insurance covering the entire territory of the EU.

1159. The IDF also enshrines the rights and duties of the insurance intermediaries. Pursuant to Article 23, insurance intermediaries have the following rights: the right to, in due time, obtain from the insurance companies all the elements, information and clarifications necessary for the performance of their activity and for the efficient management of its portfolio; the right to be informed by insurance companies of the termination of insurance contracts in their insurance portfolio; the right to receive, in a timely manner, from the insurance companies the remuneration relating to the contracts in their insurance portfolio, as well as other amounts due to them under the contract; the right to deduct, at the time of rendering of accounts to the insurance companies, their remuneration from the premiums they collected and are authorised to collect.

1160. On the other hand, according to Article 24, the general duties of the insurance intermediaries are: the duty to only enter into contracts in representation of the insurance company when the latter has given them the necessary powers, in writing; the duty not to propose to cover or cover risk in their own name; the duty to comply with the legal and regulatory provisions applicable to the insurance activity and the insurance distribution activity and not to intervene in the performance of contracts that violate them; the duty to correctly and efficiently assist the insurance contracts in which they intervene; the duty to endeavour to prevent inaccurate or incomplete declarations by the policyholder and situations that violate or constitute fraud against the law or that indicate money laundering or terrorist financing; the duty to keep professional secrecy, in relation to third parties, of the facts that they become aware of as a result of the activity of insurance distribution; the duty to prove their registration as an insurance intermediary whenever requested by any interested party; the duty to have at their service a number of people directly involved in insurance distribution that is appropriate to the dimension and nature of the intermediary's activity; the duty to maintain or ensure that the members of the management body responsible for the distribution activity maintain an adequate level of performance by complying with the requirements for training and continuous professional development, pursuant to Article 25; the duty to define a policy for the treatment of policyholders, beneficiaries and third party victims, which operating principles are set out in a written document, that guarantees their equitable treatment, as well as the proper treatment of their personal data and complaints.

Chapter 2. Insurance Intermediaries and the Insurance Contract

§1. THE IMPACT OF THE IDF UPON THE INSURANCE CONTRACT

I. General Duties of the Insurance Intermediaries that Have a Direct Impact upon the Insurance Contract

1161. The norms on insurance intermediation as set out by the IDF have a wide scope, that encompasses both issues of administrative law (*maxime*, duties of the intermediaries vis-à-vis the public administration) and issues regarding the relationship of the intermediary with the insurer and the policyholder. The fact that the intermediary acts as a connecting point between the parties to the insurance contract leads to some of the framework on insurance intermediation directly affecting the insurance contract.

1162. That is the case of some of the *general duties of insurance intermediaries*, as set out in Article 24 of the IDF. Such is the case of the duty to correctly and efficiently assist the insurance contracts in which the intermediary intervenes (Article 24(1)(d)); the duty to deploy their best efforts so as to prevent the policyholder or insured from inexactly or incompletely disclosing the risk, as well as to prevent the infringement or the evasion of applicable laws, for example regarding money laundering or the financing of terrorism (Article 24(1)(e)); the duty of confidentiality regarding information acquired as a consequence of intermediation (Article 24(1)(f)); the duty to prove the quality of registered intermediary upon request (Article 24(1)(g)); as well of the duty to keep a record of the insurance contracts intermediated, as well as of any documents specifying the terms of the service provided to the customers (Article 24(1)(h)).

1163. The *duties of the intermediary towards the insurer*, as set out in Article 29 of IDF, stress the intermediary's role in the transmission of information between the parties of the insurance contract. In the pre-contractual phase, the intermediary should inform the insurer on the risks that are to be covered, and on their particular features (Article 29(a) of IDF). While the contract is in force, the intermediary should inform the insurer on any modification of the risks that may affect the conditions of the contract (Article 29(b) of IDF; *see* Article 93(2) of RJCS), as well as on all the premiums paid, on any returns on premiums and on any insured events occurred, according to the reporting duties undertaken in regard to the insurer (Article 29(c) of IDF); it should also be pointed out that the intermediary should inform the insurer on any fact that may affect the settlement of insurance claims (Article 29(f) of IDF).

1164. The influence of the norms on intermediation on the insurance contract is also present in the duties of the intermediary in regard to their customers. The intermediary is first and foremost bound to act honestly, fairly and professionally in accordance with the best interests of their customers (Articles 17(1) of IDD and 30(1)(a) of IDF). In line with this provision, the intermediary should furthermore inform the customer in an accurate and detailed manner, attending to the demands and needs of the customer and to the information they provided, and according to what can be reasonably demanded from the intermediary in view of their category of intermediary, as well as according to the complexity of the insurance product being proposed and the type of customer, on the insurance contract or contracts that are most suitable to the transfer of risk or to the investment intended by the customer, so as to allow them to take an informed decision (Articles 20(1), (2) and (4) of IDD and 30(1)(c) of IDF).

1165. Other duties of the intermediary should also be pointed out. That is the case of the duty to inform on the general rights and obligations that stem from an insurance contract (Article 30(1)(b) of IDF). The intermediary should also timely forward the insurer of all the information or instruction that the policyholder request them to forward (Article 30(1)(e) of IDF); they should furthermore provide the policyholder with all the explanations regarding the insurance contract, both prior to its conclusion and while it is in force and during any conflict affecting it (Article 30(1)(f) of IDF); they should also refrain from any action affecting an insurance contract without previously informing the policyholder and obtaining their consent (Article 30(1)(d) of IDF).

1166. A very relevant set of norms concerns the issue of whether the intermediary has undertaken to *provide advice to the customer*. The intermediary should inform the customer *if such is the case* and should then prior to the conclusion of any specific contract, provide the customer with a personalised recommendation, according to the type of customer, to the information they provided and to the complexity of the insurance contract recommended (Articles 20(1) and 20(2) of IDD and 31(2)(b) and 31(4) of IDF). If the intermediary undertakes to gives its advice on the basis of a fair and personal analysis, they should inform the customer accordingly. In this case, they should give them that advice on the basis of an analysis of a sufficiently large and diversified, both in view of the distributor and of the type of contract, number of insurance contracts available on the market to enable it to make a personal recommendation, in accordance with professional criteria, regarding which insurance contract would be adequate to meet the customer's needs. This analysis should not be limited to the insurance contracts pertaining to a distributor with whom the intermediary has particular connections (Articles 20(3) of IDD and 31(5) of IDF).

1167. The intermediary must comply with additional duties of information in the case of distribution insurance-based investment products (*see* Articles 40–46 of IDF, in particular Articles 40–42 and 45, and especially Articles 29 and 30 of IDD, as well as Commission Delegated Regulation 2017/2359 of 21 September 2017).[527]

527. Commission Delegated Regulation 2017/2359 of 21 September 2017, supplementing Directive (EU) 2016/97 of the European Parliament and of the Council with regard to information requirements and conduct of business rules applicable to the distribution of insurance-based investment products. On Regulation 1286/2014, regarding PRIIPs, *see* Part V, Ch. 4, §3, I, In Scholarship; *see* Paulo Câmara, Art. 40.°, Deveres de informação em especial (in: Pedro Romano Martínez/Filipe Albuquerque Matos (ed.) Lei da distribuição de seguros anotada, Almedina, 332, 2019), 332 and ff.; P. Câmara, Art. 41.°, Venda com aconselhamento e avaliação da adequação, 348 and ff; José

1168. In line with Article 22(1) of IDD, Article 31(7) exempts the intermediary that carries out distribution activities in relation to the insurance of large risks from its special duties of information, set out by Article 31. There is no exemption in regard, for instance, to the duty to inform on the insurance contract or contracts that are most suitable to the transfer of risk or to the investment intended by the customer, considering their demands and needs (Article (1)(c) of IDF, above); as there is no exemption in regard to the duties to inform in the context of cross-selling (Articles 26 of IDF and 24 of IDD).

II. The Distinction Between Different Categories of Insurance Intermediaries

1169. The IDF sets out such duties for the insurance intermediaries in general. However, some adjustments have to be made in regard to the *different categories of insurance intermediaries*. It should be reminded that, whereas insurance agents act in the interest of a certain insurer or insurance intermediary, insurance brokers act on an independent quality (Article 9(1) of IDF). The duties of vis-à-vis the insurer as set out in Article 29 should be seen from this perspective. Moreover, the brokerage contract relies on the professional expertise of the broker, on whom the policyholder places a special trust and from whom they expect qualified and independent assistance.[528] This impacts how the broker is expected to go about their duties to inform or advice the customer (Articles 30(1)(c) and 31(4) and (5) of IDF).

1170. The special statute of the insurance broker is further displayed in Article 35 of IDF, which lays down an additional set of duties for this case. Some of them can affect the insurance relationship itself more or less directly. That is foremost the case of Article 35(d) of IDF, which establishes that once the broker informs the customer that advice is provided, then they should provide advice on the basis of a fair and personal analysis, under the strict requirements of Articles 31(2)(c) and 31(5) of IDF (instead of merely abiding Article 31(2)(b) and 31(4)).

1171. The duty to suggest the adoption of measures suitable for the prevention and reduction of risk to the policyholder is also worthy of mention (Article 35(a)).

1172. Under Article 39 of IDF, ancillary insurance distributors are not subject to the same duties that bind insurance agents or brokers, but only to those duties laid down in limited number of provisions – namely, Article 23, Article 24(1)(a)–(j), (n) and (q)–(t), Article 29, Article 30(1) and 30(2), Article 31(1)(a), (b), (e)–(h), (l), and (m) and 31(2)–(8), and Articles 32, 33 and 34. This leaves out for instance the duty to comply with continuing professional training and development requirements, under Article 25.

Vasques, Art. 42.º, Venda sem aconselhamento (in: Pedro Romano Martínez/Filipe Albuquerque Matos (ed.) Lei da distribuição de seguros anotada, Almedina, 358, 2019), 358 and ff.

528. José Carlos Moitinho de Almeida, O mediador na conclusão e execução do contrato de seguro (in: José Carlos Moitinho de Almeida (ed.) Contrato de seguro, Estudos, Coimbra Editora, 2009), 184.

1173. A similar technique is used in regard to insurers acting as distributors of insurance products. Article 37(3) merely states that a number of provisions applicable to insurance intermediaries are also applicable to insurers *with the necessary adaptations*. Such adaptations are far from simple, in view of the novelty of the regime and of the role of the insurer as part of the insurance contract. The provision has received fair criticism in this regard.[529]

III. The Dominance of Information Duties

1174. Similar to IDD (*see* Articles 18, 19 and 24 of IDD), the IDF strongly relies on the role of the information duties as a means of protecting the policyholder or insured. That is the case in what regards the duty to provide the customer with the insurance product information document in regard to non-life products or with the key information document in case of insurance-based investment products (*see* Articles 20(4)–(9) of IDD and 33 of IDF, as well as the Regulation 1286/2014 on key information documents for PRIIPs). That is also notably the case for sensitive issues such as transparency and existence of conflicts of interest (Articles 19 of IDD and 31(1) of IDF) and cross-selling (Articles 24 of IDD and 24(1)(r) and 26 of IDF), where enhanced duties of information play a central role.[530]

1175. It is questionable whether such reliance in the virtues of information can be an effective approach. However, one should highlight that some duties identified as information duties go beyond such borders. That is strikingly the case for the general duty to inform the customer of the insurance contract or contracts that are most suitable to the transfer of risk or to the investment intended by the customer is a *particularly enhanced duty of information*. It is underpinned by duty a duty to specify, prior to the conclusion of an insurance contract, on the basis of information obtained from the customer, the demands and the needs of that customer (Articles 20(1) of IDD and 31(6) of IDF). It also demands that the intermediary singles out the most suitable contract or contracts according to such demands and needs. This regime somehow brings the duty to inform close to a duty to advice or recommend.[531]

529. Margarida Lima Rego, Art. 3.º, Alteração ao regime jurídico de acesso e exercício da atividade seguradora e resseguradora (in: Pedro Romano Martínez/Filipe Albuquerque Matos (ed.) Lei da distribuição de seguros anotada, Almedina, 23, 2019), 24.

530. It should nonetheless be mentioned that the duties to prevent conflicts of interest go considerably deeper in case of insurance-based investment products, in line with Arts 27, 28 and 29(2) and (3) of IDD – *see* Arts 43 and 44 of IDF. In what regards cross-selling, the law also lays down the duty to offer the customer the possibility of buying the good or service separately (Art. 24(3) of IDD and 26(3) of IDF), besides allowing the ASF to intervene on a case-by-case basis to prohibit the sale of insurance together with an ancillary service or product which is not insurance, as part of a package or the same agreement, when such practices are detrimental to consumers (Art. 24(7) of IDD and 26(7) of IDF).

531. Maria Inês de Oliveira Martins, Art. 31.º, Deveres de informação em especial (in: Pedro Romano Martínez/Filipe Albuquerque Matos (ed.) Lei da distribuição de seguros anotada, Almedina, 275,

1176. The prevention of mis-selling is furthermore flanked by product oversight and governance requirements.[532] Insurance undertakings, as well as intermediaries which manufacture any insurance product for sale to customers, are bound to maintain, operate and review a process for the approval of each insurance product, or significant adaptations of an existing insurance product, before it is marketed or distributed to customers (Article 25(1), paragraph 1 of IDD). Article 25 of IDD, which sets out the requirements of product oversight and governance requirements, was transposed not to the IDF, but rather to Article 153(2)–(9) of LBIR, which refers only to insurers. However, under Article 24(1)(m) of IDF, intermediaries must also comply with Article 153 of LBIR whenever they manufacture any insurance product for sale to customers.

1177. In any case, insurance intermediaries should also have product distribution arrangements containing appropriate measures and procedures to obtain from the manufacturer all appropriate information on the insurance products they intend to offer to their customers, and on their product oversight and governance policy, and to fully comprehend those insurance products as well as their target market (Article 24(1)(n) of IDF).

1178. These provisions are complemented by Commission Delegated Regulation 2017/2358 on product oversight and governance requirements.[533]

1179. The duties of insurers or intermediaries in regard to product oversight and governance are not applicable when insurance of large risks is at stake (Article 153(9) LBIR).

§2. Relevant Provisions of the RJCS on Insurance Intermediation

1180. The RJCS also provides for the issue of insurance intermediation, in its Articles 28–31.

1181. From the onset, one should clarify that the references made by the RJCS to insurance intermediaries are construed as encompassing insurance agents, insurance brokers and ancillary insurance intermediaries, although only the first two categories would qualify as insurance intermediaries under the IDF (Articles 4(c) IDF and 2(4) IDD). The term 'intermediary' has a broader sense than that which is set

---

2019), 275; *see* generally Michael Heese, Beratungspflichten, Eine rechtswissenschaftliche Abhandlung zur Dogmatik der Beratungspflichten und zur Haftung des Ratgebers im Zivil- und Wirtschaftsrecht, Mohr Siebeck, (2015), 483.

532. M. Lima Rego, Art. 3.º, 25–26; M. Lima Rego, Influência da regulação, 153 and ff.

533. Commission Delegated Regulation (EU) 2017/2358 of 21 September 2017 supplementing Directive (EU) 2016/97 of the European Parliament and of the Council with regard to product oversight and governance requirements for insurance undertakings and insurance distributors.

by the definitions laid down by the IDF and the IDD; moreover, there would be no sound reasons not to apply the Articles 28–31 to ancillary insurance intermediaries, where their requirements are fulfilled.[534]

1182. Article 28 states that in case of intervention of an insurance intermediary in the conclusion of an insurance contract, the framework on insurance mediation – currently the IDF – further applies.

1183. Article 29 establishes that the duties of information set out in the special norms on insurance mediation do not replace, but rather accrue to the pre-contractual duties of information and clarification set out in Articles 18–26. In other words, the insurer remains bound to its duties to inform the policyholder under the RJCS, whereas the IDF lays down the duties that are directly applicable to the intermediary. If the insurer relies on the intermediary to fulfil its duties and the latter does so defectively, the insurer will not be discharged of its liability towards the policyholder, under the norm on vicarious liability in contract (Article 800 of the Civil Code).[535] The same principle applies to the duties set out in the LSCT, which bind the insurer in its quality of drafter of the general terms.[536]

1184. It should in any case be pointed out that Article 22(4) sets aside the special duty of clarification of the insurer towards the policyholder under Article 22 in case an insurance intermediary intervenes in the negotiation or conclusion of the contract.

1185. Insurance intermediaries only have authority to represent the insurer in the conclusion and performance of the insurance contract *when such powers are conferred to them by the insurer in writing*. That would be self-evident in regard to insurance brokers, in view of their acting in the interest of the policyholder, and of their independence in regard to the insurer. However, it also applies in regard to insurance agents (Articles 16(1)(a) and 24(1-)(a) of IDF; 4(1)(e) and (1)(f) of Regulatory Standard 13/2020-R of ASF), as well as in regard to ancillary insurance intermediaries (Articles 20(1)(a), 24(1)(a) and 39 of IDF; 17 and 4(1)(e) and (1)(f) of Regulatory Standard 13/2020-R of ASF). Moreover, even when the intermediary is granted powers to represent the insurer in the conclusion of the contract, that does not necessarily entail the attribution of authority to decide on behalf of the insurer on the acceptance of a certain risk, or on the terms of such acceptance; this should be clarified in the contract with the insurer.[537]

534. Eduarda Ribeiro, Art. 29.º, Deveres de informação específicos (in: Lei do Contrato de Seguro anotada, Almedina, 202, 2020), 202; Eduarda Ribeiro, Art. 30.º, Representação aparente (in: Lei do Contrato de Seguro anotada, 4. Ed, Almedina, 206, 2020), 207.

535. STJ 26 January 2021, 969/18.9T8GMR.G1.S1 (Maria João Vaz Tomé). In scholarship, *see, for instance*, Pedro Romano Martínez, Representação aparente no âmbito da mediação de seguros – Anotação ao acórdão do Supremo Tribunal de Justiça de 1 de Abril de 2014, 5, Jurismat, 27 (2014), 58–60.

536. TRG 28 September 2017, 6155/15.2T8GMR.G1 (Maria da Graça Andrade).

537. E. Ribeiro, Art. 30.º, Representação aparente, 213.

1186. Article 30 addresses the cases where a person, who may or not act as an authorised insurance intermediary for a certain insurer, purports to act as its representative without having authority to affect its position. This has proved a matter of considerable relevance.[538]

1187. The general rule in this case is that an act does not affect the legal position of the insurer, unless the insurer ratifies it (Article 268(1) of the Civil Code). In particular, an insurance contract concluded by the intermediary to whom no such specific authority was conferred is not binding upon the insurer, unless the insurer ratifies it (Article 30(1)). The contract is however deemed ratified in case the insurer does not communicate its opposition to the policyholder, within five days after becoming aware of the contract and of its content (Article 30(2)). This corresponds to the general cases identified by scholarship as those of 'tolerated representation', where it is generally held that the purported principal can be bound to the contract.

1188. Article 30(3) sets out a special rule for the cases where there are ponderous reasons, which, under an objective judgment and considering the circumstances of the case, justify the trust placed by a policyholder acting in good faith in the authority of the intermediary, provided that the insurer has also contributed to justify such trust. This solution expresses the cases generally identified as those of 'apparent representation', where the purported principal is generally deemed not to be affected by the act.

1189. In fact, since the Law on Agency Contract[539] laid down in its Article 23 a norm accepting the general principle of 'apparent representation', relevant scholarship has deemed the norm generally applicable by way of analogy to commercial contracts of cooperation, on the grounds of the principle of good faith.[540] Some authors and court decisions held this as applicable to the context of insurance intermediation.[541]

1190. However, the prevailing case law has refused this extension, apparently approaching insurance mediation as a specific contract type – instead of seeing it as a category that encompasses different contracts, namely agency and brokerage.[542]

538. *See, for instance*, the case law quoted by STJ 13 April 2021, 2347/18.0T8VRL.G1.S1 (Rosa Tching).
539. Decree-Law 178/86, of 3 July.
540. *See* Carlos Alberto da Mota Pinto/António Pinto Monteiro/Paulo Mota Pinto, Teoria Geral do Direito Civil, Coimbra Editora, (2005), 551.
541. STJ 1 March 2014, 4739/03.0TVLSB.L2.S1 (Paulo Sá); P. Romano Martínez, Representação aparente
542. J. C. Moitinho de Almeida, O mediador ..., 156–157; on its turn, José Vasques, Novo regime jurídico da mediação de seguros Coimbra Editora, (2006), 69 and 76 considered that an insurance agency did not qualify as an agency *proprio sensu*, but as a contract analogous to agency.

Moreover, mediation was deemed not to qualify as a distribution agreement[543] – which, in fact, seemed to disregard the fact that mediation can take place through agency.

1191. Article 30(3) has, therefore, brought legal certainty to a question that was relevant and arguably not duly settled. In its regard, the question of which circumstances might justify the trust of a reasonable policyholder on the authority of the pretence intermediary has been specially discussed. In general terms, the more valuable the insurance contract, the more effort the policyholder is expected to deploy in enquiring on the authority of the mediator.

1192. In view of the fact that legitimate insurance intermediation does not per se entail the attribution of powers to represent the insurer, the courts have considered that it does not suffice that the pretence representative uses letterhead of the insurer, or even that they are in possession of policy forms pertaining to a certain insurer or has the power to receive and forward insurance premiums regarding a certain insurance contract.[544] Differently, if the mediator's business premises display the logo of the insurer and create the appearance of belonging to the insurer, then the policyholder's trust shall be deemed reasonable.[545] The fact that the insurer granted the pretence representative access to their exclusive platform and gave them permission to issue and cancel contracts through that platform is deemed sufficient ground for such trust, which the insurer is furthermore deemed to have fostered.[546] The insurer has also been considered as having fostered such trust when it had through a great number of years allowed the intermediary to practice a very broad array of acts in its interest – which in practice encompassed all acts relevant to the conclusion and performance of the insurance contract.[547] This has been especially taken into consideration in cases where the intermediary acted exclusively for the insurer at stake, and used its logo on the premises, as well as its letterhead and forms; all which created a very high risk of the intermediary being taken as an employee of the insurer, which the latter should have warded off.[548]

1193. The Supreme Court has also applied Article 30(3) to a case where a person purporting to represent the insurer had agreed with the policyholder on a special discount on the premium.[549] Although said person did not have authority to bind the insurer, which had at first proceeded to collect the standard premium from the

---

543. *See, for instance*, STJ 18 December 2007, 07A4305 (Urbano Dias); TRL 17 December 2014, 432/08.6TASCR.L1-3 (Rui Gonçalves); STJ 31 March 2016, 432/08.6 TASCR.L1.S1 (Souto de Moura).
544. TRP 24 September 2019, 15351/14,9T8PRT.P2. (Rui Moreira); TRC 11 September 2020, 319/18.4T8CTB.C1 (Felizardo Paiva); STJ 13 April 2021 (*see above*).
545. STJ 13 April 2021 (*see above*), in line with Luís Poças, O novo regime da mediação de seguros: aspectos gerais (in: Estudos de direito dos seguros, Almeida e Leitão, 119, 2008), 222–223.
546. STJ 13 April 2021 (*see above*).
547. STJ 26 January 2017, 656/11.9TVPRT.P1.S1 (Tavares de Paiva).
548. TRG 17 December 2020, 1223/19.4T8BRG.G1 (Afonso Cabral de Andrade); similarly, TRG 19 November 2020, 2347/18.0T8VRL.G1 (Jorge Santos).
549. STJ 24 November 2020, 13495/16.1YIPRT.G3.S1 (Ana Paula Boularot).

policyholder, ensuing claims presented by the policyholder to the pretence intermediary, and forwarded by the latter to the insurer, the insurer had, on several occasions, accepted to return the value of the discount to the policyholder. In this regard, it does not seem to stand to doubt that the policyholder had reasons to trust in the authority of the intermediary, but it does seem striking that the case was brought under Article 30(3), instead of under Article 30(2).

1194. Article 31 provides for the effects of communications made by or provided to an intermediary acting with authority to represent either the policyholder or the insurer. In case an intermediary with authority to represent the policyholder receives any information or documents intended for the policyholder, they are deemed to have been delivered directly to the policyholder (Article 31(1)). The same applies, *mutatis mutandis*, in case of a representative of the insurer (Article 31(2)). Some scholarship considers that Article 31 is itself the source of such powers as to represent the policyholder or the insurer, whatever the case, for the limited purposes of receiving or providing information or documents. Other authors consider that Article 31 is not the source of such powers per se, but rather applies only when the policyholder or the insurer has granted the intermediary with authority for the conclusion of the contract, or when Article 30(3) applies.[550]

550. *See* respectively E. Ribeiro, Art. 31.º, Comunicações através do mediador de seguros, 224–225, and Júlio Manuel Vieira Gomes, O dever de informação do (candidato a) tomador do seguro na fase pré-contratual à luz do Decreto-Lei n.º 72/2008, de 16 de Abril (in: Rui Pinto Duarte/José Lebre de Freitas/Assunção Cristas/Marta Tavares de Almeida/Vítor Pereira das Neves (ed.) Estudos em Homenagem ao Professor Doutor Carlos Ferreira de Almeida, II, Almedina, 2011), 416–418.

Part VIII. Reinsurance, Co-insurance and Pooling

Chapter 1. Reinsurance

Maria Inês de Oliveira Martins

1195. Unlike other legal systems, the RJCS has a specific section on reinsurance – namely, Chapter VI of Title I, comprising Articles 72–75.

1196. According to the RJCS, reinsurance is the contract under which the reinsurer undertakes to cover risks pertaining to the insurer or to another reinsurer (Article 72 RJCS). This concept is in accordance with LBIR, which defines reinsurance as the activity consisting in accepting risks ceded by an insurance undertaking or third-country insurance undertaking, or by another reinsurance undertaking or third-country reinsurance undertaking (Article 5(1)(g) LBIR).

1197. These definitions are fundamentally instrumental to setting out the scope of application of each of the statutes. They are furthermore coherent with the widespread concept of reinsurance as insurance taken out by the insurer.[551] Reinsurance is an indemnity insurance that covers the insurer's risk of having certain liabilities arising in its balance sheet; it therefore bears some resemblance with the risk hedged by liability insurance.

1198. In practical terms, however, Article 73 of RJCS solves the central issue that would be handled by the debate on the nature of reinsurance, since it establishes that the RJCS applies to reinsurance contracts. In its wording, the relationship between the insurer and the reinsurer is regulated by the reinsurance contract, and in supplementary terms, by the RJCS.

551. Margarida Lima Rego/Diogo Costa Seixas, O contrato de resseguro (in: Margarida Lima Rego (ed.) Temas de Direito dos seguros, A propósito da nova Lei do Contrato de Seguro, 2 Ed, Almedina, 287, 2016), 288–292; Eduarda Ribeiro, Art. 73.º, Regime subsidiário (in: P. Romano Martínez (ed.) Lei do Contrato de Seguro anotada, 4 Ed, Almedina, 332, 2020), 332; Carlos Ferreira de Almeida, Contratos III - Contratos de liberalidade, de cooperação e de risco, Almedina, 3 Ed. (2019), 271–272.

1199. The reinsurance contract is naturally the main source of regulation of the reinsurance relationship. That would be the case anyway, under the general principle of freedom of contract. But it is even more so in regard of such a contract, concluded by two professional parties that are specialised in offering insurance contracts. Moreover, reinsurance contracts tend to reflect the international scope of the business, and to conform to the specific parlance and commercial practices of the branch.

1200. In spite of the central role of private autonomy in this branch, reinsurance contracts fall under the mandatory rules that apply to any contract.[552] That is the case of the norms that are an expression of public order (e.g., for insurance, Article 14, on unlawful insurance), as well of the norms that protect the conditions of freedom to contract (e.g., the norms on deceit, unfair exploitation, representation). That is also the case of the norms that derive from the principle of the binding force of contracts, or from the principle of good faith (such as the norms on liability in contract, or the LSCT). The contract must furthermore comply with the requirement of referring to an insurable risk and to an insurable interest (Articles 43 and 44).

1201. In what concerns the supplementary role of the RJCS, e.g., the rules on payment of the premium, or on the duty to disclose the risk, can be especially called upon. Some scholarship has also highlighted that the rules on liability insurance may apply by analogy to reinsurance matters. That is for instance the case for Article 140(3), which grants the victim a direct claim against the insurer, in the cases where the victim has been informed on the existence of an insurance contract and had started direct negotiations with the insurer. This norm is deemed to apply by way of analogy in case of stipulation of a claims control clause, whereby the reinsurer is granted the right to settle the claim, since in this case the reinsurer interacts with the insured as the insurer would normally do.[553]

1202. Article 74 establishes that, notwithstanding Article 32, the reinsurance contract should be stated in a written document, which identifies the risks to be covered. Under Article 32(1), the validity of the contract is not dependent upon the adoption of any specific form. Nonetheless, the insurer is required to state the contract in a written document, named insurance policy, and to provide it to the policyholder (Article 32(2)). The policy should be dated and signed by the policyholder. One can therefore conclude that the reinsurance contract is valid regardless of being stated in a written document. This form serves the purpose of proving the content of the contract (it is not a formality *ad substantiam*, but rather *ad probationem*). In any case, the reinsurer is under the duty to provide the policy in writing to the insurer.

552. M. Lima Rego/D. Costa Seixas, Resseguro, 305–306; as to the limit of public order, E. Ribeiro, Art. 73.°, 334.
553. M. Lima Rego/D. Costa Seixas, Resseguro, 317–318.

1203. Article 75(1) clarifies that unless the law or the contract provide differently, the reinsurance contract does not create any relationship between the reinsurer and the insured. This is in accordance with the principle of privity of contract (termed 'principle of relativity of contract', enshrined in Article 406 of the Civil Code). There are presently no legal provisions expressly granting a right to direct action to the insured against the reinsurer. Such a right can be granted however if one accepts the construction that extends Article 140(3) to reinsurance. As to the possibility of conferring rights to third parties by contract, it encompasses the well-known cut-through clauses, which are sometimes set out to the benefit of the insured for the case of insolvency of the insurer.[554]

1204. According to the most recent data, which refers to the year of 2017, the most prevailing form of reinsurance is that of treaty reinsurance (generally referred to as 'mandatory reinsurance'). Nonetheless, facultative reinsurance does have some expression in the aggregate of maritime, aviation and space and transport insurance. Reinsurance treaties are mostly proportional (a tendency that has increased after 2017) and surplus insurance is their dominant form, both in life and non-life insurance.[555]

554. M. Lima Rego/D. Costa Seixas, Resseguro, 316–317.

555. *See* ASF, *Relatório do Setor Segurador e dos Fundos de Pensões*, 2017, 98–101 and ASF, *Relatório do Setor Segurador e dos Fundos de Pensões*, 2020, 133 (both available at https://www.asf.com.pt/NR/exeres/1BCE3171-23D8-429F-B59E-E2C1F75788E5.htm).

Chapter 2. Co-insurance and Pooling

§1. Co-insurance

1205. Co-insurance is regulated in Articles 62–69 of RJCS.[556] Articles 70 and 71 of RJCS and 248–251 of LBIR concern community co-insurance operations.

1206. Article 62 of RJCS provides that in co-insurance the risk is covered by a single contract at an overall premium and for the same period by two or more insurers, each for its own part as co-insurer, without entailing their joint liability, one of them being the leading co-insurer.

1207. This concept sums-up the fundamental traits of co-insurance, which are elaborated upon by the ensuing provisions. The fact that co-insurance is a *single insurance contract*, and not a collection of insurance contracts, is further highlighted by Article 63, which states that co-insurance gives rise to a single insurance policy, which is issued by the leading co-insurer, and which should state the proportion of the participation of each co-insurer in the risk covered or in the amount of insured sums.

1208. Another central feature of co-insurance is that the liability of each of the co-insurers is strictly separated. There is no joint and several liability in co-insurance, and this fact should be apparent in the insurance policy. Article 64 clearly states in this regard that each of the co-insurers is only liable to the extent of the proportion of the risk it covered, or the proportion of the insured sum it undertook to pay.

1209. Articles 65–69 clarify the role of the leading co-insurer, both in the external relationships – namely, with policyholders – and in the internal relationships – namely, among the co-insurers.

1210. Articles 65, 68 and 69 refer to the relationships with policyholders.

1211. According to Article 65(1), the leading co-insurer has the responsibility to perform several functions, both in its own name and in representation of the other co-insurers: (a) to receive the initial disclosure of the risk, as well as their subsequent notifications on the aggravation or reduction of that risk from the policyholder; (b) to assess the risk to be insured, and to set the premium and the terms of coverage; (c) to issue the policy, notwithstanding the fact that it should be signed by all the co-insurers; (d) to collect the premiums, and issue the due receipts; (e) to undertake all legal action in case of default on the premium; (f) to receive the notification of the insured event and to settle the claims; (g) to accept and to propose the termination of the contract. Under Article 65(2), the co-insurers may agree to attribute other functions to the leading co-insurer. Under Article 65(3), in case it is

556. On the origin of these provisions, *see* Eduarda Ribeiro, Art. 62.º, Noção (in: Lei do contrato de seguro anotada, 4 Ed., Almedina, 301, 2020), 301 and ff.

stipulated that the leading co-insurer can settle the totality of the claim, in its own name and in representation of the other co-insurers, then the co-insurers, derogating Article 65(1)(c), can also stipulate in writing that the policy shall be signed by the leading co-insurer alone in their representation, as long as the policy mentions the agreement between all co-insurers.

1212. Article 68 establishes that the claims can be settled under two different procedures, according to what is expressly set out in the policy: either the leading co-insurer settles the claim entirely, in its own name and in representation of the other co-insurers; or each of the co-insurers settles part of the claim, according to the proportion of the risk it undertook to cover or to the part of the insured sum it undertook to pay. According to Article 69(1), court actions should be brought against all co-insurers; however, when the contract stipulated the procedure set out in Article 68(b) and the action concerns a specific claim, then it can be brought exclusively against the co-insurer concerned. According to 69(2), the co-insurance contract can establish that any action should be brought against the leading co-insurer, who will then act as the procedural surrogate of the other co-insurers.

1213. Articles 66 and 67 regard the internal relationship between co-insurers. Article 66 establishes that in regard to every co-insurance, co-insurers should define their mutual relationships and of each one of them with the leading co-insurer by express agreement. Without prejudice to Article 65(1), the agreement should provide at least for: (a) the value of the management fees of leading co-insurer, in case they are due; (b) the modus for the leading co-insurer to inform the co-insurers and account for its actions before them; (c) the system adopted for claims settlement. Article 67 establishes that the leader is responsible before the co-insurers in case of non-compliance with its functions.

1214. The rules on co-insurance clearly draw from the Portuguese rules on the consortium contract, and namely on one of its forms: external consortium (Decree-Law 231/81, of 28 July, Articles 1, 2, 5(2)). 'Consortium' is defined as the contract under which two or more persons mutually undertake to perform a certain activity in a concerted way or to make a contribution that will allow them to pursue concertedly a certain purpose (e.g., to take preparatory actions in regard of a certain undertaking, or to prospect certain natural resources) (Articles 1 and 2). There are two modalities of consortium: external consortium, where the existence of the consortium is apparent to the third parties that contract with the members of the consortium, and internal consortium, where the existence of the consortium in not apparent to third parties (Article 5). The members of external consortia can be represented before third parties by a consortium leader (Articles 12–15). The members of the consortium should not be presumed to be joint and severally liable before third parties (Article 17).

1215. Due to the clear kinship between co-insurance and external consortium with stipulation of a consortium leader, the provisions on consortium may supplement the contract if needed.

1216. Community co-insurance operations are defined in Article 70 as operations where the risk is covered by a single contract at an overall premium and for the same period by two or more insurers established in different Member States of the EU, each for its own part as co-insurer, without entailing their joint liability, one of them being the leading insurance undertaking. Article 71 adds that such operations are only allowed in regard to large risks. In case the co-insurance contract is concluded in Portugal, Article 248 further requires that the leading co-insurer complies with the norms on freedom to provision of services by insurers that have their head office located in a different Member State.

§2. Pooling

1217. Unlike co-insurance, pooling agreements are not mentioned by the RJCS. The term 'pooling agreements' seems to be loosely used to refer to different mechanisms by which insurers agree to combine their resources to cover certain risks, under the general principle of freedom of contract. The term is sometimes used to mention agreements between co-insurers, by which they undertake to share in the risks of a set of different co-insurance contracts, and not of a single co-insurance contract.[557]

1218. The term can also refer to structures whereby, unlike what happens in co-insurance, the fact that several insurers bear the consequences of the insured event is not apparent to the policyholders. In these cases, only the insurer that took out the insurance contract remains liable towards the policyholder; however, it shares the risk undertaken with other insurers.

1219. This may refer to cases of reinsurance, where the insurer shares part of the insured risk with several other insurers or reinsurers (reinsurance pool).

1220. It may also refer to cases where several insurers bring part of their insurance business into insurers' pool, agreeing to share in the aggregate losses or profits according to a certain proportion.[558] In case the insurers jointly manage the assets generated by the premiums, it can be said that the traits of the concept of company are present (Article 980 of the Civil Code):[559] there is pooling of resources for the

557. E. Ribeiro, Art. 66.º, Acordo entre os co-seguradores, at 313.

558. German scholarship tends to qualify these pools as civil law companies (Christian Armbrüster, Vorbemerkungen zu § 77: Mitversicherung (in: Prölss/Martin, Versicherungsvertragsgesetz: VVG, 31 Ed., C. H. Beck, 2021), http://beck-online.beck.de/ (accessed 30 Nov. 2021), 2; Christoph Schücking, § 4 Unterscheidung nach dem Gesellschaftszweck (in: Hans Gummert/Lutz Weipert (ed.) Münchener Handbuch des Gesellschaftsrechts 1, 5 Ed., 2019), http://beck-online.beck.de/ (accessed 30 Oct. 2021), 34–36, 78. Considering the concept of company adopted in Portuguese law, that refers to the joint exercise of an economic activity, some distinctions must be made. Moreover, when the activity undertaken is of commercial nature, the company undertaking it is deemed a commercial company, even though not incorporated as such.

559. Article 980 of the Civil Code establishes that the contract which creates a company is an agreement whereby two or more persons undertake to contribute with goods or services for the joint pursuit of an economic activity which is not the mere enjoyment or benefit of certain assets, with the

joint pursuit of an economic activity, with the purpose of sharing the profit resulting thereof, and the obligation to share in the losses which may occur. The insurers can then be said to be running an informal commercial company, and company law may apply.

1221. If the insurers manage their assets separately, and merely agree to pool the results of their activity, there will not be the joint pursuit of an economic activity that is characteristic of a company. The pool will then arguably have the nature of a mutual-type association.

purpose of sharing the profit resulting thereof. Art. 994 adds that a contract term exempting a partner from bearing the losses is deemed unlawful. Although these norms belong to the Civil Code, they are also the basis for the concept of commercial company (*see* Jorge Coutinho de Abreu, Curso de Direito comercial, II, Das sociedades, Almedina, 7 Ed. (2021), 23 and ff.).

Part IX. Taxation of Insurance

Joana Neto Anjos

1222. Regarding taxation of insurance one must consider that both insurance undertakings and consumers must pay an indirect tax on insurance (stamp tax) and several other taxes ('taxas parafiscais'), that actively contribute to the financing of certain public services and benefits of extreme importance and social utility.[560]

1223. In addition, Portuguese law envisages partial deductions of some insurance premiums, as well as tax benefits, in the framework of the personal income tax (CIRS), approved by Law 82-E/2014, of 31 December.

560. On the regulatory and institutional framework of rates in the insurance sector, *see* Rogério Fernandes Ferreira e João Parreira Mesquita, *As Taxas de Regulação Económica no Setor dos Seguros* (in Sérgio Vasques, *As Taxas de Regulação Económica em Portugal*, Almedina, 2008), p. 430.

Chapter 1. Taxation

§1. Stamp Tax

1224. Stamp Tax is a consumption tax that is levied on certain acts and contracts. The Stamp Tax Code, approved by Decree-Law 287/2003, of 12 November, established that insurance undertakings must pay a stamp tax to the State both regarding the amount of insurance premiums, cost of policy and other amounts collected with the insurance premium or separately, as well as on the commissions paid to insurance intermediaries (after the amount of the tax has been deducted) (Article 2(1,e) of the Stamp Tax Code).

1225. The General Table of Stamp Tax annexed to the Code envisages different rates with regard to the insurance contract and risks insured. The rates applying to the total amount of insurance premiums, the amount of the cost of the insurance policy, or to any other amounts received by the insurance undertaking are the following:

(1) caution insurance: 3% (No. 22.1.1. of the General Table);
(2) accident insurance, health insurance, credit insurance and any type of agriculture and livestock insurance: 5% (No. 22.1.2. of the General Table);
(3) goods in transit: 5% (No. 22.1.3. of the General Table);
(4) ship and aviation insurance: 5% (No. 22.1.4. of the General Table); and
(5) any other type of insurance: 9% (No. 22.1.5. of the General Table).

1226. In addition, the stamp tax rate on commissions paid to insurance intermediaries is 2% (No. 22.2 of the General Table).

§2. Other Tax: 'Taxas Parafiscais'

1227. Tax to fund the FGA. About 2.5% of the mandatory premium for motor insurance liability coverage goes to fund the FGA, which is an autonomous public fund managed by the ASF. This mechanism serves to indemnify those injured by accidents, when the person responsible is not known or does not have an insurance contract. Pursuant to Article 58(1,a and 2) of Decree-Law 291/2007, of 21 August, the contribution in favour of the FGA results from the application of a percentage of 2.5% on the commercial premiums of processed direct insurance contracts under the mandatory coverage of motor vehicle liability insurance. Also, in accordance with Article 58(1, b and 3), the contribution resulting from the application of a percentage of 0.21% on the total amount of commercial premiums of all 'motor insurance' contracts processed each year also constitutes FGA revenue, intended for road safety.

1228. Tax for the National Emergency Institute (INEM). INEM is a public institute, which is assigned all urgent or emergency activities, including the pre-hospital assistance system, transport and hospital reception. Among other sources of revenue, INEM is financed by the amount referred to Article 25(b) of Decree-Law 167/2003, of 29 July, that is 1% of premiums or contributions related to life, health, personal accidents and automobile insurance.

1229. Tax for the National Emergency and Civil Protection Authority (ANEPC). The ANEPC's mission is to plan, coordinate and execute emergency and civil protection policies, namely the prevention and response to serious accidents and catastrophes, protection of populations and coordination of civil protection agents. Pursuant to Article 27(2,f) of Decree-Law 45/2019, of 1 April, the ANEPC has its own revenues, which include the following percentages on insurance premiums: 13% of the gross premium value paid for fire insurance and dangerous goods transport insurance (including cargo insurance and vehicle insurance specifically intended for this type of transport) and 6% on the value of the gross premium paid for crop and livestock insurance, including the value of bonuses.

1230. Tax to finance FAT. FAT is a fund managed by the ASF and aims to guarantee the payment of wages in arrears, in the event of company bankruptcy, and to guarantee the payment of insurance premiums for companies that, within the scope of a recovery process, do not manage to do so. Pursuant to Article 3(1,2) of Decree-Law 142/99, of 30 April, the following constitute FAT revenues: a percentage to be charged by insurance companies to policyholders on workers' wages, whenever premiums of the category 'work accidents' are processed; a percentage to be charged by the insurance companies on the amount corresponding to the capital of pensions redemption in payment on the date of 31 December of each year, as well as on the value of the mathematical provision of supplementary benefits for the assistance of a third person, in payment to the date 31 December of each year. These percentages must be set annually by order of the Minister of Finance.

Chapter 2. Tax Deduction and Tax Benefits

1231. The CIRS and the Tax Benefits Code ('EBF') provide for certain tax deductions and benefits for insurance.

1232. Health insurance. CIRS, in Article 78(C), provides that 15% of premiums paid with health insurance are deducted from the personal income tax, up to a maximum limit of EUR 1,000.

1233. Home insurance or home multi-risk insurance. Home or multi-risk home insurance does not entitle the policyholder to personal income tax benefits or deductions. The only exception is for landlords, but only if they opt for autonomous taxation of their property income. In this situation, these multi-risk insurance premiums can be deducted from rental income as they are considered maintenance expenses, in accordance with Article 41(7) of the CIRS.

1234. Motor vehicle insurance. There is no right to personal income tax benefits or deductions on auto insurance.

1235. Life insurance. Contrary to the previous regime, it is not possible to obtain personal income tax benefits with life insurance. There are, however, three exceptions to this rule. First, according to Article 87 of the CIRS, a taxpayer with a disability can deduct 25% of the premiums paid for Life insurance with death or disability coverage in his personal income tax, provided that it does do not exceed 15% of the total collection amount. Second, Article 27 of the CIRS considers sportsmen, miners and fishermen as fast-wearing professions. Respecting certain conditions, these professionals can deduct 100% of the premiums paid in life insurance within their personal income tax, with coverage for death, disability or contribution to retirement. This deduction, however, is limited to five times the Social Support Index per taxpayer, which in 2020 and 2021 was set at EUR 438.81. Thus, the deductible limit will be EUR 2,194.05. Third, in life insurance designed for retirement and in PPR, in accordance with Article 21 of the EBF, 20% of paid premiums are deductible from the personal income tax, with a maximum limit of EUR 400.

1236. Personal accident insurance. Under Article 27 of the CIRS, only a worker who is a fast-wearing professional can deduct 100% of the premiums paid in personal accident insurance on their personal income tax. This deduction is, however, limited to five times the Social Support Index per taxpayer, which in 2020 and 2021 was set at EUR 438.81. Thus, the deductible limit is EUR 2,194.05.

1237. Finally, one should note that the total value of deductions and tax benefits that originate from health, education, billing, property charges and household and maintenance costs is limited. Article 78 of the CIRS contains information on this point, providing for a ceiling that cannot be exceeded depending on the taxable income of each household.

Part X. Risk Management and Prevention

Maria Inês de Oliveira Martins

1238. Activities of risk management and prevention of damage to insured 'goods' (in a broad sense) serve a different array of interests.[561] They serve the interest of the policyholder, where they cannot obtain full compensation for their damage. They serve the interest of the insurer in not having to perform, or at least in limiting the amounts they must disburse. And they serve the interest of the community in the prevention of damage, since sources of danger affecting one person may propagate to goods belonging to other persons. Therefore, risk management and prevention of damage to insured 'goods' are not regarded exclusively by insurance law, but are rather affected by a different array of norms, comprising administrative norms, criminal norms and civil liability norms.

1239. Insurance contract law itself does not specifically target risk management and prevention of damage to insured 'goods'. It does however impact them by setting out the insurer's right to modify or terminate the insurance contract in case of aggravation of the risk, and its duty to modify it to the benefit of the policyholder in case of reduction of the risk (Articles 92–94). Both the norms on aggravation and on reduction of the insured risk can incentivise the policyholder to adopt measures that decrease the degree of risk, by preventing the occurrence of damage. The norms on mitigation of damage and wilful causation (Articles 126 and 46) can also have an impact on damage prevention, as long as one considers that prevention also encompasses the period in which damage is *already imminent*, and not merely previous stages of the process leading to damage.

1240. All in all, risk prevention is mostly left to the contract and can be pursued by two different methods. The first method relies on making the acceptance of the risk, or performance in case of the insured event, conditional upon the adoption of certain measures that prevent or control the risk. This method is not very frequent in mass insurance, since it implies costs of verification that the insurer may not be able to pass on to its policyholders. It is a field where the employment of Artificial Intelligence techniques that allow for massified verification of compliance may bring considerable change. When the contract makes performance conditional upon

561. On the topic of insurance and prevention of damage, *see* Maria Inês de Oliveira Martins, Seguro e responsabilidade civil, BFDUC, 241 (2020), 245–269.

the adoption of certain risk control/prevention measures, then what was said above on contractual duties of the policyholder (Part III, Chapter 4, §2, II, B) shall apply.

1241. The second method relies on 'selling' risk prevention services in connection with the provision of insurance – e.g., advice on cyber risk management, monitoring and advising on healthy lifestyle habits, or monitoring and advising on compliance in corporate risks. These services have been particularly highlighted in recent times, in connection with increased capabilities of data processing, as well as with the urge to prevent catastrophic risks. Both sides of the market can have an interest in these services – on the side of the policyholders, since they can benefit from the technical expertise of the insurer in regard of the insured risk; on the side of the insurers, since this allows for the diversifying of sources of revenue and for the improvement of insurer-customer relationship.

1242. The provision of risk prevention services is nonetheless not exempt from doubt from a legal standpoint.

1243. First, one can debate whether the provision of such services is compatible with supervisory law, where it establishes that insurance undertakings should limit their object to the business of insurance and operations arising directly therefrom, to the exclusion of all other commercial business (Articles 18(1)(a) of *Solvency II* and 47 LBIR). Considering that this requirement has been construed very broadly – e.g., in order to accommodate all consequences of the provision of assistance insurance and insurance in kind – and considering that risk prevention is instrumental to the business of insurance and that it does not entail risks that the insurer is not able to quantify, this line of business, however, seems be compatible with supervisory norms.[562]

1244. Second, where access to insurance cover is tied to the provision of these services, the freedom of contract of the policyholder may be at stake.[563] The terms of the contract should be assessed in view of the general market conditions, and in regard to their compatibility with the norms on personal data protection (Article 7(4) of DPR), protection of commercial secrets (Articles 313–315 of the Code of Industrial Property), consumer protection (Article 9(6) of the Law on the Protection of Consumers), abuse of dominance (Articles 11 and 12 of the Competition Law) and unfair exploitation (Article 282 of the Civil Code).

562. M. I. Oliveira Martins, Seguro e responsabilidade ..., 261 and ff.
563. M. I. Oliveira Martins, Seguro e responsabilidade ..., 274–278.

Selected Bibliography

Previous to RJCS

Almeida, José Carlos Moitinho de, *O contrato de seguro no direito português e comparado*, Livraria Sá da Costa (1971).

Martinez, Pedro Romano, *Direito dos seguros, Apontamentos*, Principia (2006).

Monteiro, Jorge Ferreira Sinde, *Responsabilidade por culpa, responsabilidade objectiva, seguro de acidentes,* 2, Revista de Direito e Economia, 317 (1979).

Monteiro, Jorge Ferreira Sinde, *Responsabilidade por culpa, responsabilidade objectiva, seguro de acidentes (conclusão)* 6–7, Revista de Direito e Economia, 123 (1980–1981).

Silva, João Calvão da, *Banca, bolsa e seguros, Direito europeu e português, Tomo I – Parte geral*, 4 Ed. Almedina (2013).

Vasques, José, *Contrato de seguro, Notas para uma teoria geral*, Coimbra Editora (1999).

Vasques, José, *Novo regime jurídico da mediação de seguros*, Coimbra Editora (2006).

After RJCS

Almeida, José Carlos Moitinho de, *Contrato de seguro. Estudos*, Coimbra Editora (2009).

Cordeiro, António Menezes, *Direito dos seguros*, 2. Ed., Almedina (2016).

Gomes, Júlio Manuel Vieira, *Seguro de acidentes de trabalho : para uma interpretação restritiva – ou mesmo a revisão – do acórdão uniformizador de jurisprudência n.º 10/2001 de 21 de Novembro de 2001,* 116, Revista do Ministério Público, 5 (2008).

Gomes, Júlio Manuel Vieira, *Do dever ou ónus de salvamento no novo regime jurídico do contrato de seguro (Decreto-Lei n.º 72/2008, de 16/4)*, Cadernos de Direito Privado, 28, 3 (2009).

Gomes, Júlio Manuel Vieira, *O dever de informação do (candidato a) tomador do seguro na fase pré-contratual à luz do Decreto-Lei n.º 72/2008, de 16 de Abril* (in: R. Pinto Duarte/ J. Lebre de Freitas/ Assunção Cristas (ed.) *Estudos em Homenagem ao Professor Doutor Carlos Ferreira de Almeida, II,* Almedina, p. 387, 2011).

Gomes, Júlio Manuel Vieira, *Algumas notas sobre o agravamento e a diminuição do risco no contrato de seguro*, RDES, 1–3, p. 7 (2015).

Selected Bibliography

Martínez, Pedro Romano/ Torres, Leonor Cunha/ Oliveira, Arnaldo da Costa/ Ribeiro, Maria Eduarda/ Morgado, José Pereira/ Vasques, José/ Brito, José Alves de, *Lei do Contrato de Seguro anotada, 4. Ed.*, Almedina (2020).

Martínez, Pedro Romano/ Matos, Filipe Albuquerque (ed.), *Lei da distribuição de seguros anotada*, Almedina (2019).

Martins, Maria Inês de Oliveira, *Sobre a discriminação dos portadores de VIH/sida na contratação de seguros de vida*, BFDUC, 2, p. 749 (2013).

Martins, Maria Inês de Oliveira, *Contrato de seguro e conduta dos sujeitos ligados ao risco*, Almedina (2018).

Martins, Maria Inês de Oliveira, *El Derecho de contrato de seguro en Portugal, Un régimen en la encrucijada* (in: *El contrato de seguro y su distribución en la encrucijada*, Thomson Reuters Aranzadi, Cizur Menor, 2018, pp. 101).

Martins, Maria Inês de Oliveira, *Subrogation of the Guarantee Fund and liability of the persons failing to take out mandatory insurance: an endorsement of the prevailing opinion of Portuguese courts*, Insurance Review/Wiadomości Ubezpieczeniowe, 4 (2019).

Martins, Maria Inês de Oliveira, *Seguro e responsabilidade civil*, BFDUC, p. 241 (2020).

Martins, Maria Inês de Oliveira, *Entre a avaliação inicial do risco e o regime do seu agravamento subsequente*, Julgar, 43, p. 67, 2021.

Martins, Maria Inês de Oliveira, *Seguro de responsabilidade civil dos profissionais de saúde: Entre a autonomia privada e a protecção social* (in: A. Dias Pereira, F. Albuquerque Matos, N. Rosenvald, J. Barceló Domenech, *Responsabilidade civil em saúde, Diálogo com o Prof. Doutor Jorge Sinde Monteiro*, Instituto Jurídico – Faculdade de Direito da Universidade de Coimbra, p. 291, 2021).

Matos, Filipe Albuquerque, *Uma outra abordagem em torno das declarações inexactas e reticentes no âmbito do contrato de seguro* (in: M. Costa Andrade/ M. João Antunes/ S. Aires de Sousa (eds.), *Estudos em homenagem ao Prof. Doutor Jorge de Figueiredo Dias, IV*, p. 615, 2010).

Matos, Filipe Albuquerque, *O Fundo de Garantia Automóvel, Um organismo com uma vocação eminentemente social* (in: Estudos dedicados ao Professor Doutor Luís Alberto de Carvalho Fernandes, I, Universidade Católica Editora, 559, 2011).

Monteiro, Jorge Sinde, *Venda CIF, contrato de transporte marítimo e seguro de carga; sobre a qualidade de segurado*, RLJ, 3971, 105 (2011).

Monteiro, Jorge Sinde, *Direito dos seguros e responsabilidade civil – da legislação europeia sobre o seguro automóvel e sua repercussão no regime dos acidentes causados por veículos*, RLJ, 3977, 82 (2012).

Oliveira, Arnaldo da Costa, *Seguro obrigatório de responsabilidade civil automóvel, Síntese das alterações de 2007 (DL 291/2007, 21 Ago)*, Almedina (2008).

Ramos, José Luís Bonifácio, *O pagamento do prémio na Lei do Contrato de Seguro*, Cadernos de Direito Privado, 39, p. 3 (2012).

Ramos, Maria Elisabete, *O seguro de responsabilidade civil dos administradores, Entre a exposição ao risco e a delimitação da cobertura*, Almedina (2010).

Ramos, Maria Elisabete, *O contrato de seguro entre a liberdade contratual e o tipo*, Almedina (2021).

Rego, Margarida Lima, *Contrato de seguro e terceiros*, Estudo de Direito civil, Coimbra Editora (2010).

Rego, Margarida Lima, (ed.), *Temas de Direito dos seguros, A propósito da nova Lei do Contrato de Seguro*, 2. Ed, Almedina (2016).

Rego, Margarida Lima, *Influência da regulação institucional na contratação de seguros: O impacto do novo regime da distribuição na responsabilidade pré-contratual do distribuidor*, Julgar, 43, 151 (2021).

Rego, Margarida Lima, Rocha, Francisco Rodrigues, Bação, Fernando, Damásio, Bruno (ed.), *Estudo mutidisciplinar sobre o Fundo de Garantia Automóvel*, Autoridade de Supervisão dos Seguros e Fundos de Pensões, 2021 (https://www.asf.com.pt/NR/rdonlyres/CCD9CE3D-E70F-4E66-85F6-3BF3B8581160/0/FGA40Anos_LC_web.pdf, retrieved 10 November 2021).

Rocha, Francisco Rodrigues, *Do princípio indemnizatório no seguro de danos*, Almedina (2015).

Rocha, Francisco Rodrigues, *Algumas notas em torno da cláusula CIF e do seguro de transporte de mercadorias* (in: Januário da Costa Gomes (ed.), *Temas de Direito dos transportes, III*, Almedina, p. 247, 2015).

Poças, Luís, *Estudos de direito dos seguros*, Almeida e Leitão (2008).

Poças, Luís, *O dever de declaração inicial do risco no contrato de seguro*, Almedina (2013).

Poças, Luís, *A delimitação do risco coberto no seguro de mercadorias transportadas* (in: J. Costa Gomes (ed.), Temas de Direito dos transportes, V, Almedina, p. 495, 2020).

Selected Bibliography

Index

The numbers here refer to paragraph numbers.

Aggravation of the risk
  communication of, 558–585
Agreement on jurisdiction, 102
Agricultural insurance *see* Crop and livestock insurance
Alternative dispute resolution (ADR), 179, 191–196, 209
Arbitration, 7, 17, 175–196, 431, 733, 895
ASF, 24, 26, 69, 97, 178, 238, 239, 241, 262–265, 276, 277, 279, 280, 283, 284, 286, 287, 289, 290, 292, 293, 295, 296, 298–300, 302, 305, 306, 308, 309, 311, 312, 314–317, 323–327, 335, 336. 339, 347, 465, 675, 831, 838, 865, 914, 947, 965, 990, 993, 1066, 1068, 1101, 1102, 1105, 1119, 1123, 1148, 1153, 1155, 1157, 1227, 1230
Assistance insurance, 388, 942–944, 1243
Aviation, 102, 898–906, 1204

Beneficiaries, 735–736, 1091–1103
Bodily injuries insurance *see* Personal accidents insurance
Branch offices
  of insurance or reinsurance companies headquartered in another Member State of the EU, 259, 294–299
  of insurance or reinsurance companies established in a third country, 300–309
Brussels Ia, 98–103, 134

Capital redemption operations, 88, 720, 1065, 1101, 1105, 1120–1122
Catastrophe insurance, 918–923
Caution insurance, 46, 643, 933–938, 1225
CMIA, 88, 946
Co-insurance, 100, 508, 1205–1218
Collective insurance *see* Group insurance
Commercial Code
  1833, 39
  1888, 42, 43, 45, 47, 88, 844
Compulsory insurance
  and uniform contractual clauses, 838, 865, 869, 990–992, 1006
Conflict autonomy, 119, 121, 142, 154
Conflict rule, 104–107, 112, 113, 117–119, 121, 123, 125, 127, 129, 130, 132, 135, 142, 145, 150, 158
Consumer protection law, 402
Contra proferentem, 374, 380, 414, 1038
Contracts of adhesion *see* Standard contract terms
Contractual duties to control the insured risk, 619
Credit insurance, 199, 483, 621, 924–935, 937, 1225
Crop insurance, 508
Crop and livestock insurance, 1229

Damages insurance *see* Indemnity insurance
Delay in performance
  by the insurer, 622–629
Direct claim, 101, 133, 134, 251, 861, 978, 1201
Disclosure of the risk
  infringement of the duty, 545–557
Duty to mitigate the loss *see* Mitigation of loss

European system of financial supervision, 316

FGA *see* Motor vehicle guarantee fund
Financial stability, 316, 318, 340, 341
Fire insurance, 508, 830–840, 1229

Index

Fixed sums insurance, 382–384, 386, 453, 643, 688–691, 735, 736, 1031, 1033, 1036, 1038, 1048, 1086

Global business volume, 26, 265
Good faith *see* Insurance contract and good faith
Goods transportation insurance, 508
Group insurance
  contributory and non-contributory, 746–754
  and right to terminate or modify the contract, 773–783
  and duty to inform, 784–800
  and exclusion of the insured, 771–772
Guarantee Fund
  and Workmen's compensation fund, 1013–1015
  and Motor vehicle guarantee fund, 961, 965–977

Health insurance
  branch, 270, 271, 359
  contract, 508
Home insurance
  multi-risk, 833, 1233

Indemnity
  insurance, 638–687
  insurance and personal insurance, 1032
  insurance versus fixed sums insurance, 1031, 1033, 1034, 1036, 1038, 1048
  principle, 638–648
Income tax
  and taxable income, 346
  corporate income tax, 343–346
  taxable profit of insurance, 348
Industrial injuries, 988
Information duties, 692–720
  and pre-contractual disclosure of the risk, 703–714
  in group insurance, 714
  of insurance intermediaries, 707
  of the insurer, 692–720
  on the aggravation of risk, 558–585
Injured third parties, 335, 854, 862
Insurable interest, 37, 40, 352, 353, 381, 441, 442, 445, 446, 450, 454, 596, 671, 722, 724, 728, 740, 848, 1035, 1200
Insurance and reinsurance business
  authorisation, 52, 272–313
  and programme of activities, 282, 284, 285, 302, 303
Insurance and reinsurance companies
  limited by shares, 259, 260, 263, 279–290, 292, 293
  minimum capital requirement, 282, 284, 285, 301–303, 309, 311, 319–321
  mutual, 252–261, 279, 291–293
  prudent management, 282, 309
  public or publicly owned, 259, 262, 279
  solvency capital requirement, 282, 285, 301, 303, 311, 319–321
  versus limited liability cooperative, 261, 291
Insurance and reinsurance distribution (IDF), 707, 1146, 1150, 1151, 1153, 1159, 1161–1179, 1181–1183, 1185
Insurance and reinsurance intermediaries
  and insurance agents, 27, 486, 1151, 1154, 1169, 1172, 1181, 1185
  and insurance brokers, 1156, 1157, 1169, 1170, 1181, 1185
  ancillary insurance intermediaries, 1152, 1153, 1158, 1181, 1185
  duties, 1161–1168
  registration, 1153–1160
Insurance and reinsurance market
  and freedom to provide services, 311
Insurance-based investment products, 72, 695, 1065, 1073, 1117–1119, 1167, 1174
Insurance claim, 398, 486, 604, 650, 685, 709, 733, 1163
Insurance contract
  and good faith, 217, 378, 393, 395–397, 406, 421–425, 460, 540, 542, 593, 601, 607, 614, 618, 630, 634, 647, 652, 664, 667, 694, 843, 857, 859, 950, 1043, 1188, 1189, 1200
  and risk transfer, 353
  conclusion of the insurance contract, 488, 996
  interpretation, 222, 361–380, 908
Insurance for the account of a third party
  and for the account of whom it may concern, 726, 727, 847
Insurance policy *see* Policy
Insurance warranties *see* Contractual duties to control the insured risk
Insured event
  and duty to mitigate the loss, 619
  deliberate causation, 477–483

communication of the insured event, 602–615
Insured sum, 483, 540, 589, 591, 600, 621, 638, 643, 653, 662, 663, 669, 671, 674, 707, 716, 725, 849, 850, 857, 957–961, 967, 978, 1054, 1055, 1060, 1079, 1207, 1208, 1212

Large risks insurance, 501, 521, 659
LBIR, 23, 71, 87, 97, 175, 176, 178, 197, 257, 260, 261, 278, 280, 291, 315, 318, 320, 321, 323, 331, 335, 338, 339, 342, 351, 494, 720, 924, 982, 1146, 1176, 1179, 1196, 1205, 1243
Legal Aid Insurance, 890–897
Liability insurance
commercial liability insurance, 875–880
environmental liability insurance, 885
private liability insurance, 864, 868–869
professional liability insurance, 745, 864, 870–874
Life insurance
and right to insurance benefits, 1059, 1082, 1101, 1104–1110, 1122
and surrender value, 508, 766, 1084, 1086, 1096, 1104–1110, 1118
capitalisation insurance, 1059, 1105, 1107, 1118
contract, 88, 521, 766, 810, 1058–1066, 1072, 1088, 1092, 1106
branch, 72, 74, 88, 89, 281
branch and non-tied deferred capital insurance, 266
branch and non-tied PPR, 266
contract, 88, 521, 766, 810, 1058–1066, 1072, 1088, 1092, 1106, 1235
group life insurance, 778, 779, 1109, 1111–1116, 1145
temporary, 1059
whole life insurance, 358, 1059
Livestock insurance, 508, 521, 910–918, 923, 1225, 1229
Loss of benefits insurance, 841–843, 940
LSCT *see* Standard contract terms
Lugano Convention, 98, 100–102

Mandatory rules, 125–127, 150, 158, 897, 1200
Mass risks insurance
versus large risks insurance, 197–204
and semi-mandatory provisions, 203
Mediation, 61, 73, 108, 180, 186–189, 191, 195, 196, 273, 316, 1148, 1149, 1150, 1182, 1183, 1190
Mitigation of loss
and reimbursement of expenses, 1040
Motor vehicle guarantee fund, 961, 965–977
Multi-risk insurance, 831, 833, 941, 1233
Multiple insurance, 252–261, 279, 291–293
Mutual insurance or reinsurance companies, 259, 261, 279

National audit supervision council, 316
Non-life insurance, 63, 79, 116, 157, 159, 252, 263, 265, 269–271, 281, 285, 303, 1204

Occupational diseases, 48, 987–1021, 1028
Over-insurance, 381, 389, 444, 653, 662–670, 677, 985

Pension funds, 24, 71, 74, 82, 89, 210, 255, 257, 274, 276, 277, 316, 1013, 1113, 1123–1142
Period of coverage, 858
Personal accidents insurance, 448, 810, 1024–1027, 1031, 1032, 1040, 1046, 1048, 1065, 1101
Personal data
and health data, 94, 390, 487, 539, 696, 1160, 1244
Personal insurance, 68, 119, 122, 126, 381, 382, 385, 387, 388, 390, 514, 601, 655, 677, 688, 691, 718, 719, 739, 742, 744, 784, 1032, 1036
Policy, 533–621, 767–770
Policyholder, 533–621, 767–770
Pooling, 1217–1221
Premium
default on, 66, 518–532, 1085, 1088
payment by third parties, 515
special regime, 191, 729, 995, 1137
Prevention, 57, 95, 207, 274, 316, 359, 463, 473, 480, 944, 991, 1171, 1176, 1229, 1238–1244
PRIIPS *see* Insurance-based investment products

(Public order
and good morals, 472, 476

Recognition and enforcement of judgments, 98

Reinsurance contracts
  and claims control clauses, 1201
  and cut-through clauses, 1203
  and pooling, 1195–1221
Right of recourse, 480, 661, 862, 962–964, 971, 975, 978
Risk
  and insurable interests, 352, 353, 454, 596, 724, 1035, 1200
  assessment, 486, 751, 930
  inspection, 486, 801
  insurable risk, 439–483, 744, 1200
  management, 1059, 1134, 1238–1244
  modification, 560
  pre-contractual duty of disclosure, 533–558, 579, 584, 1075
  prevention, 57, 1171, 1238–1244
  questionnaire, 97, 535, 540
  systemic risks, 316
Rome I, 104, 106, 108, 129–137, 139, 141–145, 147, 148, 151–154
Rule of substantive private international law, 128

Savings for Education or Retirement Plans, 89, 1131, 1137–1142
Settlement of the insurance claim, 398
Social security, 134, 987, 994, 1016, 1143–1145
Solvency II, 71, 79, 106, 116, 153, 197, 318, 339, 891, 942, 944, 1067, 1072, 1120, 1243
Space, 904–906
Sports
  and occupational accidents insurance, 866, 996–999
Standard contract terms (SCT), 76, 193, 212, 213, 215, 219, 222, 368, 380, 401–438, 714, 778, 790, 984
Subrogation, 68, 132, 656–661, 690, 861, 932, 971–977, 1036, 1037
Supervision of insurance and reinsurance companies, 322–328
Surrender value *see* Life insurance and surrender value
System of prudential supervision, 256

Tax
  benefits, 1137, 1139, 1142, 1223, 1231–1237
  deduction, 1137, 1139, 1231–1237
  for the national emergency and civil protection authority (ANEPC), 1229
  for the national emergency institute (INEM), 1228
  Indirect tax on insurance, 1222
  Personal income tax, 1223, 1232–1236
  Stamp tax, 1222, 1224–1226
  to finance FAT, 1230
  to fund the FGA, 1227
Technical reserves, 285, 303, 329–335
Technical provisions, 285, 303, 317, 320, 321, 330, 332–334, 337, 338, 347, 348
Termination of the insurance contract, 223, 236, 519, 731, 734, 801–829
Theft and embezzlement insurance, 907–909
Transport insurance, 504, 844–852, 1204, 1229

Under-insurance, 381, 389, 671–677, 687
Uniform contractual clauses *see* Compulsory insurance and uniform contractual clauses
Unmanned Aircraft Systems, 904–906

Valued policies, 678–687

Workmen's compensation insurance
  for employees, 997–1006
  for independent workers, 1007–1012

Made in the USA
Monee, IL
13 September 2026

62974258R00190